Start With a Dream

A Drummer's Journey from Rock & Roll to TV to Broadway

by

Joey Cassata

START

with a DREAM

A DRUMMER'S JOURNEY... FROM ROCK & ROLL TO T.V. TO BROADWAY

Joey Cassata

Start With a Dream

A DRUMMER'S JOURNEY FROM ROCK & ROLL TO T.V. TO BROADWAY

Published by Satta Entertainment
Book design by Joey Cassata
Cover design by Joey Cassata
Front Cover photo by Kerry Duker
Peter Criss images by Chris Hoffman
Back cover photo by Stormgod photography
Book proofreading by Anthony Muscarella & Bill Deaver
Edited for Political Correctness by Madalyn Cassata
Edited by Joey Cassata & Sarah Tyrell
Unless otherwise noted, all photographs are from the personal collection of the author

DELUXE EDITION

★★★

Author's Note:

The entirety of this book was written on the Academy bus line from N.J. to Port Authority bus terminal in NYC while doing performances for Natasha, Pierre and the Great Comet of 1812 at the Imperial Theater. Every last word was written by myself, Joey Cassata. This is my life story and the details inside are my perspective and memories on all events.

★★★

*A special thank you to
my Mom Barbara Cassata
and
my wife Madalyn Cassata
for making it all possible and always
encouraging me to follow my dreams.*

"Joey sounds just like Eric (Carr) when he's singing and playing the drums".

-Paul Stanley, KISS

"Joey is 'that guy'. That guy you want in your band, that guy you want in your show, that guy you want to hang out with. Joey is the total package!"

- Dee Snider, Twisted Sister

"From International Rock & Roll Stages to TV to Broadway, Joey Cassata lines em' up and knocks em' down no matter what he's doing...
Joey is not only a great drummer, but also one of the funniest guys I know and I can't wait to read his stories! (even the ones I've already heard)"

-Mike Portnoy, Dream Theater

"Like me, Joey Cassata loves music, wrestling and comedy. Plus, he's a killer drummer and a great guy with an 'always be hustling' attitude. Now if he would only do something about that nose.... Anyhoo, READ THIS BOOK!"

-Chris Jericho, WWE

"I always look forward to seeing Joey. He's a great drummer and it's always a treat to get to watch him play. But it's also just as much fun to hang out with him and swap stories. Had a blast doing Z Rock with him, as well as many great times over the years!"

-Eddie Trunk, That Metal Show

I've had the great pleasure of knowing Joey for years. An absolute gentleman and an incredible drummer. It takes a great depth of musical knowledge to work with the Trans-Siberian Orchestra.... Joey possesses not only that but an amazing work ethic as well. (And he's Italian!)

-Al Pitrelli, Trans-Siberian-Orchestra

"Joeylicious is laugh out loud funny!"

-Mick Foley, WWE

"Whenever I looked up and saw that Joey was on drums, I got a sense of comfort knowing the show (The Great Comet) was in good hands".

- Josh Groban, Great Comet

"Joey Cassata is one of those unique individuals who is good at multiple things like music, sports, art, acting, writing, etc. That diversity coupled with his down to earth personality and wicked sense of humor makes him one of those guys that everyone just loves to hang out with. I've had the pleasure of working closely with him for 10 years and developed a high level of respect for him personally and professionally. He may not have realized it, but he was like a big brother to me that whole time. I wish him all the best in his career and in life."

- Paulie Z, ZO2

"Joey is a kick-ass-rock drummer! He puts his heart & soul into any gig he's called for. He can play "fancy" he can play "soft" but, I like when he plays "hard" and rocks that groove solid with great feel! And I'll ruin his wrestling reputation by adding he's a "sweetheart!""

-Billy Amendola, Modern Drummer Magazine

"Joey came into my world via the Late Great David Z. We hit it off immediately. Once we, The Trans-Siberian Orchestra, became aware of his drumming ability, he became my backup for the drum position in TSO east, and also TSO West. He had to not only learn and rehearse two drumming styles, but also two different show arrangements. He covered them both perfectly. He was easily my favourite character on "Z Rock"! Joey's always a gentleman, always funny, always a class act. One of the true gems you meet along the way."

-Jeff Plate, Trans-Siberian-Orchestra

"Joey Cassata is one of those multitalented individuals whose skills behind the drums are equally matched by his ability to consistently style his hair to perfection and achieve the ultimate year round tan."

– Vic Salazar
(Drummer, Founder of Vic's Drum Shop)

"The most admirable thing about Joey is his balance of family and work. It's something many entrepreneurs struggle with. In many ways I admire my brother, as a person, as a musician and a fellow creator. (Just don't tell him that!)"

-Carlos Espada, Kissnation

"A truth telling, no BS'ing, rockstar of a drummer who undeniably lives in the pocket of the groove... From acting, to singing, to wrestling, is there anything this guy can't do?"

- Lucas Steel, The Great Comet

"Playing the first time with Joey reminded me of when I bought my first sports car. Up until then I had been putzing around the neighborhood in an old jelopy. Then Joey came along, I was forced to redefine the term Drive. He brought an energy and fire that was contagious".

-Tommy Snyder, Playground

"What a lot of people don't know about Joey is that underneath all that tough exterior is guy who sacrificed and struggled for many years to get where's he's at. A sensitive father, husband, artist and a good friend who's always made the time to help out the people he cares about.

-Steve Kerasotis, Playground

"Joey's playing on Comet was extraordinary...always locked into the pocket, whether wailing away in a funk feel or playing a cheesy Broadway waltz. I was always awed by his ability to lock in with electronic beats, keeping perfect time with the machine while humanizing and breathing life into the groove. And Joey was a great presence in the room, no bullshit, just joy and camaraderie and consummate musicianship. We shared a little moment whenever I played Pierre in the show, where I would drunkenly stumble past the drum box during a wild electronic club scene... was always such a wonderfully grounding moment, to see Joey and his big smile and raise a glass to him, knowing the music was in profoundly good and rocksteady hands".

- Dave Malloy, Composer of The Great Comet

"I met Joey almost a decade ago, when we both worked for the Trans Siberian Orchestra. From our first rehearsal together, I was blown away by Joey's pocket! It almost made up for his personality. When I started music directing shows on Broadway, Joey was the first person I called to play with me. He is hands-down my favorite drummer to be on any gig with. And my favorite person to drink with after (and before) the show.

-Or Matias, Music Director, The Great Comet

"Joey is the real deal. He is someone you would jump at the chance to work with. Why? Because he is a champion both onstage and off. Joey fosters a sense of community and family, along with a healthy dose of humor, which translates onstage as being part of group that truly enjoys being together while making great music. I could fill an entire book about Joey's skillset, talent, and musicianship, but suffice it to say, he is second to none — sensitive when the style requires it, and of course SLAYS the drums when it's time to rock! You couldn't ask for a better player or person than Joey, and I am proud to know him as a colleague and as a friend".

- Matt "The Slayer" Doebler, Associate Conductor, The Great Comet

"Growing up with Joey, he always had a set of drums in his room, (actually, I think when he was born, instead of the family getting a crib for his room, they just sat him at the drums and handed him some sticks). It was amazing to listen to how good he was at such a young age. As we got older, Joey started playing in bands that would play shows in bars and night clubs. I was so happy for him, but honestly, it was the greatest thing to happen to ME. I got to see my best friend on stage rocking and watching the crowds go crazy, while acting like a complete drunken fool, they were legendary nights to say the least. The after parties were movie script worthy! There wasn't a show or a band that I haven't seen him play with to this day, but those early years with Playground were easily some of the wildest and most memorable.

He's come a long way from those days though. Whether it was a show at L'Amour in Brooklyn, The Stone Pony in Jersey, opening for KISS or the bright lights of Broadway, Joey has always lit up the crowd. I'm glad I've been able to be a part of it all, but I'm really happy to call Joey my friend. Booooooooommmph!!!"

-Rob Scally, Lifelong friend

"I've watched Joey follow his dreams his whole life - from a sweaty six year old banging away to KISS records in our bedroom, to sneaking into bars to play gigs at 14, all the way to being on tour with KISS and watching him perform at the Tony's on TV. Whatever the future holds I am sure Joey will be sitting behind his kit smiling and twirling his sticks

-Dan Cassata, Brother

"I am so very proud of Joey and all of his accomplishments and admire him for his continuous strength and determination notwithstanding all of the loss and struggle he has had to face in his life. He is so deserving of continued success and of all that makes him happy. He is not just an undeniable talent, but a person who will never compromise who he is and what he believes in. He is hard working and will accept nothing short of perfection when preparing for his next project or gig. But above all, his love and devotion to his family are what we cherish most. He means the world to his children and to me, and we love him more than words can ever describe. We cannot wait for the next chapter and are proud to be part of his story"!

-Madalyn Cassata, Wife

Follow along Start with a Dream with the video link below

http://www.youtube.com/c/SattaEntertainment

Playlist: START WITH A DREAM

▶ YouTube

Joey Cassata: A Video History

1 - Playground - Third Heart Video   1990
2 - Playground - Live at Lamour   1991
3 - Exposed - Package to Go   1993
4 - In The Flesh - Terminal Reality   1995
5 - Dogfish - White Rabbit   1996
6 - Valentine Smith - Lord She Bores Me   1998
7 - Hampton's Wiffleball   2000
8 - KISSNATION - VH1's Mock Rock   2001
9 - KISSNATION - Detroit Rock City   2002
10 - Sevenwiser- Punisher Soundtrack - Sick 2003
11 - ZO2 - First Video - Takin' Me Down   2003
12 - ZO2 - Living Now - Rock the Nation Montage 2004
13 - ZO2 - Live in Hidalgo, Texas   2004
14 - ZO2 - Ain't it beautiful   2006
15 - Z Rock clips - 2008
16 - MTV's - Silent Library   2008
17 - Z Rock - Z Wrestler Bloopers - 2009
18 - ZO2 - Presenting at the Spirit Awards
19 - ZO2 - No Way Out   2009
20 - ZO2 - That's What's Up   2011
21 - ZO2 - I Will Be Alright
22 - Victor - Animated series trailer   2014
23 - Wrestling with Joeylicious - Rowdy Roddy Piper 2015
24 - Wrestling With Joeylicious - Trailer   2017
25 - The Great Comet - Tony Awards   2017

All episodes of Z ROCK can be seen at:
facebook.com/ZRock

Table of Contents

Making my Idol
Peter Criss crack up!

When I picked up the sticks and began my journey of being a drummer I never thought that I would inspire others to do the same.

It is such a blessing to have inspired Joey to become a drummer. I am honored and blessed that I am a part of his journey.

Please read his book and learn what it took for him to make his dreams come true !!

God Bless,
Peter Criss

This book is dedicated to

my beautiful children

Angelina and Joe

PROLOGUE

Throughout my life, there have always been moments where everything seems to freeze, and though these moments don't happen often, they usually signify something special. In fact, when these special moments happen, nothing else in the world seems to matter except for what I am focused on at that exact point in time, which is why I like to call them my "Frozen Moments."

I remember standing in the middle of San Antonio's Verizon Wireless Amphitheater and looking up into the night sky, my eyes are met with what looks to be beautiful colorful raindrops beginning to fall. It was 10:40pm and I could hear massive explosions echoing throughout the night air. Before I knew it, a "Frozen Moment" occurred: everything falling from the sky began to slow down, and suddenly the world as I knew it came to a halt. The explosions went quiet, the rain became non-existent, and it was almost as if the people around me weren't there at all.

As each of the hairs on my arms began to rise from sheer excitement, I could feel my heart starting to beat like a giant bass drum inside my chest. A sudden calmness came over me and I started to look around, wondering how I got here. Was this really happening? It seemed as if everything in my life had led up to this exact moment.

That colorful "rain" was confetti being shot out over a crowd of 15,000 screaming fans. The explosions were pyrotechnics being concussed on a massive stage, and I began to feel a sense of euphoria knowing that my band ZO2 was on tour with the legendary rock band KISS!

Standing in the middle of what seemed like an endless sea of fans, I watched KISS play their anthem "Rock & Roll All Night." This was truly one of my best "Frozen Moments," and as I stood there watching, I couldn't help but feel as if everything I'd worked for my entire life led me to the exact spot, this exact moment - frozen in time.

These moments are so special in my life. I feel like time actually stops and I can live and breathe in that moment for a few brief seconds. I am so thankful for this gift, because over my lifetime, I recognize these moments as events that actually define who I am. These moments give me a focus and drive that helps me to achieve whatever it is that I need to accomplish. I'll never forget the first time this happened to me...

San Antonio Texas, 2004

CHAPTER 1

THE BEGINNING

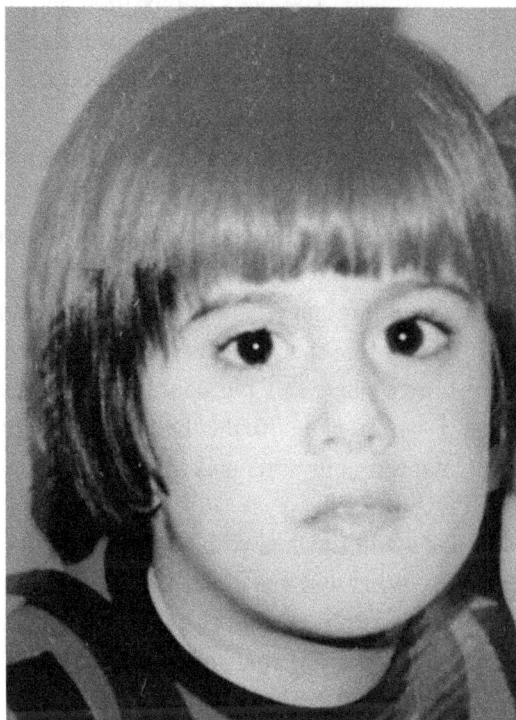

...I was 5 years old.

I don't have many clear memories from when I was a small child, particularly before the age of 8. However, I remember vividly the day which would turn out to be the one that would shape me and the rest of my life forever.

It was July 25, 1979. My family was in route to the world's most famous arena, Madison Square Garden. I'm not even sure I knew why we were going or what was even happening. My brother Danny seemed very excited, but I was kind of just along for the ride. I was probably most excited about grabbing a hot dog once inside the arena.

4

I was a pretty chubby kid and my favorite food was hot dogs, or as I called them "Frah ahs," short for frankfurter, I think. I remember there being many people there, more than I've ever been around before. After all, this was the first time I'd ever been in a big arena or stadium. There seemed to be an excitement in the air, almost electricity exuding from all the people walking around. The lines to buy food and t-shirts were 10 people deep. There was an image with which I was vaguely familiar on the t-shirts, but I didn't really have any feelings about it. Like I said earlier, I was most excited for my hot dog.

Once we finally made our way through the concession stands and I received my jumbo hot dog, I thought my night was over. I was as happy as a five-year-old chubby boy could be. We could now leave and go home whenever my family was ready.

We entered the arena through a small black curtain and I couldn't believe my eyes. It looked like the biggest place in the whole world. I couldn't understand how a place this big could even be built, or why. The electricity that I was feeling in the hallways was magnified a hundred times over. We took our seats and I waited to see what would happen next.

By then, I was just about finished with my hot dog and I could start to focus on other things. What was that giant stage for? What were those enormous speakers hanging from the ceiling? Why was everyone cheering and seemingly preparing for something to happen? I didn't understand, but I started to feel excited myself.

The lights went out and the crowd, of what seemed to me like a million people, erupted into cheers. Everyone stood. It was hard for me to see, but I managed to find an opening and anxiously watched the giant stage to see what would happen next. A loud voice began to scream, "You wanted the best, you got the best, the hottest band in the world: KISS!"

I was hit with a wave of sound that crashed through my body. I saw what looked to be super heroes on the stage playing instruments.

One was dancing and screaming into the microphone, and one looked like an alien from outer space. One was scary and looked like a monster or a demon, but the one that I was most drawn to looked like a cat and was playing the most gigantic drum set I'd even seen. I stood for

the next 2 hours in absolute awe. I couldn't believe what I was hearing and seeing. It was amazing!

Toward the end of the show, the Cat and his drums began to lift into the air. This is when my very first "Frozen Moment" happened. As the drum riser was about to reach its peak at about 30 feet in the air, with the Cat behind the drums banging, and hundreds of fireworks exploding all around the arena, everything came to an abrupt halt.

I didn't know what was happening, but all of a sudden I felt as if I was the only person in the massive arena. My breathing was slow, and a chill went through my body. I wasn't scared, though; instead, an easy calm over took me. I looked around and saw a crowd in awe at what was happening on stage. They looked at this super hero band and cheered them and loved them beyond belief. My eyes were focused on the Cat and his massive drum set, high in the air.

There was something so magical about the sound of the drums. With the Cat behind the monstrous drum kit, it looked like he was almost piloting this great spacecraft as it lifted off into the air.

Right then, during that "Frozen Moment," I knew that my life would never be the same. Someway, somehow, that is what I had to do for the rest of my life!

I don't even fully recall leaving Madison Square Garden that night. I was in a daze the whole way home. My mind was racing with images and sounds that I was still trying to fully process and comprehend.

As soon as we got back to our house in Brooklyn, on East 38th Street, I asked my brother Danny if he had any KISS albums. I don't recall the exact moment or the how or the when, but he gave me his copy of KISS *Double Platinum*. It was a greatest hits package that had been released a year earlier.

Peter Criss behind his massive drumkit 1979

It was magical looking! It was like holding a real platinum album, or so I thought at the time. The double gatefold album was made out of some sort of mylar mirror finish. It had the words "DOUBLE PLATINUM" in bright red letters on the front and the word "KISS" was in a mirror-type finish, slightly raised off the background. The KISS logo looked almost camouflaged on the cover. It was hypnotizing.

Once opened, the double gatefold album was even more incredible on the inside. It had the four KISS members' faces along the top: Gene, Paul, Peter and Ace. Underneath each face were the song titles written in black. I didn't really know any of the songs yet, but I did remember a few titles from the concert.

The two that really stuck out for me were "Detroit Rock City" and "Love Gun." I immediately ran to the living room and put those songs on first. I blasted song after song and began reenacting the moves each KISS member was doing at the concert.

When it came time to do my impression of guitarist Ace Frehley, I decided it was a good idea to stand on the back of the couch and jump off, attempting to land like Ace did at the concert, on his knees while leaning all the way back. This brilliant move fractured my hip.

Thankfully, it was a little stress fracture and didn't require the typical half body cast to fix.

I convinced my mom to let me take the living room record player into my bedroom while I was healing. Over the next few weeks, I stayed in there day and night listening to this amazing mind-blowing music. I had the whole record memorized very quickly. I would hold and examine every inch of the album, reading every little liner note written on it. I wanted to know every detail I could about the band. What was Rock Steady? What was Casablanca? Who was Bill Aucoin? These were all words written inside, but I had no idea as to their meaning.

After my hip was finally healed, I noticed that because I had been holding and handling the album so much, it was starting to look terrible. Smudges from my fingerprints were starting to take away the magical glow it had when I first opened it.

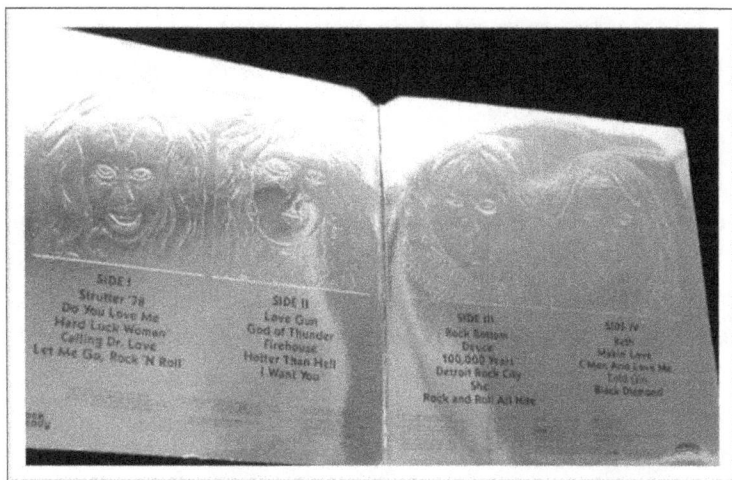

My very first record. KISS Double Platinum.

I thought to myself, "Oh my God, what do I do?" The answer hit me pretty quickly: go ask my mom. She knows how to clean everything!

I ran straight to my mom, who was, of course, in the kitchen cooking. When I was a kid, I ran everywhere; I never walked. Why would I waste time walking when I could run and get there faster? I showed her the album with all of the smudges. Without hesitation, she reached under the sink with one hand while stirring a large pot of sauce on the stove with the other. She pulled out a bottle with some sort of blue liquid in it. I asked her what it was and she said, "Just spray it on the album and it will wipe all the smudges away."

I had the solution. I grabbed a Scott towel. (In my house, we called all paper towels "Scott towels" for some reason. I think it was the name of one of the popular brands of paper towels at the time. Still to this day, I refer to any paper towel as "Scott.") Anyway, I grabbed a Scott towel and ran back to my room with the strange blue liquid.

Once back in my room, I noticed that the album was still playing and I could hear the song "Hotter Than Hell." I sat next to the record player and sprayed the blue liquid all over the cover of my most prized possession.

As I let the liquid set in, I looked once more at the bottle. It said Windex Window Cleaner. That sounded right to me. After all, this *Double Platinum* album was way shinier than any window! Once the liquid sat for a few moments, I began to wipe it away using my Scott towel. After a few wipes, I held my baby up, and it looked as good as new. I was elated with joy.

I continued this routine every single day for about two months, or whenever anyone happened to touch it and leave dirty, nasty fingerprints. After a while, I started to notice that the red writing on the cover looked a little duller. The same was happening to the black song title lettering on the inside. I also came to the harsh reality that the album wasn't actually made out of platinum after all: it was just plain old cardboard that was now water logged and starting to warp from all of my Windex applications. After all these years, I still have my completely faded, no lettering to be seen, water-logged version of KISS's *Double Platinum*. And I still love it!

Christmas 1979 was next, and it was pretty easy for me to pick out what I wanted for Christmas that year. The only thing on my mind was a set of drums!

There was no question about what instrument I was going to get. When Peter Criss' drum set rose into the air, all other instruments look lame. So that Christmas, 5 months after I attended the KISS concert at Madison Square Garden, I received my first drum set. I was only 5 years old. The drums were just a small, little kid set, but I knew if I was ever going to be like Peter, I had to start somewhere. It was a silver 5-piece set which included a bass drum, snare, two toms, and a floor tom.

The first time I sat down behind the kit that Christmas morning, I remember looking down and seeing the bass drum foot pedal. I thought to myself, "What the hell is that for?" I had no idea you had to play the drums with your feet too, thinking it was all hitting with your sticks. I knew right then that this was going to be harder than I thought.

I remember the pedal being a sort of thin plastic that I could never really hit hard enough to get a good thump. People say that today I'm an extremely loud drummer and maybe that's why. I used to stomp on that little plastic pedal as hard as I could, about 1,000 times a day back then.

I didn't let the new obstacle of using my feet damper the excitement I was feeling. It's funny, even at 5 years old, I knew that I had to work hard and practice and be disciplined if I wanted to play as well as Peter Criss and maybe be in KISS one day. I'm not sure most 5-year-olds think like that or have that kind of game plan for the rest of their lives, but I definitely did!

CHAPTER 2

SHAPING A DREAM

Christmas 1979 when I received my first set of drums.
Let the journey begin...

Family life over the next few years was a little tough. My mom and dad got divorced, and my mom was forced to raise her two sons on her own. It's weird: I remember the KISS concert and my first drum set like it was yesterday, but I have no recollection of my father ever living in the house with us. To be honest, the next couple of years are a bit hazy. Like I said, things were tough, especially for my mom.

Barbara Cassata was the best mom anyone could ever ask for. She did everything for her two boys after my father left. We never had much money growing up and my father rarely gave us anything or even saw us. We did see him on the occasional birthday or holidays like Christmas, but even then, it wasn't a guarantee.

My mom was always fighting with my father to give more — not for herself (she never wanted anything from him), but for his sons. All she ever wanted was for him to take care of us but he never really did.

It was a constant   struggle for my mom.

My brother and I both went to Catholic grammar school in Brooklyn run by nuns. I remember being called to the office almost every month during the first and second grade. Once I got to the office, the principal, who was a nun named Sr. Marie (and note that I could've written a whole chapter on this witch) would ask me, "Do you know why you were called to the office, Joseph?" "No, I have no idea," I would reply. She would then explain to me that my parents didn't pay the tuition and that soon I wouldn't be allowed to go to class or to see my friends ever again if they didn't pay immediately.

The best mom in the whole world, Barbara Cassata.

I'm not sure that I ever really understood exactly what she meant. I don't think I grasped the concept of money, or even knew what tuition was. Looking back, I realize that was a horrible thing to do to a little 7-year-old kid. She was basically trying to terrify me so I would go home crying and tell my parents to pay the tuition or I would be kicked out of school and never see my friends again. But it never worked; even at that age, I knew when someone was trying to manipulate me.

This same scenario repeated itself often over the next few years. And this is exactly what started my hatred and horrible relationship with the only person I've ever truly hated in my life: Sr. Marie!

My mom struggled paying even the basic bills. We were constantly having our gas, electric, and phone services turned off. It was hard. I remember nights when it was freezing in our house because we had no

My brother Danny and me with our grandparents Joseph and Angelina Taddonio, 1975

heat. Again, I'm not sure I really understood why we had no heat and no lights, but I knew that it was crushing my mother to have to live like this. She was always crying and upset. But, even through all of this, we still loved each other and always had fun together.

When things got really hard, my grandparents, my mother's parents, would come and stay with us for a few months. They lived in a little apartment on Carmine Street in Greenwich Village, Manhattan. When they stayed with us, I think we would live off of their social security checks. They were always good to us and I loved them very much.

I was named after my grandfather Giuseppe Taddonio. (Giuseppe is Joseph in Italian.) He was the sweetest, kindest man I ever knew. All he ever wanted was a glass of wine and a cigarette. I remember hearing that my grandfather played the drums when he was younger, but I can't really say for sure. He came over from Sicily when he was 12 and eventually became a well-known butcher in Greenwich Village.

My grandmother Angelina Taddonio, on the other hand, was a crazy, hot-headed old Italian lady that would fight with everyone. She was a seamstress who could sew or patch up anything! She was constantly crocheting and making things for around the house, including blankets, pillows, doilies, and so much more. I'm not even sure exactly what a doilie is, but I remember my mom referring to everything my grandmother ever made for the tops of our furniture as doilies. What the hell is a doilie exactly?

My grandmother also crocheted hundreds of dresses for dolls that she would then donate to the church every year. I think if we asked her to crochet us a car she could have done it! My grandparents were great, and they helped us get through a lot of tough times.

Even though we didn't really have money to do much, we always found a way to make it work. One summer, when my cousins Joey and Jodee were visiting from Boston, we wanted to go to the movies to see Friday the 13th part 3. Yes, I was only 8 years old and was allowed to see Friday the 13th! Times were different then. My mom even took me to see Scarface in the movie theater when I was 9. Great flick for a 9 year old!! Anyway, we wanted to go the movies but didn't have enough money, but we did have a giant jug of pennies in our hallway, so one day we cracked that open so we could all go.

Back in those days, you had to hand roll each dollar of pennies before the bank would trade them for dollars. There were no automatic machines to just dump change into. I think we started rolling pennies on Friday morning and finally had enough for movies tickets by Saturday afternoon. We struggled, but we made it work. We always had a great time and a loving family.

In the fall of 1981, I was shopping in King's Plaza Mall with my family where my brother and I always went to Sam Goody on the second floor to check out all the new albums. Danny was 5 years older than I was, and I looked up to everything he did– especially music. Anything he told me about a band or a musician I took as absolute law. If he told me Randy Rhodes was the fastest guitarist in the world, then it was true.

I didn't really have any interest in any other band but KISS, so I would always sprint over to the K section of the records. I was slowly closing in on owning every KISS album, but still was still missing a few. Being only 7 at the time, it was still hard to come up with enough money to buy an album.

I couldn't wait to get to the mall because I'd been saving and finally had enough money to buy another KISS record. As I was excitedly looking through the options, I came across something that definitely wasn't there last time.

Back in the 80's, it was hard to find out when new records were being released: you'd either have to know someone who bought it already, or you'd see it for yourself at the record store.

When I woke up that morning, I'd never dreamed a new KISS album would be out. Sure enough, though, in my hands was an album

Me and my brother Danny, 1981.

with a picture of a hand knocking on a giant wooden door. It had the KISS logo in the corner, but to my astonishment there was no picture of the band on either the front or the back. This had me worried. What should I do? This was a major, life-altering decision for a 7-year-old: do I buy an album that I still needed like *Hotter Than Hell* or *Dynasty?*,

My record store growing up. SAM GOODY!

One of my favorite things to do. Shop for KISS records!!

or do I buy this new unknown album called *Music from The Elder*? I couldn't even be 100 percent sure this was a real KISS album.

I'd been to record stores near my grandparents' apartment in Greenwich Village and they had records called bootlegs. I'd bought a few of those before and was extremely disappointed in the sound quality. What do I do? I ran over to my brother to ask for his advice; after all, I thought he knew everything there was to know about music and he was the one who introduced me to KISS in the first place. After explaining to him my dilemma about being afraid it wasn't a real KISS album, we came up with a pretty good plan.

Since my brother had his Sony Walkman, I would buy the cassette copy of *The Elder*, then as soon as we left the store, I would immediately test it in his Walkman. Even though I didn't really want the cassette, because all of my other KISS albums were on vinyl, I agreed with the plan. If it sounded like a bootleg, I would just return it and buy *Dynasty* instead.

I made my purchase and nervously opened the cassette right outside of Sam Goody. To my joy, the first song, "The Oath," kicked in and it sounded fantastic! This was now the first cassette I'd ever bought or owned.

Back in the 80's, two of my most cherished possessions were my Sony Walkman and my small boombox radio. I went everywhere with one of them, and now I had a store-bought cassette to play in them.

The Elder was much different than any other KISS albums I had, but it was still amazing in its own right. I think anything with the KISS name on it back then would have blown my mind.

While still in the mall, I began reading the inside of the cassette cover and saw something that put me into a state of shock. Under the band listing it said: Paul Stanley: Guitar, Vocals; Gene Simmons: Bass, Vocals; Ace Frehley: Lead Guitar, Vocals; and Eric Carr: Drums,

The first album I ever bought, KISS "The Elder."

Vocals. What? Who was this Eric Carr and where was Peter Criss??? I needed to know more immediately. But how?

I ran over to the newsstand that was located in the center of the mall to see if they had any magazines featuring KISS. Of course, I didn't have any money to buy one, but I thought I could at least look through a few to see if I could find out any information on this mysterious drummer named Eric Carr. To my utter disappointment, there were no magazines with any KISS stories. In 1981, it wasn't cool to like KISS, so magazines didn't include much coverage of them.

I strolled home, lagging behind my mother and brother. I needed to see what Eric Carr looked like. Did he look like Peter? Did he look different? Did he even wear makeup?

Listening to *The Elder* from then on was a totally different experience. I was constantly imagining what this Eric Carr looked like, what kind of drum set he had. Everything he played sounded superb. From the pounding double bass in "The Oath," to the complex instrumental "Escape from the Island." In a strange way, this mysteriousness got me even more into KISS than I'd ever been before.

One song in particular had a big impact on me. It was the last song on the album called "I". The lyric was something that I would live by for many years to come. Actually, it's still something that I follow today. It went... *"I believe in me, and I, believe in something more than you can understand, YES I BELIEVE IN ME"*!

Over the years, I would always sing it to myself whenever someone told me to give up on my dreams.

Danny, my mom, and me holding my boombox sitting on our stoop in Brooklyn, 1981. I'm listening to KISS's "THE ELDER"

It was over a year before I finally saw what the mysterious new drummer looked like. It happened on another fateful day of going to the mall with my mom and brother. It was the same routine: my mom went off shopping, even though I think she mostly just took us there for a day out of the house, seeing as how she didn't really have any money to shop for herself.

After breaking off from our mom, Dan and I sprinted to Sam Goody once again. Upon entering the store, Dan went left and I went right – straight for the K section. I definitely wasn't expecting anything special that day; I was just excited to look through all of the albums. I had no money to even buy one to fill my collection. Sure enough, when I was looking through all of the KISS albums, there was nothing different.

After about 20 minutes or so I met back up with Dan, who was looking at some Judas Priest records. He, like almost everyone else on the planet, didn't really like KISS anymore.

On the way out of the store, very nonchalantly, my brother asked "Hey, what's that?" "Where?" I responded. He pointed to the side of the store where they had some new releases. That's when I saw it—the image that had been eluding me for over a year. I jetted, another term from back in the early 80's, as fast as I could over to the rack and grabbed the album. It was beautiful. It had a purple/blue glow with the four KISS faces on it, Paul, Gene, Ace, and who I was assuming was Eric! He looked awesome. I didn't really know what he was supposed to be, but I knew he looked super cool. The letters in the upper right-hand corner said *Creatures of the Night*. I couldn't believe what I was holding. Not only was it a picture of Eric Carr, but it was a new KISS album!

But wait, I had no money to buy it and neither did my brother. "Oh no!" I said. Panic mode set in. I had to find my mom to see if she had any money at all. I could not, would not, leave the mall without that album.

I went to the counter and said to the salesperson, "Please hold onto this. I will be right back to buy it." He looked at me like I was crazy and said, "Kid, there are a hundred on the shelf. Nobody's buying the new KISS album, trust me." I got angry and made him hold onto it anyway. My brother and I booked out of Sam Goody in search of my mother ("Booked" or "Book it" was a slang term back in the 80's for run fast). Even my brother thought I was crazy, but he had no choice but to follow me because I was going as fast as I could to find my mom before all of the KISS albums were gone!

We finally found my mom outside of her favorite women's clothing store in the mall, Joyce Leslie. I explained to her all about the KISS album, about seeing Eric Carr for the first time, and how I would die if I didn't get that album today. My mom, without hesitation, went into her bag and gave me ten dollars. She knew how much it meant to me.

That's who my mom was. It was probably her last ten dollars, money she was hoping to use to buy something for herself. Instead, she gave it to me for the new KISS album. She would do anything for her sons.

When I got home, I don't think I left my room for the next 20 hours straight. All I did was listen and stare at that cover, more specifically at Eric Carr's face. The sound of Eric playing the drums on the *Creatures of the Night* album was the biggest, most thunderous sound I'd ever heard. After hearing that, I knew my small, now semi-broken drum kit was not going to cut it.

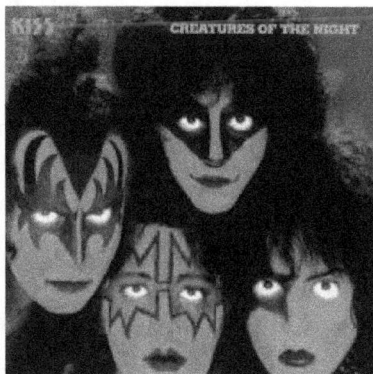

The drum set that I got for Christmas a few years earlier was in pretty bad shape. It was falling apart and barely usable. I just had to get a new kit! My birthday wasn't too far off and I begged my mom for a new kit. I told her I wouldn't ask for anything for the next 5 birthdays and Christmases if I could just have a new drum set so I could practice and sound like Eric Carr. I have no idea how she did it, but, sure enough, on my ninth birthday, I got a brand new drum kit! I believe she probably tortured or maybe even threatened my father to somehow give her money for the drums. There was nothing my mom hated more than having to ask my father for anything. But in this case, I think she swallowed her pride so she could make her son's birthday perfect. And perfect it was!

When I woke up that morning, I went into one of our "spare rooms" to find a burgundy-red, 5-piece Shock drum set. In my house in Brooklyn, we had two empty rooms on the first floor that we called our "spare rooms." When my dad still lived with us, he semi-finished our gigantic attic and made it into two very large bedrooms — one for mom and dad and one for me and my brother. The two rooms on the first floor were our old bedrooms that were eventually supposed to be fixed up.

Once my dad left, he never came back to do anything with the old rooms or even finish the new ones. So, the whole time I lived in my house, we basically had two rooms we didn't use. I found a few good uses for them over the years, making the first one my new "Drum Room."

When I saw my new drum set, my heart was immediately filled with all the happiness in the world. My mom came through for me like she always did. I guess my father didn't want her to get all the credit, so he made sure he showed up that day with his brother, my Uncle Charles, to set the drums up.

My Uncle Charles was a really good guitar player who also played drums. He always told us stories about how he used to jam with the band Twisted Sister when he was younger. I always thought of him as kind of a celebrity because of this. I used to think, "Wow! Someone who actually made it in the music business." I guess that in my little kid brain, jamming with Twisted Sister meant you'd made it.

It didn't even bother me that my father was there to take credit for giving me the drums. Nothing was going to spoil this day, the day that marked the moment I could begin my training to sound like Eric Carr.

My uncle proceeded to set up the drums and then he showed me how to tune them. "Tune them?" I asked. I had no idea that drums even needed to be tuned. I thought that was only for guitars and stuff.

As soon as they were ready and tuned, I sat behind the set and started to play the KISS song "I Love It Loud" from the *Creatures of the Night* album. Well, at least I thought, I was playing it. I have a feeling it was pretty bad. I quickly realized that this was nothing like the kiddie kit I had when I was five; this was much harder to control and to maneuver.

That was okay because nothing could stop me now that I had my new set and my *Creatures of the Night* album to practice to. I would work day and night until I was as good as Eric Carr, and nothing would distract me or throw me off course. Or so I thought.

CHAPTER 3
AND THEN THERE WAS
WRESTLING

One Saturday morning, I was home watching TV, flipping through the channels. Now, when I say flipping through the channels, I mean I was sitting 5 inches away from the TV and cranking the dial to change between the only channels we had: 2,4,5,7,9, and 11. If I was really desperate, I'd go to channel 13 which mostly had garbage on. Sometimes, I could even go to the UHF channels and get a 3/4 scrambled signal of something.

While cranking the dial, I stopped on Channel 9, otherwise known back then in our area as WWOR-TV. Something was playing that I'd never seen before– some kind of fighting. Two guys were in a dirty looking ring and they were beating the crap out of each other. It was fantastic! A 9-year-old boy is very impressionable, and this definitely made a big impression on me.

I admit that I have a bit of a compulsive personality in some regards. When I like something, that's all I can think about, and I instantaneously fell in love with this thing that the TV announcer called WWF Wrestling!

Along with KISS and drums, wrestling became my new obsession. The fighting in the ring was amazing, but what I really fell in love with was the over-the-top personalities! The characters onscreen were larger than life.

I'd never seen anything like it. And as much as I liked KISS, I don't think at that point that I'd ever even heard them speak. I just loved their music and their super-hero look. These wrestlers were different. It was their talking and their personalities that I loved.

Because my dad left us at such an early age, I never really had a male role model or someone from whom to imitate behavior. Good or bad, these wrestlers filled that void. I think my personality, even until this day, is based mostly on 80's wrestlers.

The first wrestler to catch my eye was Jimmy "Superfly" Snuka. He was this wild man from the isle of Fuji, built like a god, and he would fly through the air and splash down onto his opponents as his finishing maneuver. The other wrestler who caught my attention was someone they referred to as "The Eighth Wonder of the World." I didn't know what the hell the other seven wonders were, but the eighth was something to behold. His name was André the Giant. He was easily the biggest human I'd ever seen.

After a few weeks of watching my new favorite show, I went to school and started telling my friends about WWF Wrestling. Nobody had really heard of it. Just like KISS, I was the only one interested. That was until one day I saw Richie Pollo riding his bike on my block, wearing a shirt with the WWF logo on it.

Richie was a few years older than I was and we never really hung out or had anything in common. Until that moment. I stopped him and asked, "Hey Richie, where did you get that shirt?" He told me that he went to see WWF Wrestling live at Madison Square Garden last month and that he bought it there. My heart started beating uncontrollably. Excitement filled every inch of my body. "Went to see it live?" I asked excitedly. I had no idea such a thing was even possible; I only knew WWF Wrestling as a TV show that I watched on Saturday mornings. He then told me that wrestling was at Madison Square Garden every month and that we should go. My mind was blown.

I could see Superfly and André in person, just like I had seen KISS a few years earlier? I knew what I had to do next. I ran home and begged my mom to find out how we could get tickets to see wrestling at Madison Square Garden.

My mom was already well aware of my new obsession with wrestling. Even though these big things would come up periodically, I never really asked for much as a kid. I never had new clothes or crazy amounts of toys. So, when I did ask for something, my mom knew it meant a lot to me. She said we would go to King's Plaza Mall tomorrow after school to Ticket Tron and inquire about going. I was so excited that night that I didn't sleep a wink.

The next day was one of the longest school days ever. Every click on the clock seemed to take an eternity. Finally, at 3pm, the bell rang and I jetted home as fast as I could. I yelled up to my mom, "Mom I'm home!" She came down and since we didn't have a car when I was a kid, we started the long walk to the mall. In fact, after my dad left, we never drove anywhere, since my mom didn't drive anyway. I never thought twice about it. It was just the norm for us.

We finally arrived about 25 minutes later and entered through the giant entrance. Ticket Tron was the first store on the right. It actually wasn't really a store at all– more like a window that you went up to with a salesperson behind it.

My mom asked the woman behind the window about wrestling at Madison Square Garden. The clerk told her it was at MSG the last Monday of every month. I said, "Oh no, that's almost a month away!" But when my mom asked, "Do you still want the tickets?" I think I screamed "Yes!" as loudly as I could. The whole mall probably heard me.

My mom bought three tickets for WWF Wrestling live at Madison Square Garden for November 21, 1983. Only one question remained: how was I going to make it through the next few weeks? It seemed like an eternity.

Over the next month, I worked with my new-found friend and neighbor Richie to create different signs to take to Madison Square Garden. I didn't really understand this concept at first. Richie explained to me that everyone brought signs to hold up during the matches so the wrestlers could see them. Some signs would express how much you loved a particular wrestler, and some signs would announce how much you hated them.

The first sign I made was for my favorite, Jimmy "Superfly" Snuka. It was on a big piece of white oak tag and had his name with two drawings of his hands. Snuka would always do the "I Love You" sign language symbol with his hands, right before he jumped off of the top rope. It was the coolest thing ever. I made my mom draw the hands for my poster, since she was a great artist, as was my brother. I had some drawing skills, but I never really got that gift. I thought my sign was perfect!

Richie and I would get together every day to go over what we would do and what we would yell as the wrestlers came out for their match. It was such a magical time– being a kid and not having a care in the world.

During those years, they didn't announce who was wrestling until you got to the arena and bought a program with that night's matches listed in it. We both assumed the WWF champion, Bob Backlund, would be defending his title that night, and I was hoping more than anything to see Jimmy Snuka jump off that top rope.

Finally, the big night arrived. I remember being in school that afternoon and not being able to concentrate on anything. All I could think was, "In a few hours, I'll be in the same building as 'the Superfly'!"

Later that night, at about 6pm, my mom took Richie and me to Madison Square Garden. We took the B12 bus to the D train and about an hour and a half later we arrived at "The World's Most Famous Arena," Madison Square Garden, the same place that had changed my life just four years earlier when I saw KISS for the first time.

I remember the smell of hot pretzels cooking at all the vendor carts right before entering the building. Now, to this day, whenever I smell a pretzel, I immediately flash back to the Garden and watching wrestling. I also specifically remember entering on 8th Avenue between 32nd and 33rd Streets, and that Richie and I were beaming with excitement.

Richie was showing me all the different merchandise stands as we entered. I begged my mom for a Superfly t- shirt, but unfortunately, it was $20 and way over our budget. The only thing that we could afford was a program. It had a picture of the "Masked Superstar" on the cover, but more importantly, inside it had the matches that were going to be held that night. I nervously scrolled down in hopes that The Superfly would be on the card. To my delight, he was wrestling Sgt. Slaughter.

While walking the long, winding hallways of The Garden to get to our seats, a side door opened and out walked a familiar looking figure. It was Arnold Skaalund, manager of WWF champion Bob Backlund. Richie and I started slapping each other and began awkwardly pointing at Mr. Skaalund. He gave a kind wave of acknowledgment and went on his way. I couldn't believe that the WWF World Champion's manager just passed us in the hallway. If this was what going to see wrestling live was all about, I was in for the time of my life. We got to our seats right as the action started.

Since my mom could only afford seats up in the blue section — the cheap seats — the ring seemed like it was a mile away. Back in 1983, wrestling didn't have a cool elaborate set like it does today. There was no big ramp for the wrestlers to walk down, either, and this was before the wrestlers even had entrance music.

The first wrestler introduced was the Italian Salvatore Bellomo. We were so high up that I couldn't even see him walk to the ring. He was just walking down a simple walkway that was covered by a sea of people.

Salvatore was set to battle the evil Butcher Vachon. I don't remember much about the actual match except for the first time I heard Salvatore hit the mat after a body slam. It was so loud it echoed through the entire arena. I thought to myself, "Holy cow, that must have hurt. Maybe these seats would be okay after all." A few minutes into the match, I was so immersed in the environment that I totally forgot I was up in the nosebleed seats. Richie and I were screaming at the top of our lungs. I was reading my program and counting how many more matches until The Superfly fought. After a few more exciting matches, the time had come—the villainous Sgt. Slaughter against my favorite, Jimmy "Superfly" Snuka.

I quickly pulled out my sign and held it up screaming, "Superfly! Superfly!" I quickly realized that there was no way in hell Snuka could see all the way to where I was sitting. Still, that didn't matter: I still held it high and proud. The match was a 20-minute draw, which was a little disappointing, but still absolutely amazing to see The Superfly live and in person.

The next and final match of the night was WWF Champion Bob Backlund versus The Masked Superstar. Bob was a great champion but a little plain for my taste. I still rooted for him, though—and I went crazy when he pinned the Masked Superstar in just under 18:00 to retain the WWF championship.

I was now officially hooked! I would somehow have to get back to MSG every month to see wrestling. Every waking moment from then on out was dedicated to three things: KISS, drums, and wrestling.

My brother and I shared a room in the attic; he had one side and I had the other. It was actually a pretty huge room, so we basically divided the room in half. When I walked through the door, my side was on the left and his off to the right. I proceeded to cover every inch of wall space with Kiss and WWF posters. I even covered my side of the ceiling! All I could think about was getting back to Madison Square Garden that next month, even admitting that I'd been neglecting KISS and my drums a little bit.

Seeing concerts & Wrestling at Madison Square Garden in the 80's changed my life.

CHAPTER 4

TWO PASSIONS
TWO DREAMS

One morning, after lining up in the school yard, my friend John Wasson approached me, and in an excited voice he said, "Dude, did you see the new KISS album?" I said, "What new KISS album? You mean *Creatures*?"

John grabbed me by the shoulders and replied, "No! It's called *Lick it Up* and they took their makeup off!" My face went white. "What did you say?" was my only response. Wasson replied, "Dude! I got the album last night. They took their makeup off!"

I couldn't believe what I was hearing. Not only was there a new KISS album with all new music I'd never heard, but, THEY TOOK THEIR MAKE UP OFF!!??? Just then, our third-grade teacher, Miss Vining, stood in front of the class with the same stern look she gave us every morning, as if to say, "That's enough. I'm here and it's time for you to behave."

I couldn't stop thinking about what Wasson had just told me. What did KISS look like without their makeup? Did they still have crazy superhero type costumes? Did the music sound the same? I just knew I had to get to the mall immediately to see this album, plus I had to scrape up enough money to buy it. I also had to get wrestling tickets for the new

WWF event at the Garden later that month. Lucky for me, it was December and Christmas was just around the corner!

After spending the next 8 miserable hours in school trying to think of how to tell my mom that I needed my Christmas gifts early so I could buy the new KISS album and get tickets for WWF, the bell finally rang. I jetted home as fast I could and ran to the kitchen to see her.

After a long, hard sales pitch, my mom said yes. I really have no idea how she did it all the time. We never had any money, but somehow every time I really wanted something, she found a way to get it for me.

I called one of my best buddies, Rob Scally, to ask him if he wanted to come to the mall with me to buy the new Kiss album and if he wanted to go see wrestling at MSG later that month. I'd been trying to sell this wrestling thing to all my friends at school ever since seeing it the first time on TV. I'm not sure Scally was that into it yet, but he asked his mom if he could go and she said yes.

I met Scal, what I called him for short, on my corner and we quickly "booked it" to the mall. Along the way, we talked about wrestling and I also explained to him about the new KISS album – and the fact that they'd taken their makeup off. Now he was excited too because at that point nobody had ever seen the band without the makeup.

Once we got to the mall, I had to make a decision. Do I grab the wrestling tickets as we walk in to assure better seats, or do I run straight for the KISS album? It was close, but first I had to see what KISS looked like without their makeup. Scally and I bolted at top speed to Sam Goody's. Since Scally at the time was much skinnier and way faster than I was, he got there first. But because I was so familiar with the store, I b-lined straight to the new release section. That's when I saw it.

If it wasn't for the KISS logo in the top left corner and for a picture of someone sticking out his tongue, I would never have known it was KISS. The cover featured four regular looking guys in street clothes standing in front of a plain white background. It was the exact opposite of the *Creatures of the Night* cover that had blown my mind a year earlier.

In fact, it was very disappointing. Scally finally made his way to me and the first thing he said was, "That's KISS?" Of course, I bought the album anyway, but my excitement and being in awe of my idols faded a little bit at that moment.

We left Sam Goody a little down, but quickly remembered that we still had to go buy our wrestling tickets. We once again ran top speed to the downstairs entrance where Ticket Tron was. I don't think as kids we ever walked anywhere, especially when we were excited. We approached the ticket window and slapped down our money and said, "Give us the best tickets you have for WWF at the Garden for Dec 26th." The ticket agent took our money and printed our tickets. We looked at the numbers on the tickets but didn't know how to figure out where the seats were, so we asked him to show us.

To our disappointment, our section was way up in the nosebleed blue seats again. Scally gave me a slap on the shoulder and said, "See, we should have gotten the tickets before buying that KISS album." I hate to say it, but after looking down at my plain white KISS album with four ordinary looking guys on it, maybe Scal was right.

Over the next few weeks, I really tried to get Scally into wrestling. He would come over and watch on Saturday mornings and I taught him about each guy and about the difference between the good and the bad guys. He was definitely enjoying it with me, but I quickly realized that no one had the same passion or excitement as I did for the things that I loved. This would be a common occurrence throughout my life.

The day had arrived. All the way to MSG on the train, Scally and I fake wrestled. Every time we got too rough, my mom would give a quick "knock it off" look, mainly because she didn't want me to hurt Scally. You see, when I was 9, I was very large for my age, about 5 feet six inches and 125 pounds. I know that doesn't sound big, but when all of the other kids were about four feet seven and only 70 pounds, it made a huge difference. Scally was probably even smaller than that, which is actually what made wrestling with him so great. I could do all the moves the real wrestlers did on him, including Body Slam, Suplex, and the Samoan drop.

Once we got to the Garden, I knew more of what to expect. As soon as we entered, I hunted down the guy with the programs and quickly bought one to see the matches on the card that night. "Yes!" I exclaimed. The Superfly was fighting again and tonight in a tag team match: Superfly and Bob Backlund's manager, Arnold Skaalund, versus the intercontinental champion The Magnificent Muraco and his manager, Captain Lou Albano.

"YES!"

I'd watched this feud develop every Saturday morning on channel 9. A feud that epitomized everything about good and evil for a wrestling fan. Jimmy Snuka was everyone's hero and The Magnificent Muraco was the villain that you loved to hate. He was in good shape but had a bit of a belly. He carried himself like a slob and enjoyed every minute of it. Muraco would spit, scowl, and even eat a hot dog on occasion as he was finishing off his opponents. Also, unlike Snuka, who was monotone during interviews, Muraco was loud, obnoxious, and cocky.

It was inevitable that these two warriors would collide at some point, since Muraco was also managed by Snuka's former manager and rival, Captain Lou Albano. It all started when the Magnificent Muraco was a guest in a segment called "Roger's Corner." Former WWF champion Buddy Rogers was interviewing Muraco and in the meantime, and off-camera, Jimmy Snuka was entering the ring for his match. Muraco took this as a sign of disrespect and approached the ring to begin screaming at Snuka, who just smiled at Muraco. Muraco returned the gesture by spitting at Snuka, and this made Snuka lose his mind. The two brawled on the floor with Snuka ripping Muraco's clothes off.

The battle lines were now drawn and the war was on. I couldn't believe I was going to get to see them go at it in person. Then finally, it was time for WWF Champion Bob Backlund to defend his title against the evil Iron Sheik. Much like The Snuka/Muraco feud, I'd been watching this one develop on Saturday mornings. The Iron Sheik was a cocky Iranian who despised everything about America and Americans. He always boasted about how he was an Olympic wrestler in Iran and was stronger than any American wrestler. Every week, The Sheik would do a test of strength using two, 75-pound Persian clubs, offering anyone $2,000 to swing the massive clubs above their heads as many times as he could — and no one ever even came close.

The Saturday morning right before the Sheik's title match at the Garden, he began his challenge again, calling for anyone to come try to swing his Persian clubs. Suddenly from behind the curtain sprang WWF Champion Bob Backlund. The Sheik and his manager "Classy" Freddie Blassie seemed insulted that Backlund would even attempt the feat of strength.

Backlund entered the ring and approached the clubs. The Sheik and Blassie stood behind, looking smug and arrogant knowing this skinny American had no chance of defeating the Sheik. Bob proceeded to lift the clubs over his head; he seemed to struggle at first but once in a rhythm, he looked like he could actually beat the Sheik. Just before surpassing the Sheik's number of swings, the Sheik attacked Backlund from behind, causing one of the heavy clubs to land squarely on his back. The Sheik and Blassie left the injured Backlund face down in the ring as they smugly walked back through the curtain. They knew that with Backlund injured, they just gained a massive advantage in the upcoming title match.

The title match that night at The Garden lasted just under twelve minutes. I knew the end was near when the Sheik got the injured Backlund into his finishing maneuver, the dreaded Camel Clutch! The painful maneuver consisted of the the Sheik sitting on top of a competitor's back and then wrenching his neck backward with all of his might. Anyone else would immediately tap out to such a brutal move, but not the champ: Backlund refused to give up, even though he was in excruciating pain. With his back injury, the move was likely causing permanent damage, so finally, Backlund's manager stood on the ring apron and threw in the white towel. This was to signal the ref that he was giving up on behalf of Backlund and in essence forfeiting the WWF title. I couldn't believe my eyes. Backlund had been the champ for almost 6 years and now it was all over. The evil Iron Sheik had the championship.

Scally and I left the arena that night absolutely devastated as the Sheik and Blassie celebrated in the ring to an arena full of boos. Who could possibly save us from the tyranny of the Sheik and his vile manager Freddie Blassie?

I moped around for the next two weeks. Looking back, it's pretty funny, but for a 9-year-old, this was a tough time. First, KISS had taken off their makeup and now the WWF had a champion that I loathed. I reluctantly plopped myself in front of the TV on Saturday, January 7th to tune into wrestling.

Bob Backlund, still not 100 percent from his injuries sustained by the Sheik, was set to face off against Samoan number 3, Samu. The Wild Samoans always appeared together and this day was no different. Samu was accompanied by his brothers, Afa and Sika, and their manager Captain Lou Albano.

Every time Backlund tried to enter the ring, the Samoans would surround him. He was clearly outnumbered. Maybe when he was fully healthy, he would have been able to take on two Samoans, but never three! Backlund left the ring disgruntled. He seemed to simply quit the match due to the unfair circumstances.

Moments later, he came back followed by an enormous man exploding through the curtain behind him. It was someone I'd never seen before on WWF television, but I did recognize this behemoth. It was Thunderlips from the movie *Rocky 3*. What was he doing there?? I was immediately excited to see what would happen next.

Backlund seemed to have brought this man the announcer called Hulk Hogan as back-up against the Samoans. The match began and Backlund quickly gained the upper hand, but just as Backlund feared, the Wild Samoans interfered and began stomping on him. The man they called the Incredible Hulk stormed the ring and single-handedly took out all three Samoans and Captain Lou!

This was the most exciting thing I'd seen on wrestling yet. Dare I say, it was even more exciting than my favorite "Superfly" Snuka. The Hulk's energy was off the charts and absolutely exhilarating. The Samoans quickly fled the scene as the announcer came out to interview Backlund and the mysterious Hulk Hogan.

As exciting as Hulk's antics were in the ring, he was even more explosive when he spoke into the microphone. He began ripping off his t-shirt off as he proclaimed, "Hulkamania is here!"

I was instantly hooked and had a new hero to root for. The next week it was announced that Backlund was still too injured for a rematch against the Sheik at Madison Square Garden in January. Instead, Hulk Hogan would step in to take Backlund's place for the Championship.

When I heard them make this earth-shattering announcement, I lost my mind. I could not miss this for anything in the world. My new hero, Hulk Hogan, was going to get revenge for his friend Bob Backlund against the Iron Sheik. And, this was all happening two days after my tenth birthday. I once again had to beg my mom to get me tickets for my birthday.

WWF Champion Bob Backlund & Hulk Hogan

On January 23, 1984, my mom, my brother, Scally, and I once again went to The Garden to see WWF Wrestling. The under card was pretty much a blur because all I could think about was Hogan getting his hands on the Sheik.

The smug Sheik strutted down the aisle wearing his signature red and white turban, followed by his disgusting American traitor manager, Freddie Blassie. Suddenly, there was a sound in the arena I hadn't heard before: a loud guitar chug started playing through speakers that hung high in the rafters. I recognized the song right away: it was "The Eye of the Tiger" from *Rocky 3*. This was the first time I'd heard a wrestler come to the ring with entrance music, and it added even more excitement and anticipation to Hogan's entry. After a few bars, Hogan came bursting through the curtain like a wildfire. Pandemonium broke loose inside Madison Square Garden.

The Hulk didn't even wait for the Sheik to take his turban and robe off. As soon as the bell rang, Hulk was pounding him with punches and kicks. Hogan was in complete control of the champion until the Sheik

Scally and I having fun in the schoolyard. A few hours later we would be at MSG to watch Hulk Hogan.

finally caught him with his Iranian boot—the one with a large spike on each tip, with which he famously kicked his opponents. I never understood how this was even legal. I was outraged: one kick from the boot and Hogan went down. The champion began working on his back with a slew of kicks, and I knew right away what he was doing. He was weakening his back to set Hogan up for the devastating Camel Clutch that had defeated Backlund just a month earlier.

Scally and I began screaming to Hogan to warn him what the Sheik was doing. Unfortunately, we were once again in the nosebleed seats, and our hero Hogan couldn't heed our warning.

Finally, after a few minutes of pounding on the small of Hogan's back, the Sheik locked in the Camel Clutch in the center of the ring. I screamed in horror "Nooooo!" knowing full well that it was over. Nobody ever escaped from the Camel Clutch.

Hogan was in excruciating pain and it was only a matter of time before he gave up. Scally and I were devastated. The ref kept asking him if he was giving up, but Hogan didn't respond, at least not until I saw his two index fingers begin to wave back and forth as to say, "No, No, No!" Hogan began to shake and reach down inside for some sort of extra internal power. Somehow, he muscled his legs back underneath him and gained leverage. Moments later, he was getting to his feet as the Sheik held on to his back.

The Hulk began to shake more and finally slammed the Sheik back

Hulk Hogan winning the WWF Championship, 1984.

into the turnbuckle, sending the Iranian down like a ton of bricks. The crowd went wild. Hogan slung himself into the ropes, bounced off then flew into the air to deliver his massive leg drop. He got on top of the Sheik, hooked his leg, and the ref counted 1,2,3. It was over!!

In 5 minutes and 40 seconds, Hulk Hogan had become the new WWF Champion! Scally and I were screaming and hugging with joy; even my mom, who didn't really care about wrestling, was clapping. Hulkamania was runnin' wild!

As Hogan held up the beautiful green WWF championship title to the crowd it happened: suddenly, I could feel myself breathing slowly and deeply and I could hear my heartbeat pound like a drum in my chest. I turned to my mom and Scally and they seemed to be frozen. It was my second "Frozen Moment." I wasn't quite sure that it had really even happened years earlier when I saw KISS. I thought maybe I had just dreamed it or maybe it was just my 5-year-old brain playing tricks on me. It was none of that. It was reality. I somehow had the ability to savor a moment in time and to take in my surroundings when something impressionable happened to me. I'm not saying I had super powers or anything, obviously, I just think I have an innate ability to recognize when a special moment, a life-altering instance, was happening to me.

Was a wrestler winning a championship a "life-altering moment?" Maybe not, but for me, something had just happened that would hold an impression on me forever.

I now had the building blocks of what would be my dreams and goals for the rest of my life. Seeing KISS and hearing Peter Criss play his drums changed me; now, nearly 5 years later, watching Hulk Hogan win the WWF championship had also changed me.

Now that I had two very distinct goals and ambitions in life: becoming a drummer and becoming a wrestler. It was time to get serious. I already had a full room dedicated to my drums, but how was I going to train to become a wrestler?

I thought to myself, "I need a wrestling ring," but obviously buying one was out of the question. And back in the 80's, there were no professional wrestling schools to train to become a pro wrestler. I didn't know what to do.

I explored amateur type wrestling to get started. The problem was that even though I was only 10 years old, I was very big. Because of my size, they wanted me to wrestle in my weight class, which meant high school kids. I thought, "Sure, why not?" but my mom wasn't having it. She didn't want her 10-year-old baby boy fighting kids 15 and 16 years old.

So, what could I do? Finally, it occurred to me. I would get wrestling mats and cover my other "spare room" with them, wall-to-wall. I just had to wait until the next holiday to ask for the mats as a present. If it wasn't for Christmas and my birthday, I'd never have been able to do anything. So, until Christmas rolled back around, I'd have to wait to start on my training to become a professional wrester.

My school binders in 4th & 5th grade.
Wrestling & KISS!

CHAPTER 5

PRACTICE. PRACTICE. AND LIP SYNC

Growing up, my family always had pets and absolutely loved animals. Over the years, we had dogs, cats, snakes, lizards, fish, frogs, salamanders, and turtles. I remember one time we even talked about getting a monkey. I don't think my mom was really serious, but it was discussed.

We had a cat named Tabby and she was the meanest, craziest cat ever, but we loved her. One afternoon, my mom was upstairs taking a nap and I heard her screaming at the top of her lungs. I ran to see what had happened and to make sure she was okay. It turned out that while she was taking a nap, Tabby crawled up next to her and bit her on the face. That was just Tabby. Like I said, she was mean.

On March 18, 1984, The Cassata's gained a new family member: our dog Yukon. Yukon was an Alaskan Malamute puppy and was still small when we picked him up at the breeder. He looked like a tiny ball of fur with giant paws. He sat on my lap and cuddled with me the whole way home and we bonded right away. From that moment on, he really became not only my dog but my best friend!

Yukon grew pretty fast over the next 6 months and was rapidly approaching 130 pounds. Not only did I have my new best friend to spend every day with, but Yukon also became my wrestling practice partner. Unfortunately, he was more than a match for young Joey. One day, while play wrestling, Yukon knocked me over and I broke my wrist.

My dog and best friend, Yukon.

Christmas of 1984 was great. Not only did I get my new wrestling mats but I also go the brand new KISS album called *Animalize*! By then, my two rooms were set as well: side by side, I had my drum room and my new wrestling room that I christened "Madison Square Room."

Day and night, I would practice my drums to the latest KISS album and then go to "Madison Square Room" to practice my wrestling moves with Yukon. Soon enough, my friends and I started our own wrestling league and even made a few homemade championship belts.

My favorite championship was the Battle Royal champion when 7 or 8 of my friends came over and we beat the hell out of each other. There were no pins or submissions in a Battle Royal match. In our version, a competitor would have to throw his opponent out of the room to eliminate him. Because I was so much bigger than everyone else, I quickly became the undefeated Battle Royal Champion and also the Heavyweight Champion.

Just to be fair, I let some of my other friends hold some of the lesser belts. My good friend since kindergarten, Brian O'Grady, became Intercontinental Champion and Scally and another friend Jimmy Price became Tag Team Champions. Everything was really starting to take shape: I was getting really good on the drums and because of my size, it was inevitable that I would become a professional wrestler.

The next few years was more of the same. As much as I could, every time either wrestling or KISS was in town I went to see it live. It got so out of hand that my mother eventually told me I was allowed to go with my friends, on our own, so she didn't have to chaperone. Plus, she would be saving money by not buying a ticket for herself.

Can you imagine that? I was only about 12 years old and my mother was not only letting me go to Madison Square Garden in Manhattan with my friends, but also to what was known as the Meadowlands, Brendan Byrne Arena in New Jersey.

It was actually pretty scary. I don't think my friends ever told their parents that my mom wasn't coming. I can't imagine that they would have been allowed to go. Times Square was a much different place back then, with drug dealers and hookers on every corner.

I remember my mom told us, "Stay close together. Don't talk to anyone and don't look anyone in the eye." I think we were too young and naïve to even think about being scared. All we knew was that we were going to see KISS or Hulk Hogan! The only problem I was having was that because I was so obsessed with both wrestling and with KISS that I had to alternate friends every month because no one wanted to go as much as I did.

My brother always had a paper route growing up and I would always try to tag along so I could make a few dollars to spend at Madison Square Garden.

By the time 1986 rolled around, heavy metal music had really started to take over. I was not only listening to KISS but many new bands too: Twisted Sister, Ratt, Motley Crue, Stryper, Bon Jovi, Def Leppard, Autograph, and many more.

Of course, KISS was still my favorite, and now that all of these other bands, and the genre itself, were becoming mainstream, most of my friends were starting to get into it too.

Growing up, I had the greatest group of friends ever. We did everything together, kind of like the clan in the movie *Stand By Me*, or maybe my group was more like the kids in Porky's! Ha Ha. The friends I made in grammar school are still my best and closest friends 35 years later. We were a pretty wild group with many different personalities.

First, I was the rocker kid who was super big for his age. Growing up all my friends called me "Satta". Short for Cassata.

Scally was a jock and into basketball. He had very strict parents and was always trying to figure out a way to do things with us without getting into trouble at home.

Brian O'Grady, who everyone called "O.G." came from an Irish family with 4 crazy brothers. He was an absolute nut and had been a great friend since the first grade.

Top to bottom: Scally, Jason, Kenny, Todd, Me
Bobby, O'Grady, James, Jimmy and Damien.

Parasimo was equally crazy in his own right. Phil would always come over and tell my grandmother how bad I'd been in school that day. In actuality, he was telling her about all the bad things he'd done in school that day. Phil was also a compulsive liar and still is to this day.

Jason Pers might have actually been clinically insane. He was the kid who would dive off of my fireplace and do a belly flop on to the floor, like he was jumping into a swimming pool. Jason's mother was also very strict and obsessed with his school work. Our group hated it because she constantly called our parents to discuss study groups or extra classes we could take to get ready for high school. We would always yell at him "Tell your mom to stop calling our moms!"

Brian Daly was the other "big kid" in our group. Daly was very calm, which I never understood because the rest of his family were nuts. He had 5 younger brothers and one older sister. Two of Daly's brothers, after seeing the movie *Home Alone*, decided to break into their neighbor's house and run the water faucets just like the "Wet Bandits" did in the movie. Nuts!

Jimmy Price came from a family of older brothers. He and I always had a contest about who could be absent more days from school in any given year. At least once a week, I would play sick by shaking the thermometer the opposite way causing the temperature to go up rather than down. I would call Jimmy that morning to let him know, and then he would cut school and come over to watch TV all day. One year, he was absent 53 times and I totaled 56. We watched a lot of *Leave it Beaver* and *Gilligan's Island* that year.

James Myers was the son of our basketball coach. Overall, I think he was probably the quietest of the group. Where most of us had huge personalities, James went with the flow.

Rob Gardner was another crazy kid! I guess we were all a little nuts. Rob and I would call each other every night at 11:30 to watch our favorite show the Honeymooners together on the phone. It's still my all-time favorite show!

Then there was Bobby Howell. Bobby loved to play army and climb trees or roofs (a hobby we called "roofing" in Brooklyn). He also loved to skitch, which is when you grab on to the bumper of a car, after a good snowfall, and let the car basically drag you down the street. Looking back, skitching was really an insane thing to do–sort of like skiing without the skis but attached to an unknowing car. Crazy! Not surprising, Bobby would go on to be a big time Navy Seal.

Rounding out the main group of closest friends was Damien. We had many more within our group, but these guys were the closest and remained friends our whole lives. Damien was the only one who didn't attend our Catholic school, and he was also a year older than we were. He was never as wild as the others, but he still got into trouble, like the time he got beat up with a meat tenderizer. That story always made me laugh. He had marks all over him like chopped meat.

A crazy thing we all used to play was a game we called "Pass Out". The way to play "Pass Out" was easy. First, one person would hold their breath, and then another person would firmly press their index fingers on either side of that person's neck. Essentially cutting off blood flow to their brain. This caused the person to lose consciousness within a few seconds.

What a sick game for kids to play! We had no idea how dangerous this really was. All we knew, was that it was hilarious when one of us would pass out. Particularly the one time our friend Rob passed out and fell face first into Jimmy's dog Spike's pile of dog shit! We must have laughed for 2 years straight! Come to think of it, we still talk and laugh about that story.

One day during sixth grade, O'Grady came up with the idea of being in the talent show at our school. After talking over a few ideas, I suggested we dress as KISS and play my all-time favorite song, "Detroit Rock City." I really said it more as a joke because none of my friends played an instrument. But nobody was laughing. Everyone thought it was a great idea.

We originally played with the idea of actually buying instruments and learning to play the song. That was quickly scrapped when we figured out how much guitars cost. We then came up with the idea of lip syncing to the song.

At first, I was against it because I could actually play. But I realized soon enough that the only way to perform as KISS, with my best friends and in front of the whole school, was lip syncing. We planned to dress up as KISS, in full makeup and costumes, and just pretend to be playing our instruments. With only a few months to prepare, we had a lot of work to do.

The first task was to choose which version of "Detroit Rock City" we would do. Knowing I was the biggest KISS fan in town, my friends left the details to me. I chose the Alive 2 version; to me, that was not only the best version, but it also had the perfect intro for us to come out to: "You wanted the best, you got the best. The hottest band in the world, K I S S!"

I was also in charge of choreography. The problem was, in 1986, we had no access to live footage of KISS, with full makeup, to watch and study. Luckily, a few months earlier, KISS *Animalize Live Uncensored* had come out on VHS. Of course, I owned the tape and every day after school we got together at my house to rehearse and study the video. The band consisted of the following:

Kiss Cover Band for Talent Show
Brian O'Grady - Paul Stanley
Jimmy Price - Ace Frehley
Bobby Howell - Gene Simmons
Joey Cassata - Peter Criss

Scally took on the role of quasi-manager and the one who watched us practice to make sure everything was perfect. He would also report in on a rival band that was dressing as Motley Crue in the same talent show. We practiced for about a month and then found out we actually had to audition to be part of the talent show. We weren't worried. We were ready, and we were great!

Our costumes were all set. Since I had been both Gene and Ace for Halloween a few years earlier, those costumes were easy. Even though I was 6 and 7 years old at the time, they would fit my friends because I was about the size of an 11-year-old back then.

Brian's mom came up with a pretty cool looking outfit for him to wear and I wore one of my mom's old one- piece jumpsuits as Peter Criss. It was perfect, with a zipper going up the front that I could leave open, just like Peter's outfit during "Destroyer."

My mom, who had done my makeup for past Halloween costumes, was going to do all of our makeup. The audition was set for after school on March 10, 1986. The plan was to rush to my house after school and start getting ready.

Around this time, my mom had just started a new job working at Boops video store, 2 blocks from my house. The night before the audition, she found out that she had to go into work that day and wouldn't be able to apply our makeup for the audition. This was a disaster! How could four 11-year-olds possibly apply their own makeup? We had no idea what we were doing, but we had no choice.

After school Jimmy, O'Grady, and I ran to my house to get ready. Bobby said his mom was going to apply his makeup. After an hour, we were finally ready. We looked terrible! The makeup was all smeared, where black was running into white, and our lips and half of our chins were covered in red lipstick. Then, Bobby walked in.

As bad as we looked, he looked even more ridiculous. To draw Gene Simmons' makeup design, his mom had him put his hands on his face and then she traced them. So, he basically had two giant black hand prints on his face. This actually cheered us up. It was only the audition and we knew we would do great.

On the way to school, we had to pass by my mom's video store. She came out to give us a big good luck yell as we ran by, which gave us the little extra bit of confidence we needed.

Once at the audition, we only got to play for a few seconds. It turned out that the audition was really just a formality. They wanted to make sure everyone entering the talent show was serious and had something prepared.

For the next few weeks, we rehearsed nonstop, day and night. Even though this was just a lip sync performance, it was my first real performance in front of a live audience. It meant the world to me, and I wasn't going to mess it up. I had to make sure we were perfect. And, we were! That was until Bobby, our Gene Simmons, wasn't allowed to perform with us anymore.

My friends and I used to play this horrible prank game when we were kids: ring and run. Ours, though, was more of the Brooklyn version, which we called kick and run.

Most people in Brooklyn at that time had screen doors in front of their regular wooden front doors to their house. Screen doors were pretty flimsy and made out of a thin piece of metal. The way the game was played was we would pick a house with a good screen door. One member of the group would walk up to it, ring the bell, and then kick the screen door as hard as he could. In essence, he totally annihilated the screen door. Then, we all ran as fast as we could.

For some reason we thought it was a lot of fun. But on the night when it was Bobby's turn, he picked a house a few doors down from where our friend Jimmy (our Ace Frehley) lived.

All went according to plan: Bobby went up, rang, kicked, and we all ran. We thought nothing of it until the next day when at rehearsal, Jimmy informed us that his neighbor saw Bobby do it, which naturally didn't sit well with Bobby's parents once informed about what their son had done. Not only was Bobby punished for kicking in the door, but he was also not allowed to participate in the talent show. We were only a few days away from the performance and we had no Gene Simmons. Luckily, our other friend James Myers stepped up and said he would do it.

Finally, the day of the talent show arrived and I was super excited, but there was still a lot to do. Even though this was just a lip sync performance it gave me my first look into what it took to put on a rock show. First things first, I had to pack up all of my drums.

I'd never broken down my drum kit before and I had no idea where to even begin. I actually didn't even know it could be broken down.

My brother and his friend Jimmy Whelen took apart the drums as best as they could and started to load them into one of my friend's parents' cars. I didn't have cases or anything. Needless to say, the drums got pretty scratched on the way to the talent show, but that wasn't the biggest problem. Once we got there and unloaded, and while I was putting the drums back together, I realized I couldn't mount the toms to the bass drum; the arm seemed broken.

Looking back, I believe my brother just lost one of the wing nuts and maybe a spring, but I was sure at the time that he had completely broken my drums. I didn't have time to be pissed because we had to set up and start getting ready. Luckily, I wasn't really hitting the drums that night, so I just propped the toms on the bass drum which caused even more scratches.

While we were lining up our instruments, the point person for the talent show came over to ask, "What are you guys doing? Why aren't you setting up on stage like everyone else?" I answered, "We aren't going to use the stage to perform on."

I set up my drums in front of the stage on the gym floor. Because the whole school would be watching from just the bleacher seats on either side of the gym floor, I decided to use the whole gigantic gym floor as our stage, so we could be closer to the audience. Even then, I knew we had to stand out from everyone else. I didn't want to be lumped in with all of the other lame acts on the same stage. I wanted to be different.

I initially came up with this idea from watching the aforementioned KISS *Animalize* video. They opened that show with the same song we were doing, "Detroit Rock City." They came out on a platform over the drums to start during the "You wanted the best, you got the best" speech. Then, the drummer (Eric Carr) jumped down from the platform and the remaining members started the opening riff while standing above the drummer. It was a very cool visual that I wanted recreate using the stage as the platform above the drums.

Once our gear was in place, we moved backstage to put the makeup on. This time my mom was there to help. An hour later, we were ready and looked amazing!

Everyone backstage was raving about how great our makeup and costumes were. I thought to myself, "We can't be stopped. This talent show is ours!" While waiting our turn, our rival band, Motley Crue, was about to start.

The band consisted of a few of our classmates. They were performing the song "Smoking in the Boys Room." They looked awful—bad costumes, bad wigs. Once they started their performance, it was clear that they barely knew the song.

We were trying to be respectful, but 11 and 12-year-olds' idea of that is much different than adults. We were openly laughing from off stage, at least until the middle drum acapella chorus section of the song started.

The band began to raise their hands in the air and signal for the audience to clap along with them to the beat. It worked like a charm: the grammar school crowd obliged and began a huge audience participation clap that was roaring loud. Our laughter came to an abrupt halt. We were suddenly a little worried. Even though we were clearly more prepared and looked way better, this crowd participation part was a big hit, and we were unsure if we could follow it, or if we had anything to match it.

Once the Motley Crue band was finished, we took the stage. This was it—my first real performance (sort of) playing the drums in front of a live audience. Before we even started the song, we got a pretty good reaction because of how good we looked. But I knew it wasn't enough. We took our places at the edge of the stage above my drum set, which sat waiting below. We raised our hands high in unison and heard, "You wanted the best, you got the best. The hottest band in the world: KISS!" My jump down from the stage was modeled on Eric Carr's antics in the *Animalize* video and I took my place behind my drum set.

The chugging riff of "Detroit Rock City" started and the show had begun. We were perfect. Everything we rehearsed was going according to plan, and we were completely in sync. Even our new addition James was great on bass. Using the gym floor was working out well too, keeping us much closer to the crowd than all of the other acts, which I think we used to our advantage. The only problem was that the crowd wasn't really doing anything. I think they were enjoying our performance, but because we didn't have a big crowd participation part, we didn't get the reaction that Motley had received. That was until the bridge.

Our Paul Stanley, Brian O'Grady, took control. He went completely off script and away from everything we had rehearsed. Once he was free from the mic (the bridge had no vocals), he proceeded to go over to one of the most hated and feared teachers in the whole school, our sixth-grade math teacher, Mrs. Cook.

Mrs. Cook had one lazy eye and was notorious for yelling and pointing at someone in class, while simultaneously looking at another because of her lazy eye. This always confused not only the person she was really targeting, but also the person on whom her lazy eye was focused. This resulted in both parties getting into even more trouble.

O.G. proceeded to approach the evil Mrs. Cook, and once within striking distance, he started sticking out his tongue like Gene Simmons, even though he was playing Paul Stanley. Mrs. Cook was appalled and clearly angry—and so was I. Being a die-hard KISS fan, I knew that Paul Stanley would never stick out his tongue like Gene. It was blasphemy. I wanted an authentic KISS performance and this wasn't it. I was already preparing my lecture in my head when all of a sudden, the audience completely erupted with laughter and cheering.

They all knew Mrs. Cook and her reputation as one of the meanest teachers in the school. If they didn't personally experience one of her "Lazy eye pointing while looking at a different person" outbursts, they had certainly heard about it from other students. The crowd absolutely loved that she was having a tongue wagged in her face.

After a few moments, and to everyone's shock, Mrs. Cook seemed to start enjoying it. She was smiling and even started to stick her tongue out. The crowd noise was twice, if not three times louder than the crowd participation that the Motley Crue band had gotten. O.G. had saved the day!

There was no winner crowned for the talent show, but we knew, like everyone else there, that we had won.

I learned a lot from that first live performance. First, never let your brother and his friends move your drums. Second, and this is a lesson I've kept with me all these years, is that you should never be so over prepared that you aren't able to change things on the fly—to play to the wants and needs of a particular audience on any given night. I've played with many musicians over the years who would always want to over rehearse (yes, there is such a thing). Then when it came time for the show, they weren't able to jam or change the set list because they were so set in their ways that they couldn't improvise. I believe that improvisation in all forms of performance art is an under-valued and under-appreciated thing. And, this little performance at my sixth-grade talent show taught me a lot about improv.

CHAPTER 6

JESUS HAD LONG HAIR

VS

Long haired Joey

The evil Sr. Marie

If I wasn't already hooked on playing the drums, after that first live performance I was completely addicted! Feeling the crowd's energy and getting all that praise made it clear: I had to get back on a stage fast.

Not only was I reassured of what I needed to do for the rest of my life, but my friends and I grew closer than ever. There was something about bonding on that stage, and all of the preparation that went into the performance that really brought us closer. And that goes not only the few who performed, but the whole crew.

It was as if when O.G., Jimmy, James, and I kicked ass at the talent show, the whole crew was lifted to another social status in our school. We became the "A" crowd that everyone wanted to be a part of. We were essentially rock stars walking down the hallway every day.

I know it sounds corny but at 11 and 12 years old, a little thing like that talent show can really make a kid popular. Sixth grade became one of the best years of my life. Even though there were two higher grades at our school, we were the kings of the school. Something came over all of us after that.

Our teacher, Mr. Green, was kind of a weird old man who we used to abuse. Don't get me wrong, we weren't necessarily "bad kids," but we knew how to push the limits. Mr. Green didn't last long because of our behavior. Rumor has it, he had a heart attack, but we were never sure.

After Mr. Green's supposed heart attack, we went through about 12 or 13 substitute teachers who would all quit after the first day because of us. We loved it! This speaks to why the power of the stage (even though it was a stupid lip sync'd performance) was so addictive to me.

In truth, I naturally have an addictive personality, which is why I've never tried a drug in my whole life. I was always afraid that I'd like it. My drugs were my drums and performing. I never needed a bigger high than that. After all of the substitute teachers quit, the school finally hired a permanent replacement, a young 22-year-old right out of college. Her name was Miss Whalen. Van Halen's *Hot For Teacher* video was still pretty popular at this point and we would always joke around with, "What if we got a hot teacher like in the video?" Well, it happened!

After Miss Whalen got there, all the boys were pretty well behaved to stay on her good side. We even volunteered to stay after class sometimes to help her clean the blackboard. An added bonus for being such good boys, was that Miss Whelen would always drive us home in her 1968 red Mustang.

Even though I was behaving better in the classroom, the rivalry with my principal, Sr. Marie, was just heating up. I already hated her because of the manipulation games she pulled about my tuition being late. Now, because of my music, I was growing my hair long and that was a big no-no in Catholic school. In fact, students weren't allowed to have the back of our hair touch the collar. What a ridiculous rule! It's not like I was dirty or my hair was sloppy; it was just starting to get a little long.

Every time Sr. Marie spotted me, she would pull me in to her office and scream that I needed a haircut. She would try to demean me by saying, "You look like a girl," Or, "You look ridiculous!" Can you believe that? This from someone who was supposed to be guiding us in our religious beliefs. She was trying to humiliate me because I looked different than what she liked.

My hatred grew to the point that now, out of spite, I refused to cut my hair. So she eventually just suspended me. Yes, you read right. She would keep a 12-year-old out of class because his hair was too long.

I didn't care. I looked at a day of suspension as a day off from school. Even though I was suspended often, it never hurt my grades because I was smart and never needed to study or do homework. While I was far from a straight-A student, I didn't even have to try to pass tests. Unfortunately, I also found school rather useless because I knew I was going to be a drummer, and/or a wrestler. This attitude made me even more rebellious: it was as if I felt I knew more than my teachers, and I was 100 percent sure I knew more than my jerk of a principal, Sr. Marie.

The first time I was suspended because of my hair, Sr. Marie sent a long note home outlining the school rules and why she thought my hair looked ridiculous. She also wrote that I needed to have it cut to school regulations in order to return to school the next day. I was nervous bringing the note home to my mom. I knew that being suspended was not something she would take lightly. I never hid anything from my mom. She along with my dog Yukon were my absolute best friends! Maybe my brother Dan a close third. Lol.

I was going to be honest and tell her what had happened. When I presented my mom with the note from Sr. Marie, I expected the worst. I assumed she would be angry and insist I cut my hair because that was the school rule. She read the note as I stood by anxiously awaiting her verdict. Once finished, she looked at me and said, "You tell that Sr. Marie, Jesus had long hair, why can't you?"

I was overcome with joy that my mom was on my side and saw how ridiculous the suspension was. In my heart, I knew she believed in me and my drums and she wasn't going to side with some repulsive nun over her son and his dreams. She proved, once again, why she was the greatest mom in the world.

I returned to school the next day with my hair exactly as it was and proceeded to march into Sr. Marie's office. Upon seeing me, her face turned red as fire and I swear there was smoke coming out of her ears. She couldn't believe that I returned without a haircut. She barked, "Why is your hair not cut like I demanded?" In a very calm voice I answered with, "Jesus had his hair long, why can't I?" This sent Sr. Marie into a frenzy like I've never seen before. She couldn't believe that I'd not only disobeyed her, but that I had a smart answer for her—an answer she probably wasn't ready for. That comeback not only cost me a full week of suspension, but it fueled the fire in the Joey vs. Sr. Marie rivalry that would last the next two years.

The only time I ever remember actually disappointing my mom was when I was an Alter boy. Scally and I were set to serve Mass one Friday and for some reason we got a really bad case of the giggles.

Earlier that day we were laughing at a girl's name from our school. Her name was Martha Bartha. Now Martha was sweet as can be, but whenever Scally and I said those two names together we laughed uncontrollably.

Later in the day, my mom came to see her baby boy serve Mass. She was so proud of me and even had all of her friends come to see what an angel boy she had serving God.

About 10 minutes into Mass, while Scally was holding the bible for the priest to read, I quietly whispered… "Martha Bartha". This sent shockwaves down Scally's spine and he began laughing uncontrollably which caused the bible to shake, which also caused the priest to be unable to read it. Needless to say he wasn't happy! He screamed at us to move back to our holding area while the Mass continued. Unfortunately for us, him and the rest of the church, that made matters even worse. Scally and I couldn't stop laughing and now we were so loud the whole church could hear us. This caused the priest to finally throw us off the alter and we weren't allowed to serve mass again for quite a while.

It's a very funny story, but at the time my mother was furious and absolutely mortified!

Now that my friends and I were kings of the school and heavy metal music was the most popular music around, we agreed to officially start our own band. There was a music store on Flatbush Avenue called King James Music. Every day after school we walked over to look in the window at the different guitars for them to buy.

The plan was simple: once they bought the guitars, we would practice day and night to become the biggest band in the world. We might even tour with KISS one day! That was our dream.

Unfortunately, I realized quickly that nobody had the same drive that I had. I would let nothing stand in my way, not school, not lack of money, not the pain of hard work, and not someone telling me I was crazy for thinking I was going to be a rock star. If anything, all of those things drove me more.

Whenever someone said, "You're nuts!" or, "All you think about is wrestling and drums," or, "Cut your hair. You're never going to be a professional drummer!" the more I wanted to show them that I would do what I wanted and become the world wrestling champion and a famous drummer! My focus never wavered.

My KISS themed denim jacket all through grammar school.
I wore this every day for at least three years.

CHAPTER 7

NO LIGHTS. NO DRUMS. NO PROBLEM

S THOMAS AQUINAS

Ever since the talent show a few months prior, my drum set sat broken in my room. Several more pieces were lost or broken when my brother and his friend brought them back home. The cymbal stands barely worked anymore, the bass drum legs didn't support the weight of the toms, and the chain for the bass drum pedal snapped. Basically, my drums were a mess. But that wouldn't stop me from playing.

I had a temporary solution. I propped the drums against the wall for support. One side of the bass drum leaned on my back bedroom wall so it could support the weight of the toms leaning against it. I wedged my cymbal in between one of the toms and the wall vertically: this would serve as my hi-hat and my crash. My floor tom wasn't functional at all, and I now had to kick my bass drum instead of using the pedal. It was all pretty horrible, and I knew it was time to get a new drum set. Unfortunately, it wasn't the right time to ask for one.

Life at home was getting hard about now. I could tell more than ever that my mom was really struggling to pay the bills. We constantly had our electric turned off because we were behind on payments. Sometimes we went a few days without lights, so we sat around and used candles after sunset. We had our gas turned off a few times as well. Luckily, I don't remember it ever being in the dead of winter, which would have made it unbearably cold.

I even remember going the whole summer of 1986 without a phone. My brother and I used to tell our friends that my mom shut it off on us because we used it too much and we didn't appreciate it, but that was just a cover up.

Even with all these financial problems, life at home was still great. We loved each other and always took care of each other, and we didn't need material things to make us happy. I remember coming home from school every day and finding a picture my mom drew waiting on the steps for me. She was a great artist! It always had a little saying like "You're my world" or "I love you to the moon." When I saw things like this and the love my mom had for us, none of that financial stuff mattered.

Still, I knew it killed her inside to have her sons go through it, but I wouldn't have traded my childhood with my mom and brother and Yukon for anything. As corny as it sounds, we didn't need lights: we had love.

So, for Christmas and my birthday that year, I didn't have the heart to ask for a big present like new drums. Somehow, I knew my mom would sacrifice something else to get them, and I couldn't do that to her. Instead, I knew I was going to receive Confirmation in the spring of seventh grade and I could ask my sponsor to get me my drums.

In the Catholic religion, Confirmation is the last of the four initial rites, after Baptism, Penance, and Holy Communion. For Confirmation, a candidate picks a Confirmation name and someone to sponsor him or her—and that sponsor acts almost like a godparent, someone who is an outstanding Catholic who can guide you in the faith. Naturally, I picked my cousin Joey from Boston.

I think Joey was the furthest thing from a good Catholic as one can get. During his summer visits, with sister Jodee, he always had some new illegal scheme up his sleeve.

Me and Danny with our cousins from Boston, Joey & Jodee

One time, Joey took me to Times Square to buy a cell phone on a stolen credit card. Mind you, this was the 80's and way before cell phones were an everyday item. Back then they cost thousands of dollars and were only for the mega rich. They also weighed about 20 pounds.

When he tried to make the purchase, the store owner immediately called the cops because he knew it was a stolen credit card. My cousin and I had to run top speed through Times Square to avoid getting arrested. I was probably 10 years old at the time, but it didn't matter: I always looked up to him and that's who I wanted as my Confirmation sponsor.

It was tradition for a sponsor to buy a pretty big gift in celebration of a young Catholic finishing his sacraments. And I had just the present in mind. I went to Sam Ash Music and picked out a brand new drum set.

I still didn't know much about the different brands of drums or what was good and what wasn't. I basically picked the biggest set they had on display in the store: a 7-piece Tama Swingstar.

It just so happens that it was burgundy red, the exact color of my old drum set. It was gorgeous! The one problem was its price tag: $799. I didn't really have a great concept of money yet, but I knew that was a lot. I only hoped it wasn't too much for my cousin to spend. I told my mom and she thought it was way too much. She said that I should just ask Joey for money towards the drums, which I thought was a good idea. Still, deep down I was still hoping he would get me the whole set. So, I continued to play my propped up, broken down drums for the next few months, anxiously awaiting my Confirmation.

I went at least once a week to Sam Ash Music to look at the drums. I would bring my friends and show them the kit I was getting for Confirmation.

In May of 1987, at the end of the day of my Confirmation, my cousin Joey gave me an envelope just before he, my Uncle, and my cousin Jodee drove back to Boston. I was exploding and wanted to open it immediately, but my mom made me wait until they left. Once they pulled away, I ripped that thing open so fast, already figuring out how I would pick the drums up later that day. To my disappointment, there was only $100 in the envelope.

Looking back, that was a very generous gift and it would have been insane for him to give me an $800 present. But I didn't understand that then, and I was crushed. I really thought I was going to be able to buy my drums. Instead, I wasn't even half way there yet. My mom told me to put my money someplace safe and to start saving up the rest, which I thought that was next to impossible. How was I going to save another $700?

I even contemplated selling my comic book collection, which I started back when I was 5 years old. I had a lot of major Marvel issues, but I knew it wasn't the right time to sell them. My brother and I always said we would probably sell our collections to buy a house one day.

I remember staring at my poster of Eric Carr every day and asking it: "How will I ever be a great drummer like you if I don't even have a real drum set?"

I decided that I needed to get a job! But who was going to hire a 13 year old kid? I went to all of the local Pizzerias and asked if they needed any help. Finally, when I went to the last one on the outskirts of my neighborhood, they agreed to hire me! I was going to be a pizza delivery boy and hand deliver pizza on my bike. I even convinced my good buddy Scally to come along most nights. This, along with the tip money that I would make being an Alter boy was my source of income to put towards my drums and my dreams.

Around this time, in seventh grade, I started to realize that my friends were starting to catch up to me in size, which told me I wasn't going to be this giant like everyone thought I would be. This, along with the after-effects of playing the talent show, really tipped the scales in favor of drumming full-time over wrestling.

I still loved wrestling with all my heart, but there was no way to wrestle anywhere and get good at it. There were no pro wrestling schools or classes in the late 1980's, which meant there was no way to master my craft. I still wrestled periodically in "Madison Square Room" with my friends, but I really started to focus more than ever on my drums.

That same year, KISS released the video *Exposed*. This was a mind-blowing, earth-shattering thing because it was the first time since seeing them live at Madison Square Garden that I could watch KISS in their makeup. This time, though, I had the power to play it over and over again! And, boy, did I play that video tape non-stop. Anytime someone came over I made them watch it, and that goes for friends, relatives—anybody.

Now, I had the basis of everything I needed. I had the full concert videos *KISS Animalize Uncensored* and *KISS Exposed*, showing them in makeup and all of their glory.

Even though I spent every waking minute thinking about my drums, because I still had no real drum set to practice on, I started to spend a lot more time with friends and not locked up in my room practicing. This turned out to be a blessing in disguise.

My friends and I became inseparable between sixth and eighth grades. Thinking back, I might not have gotten as close to them if I'd had my brand new drum set to play on every day. Like the Rolling Stones said, "You can't always get what you want, but sometimes you get what you need."

My friend Jason Pers always had regular sleep overs at his house, and one of our rituals was to put on a concert. The group of girls that we hung out with would come over earlier in the day (they weren't sleeping over), and we would essentially put on a full rock concert for them. It was just pretend and lip sync, but it was so much fun.

The girls sat on the floor in front of us and yelled their heads off as we performed all the biggest songs on the radio at that time. Bon Jovi's new album *Slippery When Wet* was especially huge, and of course, we always threw in a few KISS songs. Once again, and I know this sounds silly, but these types of things really shape a kid at this age.

This really started to teach me how to perform in front of an audience. It was the perfect scenario: I combined my best friends in the world with the thing I loved to do more than anything, perform and play the drums. These goofy things would solidify all of our friendships for years to come.

After saving for my new drum set for the rest of the year, I'd saved another $400. I was up to $500, still a long way off from the $800 I needed.

I had to try and ask for the rest as a combo Christmas and birthday present. So, I did. My mom said she couldn't make any promises and said that at the very least she would give me more money to put toward the new kit. Christmas came and went and now it was time for my birthday.

I woke up the day of my fourteenth birthday and my mom gave me a card with money toward my drums. It was an amazing gift but left me still short of my target amount. I went to school that day feeling down: it had been more than a year ago since my old set had been broken. I'd been banging around on my propped-up drums for way too long.

I was starting to worry that I wouldn't even remember how to play a real kit anymore. When I returned from school that day, I went straight up to my room to think about how I was going to raise the money for my drum set.

There was a basketball game that night at school, but I called Scally to tell him that I didn't feel good and that I wasn't coming. A few minutes later, Scally called back and my mom answered before I could. I heard her say, "He's not sick and he's coming to the game." I was mad and yelled, "Why would you tell him that? Now I look like a liar!"

My mom insisted that I stop sulking and go to the game, so I reluctantly went. Being around my friends did help me feel a little better, and I realized why my mom had made me go. Still, I was a little surprised nobody was making a big deal that it was my birthday. A few of my friends nonchalantly said happy birthday but nothing big.

After the game in the locker room, I couldn't find one of my sneakers. I saw a few kids laughing and knew they must have played a joke. I looked everywhere for about 15 minutes and finally found it in the showers. When I came out of the shower from retrieving my sneaker, almost everyone was gone.

My friends and I usually walked home together so it was a little weird that they left without saying anything, especially on my birthday. I thought it was a little odd. I left the school gym and started to walk home and began to remember why I was down in the first place: I didn't have my new drums.

As soon as I walked in my front door, I knew something was up. My front hallway was the place my brother and I always kept our bikes, but now there were about 10 bikes sitting there, and I recognized a few. I walked upstairs to find a giant surprise birthday party waiting for me!

I ran over and gave my mom a big hug and told her I was sorry for being depressed about not getting my drums. She smiled and told me, "Go up to your room for a second."

I walked up my stairs with most of my friends trailing behind me. I opened the door to my room to find a brand-new drum set waiting for me, fully set up and ready to go. I was speechless. How did she do it? Not only how did she afford to get it for me, but how was it all set up so perfectly?

It was a dream come true. I had my mom, brother, Yukon, and all of my friends around me. They shouted and wanted to hear me play. I was a little leery about playing because I hadn't played on a real kit in almost 2 years. Do I even remember how to play a real kit? I thought to myself. Also, this kit was massive, or it at least seemed that way to me back in eighth grade. It had four rack toms, which I'd never tried before. Still, I couldn't get out of this: they wanted me to play. So, I said, "Screw it!" and jumped behind the kit and started to pound away.

It all started to quickly come back to me. I realized I was actually better than before my old kit had broken. Thanks to the time I spent practicing on my broken kit and air drumming with just my sticks, I'd somehow learned more control than I'd ever had before. Plus, it was simply easier to play on an actual kit than on a broken one.

Using the bass drum pedal was infinitely easier than kicking the bass drum with my foot while standing. Everyone agreed and thought I sounded great. I think I even saw my mom crying with joy to see how happy I was. She had come through once again for her baby boy.

After a month or two of rigorous practicing to *KISS Alive* and *KISS Alive 2* on my new kit, I felt I was playing really well. I had both of my favorite albums down pat. I loved playing along to all of my favorite songs more than anything. I actually think this is the best way for kids to learn and practice drums, since the instrument is about time, feel, and playing what's good for the song. Drums really aren't about chops and how much you can do. The only problem was I didn't know any other kid who played an instrument.

My 13th Birthday Party!

7th Grade class picture

CHAPTER 8

THE BATTLE OF THE BANDS

I knew the next step in becoming a successful drummer was to play with other musicians in real bands. As luck would have it, in March of 1988, my friend James Myers called to tell me that his neighbor had a band and they were looking for a drummer. I was interested right away.

I went immediately to talk with them about auditioning. I spoke to the guitar player, Ray Connelly, who told me that the name of the band was Menace and they had a show at a high school battle of the bands in a few months. He asked me to learn a few cover songs and come down to audition later that week. I was so excited to be talking to someone in a real band that wanted me to audition, that I didn't even ask him what kind of music they played.

Once he gave me the songs to learn, I quickly realized what kind of music they were into. They were two Metallica songs and an Anthrax song. I knew of both bands because my brother was into them, but I personally wasn't a big fan. They were what was considered Thrash Metal, which was much heavier than I was used to.

Ray asked me to Learn "Master of Puppets" and "For Whom the Bell Tolls" by Metallica and "Medusa" by Anthrax. I wasn't really familiar with any of the songs, but I told Ray I'd absolutely be there to audition. Even though it wasn't my type of music, I couldn't pass up the opportunity to play with a real band. As soon as I hung up, I asked Dan if I could borrow his Metallica and Anthrax albums.

"Master of Puppets" was the first one I listened to. The first thing I noticed was it was over 8 minutes long. I also noticed some double bass beats and fills, things I hadn't yet ventured into. I wasn't sure if I would be able to play the song without double bass.

Of course, looking back, it would have been easy to play the song without the small double bass parts, but back then I thought it would be impossible to pull off. Not only did it have double bass, but if this band was into this type of music, they would definitely expect me to be able to play double bass in the future. What was I going to do? A few days wasn't enough time to learn double bass. Besides, my drum set only had one bass drum and I wasn't about to buy another one.

Over the next few days, I learned the songs as best as I could, even though I didn't really like them. I came up with a plan to tell the band that I had injured my left foot so I wouldn't have to attempt any double bass. I went to meet the guys in Menace at Sink the Pink Studios on Flatbush Avenue.

I first met the guitarist, Ray. Since he was the person I'd been speaking to on the phone, I felt I knew him already. He seemed like a genuine guy. His brother Ken, the singer, came next. He was also nice but definitely not what I was expecting in terms of what the singer might look like. Even though my hair wasn't very long yet, I think I basically still looked the part of a rock and roll drummer. Ken, however, was a heavy-set guy with short hair and a very ordinary look. Come to think of it, Ray also seemed ordinary to me, at a time when I imagined a band to look like, well—a band. All my friends were jocks and that's kind of how they looked. So here I was, excited to meet an actual band, with the assumption that they would look like they played rock and roll. I was a little disappointed.

Next I met the bass player and another guitar player. Both looked more like rock and rollers, but the kind that I didn't necessarily like. They had more of that dirty "thrash metal" look. I was definitely more of a

64

"hair band" rock guy. They were all also much older than me, something I'd notice as a trend throughout my years of playing. Almost everyone in every band I was ever in was older than I was.

The first thing I did was inform them that I had twisted my ankle the day before. But, not to worry, it was just my left ankle so I'd be fine to play. I just can't play any double bass tonight. They said, "No problem." My plan worked like a charm.

This was the first time I'd ever been in a real studio rehearsal room. It was very cool, complete with a full set up of gear for everyone. There was a wall of guitar and bass amps to choose from and the drum set was a Pearl export series. It was okay, but a little beat up.

After about 20 minutes of setting up, Ray asked, "What do you want to play first?" I said, "Let's try 'For Whom the Bell Tolls,' which was the one I disliked the least. He said, "Great, you count it off."

This was it! The first time playing with other musicians in a real band. I was beyond excited. I wasn't exactly sure what he meant by "count it off," but I'd listened to enough of KISS *Alive* to know that Peter Criss counts in "Black Diamond," so I went for it: I took my sticks and clicked them together four times and we were off.

I didn't even realize at that time that the count in was supposed to not only bring the band into the song, but it was also meant to set the tempo. I think I counted it in at the same speed as "Black Diamond."

The first thing I noticed was that the guitars were really loud. I didn't mind at all and it actually felt good that I didn't have to play lightly to hear the music properly. I'd had that problem practicing in my room to my records all the time, having to play a little softer than I liked because I either couldn't hear the song or my bass drum would actually make the record skip.

When Ken entered with the vocals, it left a lot to be desired, even for Metallica-style vocals. He wasn't a good singer. In fact, he was pretty awful. It didn't really matter to me that much; I was finally playing with a live band and even in that moment I knew that this was just a stepping stone to the next level.

We played for about two hours and they even showed me an original song they were doing. It was an instrumental called "The Universe." It was pretty weird, but once again I didn't care. This was the first original song I'd even done. I was actually making up drum beats and parts for the first time, and I loved every second of it.

After rehearsal, we talked for a bit, but I still wasn't sure what they thought of me or if they liked my playing. I definitely thought I was good enough to be in the band, but I wasn't sure what they were looking for.

The next day, I got the call from Ray who said that they wanted me to join. Even though I wasn't into the music they were playing, I still accepted immediately. I finally found other people who played instruments, and I wasn't about to turn them down.

Menace:
Ken Connelly - Vocals
Ray Connelly - Lead Guitar
??? - Rhythm Guitar
??? - Bass
Joey Cassata – Drums

I was now officially a member of my first band. From that day in March of 1988, when I joined Menace, until this day that I sit here writing this book, there has never been a period of more than a few days where I haven't been in a band in some form.

After getting the good news, I knew I had to resolve the one problem that still loomed: I needed to learn to play double bass. I still couldn't afford a new bass drum and there weren't any holidays coming where I could ask for the drum as a present. Even if there were, I couldn't ask my mom for something else after she surprised me with my new drums on my birthday.

Then it hit me! I ran to "Madison Square Room" and in the corner sat my broken down old drum set that just happen to be the exact same color as my new Tama set. I couldn't believe it. My problem was solved. I had my second bass drum all along, and I wouldn't even have to fix anything on that kit because I wasn't planning on mounting any toms to it.

The only problem left was not having another pedal for the second bass drum, but I would worry about that later. I was way too anxious to dust it off and bring it up to my room to see how it looked.

When I placed the bass drum next to the Tama drum, the color looked identical. But alas, a new problem arose. When I went to place my rack toms into position, I realized that there was now a gap between the 12-inch and the 13-inch toms, since my 13 and 14-inch toms were mounted to my Tama bass drum and the 10 and 12-inchers had a separate stand. With the newly added bass, they wouldn't reach far enough to meet with the mounted toms. Then came another revelation.

I excitedly rushed back down to "Madison Square Room" and grabbed one of my old toms and my old snare stand. Once back in my room, I mounted the tom on the snare stand and placed it in the gap between my two toms. It worked perfectly! I now had what looked like Eric Carr's set up from the *Animalize* video. There were 5 rack toms, 2 bass drums, a floor tom, and a snare. I just needed to somehow get another pedal and soon came another brainstorm about how to deal with that.

A few days later, Menace rehearsed again at Sink the Pink Studios. In the rehearsal room were tons of back-up gear, so at the end of the rehearsal, I put one of the older, beat-up drum pedals in my bag and hoped no one would miss it. It was dumb of me to do, but luckily no one noticed. It was probably a pedal no one ever used, given the condition it was in. With the new additions to my drum set, and my new pedal for my left bass drum, I could begin learning double bass. The first thing I attempted was my favorite double bass fill, the opening of KISS's "Creatures of the Night." Surprisingly, after my first attempt, it sounded pretty descent. After about two hours of fooling around with double bass, I became pretty good at it, at least good enough to play what Menace needed from me.

Menace would rehearse anywhere from two to three times a week, usually in Ray and Ken's basement. All the rehearsals were just to get ready for the battle of the bands they entered right before I joined. Unfortunately, over the next few months, the band really didn't sound any better, mostly because of Ken's vocals. I also started to notice little things in each member's playing that didn't sound right. I knew the songs pretty much inside and out at this point and could instantly hear when someone was off or out of tune, and both occurred often. Even with the band still sounding terrible, I was determined to stick it out.

I looked at every rehearsal as another step toward reaching my dreams. I knew this was just a band for me to learn how to play with other musicians.

My first official gig, at the battle of the bands, would be on June 10, 1988. This was the first of many times in my life where a gig would conflict with a family or personal event. In this case, it was my eighth-grade graduation dance.

While it doesn't sound like a big deal, but this was one of the last times my friends and I would all be together. They meant the world to me, but I knew I had to play the show. I had to learn to sacrifice these kinds of social events if I was ever going to make it as a drummer.

Over the next few months, while getting ready for the battle of the bands, my ongoing war with Sr. Marie reached an all-time high. I was suspended five times during eighth grade, and all because of my hair. It got to the point where I didn't even want to walk into the school and pass her office because I knew I would get screamed at.

She was really trying to pull some sort of weird power trip on me, but I wasn't budging. As long as I had my mom's support, there was no way I was giving in to this power-hungry piece of garbage. It may sound sacrilegious to call a nun a piece of garbage, but after all she had done to me that's exactly what she was.

She actually called a meeting with all of the teachers to try and get me expelled from school. She called me a "ring leader" and claimed that all of my friends, which she called the "bad kids" or "trouble makers," followed what I said. Getting rid of me would be for the good of the school.

I knew this was her power trip again because I wouldn't obey her like everyone else did. She had repeatedly told me to cut my hair and I had repeatedly refused. This was her final attempt at dealing with me.

My mom, along with all of my friends' moms, went up to school to fight for me and to tell Sr. Marie that I should not be expelled. Some of them even threatened to take their kids out of the school if I were expelled.

I think that was the ultimatum that saved me. As soon as it might hurt her and the school financially, she backed down and reluctantly let me stay. Of course, she knew that in a few more months, I'd be gone for good anyway. I had won this small battle but the war was far from over.

Still, more battles loomed. Two weeks before our eighth-grade final exams began, Sr. Marie grabbed me off line and told me that if I didn't get a haircut I would be taking all of my final exams in her office. So, of course, on the first day of final exams, I showed up with my hair the same way it had always been. (Actually, throughout the school year, it grew longer and longer). Sr. Marie informed me that I was to report to her office every morning during finals.

I proceeded to take my tests in her office every day. Luckily for me, earlier in the week I had found my old KISS book from when I went to see them at Madison Square Garden when I was 5 years old. I always finished my tests pretty quickly and now I had something besides Sr. Marie's ugly face to look at for the rest of the day. This infuriated her even more - one, because she saw that the tests were relatively easy for me, and two because she saw me reading a KISS book after I was done. KISS represented everything I loved and everything we fought over. It was the perfect way to dig at her without having to say a word.

Finally, the day of the battle of the bands had arrived. This would also be my first official live performance, since I didn't really count the talent show.

I was a little sad that I wouldn't be able to share one last party with my friends at the dance, but I was super excited to get my career as a rock drummer underway. I took extra care of transporting my drums this time and I didn't let my brother touch them. I still didn't have cases, but I wrapped them in blankets and put them in Ray's parents' van.

When we started to load into the school, there was another drummer warming up. He was the first live drummer I'd ever heard besides myself, and he was very good. I was a little intimidated, not so much about my own playing, but because I knew as a band we weren't very good. If this was the caliber of the musicians in this battle of the bands, we were in big trouble. Years later, that same drummer asked me for lessons after seeing me perform at a club.

My mom sat in the audience with one of her friends, excited to see her baby boy do what he loved to do. Menace was scheduled to go on third out of 6 bands. Once the second act was finished, we rushed our gear up on to the stage, set up as fast as we could, and the guitarists and bassist tuned their instruments—or so we thought. As soon as we hit the first note of the opening song, "For Whom the Bell Tolls," I heard that they were completely out of tune.

When Ken started to sing he made it even worse. He was completely flat. I was far from perfect, but I thought I played pretty well, all things considered. By the time we entered our third song, I could clearly hear boos. Unfortunately for the crowd, the third song was our long original instrumental song "The Universe".

It was not a good idea to play a 7-minute original instrumental during a battle of the bands, especially when all of the instruments were out of tune. The boos got louder and we decided to cut a song to end with "Master of Puppets," another long song. Needless to say, the response wasn't positive. I knew we weren't good, but I didn't realize that we would sound even worse than when we rehearsed.

I knew right away that was my last show with Menace. A few months of playing in the band taught me a lot. I felt comfortable playing with other musicians and I learned about the dynamics of a band atmosphere. I also knew I didn't want to play anymore cover songs. I knew that to make it, I would need to be in a band with all original material.

I saw my mom waiting outside and she looked so proud. She gave me a big hug and told me I was great. I said, "Ma, I know we were terrible." She said, "I said YOU were great, not the band." We both had a good laugh and went home.

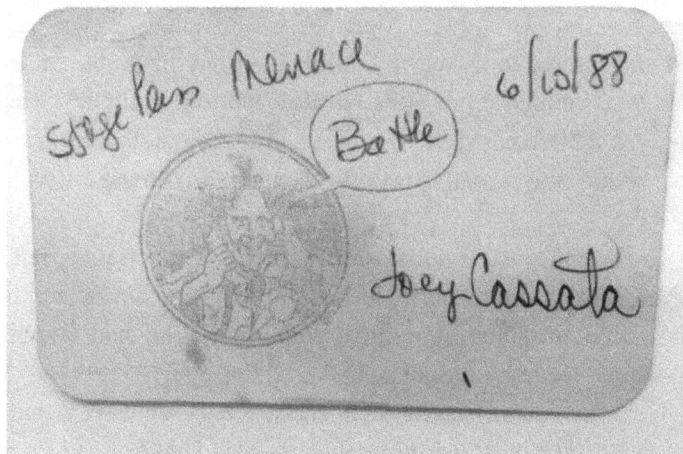

My first band Menace's stage pass, 1988.

CHAPTER 9
NOSE TO NOSE WITH THE BEAST

Hanging with my crew. Can you spot me?

A few days later, I told Menace I was officially leaving. They were upset and wanted to know why. I didn't say anything about the band not being good enough, I just spoke to Ray and told him that I was moving on to play a different style of music and all originals. By the end of the conversation, Ray was also leaving Menace and starting a new band with me.

Right away, we found a singer named Brian Hanna, but just like Ray, he didn't look the part. He was only an okay singer and he played a little rhythm guitar, but most importantly he had something we desperately needed: original songs!

Next we found bassist/keyboardist Kevin Murray. A bassist who also played keyboards was more than we could have hoped for. We were looking to do lighter, more commercial rock and the keyboards would work out perfectly.

Kevin, who we called "Mur," looked the part. Finally, a guy that played and instrument that looked like he was in a band. It was refreshing.

He started to play an original riff that he had written on keyboard and it sounded great. We all started to jam along and then Hanna started to hum a melody line and even blurt out a few words. Just like that, we had begun writing our very first song together. I couldn't believe it.

I'd always heard stories of bands just jamming and coming up with songs, but I never really understood until this moment. The song became our first original together and was called "Second Look." Mur was in.

Now all we needed was a name. I think Hanna said something like, "We just created this cool new song the first time we ever played together. Let's call ourselves Creation!" We loved it and agreed, Creation was born.

Creation Logo, 1988

CREATION:
Brian Hannah - Vocals, Rhythm Guitar
Ray Connelly - Lead Guitar
Kevin Murray - Bass, Keyboards
Joey Cassata – Drums

Before I could devote all of my time to my new band Creation, I had to finish eighth grade and graduate. I also had to once and for all beat my mortal enemy, Sr. Marie.

I already knew where I was going to high school. I made it into all the schools I applied for, and for some stupid reason, I decided to go to an all boys' military school in Manhattan.

Some of my friends were going there including O.G., Scally, and Bobby Howell. I think the main reason I went was because that's where my brother graduated and I thought if I went there, it would make my mom happy.

After taking all my finals in Sr. Marie's office, I was finally allowed to return to class for the final two weeks of school. The last few years

Creation! Kevin Murrray, Me, and Brian Hannah.

with my friends in grammar school were some of the best times of my life. We became more than friends — we became brothers. We enjoyed those last two weeks and tried to make them last a lifetime. We all knew that soon we would all be going to different schools, and while we'd still see each other, it would never be like it was.

The whole week before graduation, Sr. Marie threatened me by saying, "You will not graduate unless you cut your hair!" She was relentless up until the last second. I, of course, completely ignored the threat and enjoyed the last week with my friends. She wasn't going to ruin the
last moments I had with my buddies.

On graduation day, my mom gave me a gold drum necklace with the skin made of pearl. It was beautiful, and I loved it. I knew what it must have taken to save up for it, so it meant the world to me and I wore it with pride.

We learned a few weeks earlier during graduation practice that we would be marching down the aisle to the song "Pomp and Circumstance." I now know that most graduations play this song, but back in 1988, I only knew it as one thing: The "Macho Man" Randy Savage's theme song.

All of my friends dared me to do the whole Macho Man routine as I walked down the aisle. I couldn't disappoint them. So, as "Pomp and Circumstance" blasted over the church loud speakers, I began the Macho Man walk, as if headed to the ring to fight my opponent at Wrestlemania. In a way, I actually was.

At the end of that long walk waited my arch nemesis, Sr. Marie. Even though I was walking the aisle during the actual ceremony, I still hadn't technically graduated yet, not until she handed me that diploma.

The night I defeated my arch enemy, Sr. Marie

I saw her staring at me with her beady eyes. She was dressed in her usual attire—a dark gray suit with dirty black sneakers. Her short gray hair was spiked, and I could smell her stench from a mile away.

I knew what awaited me, so I took my time and really played to the crowd. I mostly did it to get one more laugh with my friends, and laugh they did. They couldn't believe I had the balls to actually do the Macho Man ring entrance in church during graduation.

Ever since I was little I always had the balls to do crazy stuff, or maybe it was more that I liked the attention. I remember when I was about 7 or 8, my brother and his friends dared me to run in front of our neighbor's house, while they were sitting on their porch, and pretend to take a big fall and get really hurt. They hid behind the cars to watch, while I ran top speed down the block and then took a huge fall when I reached the targeted house. The neighbors would come running and screaming with concern, "Oh my God, are you okay?" I would even shed some tears to make it look convincing. Once I really had them worried for me, I would get up and run away laughing. My brother and his friends would give me a big cheer for my amazing performance and I'd take a bow. Shy, I wasn't.

So after my graduation antics, I returned to the back of the church, where Sr. Marie grabbed me one last time and pulled me in close. I was nose-to-nose with the beast, and I could smell her disgusting cigar breath. What the hell kind of nun smokes cigars anyway? We held our ground for a few moments, then she finally spoke, "I guess you won, Mr. Cassata." Still nose-to-nose, I smiled and said, "Yes, I guess I did." I pulled away from her, grabbed my diploma out of her hands, and continued through the church doors, holding up my diploma like it was the WWF championship belt! Game, set, match. Joey wins!

The summer after eighth grade was one of the best summers of my life. Every day was spent rehearsing and writing new music with Creation or just hanging with my friends. We all knew this was the last time we'd all be together like this, so we made each and every second count. We would play stickball or football all day long, run home to eat dinner with our families around 6 o'clock, then as soon as we finished we'd meet back up to hang out for the rest of the night.

My house was usually the meeting place for everyone. Sometimes, we would just hang out on the front stoop all night. There would be about 15 of us just doing nothing for hours. Looking back, I say to myself, "What the hell did we do for that many hours just hanging on my stoop?" But, when you have friends like that, you didn't need any place to go. All you need is each other's company to have great time! The friends I made in grammar school were my friends for life! The summer of 1988 could not have been any more perfect.

The friends I made in grammar school became my friends for life

CHAPTER 10

WHEN IT RAINS IT POURS

My childhood home in Brooklyn

my
room

The last weekend of the summer meant I had to do something that I'd been avoiding for years. I had to cut my hair. I would definitely not be able to battle and beat the Catholic military school I was going to in Manhattan like I had beaten Sr. Marie. My brother warned me that they wouldn't tolerate anything against the dress code, which was basically a full suit. We had to wear our own shirt and tie everyday as well as a blazer that was part of the school uniform. The other major rule was, just like my grammar school, no hair touching the collar. What a joke. I was regretting my decision to go to this school before I even started. But I did what I had to do: I got my hair cut just above my collar and I hated it! All of my friends said they didn't even recognize me.

They hadn't seen my hair this short since the first or second grade. I just didn't look or feel like myself. Not only did I hate the way it looked, I hated having to compromise what I wanted and what I believed in just for someone's stupid rules. This wasn't a good way to start high school. It was one of the only times, if not the only, that I compromised myself. I went in to the first day of school totally resenting them already.

All was okay for the first few months until one day while on my way to class, the dean pulled me into his office and asked me to turn around. I had no idea what he wanted, but I knew it couldn't be good.

He said, "We have a problem here. Do you know what it is?" I replied, "No, I don't," with a little bit of an attitude. He said, "Your hair is way too long." I couldn't believe it. I just battled for the last 3 years against the most evil person in the world, and now I would have to start all over again.

The dean handed me a large pair of scissors. These were no regular scissors: these had the perforated edges that were used for art projects. He said, "Go cut your hair in the bathroom and come back to me in ten minutes. If it's still touching your collar, you are expelled."

I thought to myself, "What a fucking joke. Another power-hungry asshole that has to prove his worth by bossing around little kids." At first I thought, "No! I won't do it." But then I thought about my mom and how disappointed she would be if I got expelled.

So, I went to another classroom where my friend was and told the teacher that I needed to see him, and that it was an emergency. Once out of the classroom, I handed him the scissors and informed him that I needed him to cut my hair. He looked at me like I was crazy, but gladly went along. He figured at the very least this will be a great story to tell our friends.

About 10 minutes later, I returned to the dean's office with the back of my hair completely mangled, not only from the perforated scissors, but from my friend not knowing what the hell he was doing. As much as I disliked the school already, this little incident really made me feel like I was in the wrong place.

From that moment on, I was just going through the motions. I knew in my heart that I could not take another year of this school. I had to do what I wanted to do, and that was play my drums.

I never said anything to my mom, but I began cutting classes a lot. Sometimes I would just sit in the library at school just so I could write songs or read the newest issue of *Modern Drummer*. I was miserable. The only thing about the school that I enjoyed was playing on the football team, where I was co-defensive captain. I vaguely remember overhearing my coach say that he wanted me to be quarterback, but I was too big and that he couldn't waste my size. He needed me on defense.

I remember the first time we lined up in practice for a sprint. I was easily the biggest kid. The coach blew the whistle and I took off. Turns out that not only was I the biggest kid but I was the fastest. My buddy OG and I were neck-and-neck, but I pulled it out at the last second. I ran a 4.7 that freshman year of high school. Back then, I had no idea what that meant, but now I know how good that was. The football field was the only place in that school that I fit in.

Once the school year was over, I told my mom that I didn't want to go back. I knew I had failed a lot of subjects and I didn't even care. I think subconsciously I might have failed them on purpose. I told my mom that I wanted to go to a music school. She was disappointed, but she understood.

Once again, my mom not only didn't stand in the way of my dream, but she helped me open the door to get closer to it. She came home with a few school brochures one day and we both found the perfect place. It was a performing arts high school in Manhattan, the place that the TV show *FAME* was based on.

My mom called to set up an audition. I prepared a little piece and a few weeks later went down to audition. It was pretty easy, and I got accepted! Unfortunately, there was one major problem. Because I hadn't taken all of their music classes the year before and because I'd failed a lot of the subjects at my old school, I would be behind. I wouldn't have to take my whole freshman year over, but I would have to take half freshman classes and then slowly start to catch up.

The summer of 1989 was nothing like the year before. It actually turned out to be one of the worst summers of my life. One day in late August, we got a call that my grandpa had been rushed to the hospital and we needed to get over there as quickly as possible. He had been sick with emphysema for a long time because of his smoking, one of the main reasons I've never even tried a cigarette in my whole life. I grew up around constant smoking and I saw how sick my grandfather had been because of it. Even my mother was already showing signs of its effects.

My grandpa and I were always very close. He was the only father figure I'd really even known, and the sweetest, gentlest man in the whole world. He was the exact opposite of my grandmother. Ha ha. He had been in and out of the hospital for a few months, but him dying never crossed my mind. No one in my family or anyone I had ever known had died. He was in ICU the last time I saw him.

My mom, brother, and I, along with my two aunts, went to the hospital. My grandmother didn't come because she rarely left the house. Actually, the only time she ever went outside was to come and visit us in Brooklyn. When we got to the hospital, I just thought Grandpa would be like he always was when he was sick in the hospital, lying in bed, kind of weak, but still himself. He'd still be Grandpa and still be joking around with me. When we finally got to his room, someone was lying in bed with a tube coming out of his nose, red liquid pouring through it. The man lying there was swollen and looked Asian to me. My mom and aunts immediately began crying, but I was confused. I didn't understand. There was no way that this man that was lying down in bed was my grandpa! How could it be? My mom hugged me and said, "That's Grandpa, Joey. Talk to him. Let him know you are here."

As I got closer, I could see it was in fact my grandfather, but he was so badly swollen that I didn't recognize him. He was bleeding internally and the liquid coming from the tube in his nose was his blood basically draining from his body.

Even though he was unconscious, I grabbed his hand and held on more tightly than I'd ever had in my life. He began rubbing my fingers with his thumb just like he always did. He knew I was there with him. Finally, after a few minutes the nurses came and asked us to leave.

My mom told me to kiss him goodbye and tell him that I love him. And that's exactly what I did. I kissed my favorite man on earth goodbye. As soon as I left the room, I broke down like I never had before. The walk from my grandpa's room to the waiting room was the longest walk of my life.

A few minutes later, the doctor came out and told us he had passed. He said we could see him if we wanted. My mom, brother, and two aunts went, but I couldn't. It was the first time and maybe the only time in my life that I was too weak and scared. I couldn't make that walk again and see him. I regret every day not seeing my grandpa one last time.

Something else strange happened during that summer. Two people came to our house and began looking around all of the rooms. My mom explained something to us that I didn't quite understand at the time, something about how those people were going to be helping us pay the mortgage in some way. I didn't really understand, and I didn't really care. I had just lost my grandpa and that's all that was on my mind.

I would learn later that year that we might be losing our house. This news was unimaginable to me. This was my home. This was the only place I'd ever lived. There was no way we were losing it. Even though my father was rarely around, there was no way he would let this happen, was there?

The school year began and I actually totally forgot all about the house troubles. It was too unfathomable to even think about anymore, at least until later that year when the police came to evict us. They were literarily at the front door telling us we had to leave immediately! My mother somehow convinced them to give us one week to vacate.

I couldn't believe it was happening. We had one week to not only find another place to live but to pack up everything we owned. I saw this stuff in the movies, but I never thought it was real. I never thought they could actually throw a family out onto the street.

My father never paid the mortgage and sure enough we were getting evicted from the only place I'd ever called home. It was one of the most heartbreaking times of my life, and I can't imagine what my mother felt. Her sons, for whom she'd done everything, were about to be thrown out of their home.

While my brother and I began packing our lives into boxes, my mother was searching for a new place to live. I didn't know what we were going to do. If we had no money to pay for this house, how could we move to another?

After a week of crying and packing and complete disarray, my mother said she had found a small house that we could rent. It was in the Bergen Beach section of Brooklyn, about a 10-minute drive from the house we were getting evicted from. A 10-minute drive doesn't seem like much, but for a kid it might as well have been 100 miles. I would be far from my friends.

But that wasn't my worst worry. What about my drums? They were my life! My room in my current home was enormous and I could play the drums in there anytime I wanted. How could I do this in a new home? My mom assured me we would figure it out.

One week later, my biggest nightmare came true. The Marshall and the police came back to officially put us out. We had the moving van there that morning and were just about out of the house. I remember telling my friends that we had sold the house and were moving because the neighborhood was starting to go down. It was a complete lie. I was too ashamed to say we were getting thrown out because my father didn't pay the mortgage.

So, in April of 1990, my brother, my mother, my grandmother, who was now living with us full time, Yukon, Tabby, and I left our home, never to return.

This was a day that would have repercussions on my life for years to come. I was never the same after that day. I like to think I was always a loving, sweet boy who always hoped and assumed the best in people and in the world, but after the day we were literally thrown out of our home, I changed. I became angry, more unforgiving, and I downright didn't trust people.

Besides my family and friends, I had no use for anyone in the world. I made a promise to myself that day that I would bury myself in my music until one day I was a big enough star and made enough money to buy my mom her house back!

Once we moved into the new house, which was about 1/3 the size of our old house, I knew I had to start getting more serious about my music career. The performing arts school I was attending wasn't what I hoped it would be. I guess school is school, and even though I played drums for some of the day, it still felt like school. I never really became friends with anyone at the school because I didn't want any distractions from my goals. I had my friends from grammar school and I didn't really need more.

Creation was writing some good songs, but I knew that they weren't good enough to get me where I wanted to go. This is where I came up with the strategy of playing with as many people and as many bands as I could. I figured that the more people I played with, the more of a chance I'd find the right band and be able to succeed.

As coincidence would have it, Scally's brother Matt said that he had a friend that was looking for a drummer. I asked Scally to get me a tape of their songs so I could check them out first. This was another one of my new rules: no wasting time on amateurs. I needed a band that was serious, had great players, and most importantly had great songs. I got the tape and played it on my stereo, recently set up in my new room.

The tape was labeled "Seventh Heaven." I kind of liked it, and the songs sounded great! They were poppy and commercial sounding, sort of like Bon Jovi. I called Scally right away and told him to have his brother set up an audition.

The audition for Seventh Heaven would take place at the same studio where I met my first band Menace, Sink the Pink Studios. This time it would be in the big room, which was kind of famous in my neighborhood because it had a giant stage and also a giant drum set.

When I walked in and saw the stage and drums I loved it. I already felt like I had taken a step up from my previous bands. Not only were Seventh Heaven's songs really good, but they obviously thought big like I did. It's funny how little things like renting the "big room" set a perception of someone back then for me. These were the types of little things that a kid latched on to in order to form a first impression. And my first impression of Seventh Heaven was great.

I met the guys in the band and also their manager. Having a manager was another one of those things at that age that made a big impression. "Wow, a manager!" I thought. "This was serious." They informed me that they didn't have a singer yet and that they wanted to get a solid drummer first. They had asked me to bring down a tape of my playing.

I brought down a song I recorded with one of my classmates at school. We had a classroom where we could write and record our own songs. After handing them the tape with my name and phone number on it, they said, "Let's jam on the songs we gave you." Even though I hadn't yet set up my drums in my new house, I learned the two songs they had given me. They were pretty easy but I hadn't actually played them yet.

As soon as we started the first song, I knew it felt right. These guys could really play. This sounded like a professional band and was leaps and bounds above the other musicians and bands I had played in. After we jammed on their few original songs, they asked me if I could do a little solo to just show some of my chops. I definitely didn't practice for that and I didn't have much prepared, so I used an old faithful: a combination of the Eric Carr solo from the *Animalize Uncensored* video and Peter Criss' solo from *Alive*. They seemed to like it. When I was done, they said that they would give me a call and let me know if I made it or not.

The next day I planned on setting up my drums in the new house. My mom and I were in the living room polishing them when there was a knock at the door. It was the keyboardist and the manager from Seventh Heaven. It turns out that I still had my old phone number on the tape I gave them, and they had no way of getting in touch with me. Even Scally didn't have my new number yet. Luckily, Scal had already been to the new house and remembered where it was. The manager told me they didn't want even a day to go by without me hearing from them. They liked me that much. They wanted to make sure I didn't join another band before they could get back to me. They told me I was in if I wanted the gig. Of course, I said yes. They left and my mom and I celebrated. Even though we had lost our home and been forced to pack up everything we owned in a week, we still had each other and I still had my dreams.

Unfortunately, the excitement didn't last long. A few days later, I received a call from Seventh Heaven's manager. He informed me that a drummer they knew approached them and told them that his uncle could get them on the TV talent show *Star Search* if he was accepted in the band. *Star Search* was a big deal back then; it was like *American Idol* of the late 80's and early 90's. It was an opportunity they just couldn't pass up. He thanked me for everything and told me to stay in touch. I was upset but I totally understood.

About a year later I found out that they never even made it to *Star Search*. The drummer strung them along and never came through on his promise. Years after, Seventh Heaven tried to steal the song I had written that was on my audition tape. Lawyers were involved and it was messy.

In my new house, the drums were set up in my bedroom, which happened to be up front. After only a few days, we started getting complaints from the neighbors. No matter how much soundproofing I put up, it would never stop the sound from escaping the front window. It was just too loud for all of my new neighbors and I had to figure out something to do.

I had the big bedroom, my mother had the medium bedroom in the center, my brother had the basement, and my grandmother was supposed to be in the small bedroom in back. Because we had some kind of old-

84

fashioned heating system, though, the heat would come from the basement then shoot up through two large vents. This caused my grandmother's bedroom to be way too cold, and she said she couldn't sleep in it anymore. She was basically staying in my room with me every night on a pull-out sofa. Because of this, the small back bedroom wasn't being used.

My mother suggested I take over her bedroom for my drums. It was smaller than mine, so she figured we could sound proof it more easily. I would keep my big front bedroom and my mom would switch to the small back bedroom. She would really do anything for us.

Looking back, I should have taken the small bedroom for my drums and put my bed in the middle room. That would have left my mom with the big bedroom to share with Grandma. I didn't even think of it at the time and it's still something that bothers me to this day. My mother always sacrificed everything for her sons.

Even though I was still writing and playing with my old Creation bandmate Brian Hannah, I also began playing with a band called Asgard, with a guitar player that lived on my new block. I knew neither was good enough for me to do full- time, so I continued to keep my eyes and ears open for new opportunities.

This was around 1990 and the internet didn't exist yet. There were only a few ways to find new musicians to play with, like placing an ad or answering one in a local music paper. The two papers that I checked regularly were *The Village Voice* and *The Aquarian*, formally known as *The East Coast Rocker*. The only other way to find a new band was looking on bulletin boards in all of the music stores.

I answered an ad for a drummer in *The Aquarian*. It said, "Music and look in the vein of Guns and Roses." Guns and Roses were a new band at the time, and I wasn't really into their music or look, but I figured I'd give it a shot, seeing as how my new motto was to play with as many people as possible.

The band set up an audition at Ace London Studios on Quentin Road in my old neighborhood. As soon as I walked in, I knew this wasn't the band for me. They looked like rockers, but like the ad said, they had more of that dirty rock-and-roll image like Guns and Roses.

We started to play a few songs and they were actually pretty good players, but something about their whole vibe just turned me off.

The next day they called me to tell me they loved my playing and wanted me in the band. I politely said, "Thank you, but unfortunately the project wasn't for me." They couldn't understand how I was turning them down and got a little arrogant on the phone. They told me I was passing up a good thing. Still, I knew it wasn't a fit for me, so I wished them luck and the search continued.

CHAPTER 11

PLAYGROUND & WHITNEY HOUSTON'S MANAGER

I started cutting school more and more to just hang out at my favorite music store Sam Ash on King's Highway and 13th Street in Brooklyn. The only other music store that I knew of was on Flatbush Avenue near King's Plaza Mall. It was called King James Music, and it was an extremely small little mom-and-pop type place. They didn't even have enough room to set up a drum set inside. The only reason I would ever even think of going there was to get an emergency pair of sticks when I ran out.

One night I had an Asgard rehearsal, and I ran out of sticks. I asked my brother to drive me to King James to buy a pair. On the way out, I glanced at the bulletin board and saw a white piece of paper that said, "Drummer wanted for commercial rock band. Must be 18 or older." At the bottom, were about 6 or 7 little strips to rip off with the band's phone number on it. Even though it said 18 or older and I was only 16, I figured I'd take one just to see. I really didn't think much of it.

The next afternoon I called the number and said "Hi, I'm answering the ad you had in King James Music for a drummer wanted." After about 20 minutes of him filling me in on what the band was about, and what kind of music they were looking to do, the guy on the phone said that if I was interested I should come by his house to pick up a demo tape they'd just finished recording. I said, "Great, I'll be there tomorrow."

Right before he hung up he said, "I almost forgot to ask. How old are you?" Thinking quickly and remembering that the ad said 18 or older I said, "I'm 18." I then asked, "By the way, what's the name of the band?" He replied, "Playground!"

The next day, I asked my brother to drive me to Sheepshead's Bay to go pick up the demo. My mother also came along for the ride. I knocked on the front door of a small house in a neighborhood that had seen better days.

The person that answered was a tall, skinny guy with a giant head of hair. It was the guitarist Brendan Murphy whom I'd been speaking with. He gestured me inside and I obliged. I was glad to see that Brendan's image was along the lines of what I was looking for. Back in the late 80's and early 90's, image was very important.

The main reason it was important to me was that it told me right away that he was serious about being in a band. I'd already played with so many people that just wouldn't commit full time. Everyone always had an excuse about why they didn't have long hair or look like a rocker: "My job won't let me," or "My girlfriend doesn't like my hair long." Meanwhile, I almost got kicked out of grammar school and high school because I wanted my hair long. As crazy as it sounds, Brendan's image immediately told me that he was serious.

After a brief conversation, he gave me Playground's three-song demo which included the songs "Could've Been You," "Heaven in Her Eyes," and "Third Heart." I told Brendan I'd be in touch after listening to the tape. After I left, I realized he never brought up the age question again. I guess I passed for 18.

As soon as I got back home, I put the tape in my stereo and gave it a listen. The quality wasn't that great but there was something about the songs that I liked. It wasn't as polished as the Seventh Heaven demo, but I liked it.

I could tell right away why they parted ways with their old drummer. He wasn't very good. "This could be very promising," I thought to myself. Even though I was barely 16, I was at the point where I was auditioning bands rather than them auditioning me.

I called Brendan the next day and told him I liked the demo and I'd love to come down and jam. Playground set up my audition at a familiar place, Sink the Pink Studios. I hadn't yet met the rest of the band, but I was hoping they had the same type of image as Brendan. Playground rented the "big room" for the audition, a good first sign in my book.

When I got into the room, I met the other two members, guitarist Steve Kerasotis and singer Tommy Snyder. Steve had short hair but he had a cool image. Tommy looked like a typical rock singer at the time. He had long curly hair, probably a perm, and a black leather jacket with fringes. I thought to myself, "Perfect!"

Before we even started playing, I remember thinking to myself, "If these guys are even just okay, I think it can become something pretty special." They had cool songs, the right look, and so far the right attitude. As soon as we kicked into the first song, "It Could've Been You", something just felt right.

I don't know how to explain it, but every once in awhile you come across people that you just gel with. Something felt comfortable and familiar as we were playing, not only musically, but the energy in the room just felt right.

Over the years, I've always had a saying: "These are my kind of people," or "These aren't my kind of people." There are just certain people that I gel with musically and personally, and I think Playground was the first band where both happened.

After the audition, they asked me to join right on the spot and I gladly accepted.

PLAYGROUND:

Tommy Snyder- Vocals
Brendan Murphy- Guitar
Steve Kerasotis - Guitar
Joey Cassata – Drums

We began to rehearse non-stop at a place called Redline Studios in Staten Island. It was a magnificent room, almost like a giant airport hangar. It had a giant stage and the drums sounded massive, almost like Eric Carr's on *Creatures of the Night*. Not only were we rehearsing at least 2 nights a week, but I also began hanging out with the guys in the band on the other nights. We would go out to bars in Bay Ridge or in my old neighborhood, Marine Park.

Flatbush Avenue in Marine Park was a great hang out and always packed with people. Even though I was only 16, my grammar school friends and I had been hanging out there for over a year now. The bars weren't strict about asking for I.D. We regularly visited a place called The Cuckoo's Nest," a perfect fit for us.

Rehearsals were going great, but out on Flatbush Avenue was where we really started to bond as a band. The singer, Tommy, was a complete nut and had a big group of friends that would always meet us at the bar.

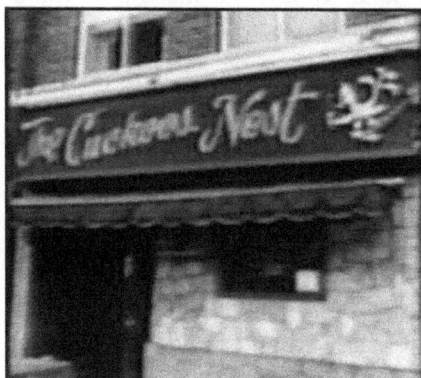

I got along great with one of Tommy's friends in particular, Ernie LaMonte. He was a short little guy with glasses, had a high-pitch voice and a lisp. He was funny as could be. Ernie would also come to rehearsals

Playground's regular hangout in Brooklyn.

because he absolutely loved the band and he prided himself on knowing everything there was to know about music.

After a month of vigorous rehearsals, things were going as well as they could, at least until I received a call from Brendan telling me that the band was over. I was in shock and anxiously said, "What? How could this be? Things were going so good. What happened?" Brendan went on to tell me that things just weren't working out.

I couldn't believe what I was hearing. I thought I'd finally found a band that not only had the same drive and passion as I had, but these were people whom I genuinely liked. I was pretty upset.

Not more than five minutes went by when my phone rang again. It was our singer, Tommy Snyder. I asked, "What the hell happened?" He replied very nonchalantly, "What do you mean?" I went on to explain that Brendan had just called and said that the band was over. He began laughing and I heard him yell to someone in the background, "Yeah, he called Joey and told him that the band was over." He proceeded to tell me that the band was not over, and that Brendan had had a meltdown and quit.

I guess Brendan was so egotistical that he assumed if he quit then the band would end. Tommy said, "Not only is the band continuing, but we want to do so with just Steve on guitar, and we already set up an audition for a bass player later in the week." I took a deep breath to process all of the information Tommy had just given me. He asked, "Are you still in?" and I said "Absolutely!"

Steve knew another guitar player named Dave Robau who said he knew a bass player looking for a band. Crazy, but that's how things worked back then: word of mouth. A friend of a friend would introduce you to someone.

There weren't that many bands and musicians in the neighborhood and somehow, they all knew each other. Dave set up an audition for the bass player in the garage of the drummer he'd been playing with, Rocky Merrolla.

This would be the first time we were playing without Brendan. Nobody was sure how it would be with only one guitarist. Before the bass player arrived, we jammed a little to warm up and quickly realized that we didn't need the second guitar player at all.

Over the years, I actually have come to dislike playing with two guitarists. Unless done perfectly, it can become messy – and noisy. Most guitar players play way too loudly, and their sound is usually pretty crappy. Multiply that by two and there comes a major problem.

Playground's first rehearsal as a 3-piece felt right. After a few songs, the bass player arrived and introduced himself. His name was Brian DeVito. My first impression was that he looked like a rocker, which was a good sign. Brian received the same three song demo that I did to learn for the audition.

Up until this point, I hadn't played any of these Playground songs with a bass player, and I immediately felt the difference as soon as we hit the first note. Not only was the guitar clear, but the songs now had a bottom that I could lock on to. We had found our bass player.

Over the course of the next few weeks, we decided that we needed to start playing live. We knew we could only get so good rehearsing in a studio night after night and that we had to test out these songs in front of a live audience.

Besides me, no one else in the band had ever played a live gig before. Even though I had played the battle of the bands, I was also new to gigging. We had no idea how to even go about getting a show. The band would get together and have meetings about how to book shows. The only thing we could think of was to get one of the local music papers and start cold-calling every club we could find. And that's exactly what we did. We must have called 2 or 3 dozen places looking for a gig.

It was basically the same conversation every time. It went something like this: "Hello, my name is Joey Cassata from the band Playground. We were wondering if you had any open dates that you needed a band for?" The club owner's response would go something like this: "Do you guys have a following? How many people did you draw the last time you played?" I would then respond, "We are a new band and this would be our first gig, but I think we would be able to get a lot of people to come to the show." The club owner would usually end the call right there with, "Call us back when you get a following."

Looking back, we were so innocent and naïve that we always told them the truth about it being our first gig. Even the terms they were using were completely foreign to us. What the hell did "a following" mean? Was he asking if we had fans? How the hell could we have fans if we've never played before? Not one club owner would ever ask us about our music or to hear a demo tape. It was always about bringing people. This was extremely frustrating to us because it was a catch 22. How could we have fans if we'd never played, but no one would give us a show unless we brought the fans. Again, we were so young and dumb that we didn't even think of considering our friends as fans. All of my friends had been dying to see me play live since I started playing drums! I'm sure the other guys in the band had plenty of friends that would come also. We just never thought of it.

After about a week of doing this, we started to lose hope, until one day Steve and I cold-called a place all the way out in Staten Island called Billy O's. We had tried all the Brooklyn and Manhattan clubs, and unfortunately no one wanted any part of us.

We were skeptical about booking a show in Staten Island; not only was it far away, but there was no public transportation. None of my friends even drove yet, since we were all still too young. It didn't matter; we were desperate and had to give it a shot. Steve started talking to the manager and I heard most of the same questions being answered.

After a few minutes, I'd lost hope, but then Steve said, "Hold on," then cupped his hand over the phone. "He wants to know if we are available August fourth." I couldn't believe it! I shouted, a little over-zealous, "Of course we are available!" Steve got back on and said "Great, we will take it."

As soon as he hung up, we started to hug like we just won the Super Bowl. We had finally secured our first gig! I immediately asked Steve what the details were. He said the guy said told us to stop by and see the place and that we needed to get another band to play with us that same night. Truth was, we didn't know any other bands, but that didn't matter. We would figure it out. First, we had to call and let the other guys know that in under two months we had our first show!

We excitedly called Tommy to tell him the great news, but when he answered he was already excited about something else. Before we could tell him the news about booking our first show, he started rambling a mile a minute—something about a big opportunity for us and Whitney Houston's manager. Steve and I looked at each other like he was nuts. We would all see each other at rehearsal later that night and decided we would discuss everything then. We didn't even get the chance to tell him about the show.

Playground was now rehearsing at Rockaway studios out in Rockaway, Queens. It was a brand-new studio that just opened. Usually our bass player Brian DeVito, whom we just called DeVito, would pick me up at my house and Steve and Tommy would go together. On this particular night, we went an hour before our rehearsal start time so we could discuss all the band business.

We filled Tommy and DeVito in about our first show at Billy O's in Staten Island come August. They were excited and had a lot of questions, but first Steve and I had to know what the hell Tommy was talking about on our phone call earlier that day. We told him, "Talk slow and start from the beginning."

He explained to us that there was a talent competition in Starrett City, where he lived, and they were looking for a band to perform. It was going to be broadcast on a local public access TV station, and Whitney Houston's manager was going to be one of the judges.

Now I have no idea why, but this news was very exciting to all of us. We thought, "Wow! Not only are we going to be on TV, but Whitney Houston's manager is going to watch us perform."

Looking back, this was absolutely ridiculous. But, at the time, Whitney Houston was one of the biggest names in music and this would be our first brush with someone who worked in the music industry. Tommy then told us that we wouldn't be performing live and that they wanted us to lip sync to our recording. We all knew there was a big problem with that last bit of info.

The demo tape they had given me to audition with was definitely not good enough for a performance of this magnitude, and we knew immediately that we needed to make a new demo. This was sometime in mid-May of 1990 and the public access TV talent competition was going to be at the end of June. That only gave us one month to record.

We decided we would only need to do one song and that would be "Third Heart." It was our most mainstream song and had a great hook in the chorus. Looking back, this was madness. It was so cost-prohibitive back in the early 90's to record just one song. We would need to book a professional recording studio on an hourly basis. The most time-consuming part of recording can be getting sounds for each instrument and then mixing after. It would have been much smarter to record 3 to 6 songs, but again, we were young and naïve. Besides, Whitney Houston's manager was going to love us and hopefully we wouldn't need another demo.

I actually miss that innocence. It was so exciting thinking everything you did was great, to never second-guess yourself and be willing to do anything. These early Playground years were some of the best moments in my musical career because of that bright- eyed, innocent attitude.

We found a recording studio out in Staten Island called Laughing Dog Studios, but we wanted to go check it out in person before we booked it. When we arrived, the first and only person we met was the owner/engineer, Dan. Dan was a kind of guy who wore old, dirty flip flops. Because we were obviously young, Dan didn't treat us with any respect. He knew we didn't know much about recording, and he tried to act like a big shot engineer.

The drum kit in the studio was a small 5-piece Yamaha kit. I was used to playing on my big kit, but more importantly, the song we were recording had some cool tom fills for which I needed my high toms. I told Dan that I wanted to bring in my own kit, but he wanted no part of it, basically telling me, "No, the Yamaha kit here is top of the line and I know how to get a good sound with it. I don't want to be messing around with some crappy kit." Again, we were so naïve that I just said, "Okay." If a producer/engineer ever tried to pull that on me today, they would have a big problem.

Even though we didn't really like Dan the engineer, and I wasn't thrilled about using a different kit, we really had no choice. We had to have a song recorded to perform in front of Whitney Houston's manager! So, we booked Laughing Dog Studios for the following weekend.

When I got home from Staten Island, I decided to call Dan and insist that I at least bring my "Roto Toms" to the recording session. Roto toms were three, small high-pitched toms that were on one single stand. I wasn't taking no for an answer. Dan wasn't happy and reluctantly agreed.

We rehearsed the song like madmen that week. We must have played it 100 times to make sure it was perfect. Even though I had a little experience recording in school, and the rest of the guys had experience recording their first demo, we were still all very new to the recording process.

For everyone reading this that doesn't know how most recordings are done, I'll offer a quick explanation. Usually, every instrument is recorded separately. The benefit of this is that if things get messed up, only that one part has to record again. There is also no bleeding of instruments on each other's microphones. If you were to record "live," where all instruments are recorded simultaneously, the band would have to be prepared to start from scratch when someone made even the smallest mistake.

This was way before there was digital recording where it's easy to punch in at any desired spot. This was all analog and on reel-to-reel tape or DAT.

Drums are the first instrument to be recorded because once the drums are recorded, everyone else can just follow and align together with that part.

The drummer wouldn't have to play the song alone, just be alone in the actual recording room. The other members of the band could be in the control room with their instruments plugged directly into the main mixing board. They would just record a basic "scratch track" while the drummer works in the sound room recording his actual take.

The drummer's main job is to keep time for the band. To help the drummer lock in to a specific tempo, which is the speed of the song, sometimes a click track is used. A click track is just what it sounds like: a clicking noise that the drummer plays along with, set to the tempo of the song.

I'd played with a click track a few times up until this point and I never really loved it. Playground did not rehearse the song to a click track nor did we even set a tempo for a click track. So obviously, going into the studio, I assumed we were not recording to a click track.

As soon as we were ready to try the first take, Dan said, "Okay, what's the tempo so I can set the click track?" I said in the talk back mic, "We aren't using a click." Dan, thinking he knew everything there was about recording, replied angrily, "You have to use a click track. Otherwise it will be too hard to mix the song later." Like fools, once again we gave in because we figured Dan the engineer and owner of his own recording studio knew what he was talking about.

Steve happened to have a copy of the old "Third "Heart demo. Dan played it for a few seconds in the control room and set the click track tempo from that old recording.

We were now ready to record even though we had never rehearsed it with the click track and didn't even know if we wanted it to be the same tempo as the old demo. Even with all these uncertainties, we were about to begin. God help us.

As soon as we started, I knew something was wrong. The beginning of the song started with big hits with drum fills in between. This is where I needed the Roto toms that Dan was so against. Immediately the tempo felt way too fast. Then, once the hits were over and we entered the musical intro of the chorus, I recognized immediately what was wrong and stopped playing. I signaled into the control room and told them that the song has various tempo changes, including the whole beginning. Unless we were going to take out an hour or two to actually map out every tempo change, we needed to scrap the click and just get on with it. Most of the other guys in the band barely understood what I was even talking about and Dan looked pissed that he wouldn't have his click track to edit with later in post-production. I didn't care what Dan wanted! This was our money and I wasn't wasting a few hours to set up a new click track.

After two takes, my job was finished. I laid down a pretty decent drum track. I wasn't happy with the sound of the drums, but moron Dan the engineer assured me that he would make them sound "huge" when we mixed. Again, I foolishly listened to him.

As much as I relished every moment during these early stages of my music career, I was still savvy enough to absorb every lesson I was learning along the way. I would never again let a producer or engineer tell me that the drum sound was going to be fixed in the mix. And sure enough, almost every one of them tried that same trick with me for many years to come. After many more mishaps for the other members of the band, the recording of the Playground "Third Heart" demo was finally finished in early June of 1990. We now had a few weeks to rehearse for our big TV debut!

We thought we needed a few synchronized, choreographed moves to make our performance really look professional. We rehearsed our moves at least three times a week at Tommy's apartment in Starrett City. I would sit on the back of the couch, so it looked like I was on a drum riser, while the other members of the band would practice their spins and dropping to their knees in unison. It felt like I was back in sixth grade again putting on concerts for the girls in Jason Pers' basement. Only this time, it was for real. Sort of.

Our friend Dave even got us into the Jewish center in Brooklyn, where his father worked, so we could use their big stage for rehearsal. Looking back, the whole thing was absolutely ludicrous: we didn't need to rehearse three little moves over and over again. Never mind that I wasn't even part of these moves and I still came to air drum behind the other guys while they did their moves. Again I say, innocence is bliss. I never even gave it a second thought. Of course, I wanted to be there. This was, after all, my band and we were getting ready as a team for the biggest event any of us had ever been a part of.

I loved every second of those long nights in the Jewish center, air drumming in front of my band mates while they practiced silly choreographed moves. We were bonding as a band and as friends. It was a priceless time that I wouldn't trade for the world.

We were now a week away from our big performance and I realized a horrifying thing: I had tickets to see KISS at Nassau Coliseum in Long Island the same night that we were doing our Public Access TV performance. I was crushed!

Kiss was currently on their *Hot in the Shade* tour and I really didn't want to miss it. But just like when I had my very first gig at Battle of the Bands and I had to miss my eighth-grade graduation dance, I would now have to sacrifice something else. This time it was KISS! I knew this was a sign of things to come. To be in a successful band or successful at anything, a person must sacrifice a big part of a personal life, and I totally understood.

After weeks of rehearsing our lip sync performance and the disaster that was the recording session, it was finally time to perform in front of Whitney Houston's manager! On the morning of the performance, Tommy called us in a panic and told us that our slot had been moved up to the evening instead of our original 8pm start. The other guys were upset, but I couldn't have been happier. This meant I would be able to go see Kiss after all!

Once we arrived at the Starrett city TV studio, we set up our equipment in a pretty small room, much smaller than the giant stage we had been rehearsing on at the Jewish Center. Once set up, we asked them to play back the demo so we could hear it and test our playing along to it. Even though we were lip syncing, I still would have to hit my cymbals to show them moving. Otherwise it would have looked completely fake.

We tested it for a few seconds and quickly realized we had a big problem: we couldn't hear the track over the loud crashing of my cymbals. The producer of the public access show told me to just pretend to hit them. Once again, a moron producer was telling me the wrong thing to make his life easier. I had seen enough videos in my day to know that nobody ever faked hitting the cymbals. It would have looked ridiculous. And to quote Jake Woltz, the head of the film studio in the movie *The Godfather*, "A man in my position can't afford to look ridiculous!"

I knew I needed to somehow mute the cymbals. Sometimes I would mute my drums using duct tape on the skins and thought maybe that would work on my cymbals. I asked one of the workers in the studio for some tape and began to apply it to the bottom of my cymbals so it wasn't visible on camera. It worked like a charm. I would use this exact method many times in my career.

We were now ready to go. From where we were in the studio, we couldn't see any of the judges or the other contestants. We just knew Whitney Houston's manager was probably right behind the door getting ready to watch us perform for the first time as a band. I think Steve, DeVito, and especially Tommy were nervous. I wasn't at all. If anything, an easy calm come over me right before we started, probably because the place I most felt like myself was on stage, behind my drums, performing and doing what I was born to do.

The host of the show came out to introduce us on camera. He was an elderly gentleman who looked a bit like Elvis. He held his mic and said, "Up next we have an up and coming band called Playground." Now that was all fine for an introduction, but what he said next for some reason made me start laughing hysterically right as we went on.

He looked directly into the camera and said, "Go for it!" I'm not sure why this was so funny to me: maybe because it was a line out of *Rocky* or maybe it was just the way he said it. Luckily, the song had a keyboard intro and I had a few seconds to compose myself. You can see my laughing at the beginning of the video on YouTube.

The performance was going great. One of the big choreographed moves was coming up, the synchronized drop to the knees. All the times that we'd practiced this particular move, we'd never actually gotten it perfectly in synch. I watched from behind my kit until finally—they nailed it! Everyone dropped in perfect synchronization. I was so proud. They delivered for the first time and in our biggest moment. It was all easy sailing from then on. We finished the song and were thrilled. All the hard work had paid off.

We just put on an amazing performance on TV (public access) and in front of one of the industry's biggest managers, but I couldn't stay to celebrate with my new band because I had to rush to get to the KISS concert. I didn't even stick around to hear any feedback.

As I was carrying my drums and rushing to the parking lot, I passed the waiting area. The one thing that caught my eye was the fact that the room was filled with little kids. A little girl in a tutu, a group of kids dressed as rappers—you name it. I really didn't think anything of it at the time because I was still so high from our great performance, and now I was on my way to see KISS.

Playground playing on public access TV, 1990

The KISS concert at Nassau Coliseum was extra special that night. I was seeing my favorite band after just having played a great show that could possible break my band into the big time. The only thing I could think of while watching was that I wanted to be up there on that stage with them!

I could see it in my head: "Playground/KISS world tour!" I slept extra sound that night knowing I was on the right path to making my dreams come true.

The next morning, I was expecting to hear from one of the guys but woke up to nothing. I called Steve to find out all of the details. First, I wanted to know what Whitney Houston's manager thought of us. Second, I wanted to know if we had won. Steve's tone immediately smelled of bad news.

He asked, "Do you want the good news or the bad news?" My answer to this question is always, "Bad news first." He told me that her manager was never there and he's not sure if he was ever supposed to be there. I couldn't believe what I was hearing. All of the work, time, and money we spent on the demo was to impress Whitney Houston's manager and there was a chance he was never even supposed to be there. I asked Steve, "Then who were the judges?" and he replied, "That's part two of the bad news. There really were no judges." I was furious. "Then, how did they pick a winner? At least tell me that was the good news. We won?"

Steve told me, "There was no winner. It was more like a kids' talent show and they didn't want to make any of the kids feel bad, so they didn't choose a winner." I couldn't believe what I was hearing. I reluctantly followed up with, "Then what's the good news?" Steve said, "The good news is that they are going to air our performance on TV in a few weeks and they are sending us a copy. So at least we will have a cool video of us playing." I couldn't help but to start laughing.

This was one of the many lessons I'd learn in the music business. Sometimes working hard and killing yourself to do something isn't the most important thing. You, meaning yourself, not a manager, and some other guy in the band, and not a friend of a friend, but you must make sure all of the back-end details are solid before thrusting into every endeavor.

I was still far from jaded, but this was definitely not an event I would be forgetting anytime soon. On the bright side, I still have that great video of us lip syncing "Third Heart" on public access TV with the amazing, "Go for it!" intro. The whole Whitney Houston's manager story actually makes the video even more enjoyable!

CHAPTER 12
STARTING TO CREATE A BUZZ

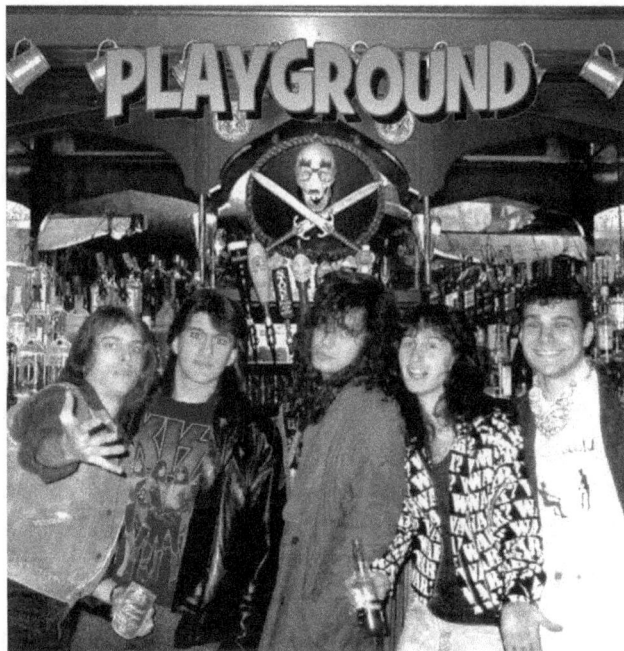

Even though the Public Access TV / Whitney Houston's manager performance turned out to be a disaster, Playground still had their very first live gig to get ready for, and we couldn't have been more psyched!

The weekend after the talent competition, the whole band went to Billy O's to meet with the owner and discuss more details. Steve, DeVito, and I piled into Tommy's car and headed to Staten Island. Of course, we had a few drinks on the way to loosen up. For some crazy reason, drinking and driving wasn't as much of an offense back in the 80's and early 90's.

By the time we got to Billy O's, we were all feeling pretty good. Remember, I'm still only 16 years old at this point, while Tommy, Steve, and DeVito were all 20 or 21. Because of how I looked, no one ever questioned it, not even the club owner who graciously greeted us at the door. I'm not sure if I ever actually heard his name, but I just assumed it was Billy.

Billy began showing us around the club, pointing out places like where we'd load our equipment in and where the dressing room was. Since this was all brand new to us, it was very overwhelming and exciting. "We were going to have our own dressing room! Holy crap!" I shouted. Again, young and innocent makes for a priceless, unforgettable time.

Billy asked us if we secured the opening band for the night we were playing. We said that we were working on it but not to worry. In actuality, we had no idea who we were going to get to open for us. Billy then asked if we brought any passes to leave with him so he could put them around the club. We had absolutely no idea what he was talking about. We said in almost unison "Passes? What kind of passes?"

Knowing this was our first gig, Billy was pretty patient with us. He went on to explain that we needed to print passes so that we could give them out to advertise our show. Again, because this was all so new to us, we asked Billy "Where would we get passes like that?" Remember, this was before everyone had a computer or even a home printer. I had never printed anything in my life. Billy told us, "Go to a local printing shop and have them printed. Put the name of the club, name of the band, date and time." After a few more minutes and a quick drink for the road, we were headed back to Brooklyn. On the way home, Steve said that he knew a printing place near the bank where he worked on Avenue U and 16th street called PIP Printing.

Now the only other problem we had was finding a band to open for us. I remember hearing from Brian Hannah, the singer for my old band Creation, who told me that our former bass player, Kevin "Mur" Murray, had a new band called Naked Gypsy and that they'd been playing gigs. Steve was in charge of getting the passes printed and I was in charge of getting the opening band.

I called Mur the next day to ask him if he and his new band were interested in playing with us. Much like Playground, Naked Gypsy was just starting out and they jumped at the chance for a gig at a new club.

A few days later, Steve and I were very excited to pick up our new passes at PIP Printing. We didn't know it at the time, but the passes looked terrible: they were all white with plain black lettering. All they said was, "Billy O's presents Playground. Saturday August 4th. Doors open at 9pm. Show at 11pm." The passes didn't offer the address of Billy O's, the phone number, or even how much it was to get in. It didn't matter, though: we weren't giving them to strangers. We were going to give them to every single person we already knew—friends, family, neighbors, the mailman…everybody!

Everyone that we handed a pass to said they were coming. My old grammar school friends were very excited to finally see me play live. Not only that, but they were excited that they were going to be able to hang out in a bar and drink. After all they, like me, were only 16 years old, and some were only 15!

Something terrible happened the day before our first show. I went grocery shopping with my mom and my cousin Rosemary, who was driving. My mom was in the passenger seat and I was in the back. After we parked, we all exited the car about the same time with my mom slightly ahead of me. While my mom's front door was still open, I reached up and grabbed the bar in between the two doors to lift myself up. While still holding the bar, my mom slammed her car door shut, immediately crushing, and trapping, my fingers in the door.

I was in such shock I didn't even scream. I calmly said, "Ma" and pointed at the car door with my other hand while my fingers were still trapped inside. My leg began to shake, and my mom started to scream as she feverishly tried to open the car door. Unfortunately, the car door was now locked, and she couldn't open it.

She started to scream to my cousin, "Joey's fingers are caught in the door!" My cousin began to fumble for her keys to open her side and then reach over to unlock the passenger side door. What was probably only a few seconds felt like an eternity. Finally, the door opened and my fingers were free. That's when the pain hit me. My ring and index fingers were crushed. We got right back in the car and rushed straight to the emergency room.

Sure enough, my two fingers were broken. As the doctor was putting my fingers in a metal splint, I told him that I had my first gig with my new band and that I couldn't play the drums with these big metal splints on. Canceling the show was never even an option in my mind. He advised me to keep the splint on or try taping my fingers together like athletes do when they need to play with broken fingers. I didn't even tell the guys in the band until they saw me the next day when we were loading up for the show. I figured they would be nervous enough without this new bit of good news.

Besides my broken fingers, the other big problem we still faced was how to get people to the show in Staten Island. Obviously, my 15 and 16-year-old friends didn't drive, and most of our other friends didn't have cars.

There's something about being young that somehow motivates you to just figure out a way to get things done. You don't over-think things, always believing that there was a simple solution to everything. For this particular problem, we would just pack anyone who didn't have a ride into the back of the U-Haul that we were renting to bring all of our equipment to the gig.

The back compartments in a typical U-Haul truck are definitely not made to carry passengers, for many reasons. First, we would have to roll down the large sliding back door and lock it from the outside. This was extremely dangerous: it meant that all the people in the back would be locked in and only able to get out if someone from the outside unlocked and opened the door. Second, there was no light in the back while the truck was in motion. This was crazy, mainly because the passengers would also be back there with all of the band's equipment. This was the first time any of us had rented a U-Haul and we didn't realize that it might be a good idea to strap everything down so that nothing slid around.

With all of the people sitting on the floor, all of the heavy equipment sliding around, and it being pitch black, it all added up to a potential disaster. On top of all of that, we had our singer, Tommy, driving the truck and he thought it would be very funny to take turns and bumps at a fast speed to make everything and everyone in the back go flying.

As crazy as all of this was, everyone actually wanted to be in the back of the U-Haul. It sounded like fun to us. So, on the night of August 4, 1990, me and about 15 other guys, along with 4 or 5 cases of beer, piled into the back of the moving truck with all of our equipment. The

U-Haul was followed by a procession of cars headed to Staten Island to Playground's very first show.

We had our army to support us and we planned on delivering for them. If every show from here on out was like this, sign me up for the rest of my life. This was going to be great!

My plan was to have a lot of my friends help me load my drums in and then stay in the club until the show started. That way they didn't have to pass the doorman who was bound to be checking I.D.'s later in the night.

Once we loaded in, it was time for my first sound check. Even though I had already played a gig at the Battle of the Bands two years before, I definitely didn't get a sound check at that show. To tell you the truth, I wasn't exactly sure what a sound check even was. The sound man told me to hit the bass drum. So I did. Once. He said, as politely as possible, "Please keep hitting it until I say to stop." How was I supposed to know that's what he meant? He went one by one to get sounds for my massive 10-piece drum kit plus my three Roto toms. So with the Roto toms, I had a total of 8 rack toms from 6 inch to 15 inch. It looked massive sitting on the drum riser, just like Eric Carr's!

After testing each drum one by one, the sound man told me to play the whole kit to see how it all sounded. I began doing all sorts of triplet double bass fills and big rolls descending on my toms. Just then the opening band, Naked Gypsy, walked in. Their mouths were hanging open. It turned out that they not only had my old bassist Mur in the band, but the singer and guitar player were from the band that I auditioned for about a year prior, the group that looked a little too dirty for me. We recognized each other immediately while I was sound checking.

When I got off stage, I greeted them very friendly even though they had been pretty upset that I didn't want to join their band. I was expecting a little hostility, but instead I got praises. They couldn't believe how good I had sounded during sound check. After sound check, I had to explain to the drummer for Naked Gypsy that he would be setting up in front of the drum riser.

This to me, was always the number-one benefit of being the headlining band. You could set up your gear and just leave it on the stage instead of having to rush to set up in between bands. I just always felt that coming out in front of the audience to set up my drums caused the show to lose a sense of mystique. The people in the audience don't want to see that; they want the show and the people on stage to be larger than life.

Later that night, after Naked Gypsy finished their set to a dull applause, I looked out from the dressing room and the club was packed! I had all of my good friends there plus my brother, and even my mom came! Once Naked Gypsy cleared the stage, the audience began shouting, "We want Playground! We want Playground!" Tommy, Steve, DeVito, and I huddled together in the back and told each other to kick ass and have fun.

As soon as we walked on to the stage, the place went wild. It's a feeling I could never describe to someone who hasn't been on stage. It's not just about being on stage and getting cheered and feeling the audience's energy. It was about knowing how hard you worked every day to get to this point — all the hours practicing, the late nights, the long train rides to rehearsal, the hundreds of hours rehearsing in your room to get better. It was all for something and this moment was it.

Before we hit the very first note, I felt a very easy calm come over me. It was a feeling that I immediately recognized. The cheering crowd began to slow, their sounds began to grow quiet, and I could feel the hair on my arms begin to raise. My heart was pounding strong, but slow and controlled. Then the moment froze. I took a deep breath and felt joy overwhelm me. I knew everything in my life had led me right to where I was supposed to be, on this stage, right now. I saw all my friends, my brother, and my mom with the biggest smiles on their faces. I knew this was just the beginning, but I was going to enjoy every second of it. Just like that, everything unfroze and we began playing our opening song "Could've Been You".

Playground was firing on all cylinders. No one seemed nervous and no one seemed overwhelmed. At one point, Steve broke a guitar string and needed our friend Dave, who was Steve's guitar tech for the night, to change the string and hand him his backup guitar. Dave was nowhere to be found. It turned out that he was in the audience partying with all of the other crazy maniacs that night.

Before the show, I was so excited to get on stage that I forgot to get myself water to drink during the performance. I quickly gestured to my friend Jimmy Gaffey, who was my roadie that night, that I needed two ice teas from the bar. This was before bottled water was a very common thing. Jimmy came back a few moments later and handed me two tall glasses of iced tea.

I quickly chugged the first one down. Because I drank it so fast, I didn't realize until I was done that it tasted weird. My moron friend/roadie got me two "Long Island Iced Teas," which were made with 4 different kinds of alcohol. Guzzling one of those went straight to my head. Luckily, I was okay and I got through the rest of the performance. Over the course of my career, I was never someone who could drink before a performance. Being a drummer, I always felt it would throw off my equilibrium and cause me to play badly.

When it was time for our final song, Tommy thanked everyone for coming and we busted into Fats Domino's "Ain't That A Shame." The crowd erupted, probably not so much for the song choice, but because they knew it was their last opportunity to go crazy.

By the time the song was over, the entire stage was filled with our friends going completely berserk. Everyone refused to leave the stage. They began chanting, "One more song, one more song!" As incredible as this was, it was a disaster because we didn't have any more songs. We'd played every song we knew as a band.

Luckily, Tommy started to sing the Van Halen version of "Happy Trails" which was completely *a capella* (no instruments, just vocals). It worked, and the whole crowd sang along. This was an absolutely perfect show from top to bottom.

After we finished, Billy told us we did a great job and handed us $52. Even though he was obviously robbing us (the place was jam packed because we had brought in about 200 people), it didn't matter. We were so thrilled with what we just accomplished that we gladly took the $52, split it four ways, and were the happiest band on the face of the earth.

It worked out to be $13 per band member. We decided to just put the money on the bar for celebratory drinks. But before I did, I took one dollar out to keep as a memento to commemorate the first dollar I'd ever made as a musician.

We were on such a high after playing our first show at Billy O's that we didn't want the party to end. By the time we got back to our neighborhood in Brooklyn at around 4 am, mostly everyone was either passed out or headed home. Tommy, myself, Playground's number-one fan Ernie LaMonte, and my two great friends Rob Scally and Bobby Howell all went to Marine Park with a few cases of beer and stayed up all night drinking and talking about the show.

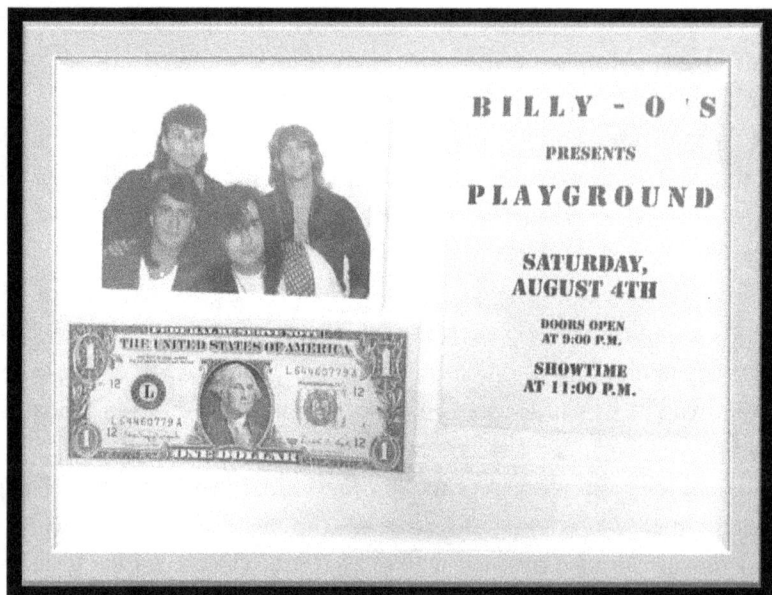

My first dollar ever earned as a musician.

We watched the sun come up while still floating on cloud nine. We even began to see people from the neighborhood walking to church. We waved hello while holding up our beer. Experiences like this really made me love what I was doing more than ever. Of course, I loved my drums and playing them was all I wanted to do, but bonding with people over what you loved to do was priceless.

After a few days of still flying high, it was time to start thinking about our next show. Now that we had a little clout by filling up Billy O's with such a big crowd, we could go to other clubs and use that as a selling point for our band. It worked like a charm. I'm not sure if the clubs ever really checked to see if we drew that many people or if it was simply that we now had confidence when making calls to the clubs. Either way, we booked two more gigs right away.

For our second show, we would play in our hometown, Brooklyn, at The Crazy Country Club located on 64th Street and 7th Avenue. The date was set for August 31,1990.

The Crazy Country Club was a semi-famous local spot. Once we booked this show, we knew it was going to be huge! And huge would prove to be a mild understatement. Because this was a local show, every person we knew could get themselves there. I think I invited everyone I'd ever met. We had everyone coming—family, friends, friends of friends, neighbors, and just about anyone from the neighborhood that heard what a great time our show at Billy O's had been. They all flocked to The Crazy Country Club that night to not only see a great show, but to be at a great party.

That's really the best way to describe the early Playground shows. They were the biggest and best parties I'd ever been to. And we were the hosts and guests of honors. Ernie said it best, "It was such a joy when Playground played. I didn't feel like I was watching a band, I felt like I was in the band!"

Ever since joining Playground, Tommy would always talk about his old girlfriend Erin, whom he was still in love with. I think every Playground song was about her in some way. Up until the night of the Crazy Country Club, I'd never met her. She showed up to the show with her new boyfriend and Tommy was a wreck because of it. He performed well, but you could see him the whole night slowly spiraling down.

After we finished our amazing set, I saw all of Tommy's friends starting to line up. I had no idea what was going on until his friend Shaun came over to me and said, "Hey Joey, come with me. There's something I want to show you." Still not knowing what was happening, I went along with it out of curiosity. At the end of the line, I saw a guy sitting in a chair while one by one, each person in the line walked passed him and spit on him.

I couldn't believe what I was seeing. The guy didn't even get up to try and leave. He knew if he did, he would probably get beaten to a pulp.

After about 40 people spit on this poor bastard, I finally asked Shaun, "Who is that guy?" He chuckled and said, "That's Erin's new boyfriend."

Even though this was a sick thing to do, I respected it. They loved their friend so much that they weren't going to let this girl parade her new boyfriend in his face at his own concert.

My friends were the same way. We had a bond that meant we would do anything for each other, and obviously so did Tommy and his friends. Because Tommy and I had the same kind of friends, I think that made us grow close.

The show was a major success! The place was sold out and then some. The headlining band didn't bring anyone. Playground sold the place out and the owner knew it. In fact, he wouldn't let us leave without booking us for another night. He offered us the headlong slot on September 26, 1990, and we gladly accepted.

We were now rehearsing in Rockaway Studios which was where all of the local bands began to rehearse. We had been there for about a month and the owner Mitch Glider had never really given us the time of day. He was kind of a cocky, nerdy guy who thought he had more power than he did.

The entertainment business is funny; nobody gives you the time of day until they think they can make money off of you. Our next session at Rockaway, following the big success of the Crazy Country Club gig, Mitch was a completely different person to us. He greeted us with open arms and told us that he wanted to talk to us after rehearsal.

He told us that he'd heard through the grapevine that we had an amazing show at The Crazy Country Club and he would love to work with us and help promote our next show. We didn't know exactly what that meant, and we told Mitch that we already booked another show for September 26 at the Country Club. Mitch said, "Great! Let me promote it for you. It'll be great!" Being the young, naïve morons that we were, we didn't realize that we absolutely didn't need Mitch at all! We didn't understand that he just wanted a piece of the action by calling himself the promoter. We were going to pack the Crazy Country Club without any help from Mitch. Another lesson learned to be put in my pocket for a later date. Even though I was only 16, I was absorbing everything about the music business that I could. All of these lessons would come in very handy down the road.

The Crazy Country Club show would now be billed as "Rockaway Studios Presents" Playground. The date was September 26, 1990. The show was our best and biggest yet. We were headlining in our hometown and the word was officially out that a Playground show was "the place to be"! The Crazy Country Club was completely sold out. We even had to sneak a few dozen of our friends in the back door because they weren't letting anyone else in. The band we opened for a month prior was now opening for us. I always remember reading stories about when KISS first started; they were opening for Blue Oyster Cult and then a few months later Blue Oyster was opening for them. Now, the same thing was happening to Playground! I always associated everything with KISS.

The Crazy Country Club in Brooklyn circa 1990

Mitch the so-called promoter jumped up on stage to get the crowd ready and to announce us. He started by saying, "Hi everyone, my name is Mitch and I own Rockaway studios." Before he could even finish his opening line the crowd began to chant, "F**k Mitch! F**k Mitch! F**k Mitch!"

Those were our friends, all right. They could spot a phony a mile away and that's exactly what Mitch was. He saw dollar signs in us and he took advantage of a young band. That chant was classic and exactly what Mitch deserved.

From the moment we hit our first note, the crowd went absolutely insane! Then, toward the end of our set another classic chant broke out. The United States had just recently entered into the Gulf War with Iraq, and Tommy decided that right before our last song he would make a political statement. He began preaching from the stage about America and how great the U.S.A was. He then started the now infamous chant that was luckily captured on video.

Tommy shouted, "F**k Iran, F**k Iran," then the whole crowd joined in with the same. The only problem was, we were at war with Iraq, not Iran. The crowd was filled with predominantly under-age kids who were very drunk at this point and would have followed any chant that we started. Tommy's sister Liz was videoing us that night, and her screaming at Tommy with, "It's Iraq, you idiot, not Iran!" is quite audible.

ROCK - AWAY STUDIOS
PRESENTS

P L A Y G R O U N D

AT THE

CRAZY COUNTRY CLUB
7th Avenue & 64th Street
Brooklyn, NY
(718) 836-4008

Crazy Country club pass. Notice the Rockaway studios presents at the

After our set was finished, one of the audience members cornered Steve in the bathroom. It was none other than our former Playground guitar player, Brendan Murphy. Brendan had left the band a few months prior after having an argument with Tommy and Steve because he didn't think the band was serious enough. He thought we should be gigging and doing more. Now just a few months later, Brendan saw what an overnight success we had become and essentially begged Steve to rejoin the band.

Steve was more than happy to have Brendan back and immediately said yes. Tommy, DeVito, and I all didn't have any strong opinions on it one way or another. We felt that since Steve was the guitar player, if he wanted Brendan back it was okay with us.

I actually didn't think we needed Brendan back in the band. I thought we sounded great with one guitar player. When Brendan originally left, Steve really stepped up and took control, even with his very quiet, laid back personality. When Brendan left, Steve really did an amazing job! Unfortunately, when Brendan re-joined, Steve once again became quiet and withdrawn. I'm not sure if it was because he was never that confident in his playing or if it was just an easier role for him to play inside the structure of the band. I personally always enjoyed Steve's playing more than Brendan's.

PLAYGROUND rehearsing at Rockaway Studios.

After rehearsing a few times with Brendan and welcoming him back, he came up with an idea of having a Playground newsletter. Remember, this is still way before email and the Internet. So, once a month, we sent a newsletter to all of our fans to let them know what was happening in the world of Playground. We named it "Letters from the Sandbox." Brendan would type it, filled with all of the pertinent information that we needed to promote. We would also all personally sign each one and hand write a special message to all of the people we personally knew.

Because we still had no money, we saved on postage by hand delivering every single letter. As crazy as that sounds, these were the wild things that I absolutely loved and have the best memories of to this day. Each band member was essentially in charge of delivering the letters to the people they knew. Because I didn't drive, our friend Ernie, who had now become a cross between band manager and band mascot, would drive me from house to house to hand deliver the "Letters from the Sandbox." I know it sounds like a miserable and tedious task, but Ernie and I had a great time.

Ernie always prided himself on his musical knowledge and loved more than anything to introduce new music to someone. We spent three straight nights together, at about 4 or 5 hours per night, and became really close friends in the process.

Again, being young and innocent was such a positive. This is something I would never even dream of doing in my later years. I would

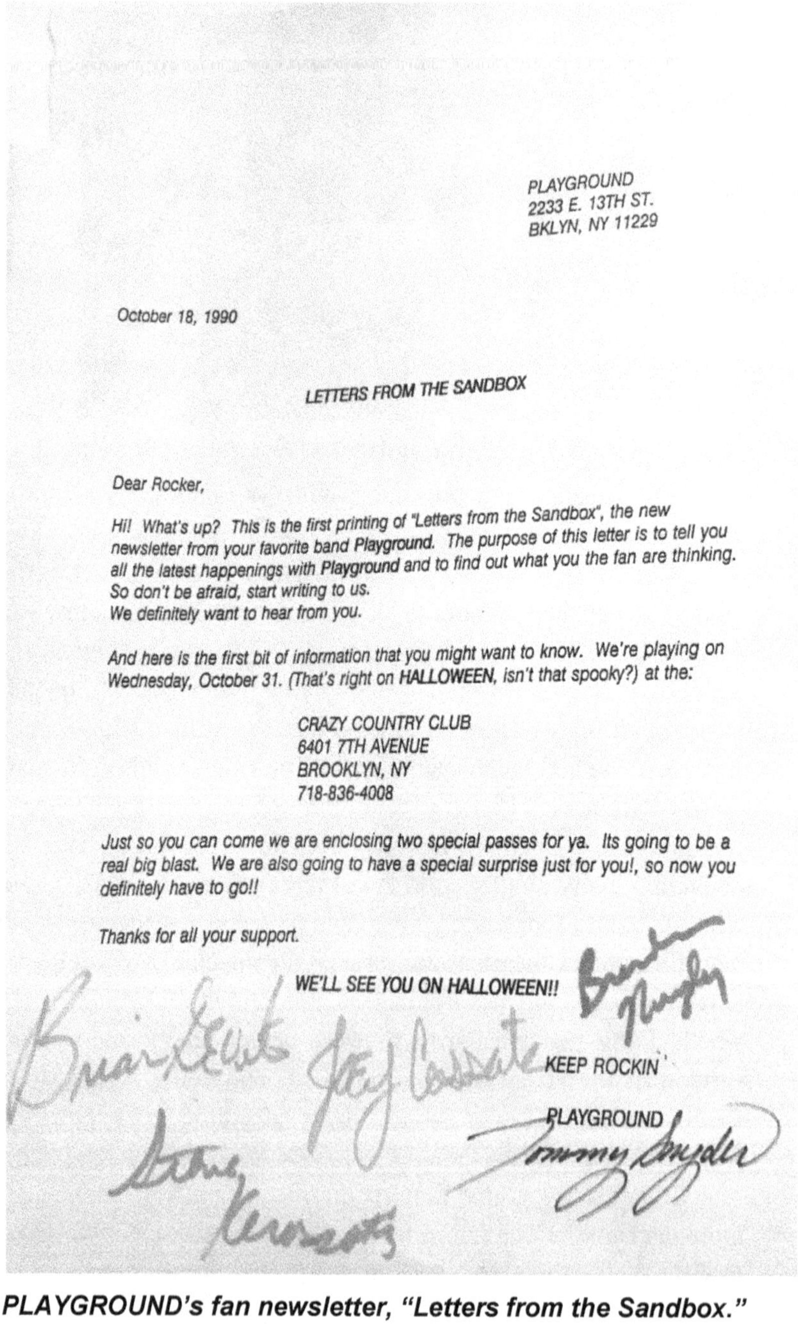

PLAYGROUND
2233 E. 13TH ST.
BKLYN, NY 11229

October 18, 1990

LETTERS FROM THE SANDBOX

Dear Rocker,

Hi! What's up? This is the first printing of "Letters from the Sandbox", the new newsletter from your favorite band **Playground**. The purpose of this letter is to tell you all the latest happenings with **Playground** and to find out what you the fan are thinking. So don't be afraid, start writing to us.
We definitely want to hear from you.

And here is the first bit of information that you might want to know. We're playing on Wednesday, October 31. (That's right on **HALLOWEEN**, isn't that spooky?) at the:

CRAZY COUNTRY CLUB
6401 7TH AVENUE
BROOKLYN, NY
718-836-4008

Just so you can come we are enclosing two special passes for ya. Its going to be a real big blast. We are also going to have a special surprise just for you!, so now you definitely have to go!!

Thanks for all your support.

WE'LL SEE YOU ON HALLOWEEN!!

KEEP ROCKIN'

PLAYGROUND

PLAYGROUND's fan newsletter, "Letters from the Sandbox."

think it was such a waste of time and energy. But because everything was so new and exciting, I was willing to do anything. Besides, what could be better at that time than hand delivering a newsletter from my new "super popular" band to all of my good friends and family? On top of that, I became close with one of my best friends for years to come. Ernie would actually play a very significant role in my life years later.

At this time, I was still so obsessed with KISS that I didn't really give older music a chance. Of course, I knew Led Zeppelin, The Rolling Stones, and the Beatles, but it wasn't until Ernie really showed me the obscure stuff from those bands that I really became a fan. Ernie never liked to show people "the hit songs" from bands; he wanted to introduce people to songs that nobody had ever heard of.

I totally understood that mentality because when I would introduce someone to KISS, I never liked playing them "Rock and Roll All Night" or "Detroit Rock City." Instead, I would play "100,000 Years" from *Alive* or "Saint and Sinner" from *Creatures of the Night*.

Ernie loved delivering these newsletters too, but for different reasons than I did. He now had a captive audience who would spend hours upon hours listening to his musical suggestions. I hate to admit it, and I'm sure he will love to hear this and never let me live it down, but I definitely credit Ernie for broadening and expanding my musical taste and knowledge.

Once all of our Letters from the Sandbox were delivered, we concentrated on rehearsing for the show and catching Brendan up to speed. After playing those few amazing gigs, we were starting to get very confident with not only our playing, but our whole show and performance. Dare I say, we were even a little cocky. We hoped Brendan, who had never played a live show before, would be able to perform well.

A few nights before Brendan's debut at our big Halloween show at The Crazy Country Club, Steve came down with a severe case of the Chicken Pox. We couldn't believe it. What were we going to do? We'd put some much time and planning into this show and into all of those newsletters we sent out. How would we even let everyone know if we had to cancel the show?

We decided we wouldn't cancel. We had played up to this point with only one guitar player; now Brendan would just have to cover all of the parts like Steve did. Steve actually made the transition much easier than Brendan did. This just further confirmed my belief that Steve was the better player.

My brother was picking up a few of my friends from the old neighborhood in his vintage white Camero, then we would all drive over to the show together. The plan was simple enough, but after almost an hour they still hadn't arrived.

We got a call that my brother was in an accident and that we needed to get to Avenue L and 57th street pre immediately! Our hearts sank.

Once arrived, we saw a massive crowd of people, but I didn't see Danny's car anywhere. I thought to myself "Oh, he probably just had a little fender bender and he already left". That was until the crowd shifted and I could see through.

My brother's car was inside of a house. Yes, you read it right! The car looked as if it hit a ramp like in Smokey and the Bandit, went airborne, flew 20 feet in the air, and landed in someone's living room. Thank God everyone was fine, but it was scene right out of a movie.

The night of Halloween 1990 was another big success for Playground. The show was completely sold out and there was a line of people down around block trying to get in. I didn't think we sounded as good or as tight as we did with Steve, but we made it work. Our crowd was so fanatical about the band and the shows that it didn't really matter if we sounded good or not. It was more about the energy and the party.

Shortly after the Halloween show that Steve missed due to the Chicken Pox, I came down with them. This gave us another little set back, but we were back in the studio by mid-November. We could begin gigging again right after the holidays. There was a great buzz and electricity surrounding everything that Playground was doing, and we wanted to keep that momentum going.

The phrase "creating a buzz" is constantly thrown around in the music industry. I have personally been in dozens of bands that have tried to create the proverbial "buzz" and it's almost impossible. It's like capturing lightning in a bottle. Playground had definitely trapped themselves a nice size bolt!

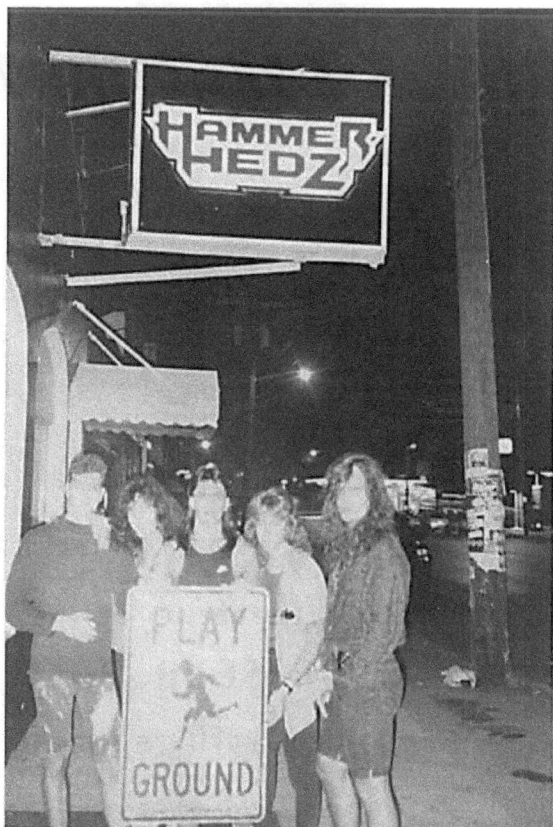

*Playground standing outside of Hammer Hedz
in Long Island, NY 1990*

CHAPTER 13

L'AMOUR & SCUD MISSLES

PLAYGROUND

Will be appearing at the

L'AMOUR SCUD BATTLE

on Friday, April 26, 1991.

Doors open at 9 P.M.

Sometime in late November, while trying to get the set list tight and coming up with some new ideas, an argument broke out during rehearsal. As usual, it started about everyone's volume. DeVito started to complain that he couldn't hear Steve's guitar because Brendan was too loud. Then, Tommy started to complain that he couldn't hear himself singing, etc., etc., etc...

The dynamic of the band before Brendan rejoined was always balanced. Steve was quiet, DeVito was loud, and Tommy and I were always just about having fun. This basically let DeVito do what he did without any contention. Once Brendan rejoined, it threw the weird balance that we had out of whack.

The problem was that Brendan had a pretty obnoxious personality, and he was a bit of a "know it all." This did not mix well with DeVito, and because they didn't mix well, my and Tommy's personalities got even louder. On this particular night, everything came to a head.

DeVito's girlfriend, Jeannette, was there and he wasn't going to stand for Brendan talking down to him. Finally, DeVito had had enough and he threw his bass across the room and walked out. Luckily for us, we were recording the rehearsal to listen back and caught the whole exchange on tape. DeVito's bass had made a deep giant "bong" sound as it crashed to the floor. Tommy quickly said "Lets try it in that key". Jeanette responded with "You're such an asshole Tommy" and ran after DeVito to try and calm him down. We laughed and just assumed that he needed a break for a few minutes and went to get some air. That wasn't the case this time. He never came back. We couldn't believe it.

DeVito called me the next day and basically said he'd had enough and was quitting the band. I urged him to reconsider. We had a great thing going and we were on our way up. But, he wasn't having it.

We found out later that DeVito was frustrated that his songs weren't being used in Playground. He actually started to jam with another local band, Big Bad Wolf, with hopes of joining them.

Playground immediately started looking for a new bass player. We auditioned a few guys and finally found our man in Richie Delfino. He was perfect. Not only was he a really good bass player but his two favorite bands were Kiss and Black Sabbath—Tommy's favorite and mine as well. We were in heaven. Before we officially made him a member of the band, we wanted to get to know him a little better. We didn't want to have the same problem with personalities clashing like we did with DeVito.

Tommy and I took Richie to hang out at The Crazy Country Club one night to see a few bands. We had such a good time and got along so well that we stayed after closing to jam with the owner. At this point, we were like royalty at the Crazy Country Club because of the massive crowds we were bringing in. After the late-night blues jam, the owner gave us his approval to sign Richie on bass.

The next weekend, we took Richie to Billy O's, back to the spot where we had played our very first show. We were once again treated like royalty. I'm sure it wasn't because these owners loved hanging around with a bunch of kids. It was because we made these guys a small fortune every time we played their club.

This time, Steve and Brendan were also there. By the end of the night we all agreed we could officially welcome Richie into Playground. The owner also wouldn't let us leave without booking another date to play. We booked February 16th, 1991, giving us about two months to get Richie ready! We all knew that 1991 was going to be the year of Playground!

We began official rehearsals with Richie right away. To save money, we began rehearsing in the small drum room in my house. The room was actually so small that the other band members would have to stand in the hallway while I was inside the room playing my drums.

Every once in a while, Steve and Tommy would sneak down into my kitchen where my mom always had something cooking on the stove. They would run back up with meatballs, chicken cutlets, or whatever they could get their hands on. This was all going on while I was in the room waiting to start the next song. I could hear Tommy trying to sing the next song with a mouthful of meatballs!

We knew that once New Year's was over we would need to start gigging heavily again. So, we began rehearsing a few times a week. Come to think of it, Steve and Tommy might have called for that many rehearsals just so they could eat my mom's cooking a couple of times a week. Bastards!

The band was invited to a New Year's Eve party at Tommy's friend Jimmy O'Brien's house. The party was filled with everyone that typically came to our shows. It was a very fun and relaxing atmosphere. Brendan and I were drinking in the kitchen while Tommy and Richie were hanging out in the basement. A little after midnight, we heard a loud ruckus coming from the basement. Tommy came bolting up the stairs and ran out the front door. Seconds later, Richie came up bleeding heavily from the nose and over his eye. He was yelling, "We have to get out of here! We have to get out of here!" Brendan and I grabbed Richie and got the hell out of there without even knowing what had just happened.

Richie told us that Tommy and a guy named Ercon had an argument and it came to blows. Because the basement happened to be filled with all of Ercon's crew, Tommy, Richie, and the few other friends of Tommy's who were down there didn't stand a chance. Not only were they heavily outnumbered, but because Richie was the new guy and nobody knew who he was, both sides were hitting Richie during the melee. Poor Richie: only in the band a few weeks and getting utterly destroyed by both opposing sides in a pretty big fight.

Tommy and Richie went to the hospital that night and both were in pretty bad shape. The whites of Tommy's eyes were dark red for weeks. He looked like one of the lizard people from the old 80's TV show, *V.* I'm not sure how Richie looked after that night because I never saw him again. He came to my house the next day to pick up his amp when I wasn't home, and that was the last we heard from him.

Playground once again stalled. First Steve's chicken pox slowed down our unbelievable momentum, and now we had two bass players quit inside of a month. We had a show booked in February and we needed to find a bass player fast.

One afternoon, while I was up in my room reading comics, the doorbell rang. I glanced out my window and saw the car of our former bass player, Brian DeVito. I quickly ran downstairs and told my mom to say I wasn't home. I hadn't seen him since he quit the band and I wanted to see what he wanted before I spoke to him.

I ran back up to my room while my mom answered the door. I heard her say, "Hi Brian, Joey's not home." Brian asked, "Can I come in anyway and talk?" This wasn't that unusual. Because we used to rehearse in my room, my mom became very friendly with all the guys in the band. Tommy would sometimes talk to my mom and grandmother about his ex-girlfriend Erin, sometimes for 2 hours while we rehearsed upstairs. My mom kindly welcomed DeVito in and sat him on the couch as if to begin a therapy session.

They began talking in the living room while I listened in the upstairs hallway. Brian began saying how he thinks he made a big mistake leaving Playground and that he misses all of us. I couldn't believe what I was hearing. After how he walked out, I never thought that was why he was coming to see me. If I had known, I would have answered the door. But it was too late now. I couldn't go downstairs and say, "Hi, I've been here the whole time." So, I just stayed hidden and kept listening.

My poor mother and grandmother had to sit there for over an hour while Brian cried to them that he wanted back in the band. My mom and grandmother really became sort of the Playground's psychiatrists. Finally, Brian left and my mom screamed up to me, "He's gone, you bastard! You can come down now!" She was just kidding. I knew my mom wasn't mad. She secretly loved being "band mom."

This was such a weird coincidence. Brian had no knowledge that we had gotten a new bass player in Richie and that he just recently quit. If Richie had still been in the band, I'm sure none of us would have cared what DeVito had to say; that wouldn't have been fair to Richie. But, we were in sort of a bind at the moment. We had a show already booked and had no leads on finding a new bass player. I quickly called the other guys to fill them in on what had transpired. They were laughing hysterically about the fact that I was hiding upstairs while poor DeVito cried to my mom and grandmother. But, we all unanimously agreed that we should take DeVito back.

We found out years later that DeVito was trying to join the local Brooklyn band Big Bad Wolf and that they simply didn't want him. That's the real reason he came crawling back to Playground.

Playground finally played its first show as a five-piece band (both Brendan and Steve on guitar) on February 16, 1991, at Billy O's, the same place we started 6 months prior. Now, and after only 6 months, we were a completely different band—not so much musically, but mentally. We were very confident and borderline cocky now. We knew the clubs wanted us because we brought so many people and we decided that we weren't going to get screwed out of money anymore. We worked out what they call a "door deal." It's when the band gets a portion of every ticket sold at the door. This was the first show where we actually made decent profit. It wasn't anything incredible, but it was somewhere around $150 per person.

Considering I was only 17 years old, this was great money for me. Of course, we blew it all once we got back to Brooklyn. We invited everyone that was at our show to come party with us after at our favorite spot, The Cuckoo's Nest. We walked in and slapped all of our money on the bar and said, "Drinks are on us for the rest of the night!" If memory serves, Ernie ordered 100 beers from the bartender that night—

all at once! It was our way of saying thank you to our fans. Playground was back!

Tommy's house at this point became exactly like the one in the movie Animal House starring John Belushi. It was 24/7 partying. We even paid his rent one month with beer can returns.

Ernie decided to tell a few Asian girls that were in attendance the night of Billy O's , that he was the bands' manager and that we were all having a party back at the "Band House" in Brooklyn. Those poor girls were stuck in Brooklyn for almost a week. Ha ha.

I think all the raunchy details involving Playground could warrant it's own book. Maybe I'll write it one day and change some of the names to protect the innocent. It might be more in line with Motley Crue's "DIRT".

Having the time of my life! Age 16

Playground began booking as many shows as possible. There was a great buzz around the neighborhood about us, and we wanted to keep the party rolling. Next, we would be returning to the Crazy Country Club on St. Patrick's Day. It was another amazing sold out show that created even more hype about the band. Everyone now knew that if you wanted to have a good time, come to a Playground show. I'm not sure if we really appreciated what we had accomplished back then.

What we created at our live shows was not only a great performance but an incredible party atmosphere. But because we were so young, we were always looking ahead for the next big opportunity, and it came shortly after St. Patrick's Day.

We heard that the legendary rock club L'amour was soon closing. But before it did, it was hosting a giant battle of the bands called "The Scud Battle of the Bands," referring to the scud missiles the Iraqi military were using against the U.S. military in the Gulf War. We quickly submitted for an entry.

L'amour was absolutely the biggest rock club around. Every major signed band had played there, including Metallica, Motley Crue, and Twisted Sister. Everyone! I just most recently saw Anthrax, Skid Row, Badlands, and Mr. Big at L'amour. The biggest and best show I'd ever scene at L'amour was when Paul Stanley from KISS did a small solo tour. That was also the first time I saw future KISS drummer, Eric Singer, play live. To play that stage, the same stage that I just saw Paul Stanley on, would be a dream come true. This was a far way off from playing in front of Whitney Houston's manager just a few months prior.

When you're a kid, there are always times when you say to yourself, "If I do that, I've made it," or "If I can just play there, I've made it." When

PLAYGROUND passes through the years

I was 15, 16, and 17 years old, if a person played L'amour, "he'd made it." Truth be told, I knew when people said, "You've made

it", that it really meant nothing. It was really more in their eyes than mine. It was just an event or a milestone that validated what you were doing in someone else's eyes. I just wanted to play my drums all the time. That to me was "making it." Doing big things and playing great shows is the easy part; it's when things are hard that a person really sees who wants to stick with it and who doesn't.

L'AMOUR
"THE ROCK CAPITOL OF BROOKLYN"
1546-62ND ST., BROOKLYN, N.Y. 718) 232-1616

SCUD
BATTLE '91

APRIL 5
DAMNABIITY
THROTTLE
CONFUSION
OUTCAST
MIND ERASER
FEAR ITSELF
MOTIVE DRIVE

APRIL 12
SHOWDOWN
KILLAR WATTS
WRETCHED WHORE
SHATTERED TRUTH
CRASH SERVICE
AWOL-SIMON SEZ
MIDNIGHT REIGN
SEDITIOUS

SHOW MILITARY I.D.
GET IN FREE

APRIL 19
REQUIEM
RAW STEEL
TRENODY
LAST REMAINS
STEEL & STONE
SINTILLION
EXALT
INSANIAC

APRIL 26
SMASH ALLEY
NAKED GYPSY
PLAYGROUND
ALCHEMYST
VAIN EXISTENCE
ROCKIT QUEEN
PERSUASION
MISTER STRANGE

718-376-0150

Even though playing L'amour was the opportunity of a lifetime, we quickly saw that it was just another way for a club to make money. They didn't care who played the battle of the bands. They didn't even ask for a demo tape. All a band had to do was purchase 100 tickets at $5 a ticket and they could play. In essence, the band had to pay them $500 to play. This was the beginning of the "Pay-to-Play" era of music. Clubs were beginning to make bands pay them to play at their clubs.

L'amour told us that we could sell the tickets at whatever price we wanted. We knew that we could easily sell 100 tickets at $10 each. So, we agreed. This being the world famous L'amour, we knew we would be able to bring a lot of people. We had to pull no punches. We set out to have the biggest show of our lives!

The next month consisted of non-stop promotion and rehearsals for the show. Every second of ever day was focused on winning that battle of the bands! We worked day and night. When we weren't rehearsing; we were out promoting to every person that would listen. We did a whole

126

new photo shoot to use on flyers that we would pass out and plaster all over town. Our "Letters of the Sandbox" newsletter mailing list had grown so big that we couldn't hand deliver anymore.

Even after all these years and thousands of shows played, I think Playground at L'amour was the hardest I have ever worked to put on any single show. Nothing was going to stop us from winning. It wasn't only about the $1,000 prize; that we planned on using for our new demo. It was also the prestige of playing L'amour and winning their Battles of the Bands. We knew this was going to catapult us to the next level. We were given the third slot out of 8 bands. We were to use all of L'amour backline equipment. We weren't allowed to bring anything because they wanted the bands to turn over quickly. I hated this: I was still at the point in my drumming evolution where I was extremely particular on how I played my drums.

Luckily for me, the band with which we played our very first show, Naked Gypsy, was on right before us. Our friend Rocky, whose garage we used to audition our bass player DeVito, was now the drummer in Naked Gypsy. I was the one that set up his audition so he kind of owed me one.

I asked him if I could set the drums up the exact way I wanted when he played so I didn't have to change anything right before Playground went on. This worked out great. Now, I wouldn't have to run out and adjust stuff right before Playground went on. Remember, I'm a firm believer of the mystery and magic feeling of a when a band first walks out on stage. We also loved going on after Naked Gypsy because we didn't think they were any good.

The crowd also knew what time slot we had. So, as soon as Naked Gypsy finished their set, the audience started to come alive. I can still feel the energy that was in the air that night. L'amour was as crowded as when I saw Paul Stanley play there. The crowd began to chant, "Playground! Playground!" More than 2/3 of the audience was there to see us. Finally, the DJ introduced us: "And here they are...PLAYGROUND!" The place went berserk.

When I got up on the drum riser and took the throne, where so many amazing famous drummers had played before me, a now very familiar sensation came over me.

I became calm. My breathing slowed, and I could suddenly hear my heart beat like a giant bass drum.

The crowd fell silent and everything began to slow down. I was experiencing another "Frozen Moment." This was a very pivotal moment in my music career and my mind and body stopped my

PLAYGROUND at L'amour in Brooklyn. Easily in my top five favorite shows of all time!

surroundings so I could enjoy it for a brief moment in time. I looked out over the sea of people in the audience, filled with my family and friends, and smiled like I had never smiled before. After a long deep breath, I was back in real time.

The crowd was the loudest I'd ever heard. We pounded into our opening song "Could've Been You" and followed it with the upbeat, poppy "Get Your Hands Away From My Girl." We had our tight 30-minute set list down to a science for this show. The high energy "Silver Lining" was next and the crowd loved it.

Then we did something no other band did that night: we slowed the set down with the amazing ballad, "Some Things Never Change." This did not calm the crowd down at all. They loved this song and they loved us. Their energy never wavered.

After the ballad, Tommy yelled, "We got one more for ya!" We blasted into our closing song, "I Don't Care" and the crowd got even crazier. Once finished, Tommy yelled, "Thank you! Good night!" I know it's cliché to say, but it felt like the crowd was going to blow the roof off of L'amour when we finished. We were later told that we had brought in the most people for any unsigned band in the history of L'amour.

The DJ couldn't believe it either. He yelled over the microphone, "Let's hear it for Playground!... Wow, that good, huh? A thousand dollars to them!" Then he paused, realizing that the battle wasn't over and he couldn't declare us winners just yet. He covered his mistake by saying, "That's the thousand-dollar question." We walked off knowing we had won. Nobody could top what we just did. This was one of the best feelings I've ever had. Knowing how much hard work we put into this show and then seeing it all pay off and hearing that amazing reaction by the crowd was pure ecstasy. There was only one thing to do while we waited: go to the bar and celebrate while the last few band performed. After that, they would officially announce Playground as the winners.

While we were celebrating at the side bar in L'amour, everyone was coming over to congratulate us. People couldn't believe that the DJ actually already announced Playground, mistakenly, as the winners. The next few bands were both just average. The final band, Mr. Strange, had a really good bass player that was kind of showing off a lot. They had no songs and the crowd was completely dead ever since we finished our set.

Once the final band finished, the DJ came on the microphone and said, "Okay, everyone. The judges are backstage tallying their votes. We will announce the winner shortly." The crowd once again began to chant, "PLAYGROUND! PLAYGROUND!" Moments later, he came back out onto the stage to officially announce the winner. He began by saying, "First, we want to think all the bands that participated. We have an unbelievable crowd here tonight and you should all be proud!" I was thinking to myself, "Yeah, we are proud. The crowd is all ours!"

He continued: "This was a tough decision, but we have a winner." The crowd began chanting again, "PLAYGROUND! PLAYGROUND!" Still, he continued, "The winner of the L'amour's Scud Battle of the Bands is …Mr. Strange!"

Our mouths hung open in shock. I actually thought they were about to say, "Just kidding. Playground!" I waited and waited, but the joke kept going. We couldn't believe it. The crowd went ballistic, booing and throwing things at the DJ and the stage. I saw Tommy storm off, mad beyond belief. I was still in shock. This was just unbelievable. We had just pulled off the greatest show we could ever put on, at the greatest rock club ever, and it didn't matter. We lost.

We were devastated. The man on the stage said on the mic, "If someone from Playground could come backstage, we want to talk with them for a moment."

"Wait, what was this all about?" I thought. We quickly assigned Brendan to go backstage to see what was happening. After about 15 minutes, Brendan came back out to fill us in on what they said. He said the promoter explained that L'amour was closing soon, but they were opening up a new club called The Cabaret. They wanted us to play on their opening night because we did such a good job tonight.

We later learned that Mr. Strange paid more money to be part of the battle, basically buying their win. But, the promoter knew that they could make money off of us because of our crowd. In hindsight, I wish we would have said, "Sure, we will play your club, if you declare us as the winners. Otherwise, forget it!" Once again, a lesson learned. It all came down to money not necessarily talent or hard work.

Soon after, Tommy came back from the bathroom with his hand all bloody. Apparently, he was so angry over our loss that he punched the bathroom wall. Needless to say, the promoter offering us a show at the new club didn't make us feel any better.

To show what we thought of the judges' decision, we decided to get up on stage, pull our pants down, and moon the promoter and the other bands as if to say, "F**ck you for screwing us over." Our fans loved this gesture and began cheering. Looking back, I always wondered if Playground had won that L'amour battle of the bands how different things could have been. I know it was only a $1,000 prize, but it was more about us putting our hearts and souls into something and coming up empty all because the promoter took a bribe. This was a big lesson learned. It wasn't always about how hard a person worked or how good a musician was. It was knowing the ins and outs and schmoozing and networking with the right people that really gets a person where he wanted to go. Don't get me wrong, I'm still super proud of what we accomplished that night and I do believe putting my heart and soul into something is a good thing. I just don't think it's the only thing. That Playground show at L'amour is still one of my top 5 all-time favorite shows I have ever played.

CHAPTER 14
NO MORE BROOKLYN.
NO MORE PLAYGROUND

Playground outside of L'amour after our big loss.

During this time, my music career was really starting to blossom. But something happened at home that once again took me away from my dream. My father had failed to pay any rent at the new house we had moved to. After getting thrown out of our old home, he promised that he would take care of the rent in the new house. Even though my mother was always struggling to find a job and make ends meet, she never asked my father for any child support. All she said was, "Please do not let these kids go through the horrible ordeal of losing another home." Unfortunately, that's exactly what was about to happen.

Our landlord would come banging on our door screaming for his money and there was nothing we could do about it. My brother and I weren't old enough to support the family and my deadbeat father was, once again, making his kids lose their home. Finally, after a few months of us not answering to the landlord, he also got a Marshall to come and serve us with eviction papers, complete with a specific date for us to leave. This time that date was only a few days after being served. We were about to have nowhere to live.

My grandmother, who had been living with us since my grandfather had died, still had her small apartment in the West Village of Manhattan, and we were going to be forced to move there. It was me, my brother, my mom, my grandmother, my giant 170-pound dog, Yukon, and our crazy cat, Tabby — all moving into a tiny apartment. We couldn't even bring our belongings. There wasn't enough space in my grandmother's apartment. We would have to put everything we owned into a storage unit.

On the day I had to leave my home, for the second time, I flat out refused. I had enough. I couldn't imagine leaving Brooklyn, all of my friends, and my band mates to go to live in a small apartment in Manhattan and having to put all of my belongings in storage. I locked myself in my room and wouldn't come out. I'm not exactly sure what I was thinking, but I just couldn't face getting thrown out of my home again. I couldn't believe my father was letting this happen to his kids again! He wasn't even there to help us on the day we were forced to get out.

I found out years later that on the day his kids were getting thrown out of their second home, my father was getting remarried, and he never even told us. I never had any use for my father, but this was when our relationship officially ended.

My mom called Tommy From Playground to come and talk with me. I was so embarrassed that this was happening that I didn't want to face my friends. Tommy really came through for me that day. He came and talked to me and told me not to worry, and that everything was going to be okay. The thing I remember most was he said, "We are going to be rich rock stars soon and we'll buy all of our moms' homes!" That cheered me up a little, at least enough to face what I had to go through. I'll never forget what Tommy did for me that day. Thank you, my friend.

My new home on Carmine Street. Greenwhich Village NYC.

After finally talking me into packing, I told my mom there were a few things that I would absolutely not let go to storage, mainly my drums and my comic book collection. My brother and I had been collecting comics since we were little, and the books were starting to be worth a good amount of money at his point. I always thought to myself, "Someday, I'll either give them to my kids or they will be worth enough to maybe buy a house for them." My mom agreed we would make room for the comics at my grandmother's apartment. Brendan, the Playground guitarist, agreed to take my drums to his house so we could begin rehearsing in his basement. Those were my two most prized possessions, my comics and my drums.

Now that they were safe, I was willing to send the rest of my belongings to storage. The thought was that we would pay for the storage facility for a few months until we could find a new place to live. So, on the morning of May 5, 1991, I was officially evicted from my second home.

After a few months of living in my grandmother's apartment, I began to realize that this was permanent. How could we ever get another house? We had no money. My mom couldn't even afford to pay for the storage facility anymore. So, once again, she groveled to my father and asked for help. Mind you, my mom could have taken my father to court many times for child support and she never did. To this day, I still have no idea why.

I wasn't speaking with my father at all at this time. He promised my mother that he would pay for the storage facility until we could figure something out. A few months later, I made some room in the apartment and I wanted to get a few things out of storage. I had a huge collection of wrestling magazines that I wanted to get, along with all of my action figures.

I had taken a few old Star Wars figures to my grandmother's apartment because they didn't take up much room, but the bulk of my collection was still in storage. I had no idea where the storage facility that was holding of our stuff even was.

One morning, I decided to call and arrange a time for me to go pick up a few things. I spoke to a woman who asked for the invoice number that was on my paperwork. My mom had given me the inventory list and I read the invoice number to the woman. I could hear her typing on the other end of the phone call. She said, "Sir, there's seems to be a problem with this account." I nervously asked, "What's the problem?" She explained, "This account was over 6 months delinquent and the items went up for auction."

If you've ever seen the TV show *Storage Wars*, you'll know exactly what that means. Basically, if and when a storage unit isn't paid for, the storage facility has the right to auction off all of the items in the unit. It turned out that once again my shitty father failed us. I found out he never made even one payment. We'd lost everything we'd ever owned!

As bad as it was when we lost our first home, this was even worse. That day I vowed I would do everything I could to get my mom a house. I also vowed that I would never be anything like my father. If and when I ever had children, I would be the exact opposite of him.

During these horrible months, Playground went on, business as usual. Right after L'amour, we played the grand opening of their new club, The Caberet. It was another spectacular crowd and a huge success. After that, we even finally went on to play in Manhattan at the clubs Bond St. and Beowulf.

We decided to rent an old school bus and turn it into the "Playground party bus" for these shows. For a flat fee of $15, a person was able to drink all the beer he or she wanted and also get a ticket to enter the club. It was not only a great way to get people into the city to pack these clubs, but it was a terrific way to make money. We were cutting out the slimy promoters and selling tickets ourselves.

The night of the Beowulf show is where I can pinpoint the first crack in the Playgrround armor. We had added a new song to our set list toward the end of all of our performances. It was a cover of Billy Joel's "Sometimes a Fantasy." When we started playing this song on the night of Beowulf, our fans began to get a little reckless. They were having so much fun, and probably were pretty drunk from the Playground party bus, that they began moshing, Brooklyn style. All that meant was they began to go nuts, pushing people, standing on tables, and eventually breaking a few beer bottles.

After our performance, we were informed by the club owner that our crowd had caused a lot of damage and they wanted us to pay for it. We absolutely refused and, as a result, we were banned from ever playing Beowulf again.

For some reason, this struck Tommy and me as funny and as weirdly great. We loved the idea of being banned from a club. It seemed like something that might happen to Van Halen or Motley Crue back in the early 80's. Brendan did not share our enthusiasm. He was pissed and called a band meeting the next night before rehearsal.

Brendan started off the meeting by basically blaming Tommy and me for not controlling our friends, which led to us being banned. We couldn't help but laugh. Tommy said angrily, "And who the hell did you bring to the show? Nobody, that's who! Without my and Joey's friends, we wouldn't even have a god damn show!" He was absolutely right.

Brendan shouted back something about being unprofessional and how bad it looked that we got banned from Beowulf. I immediately disagreed, countering with, "I think it's great! We could use it in our promotion! 'Come see Playground before they get banned from everywhere!'" I was half joking but also quite serious.

This made Brendan even more livid. He then said we were going to stop playing the new Billy Joel song because it got the crowd too crazy. I laughed out loud and replied, "Too crazy? Crazy is what we want our crowd to be, you idiot. What do we want, for them to just stand there and politely golf clap after each song? It's a rock concert. They should do whatever the hell they want!" Tommy then chimed in and said, "You know what, fuck it! You want to castrate our crowd, fine! We won't play Billy Joel any more. Watch what happens!"

Later that week, Brendan took it upon himself to send out a new "Letters of the Sandbox" to explain to the fans that we can't have what happened at Beowulf happen again. Needless to say, this completely backfired.

The next show was at a new club, Christopher's, right in the heart of our old neighborhood on 34th Street and Quentin Road. This should have been our biggest, most rowdy crowd to date. Instead, while we played, the crowd wouldn't even approach the stage. They stayed back near the bar and wouldn't come close. At this time, no one else in the band knew that Brendan had sent the newsletter lecturing our fans. We found out after we got off stage.

Tommy asked a few people why they didn't come up and have fun and that's when they showed him the letter from Brendan. We were fuming! Things were never really the same after that, not only inside the band, but also with our fan base. Playground was known from the beginning as putting on the best parties. Nothing had been more fun than going to a Playground show. Tommy and I told all of our friends that we had nothing to do with that ridiculous letter, but it still kind of sucked the life and joy out of our shows.

A few shows later, DeVito got drunk after our performance and mouthed off to a bouncer and got thrown out of the club. This caused a fight between us and him. Shortly after, we asked DeVito to leave the band. The house was starting to crumble.

In retrospect, this was a mistake. This wasn't a reason to throw DeVito out of the band. I think we were all frustrated with everything and DeVito was a scape goat. Maybe we thought that by getting someone new in the band, we could save it by changing the energy.

Boy, were we wrong. Our new bass player, Tommy Carter, worked at Rockaway Studios and was always a fan of the band.

Tommy Carter was a great player, but I never got along with him personally. There was just something about him that rubbed me the wrong way.

About this time, Steve was dating a girl named Cathy. Tommy said he had kissed Cathy before Steve had begun dating her. This little passing comment turned out to be the final nail in Playground's coffin.

Steve confronted his girlfriend and she denied ever kissing Tommy. Steve then had a huge blowout with Tommy, calling him a liar and a troublemaker. Still to this day, I have no idea if Tommy ever kissed Steve's girlfriend or not, but why would Steve even care? Tommy said it was before Steve began dating her.

I know what you're thinking: another Yoko Ono breaking up a band. You're right! Now that Steve and Tommy's relationship was all but over, the end of Playground was in sight.

Tommy Carter, Me, Tommy Snyder, Steve Kerasotis, and Brendan Murphy.

Our next and final show would be at the newly reopened L'amour. After the show, Steve informed us that he would be leaving the band. He never actually said that he didn't want to work with Tommy, he just said, "My heart isn't in it anymore." It was very fitting that our final show was at L'amour. I can still trace back that big disappointment at the first L'amour battle of the bands as our pinnacle of success. It slowly snowballed downhill after.

Playground was no more...

CHAPTER 15

"IT'S NOT HOW HARD YOU GET HIT. IT'S ABOUT HOW HARD YOU CAN GET HIT AND KEEP MOVING FORWARD." – ROCKY BALBOA

NIKO ANDUCICH
(7 1 8) 4 5 4 - 8 2 8 1
IMN Management

EXPOSED

1992 was starting out awful. I had lost my home, lost all of my possessions, and now I had lost my band. It would have been very easy to give up and just feel sorry for myself, but that wasn't in my nature. The harder things got, the more I knew what I had to do. I wasn't sad, I was angry! I was angry that my father lost another home for us, I was angry that I lost everything I had ever owned, and now I was angry that the guys in my band had let me down. I couldn't understand it. How could they let a stupid thing like a girl get between their dreams?

This was when I realized that everyone did not have the drive, passion, and determination that I had. I feel that, in a way, every other member of Playground basically gave up on their dreams that day. I think it was easier for them to say to themselves, "Playground would have been huge if we just stayed together." Maybe they were afraid of failing after Playground, maybe they just didn't want to play music anymore, maybe this really wasn't their dream. And if it wasn't their dream anymore, I totally respect that. I just knew that I had to get right back up, dust myself off, and start all over again. And that's just what I did.

A few days after Playground ended, I started answering ads again in all of the local music papers. I answered two ads that looked promising. The first one read, "Commercial hard rock band with full length cd and management looking for drummer." This was extremely exciting! CD's were still very new at this time, and for someone to have a full-length CD meant they were pretty big. Plus, the ad said they had management. Of course, this could mean anything, but back then these were some key words you'd look for when trying find a new band and weed out the crappy local bands. I left a message for the contact number. His name was Scott Rage.

The second ad I answered was for a band out in Wayne, New Jersey, called Sinister Charm. We spoke briefly and immediately set up an audition. I had to take a New Jersey transit bus to go meet them at their studio in Wayne.

Once again, innocence is amazing. I was about to take two buses and a train all the way to New Jersey to meet with a band that I had never even heard a song from yet. I was willing to do anything to find a new band and nothing was going to stop me from making my dreams come true. I never even gave a second thought to going all the way there to meet people. Once I arrived, I met with singer Tony Martino and guitarist Scott DelFino. Two Italians! I liked that already.

Sinister Charm was rehearsing in a giant old warehouse. It was actually a really cool set up. They had a cheap set of drums already set up for me to audition on. They didn't have a demo or anything, but they began showing me some of their original material and I absolutely fell in love with the songs. One song in particular I thought could be a huge hit. It was called "I think I love you." We instantly took to each other. Before you knew it, they were not only asking me to join the band, but they wanted me to stay over for the night to hang out and write some more music. I accepted. Just like that, I had found my new band.

Sinister Charm
Tony Martino - Vocals
Scott DelFino - Guitar
Joey Cassata – Drums
Bass - John ?

Sinister Charm Photo Shoot

After a long rehearsal of catching me up on all of their original material, we went back to Tony's house. That is when I really knew I made the right move in joining this band. Tony and Scott began playing me all of the acoustic and piano songs they had written. They were incredible! This was a time when the "Power Ballad" was huge. I thought that everyone of their songs could have been a huge hit on MTV.

I arrived back home and told my mom that I think I found my new band. I played her a tape of the rehearsal and she loved it. She was so happy for me and always gave me her 100 percent support. She then said, "Oh, I forgot to tell you. You have a message on the answering machine about an ad you answered."

It was Scott Rage calling me back from the ad I answered a few days prior. Even though I was happy with Sinister Charm, I wasn't going to let another opportunity slip by. I called Scott back and we talked for about 30 minutes. He was friendly, yet very business-like, which I liked. I needed to be involved with people that had the same drive and passion as I did. Scott told me that they would mail me a CD and press kit of their band Exposed so I could learn the songs for an audition the following week.

In the meantime, I had set up moving my drums that were still in Brendan's basement to Sinister Charm's warehouse. The most difficult and worst part about living in Manhattan was being away from my drums. Up until I moved, I had played my drums every single day from the time I was 13 to age 17. How was I going to learn a full CD of material without having my drums to practice on? I quickly remembered my old trick from before I was able to buy my Tampa drum set. Air drumming with my sticks was actually an amazing way to practice songs. It worked on muscle memory and helped with stick control.

I received the Exposed CD a few days later and was extremely impressed. The quality of the packaging was amazing. The artwork and the band photos looked perfect. The production sound was better than 90 percent of the CD's I owned at the time. And, most importantly for me, the drum sound was exactly the sound I wanted back then.

This was obviously a very professional band with great management and money behind them. The one drawback was that the songs were definitely not as catchy as the Sinister Charm songs. Either way, I had to at least audition for this amazing band to see what would happen. I could always make a decision about Sinister Charm after.

The Exposed songs were pretty challenging to learn, and the drum parts were very intricate. I would learn them as best as I could by air drumming and memorizing, but I knew I needed to play them at least once before I went to the audition. I rented a small studio in Manhattan for two hours to practice, and luckily the air drumming had paid off. I seamlessly played the songs on the drum kit with only a few minor hiccups that I quickly corrected.

The audition was held at the Exposed studio in the Queens "Music Building." I had never been there before, but over the years I had heard about many big bands that had rehearsed in that building. I would later learn that Exposed's room was Metallica's old room when they rehearsed in the same space. Anthrax also rehearsed right next door! When I arrived, it was not what I was expecting. It was a very run-down old building with a weird smell.

I went to the top floor and knocked on a big black door with an Exposed sticker on it. The guitarist Scott Rage greeted me, he then introduced me to the other members: singer Johnny Blade and bassist Martin Pelosi. Also in attendance was their manager Niko Anducich.

After exchanging a few pleasantries, I climbed up onto the massive drum riser that was set up in their rehearsal room. It still had their old drummer's kit set up. We plowed through the first three songs from their CD: "Rolling Thunder," "Getting Higher," and "The Countdown to Midnight." Not to toot my own horn, but we sounded incredible together! This was easily the most talented and seasoned group of players I'd played with to date.

Scott was an amazing Yngwie Malmsteen type virtuoso guitar player, but still could play that Ace Frehley sloppy blues style when needed. Marty was an excellent bass player with a lot of feel and groove. He could also complement some of Scott's technical runs in a similar way that the band Mr. Big was doing at the time with bassist Billy Sheehan and guitarist Paul Gilbert. Johnny Blade was a high powered, high range type vocalist with a sound that was popular at the time. He immediately reminded me of Geoff Tate from Queensrych. They were exactly what I was looking for!

After we jammed, I could tell that they were happy with the way I played, and they asked me if I sang at all. Up until this point, I had never sung back-up or lead, but I loved singing along to all of my favorite songs at home. John gave me a few lines to sing and try a harmony on and I did pretty well.

Next, we chatted for a bit so they could get to know me. When I told them I was 18 years old, they couldn't believe it because I still looked much older than I really was. They then told me that they were all 28 years old. Now, I was the one that couldn't believe it. I could tell they were older than I was, but I never thought by 10 years! If they were okay with me being ten years younger, then I was okay with them being ten years older. They thanked me for coming down and said they would be in touch. When I walked out of their rehearsal room, 5 other drummers were waiting to go in. It turns out they auditioned over 30 guys.

I left there thinking it was a long shot at best. I'd enjoyed playing with them, but I didn't get my hopes up. Besides, I was actually very excited about my new band, Sinister Charm.

I just recently brought my drums to their studio out in New Jersey and the original songs they had were way better than what was on the Exposed CD. Still, Exposed was just much further along in their career.

I would have to wait to see if they even got back to me before I gave it any more thought.

Another week went by and I still hadn't heard anything from Exposed. I assumed I didn't get the gig and was totally okay with it because Sinister Charm was really starting to heat up. Like I said, Sinister Charm were writing one hit song after another. If we could get a really great quality demo together, it would blow away what Exposed was doing.

It was now approaching summer of 1992. I wasn't going to graduate from my music high school with everyone else because I had started a year late. It was going to take me at least until January of the following year to graduate, which didn't really matter to me. I didn't have any close friends at the school with whom I wanted to graduate anyway. It just sucked that I had to go for another half a year. I wanted to be done with school in the worst way.

One day, after returning from school, I had a message on my answering machine from Scott Rage. He said to call him as soon as I could. I was actually a little hesitant to call him back. What did he want? I was very happy with the way Sinister Charm was progressing, and I wasn't sure what I would do if Exposed offered me the gig. Yes, Exposed was better right now, but I thought Sinister Charm had more potential.

I called him anyway to see what he wanted. Scott picked up and said, "Hey, Dude." (He called everyone dude.) "Sorry it took so long to get back to you. We auditioned a lot of guys but feel like you are the best fit. We would love you to come down to the studio this weekend to jam again and talk over details." I said, "Sure, I'll be there. Thanks!" then hung up the phone.

I now had a big decision to make. Do I join the already established band, Exposed, with a manager and a CD? Or do I take a chance on a relatively new project, Sinister Charm, which had the potential to be something special? After a few hours of thinking long and hard, I made the decision to stay with Sinister Charm because the songs were so special. I had rehearsal with them that night and I would call to let Scott know the next morning.

As fate would have it, when I arrived at Sinister Charm rehearsal that night, our guitarist Scott Delfino wasn't there. Tony informed me that Scott had just quit the band. I couldn't believe it! Things had been going so great. I asked, "What the hell happened?" Tony responded that they had gotten into a bad argument over something stupid. He said, "I honestly don't know. Call and ask him." That's exact what I did as soon as I got home.

Scott went on to explain to me that Tony was some kind of pathological liar and he couldn't be trusted. I didn't understand what he was talking about and asked for more details. "Tony told me that he was in a car accident a year ago and that was why he wore hair extensions." First of all, I didn't even know Tony wore hair extensions, nor did I care. Scott continued and said, "The story was a complete lie. He just couldn't grow his hair long so he wore hair extensions. Can you believe it, Joey?"

I said, "Hold on a second. Are you telling me that this great band is breaking up because you found out your singer and writing partner lied about why he wears hair extensions?" Scott confirmed, "I can't play in a band with a guy that lies like that." I hung up the phone and was in

absolute shock. It was like dealing with mental patients. I could see why so many bands break up: it was because they are all nuts. These two morons were going to throw away an amazing band because of hair extensions! This was even more ridiculous and petty than why Playground broke up. At least it made my next decision very easy. I went down a few days later, sometime in the late summer or early fall of 1992, to meet with the guys from Exposed, where they officially offered for me to become a member. I gladly accepted.

Once I joined Exposed, I knew I had reached the next level in my music career. Not only were they all incredible players, but they were much more professional and business oriented. The first thing they had me do was sign a management contract with their manager, Niko. Niko was a sweetheart and had been around the music industry for a very long time. He always credited himself with discovering the multi-platinum rock group The Scorpions. Me, still being only 18 years old, had no idea what I was signing but gladly signed anyway.

I quickly learned that Exposed was about one thing and one thing only: getting a record deal! They knew that's all that really mattered. Yes, playing live shows was important to make a band tight, but that's not what got you to where you needed to be anymore. It wasn't 1982 when it was possible to build a following, have the record companies hear about the buzz, then send someone from their A&R department to come and look at you. It was almost 1993 and the club scene was dead. The only way record labels could hear about your band was to submit a demo or album to the labels.

Niko had a few big connections at Atlantic Records. One was with co-founder Ahmet Ertegun, and that had something to do with their shared Turkish heritage. Ertegun has been described as one of the most significant figures in the modern recording industry, and even though at this time Ertegun wasn't really personally signing bands, Niko knew that Ertegun would pass along any recordings that Niko submitted to the head of his A&R department, Jason Flom. Flom was already credited with signing rock acts such as Twisted Sister, Saigon Kick, Skid Row and White Lion. Flom was a major player in the music industry at this point and was always looking for "The Next Big Thing." We knew Exposed could be just that!

In the exact opposite way of thinking than my previous bands, Exposed immediately wanted to record a brand new, full-length album so they could get it in the hands of Flom at Atlantic records. The guys in Exposed were always so professional about everything. They even insisted that everyone in the band have top of the line gear to play on. It was all part of the mystique that they wanted to project. In their minds, if they had the biggest and best of everything, then the perception would be that Exposed must be a huge band. "Look at all of their amazing gear. Look at their amazing rehearsal studio. Look at their amazing sounding, full-length CD." I totally agreed with this philosophy. Perception is absolutely reality!

Because of this way of thinking, they asked me to upgrade my drum set. Even though I had just recently bought a new Gibraltar rack system, I agreed it was time for an upgrade. After all, I was still using my bass drum from my old Shock set that I got when I was 9 years old. There was just one big problem: being in this new, amazingly professional band was getting very expensive!

It was now April of 1993 and I had just recently graduated from my music high school. There was no ceremony or anything. Because I graduated mid-year with just a few other students, I was basically handed a piece of paper and sent on my way. Music school was never what I'd hoped it would be. It was just another school trying to tell me what to learn and how to learn it, and I was glad to be finished. I thought briefly about going to college, but I decided, at the very least, I wanted to wait until September so I could take some time off to focus more on Exposed. Hopefully, we would be huge rock stars by then and I wouldn't have to go to college.

Like I mentioned, being in Exposed was getting expensive. Even though we had a manager, he didn't pay for anything. He had one responsibility: to get us a record deal! Band members were responsible for paying for studio rent and recording the new CD, and now the band wanted me to buy a new drum set. I knew I had to find a job immediately.

For years, my brother had been working in a hospital located in the West Village of Manhattan. One of our relatives worked there and had originally gotten Danny the job. Because he was now a valued employee, he made a recommendation for me to get a part-time position in the same department. Shortly after the recommendation, I got the job.

My hours were 3:45pm to 8pm, which was absolutely perfect. I got out at 8pm and went straight to Exposed rehearsal every night. I would now have enough money to support all the things I needed to do with my new band. After I got my job, I quickly signed up for a brand-new credit card, my very first, and went with Exposed guitarist, Scott Rage, to Sam Ash Music to buy my new drum set. Scott told me that he had a "hook up" at Sam Ash and that he could get me a good deal on a new drum set. I didn't know exactly what he meant by a "hook up," but if it meant me getting a good deal on the new set, I was in.

After doing some research, I picked out the drum kit that I wanted. I decided that I wanted to stick with Tama because that's what I had been playing for the last 5 years. I had always wanted to buy a Ludwig kit because my hero Eric Carr was playing them, but they were very expensive at the time and also not as popular in the rock world anymore. Most stores like Sam Ash didn't even have them on display, so I wouldn't know how to get a set of Ludwig's even if I wanted. I also decided on

Tama because I really loved the sound of Queensrych drummer, Scott Rockenfield's drums on their newest album, *Empire*.

I found out Rockenfield was using Tama's new flagship set, The Artstar 2, and that's what I wanted! When Scott and I arrived at Sam Ash, we were quickly greeted by Scott's friend Marco Soccoli, who was the head of the drum department. I told him what I was looking for and he replied, "I have a set of Artstars in stock!" He pulled out a blue, almost purple, floor tom for me to see and I immediately fell in love with it. The color, officially "Jewel Blue," was gorgeous. He then grabbed the Tama catalog for me to pick out sizes and configure my set up. Because of the research I had done, I knew exactly what set up I wanted — the same exact thing that Rockenfield was using in the new Queensrych video "Silent Lucidity." Marco knew right away what I was configuring.

This was so freaking exciting to me! Even to this day, getting a new drum set is always such an adrenaline rush. After picking out the sizes, Marco asked me what I wanted to do about hardware, which I hadn't even really thought about. I told him that I just bought a new Gibraltar rack about a year ago and I would probably just use that. He said, "No way! I think I got just the thing."

He went into the back room and came out with two six-foot poles. I had no idea what they were for, but I was excited. He began explaining that with these poles, a drummer could build a full cage around the set. He said, "It will look sick! Kind of a cross between Scott Rockenfeld and Blas Elias from Slaughter." I couldn't picture exactly what he was talking about, but I knew what those other drummers' kits looked like and if I could have that, then I was on board. The only problem was that I had a feeling this was way too expensive. I had a $5,000 limit on my new credit card and that's all I could spend. The drums alone were going to be about $4,800. This spectacular cage Marco was constructing in his mind was probably another $2,500, plus I needed a few new cymbals. I explained to Marco my dilemma and he told me to pick out the cymbals I wanted and we would figure something out.

I picked out a brand-new set of Zildjian customs Z's that totaled about $1,300. So, the cymbals in combination with the drums, and the new gigantic rack, meant that I was looking at close to $10,000. I wanted to get a new kit and have top of the line gear like the rest of the guys in Exposed, but $10,000 was nuts. There was no way I could afford it.

Marco did some calculations and told me that he could get me all the drums and cymbals for the $5,000 credit that I had. I was super happy and that was an amazing deal, but without the cage I couldn't set anything up. I said, "Great, but there's no way I am going to be able to afford the cage too." He said, "Joey, Paisan, don't worry about it. I'm going to throw the whole cage in on the arm." The term "on the arm" was an Italian way of saying for "for free."

What!!?? I couldn't believe it. I guess Scott really did have a "hook up." Marco and I got back in touch years later and he would become my artist rep at Vic Firth Sticks and then later at Evans Drumheads. He was the one originally responsible for giving me my very first full endorsement. Paisans for life!

I placed the order for the drums and we left that day with the full cage and cymbals. I still thought it was too good to be true. I just paid $5,000 for $10,000 worth of gear. It wasn't until my drums arrived a few weeks later that I fully believed it. Scott came with me to pick them up and we went straight to the Exposed rehearsal room to set up my massive new set.

My new Tama Artstars were incredible. I felt like I was piloting a massive spacecraft when I sat inside the 6-foot high cage. It was my dream set. Even though it wasn't anything like the drum set that I saw Peter Criss play at Madison Square Garden when I was 5 years old, when

My brand new set of Tama's with full cage! 1993

I sat behind this new set up, I remember feeling the same way I felt that fateful night at MSG when I first saw Peter's drums rise up to the ceiling.

My dreams were slowly becoming a reality. Exposed played a few shows while getting ready to record our new full-length album. I found out quickly that, although my new cage drum set was amazing, it was not very practical when transporting to gigs. One of the first shows I played with Exposed was in New York City at a place called Acme Underground. It was in the basement of a building on Bleeker Street, and when I tried to set up the cage on the drum platform, there wasn't enough height to accommodate the 6-foot poles. This was back when I still thought I needed a giant drum set to perform, and it related to the Exposed mentality of having all the best gear and showing the audience that we were "big time." My drum set turned out to look ridiculous in most of the places we were playing. Basically, no place in Manhattan could accommodate such a giant kit. I quickly reverted to a scaled down version when we played Manhattan.

Around March of 1994, we began tracking the new 10-song Exposed album. Tracking took place at Purple Light Studios on Fourth Avenue in Brooklyn. This was, of course, long before computers and Pro Tools recording software. We recorded on 2-inch tape on a 24-track board. This was to be my first real session in a big recording studio. I had done stuff with Playground and in school, but I'd never attempted to record a full-length album. Knowing that this was going to be the same process that all of my heroes went through to record their albums meant I was excited and ready for the challenge.

All of my drum tracking went smoothly. Scott's guitar work on the album was fantastic, but he overlaid so many different guitar tracks that the overall mix of the drums suffered. After several weeks of tracking, mixing, and mastering, the new Exposed album was completed. Now, our manager Niko had to do his thing: get us a record deal!

Even though the recording was a little muddy and not up to par with the first Exposed CD, I thought the songs were better on this new one, especially the acoustic guitar- driven song "Next Stop." I thought this could absolutely be a hit. We were positive Niko was going to be able to land us a record deal with this new album. We scheduled a "Record release/listening party" and invited many industry big wigs. Niko even arranged for a Limo to drive us to and from the party.

On the night of our release party, we really felt like rock stars- or at least what I thought it would feel like to be a rock star back when I was 20. We figured after that party it was only a matter of time before record labels were fighting over us, but we waited and waited and never heard from any of them. We knew, though, that Niko saved his big guns for last. He called his friend Ahmet Ertegun to set up a meeting with the head of A & R at Atlantic Records, Jason Flom.

I remember the day of Niko's meeting like it was yesterday. This was, after all, the meeting I'd been waiting for all my life. My dreams and aspirations were all in the hands of Jason Flom. He had the power to make them all come true. If he liked the band, we were set. We would have a record deal and be on tour with other bands from Atlantic by the end of the year.

I remember being in work at the hospital and not being able to concentrate on anything. If Jason liked it, I would be quitting the next day! I'm not the type that gets nervous, but when something is out of my control, then I get nervous, and this meeting was totally out of my control! Scott and I were on the phone about twenty times that day. I would call him from a pay phone every 30 minutes to ask if he'd heard from Niko.

Later that night, Scott called and said he'd finally heard from Niko. Niko said the meetings went great. Flom listened to a few songs in the office and seemed really into it. He said that he would get back to Niko in a few days. I frantically responded, "A few days?" How the hell could I make it a few days when just waiting these few hours seemed like an eternity? But wait was what I had to do.

The next few days were pure agony, but at the same time I was getting uncontrollably excited. The thought of the head of Atlantic Records sitting and listening to our new album was incredible. I would day dream all day about hearing those songs on the radio. I just knew that Flom was going to like it and I knew he was going to sign us. A few days later, Niko called a meeting at our studio. I thought, "Surely, this is to tell us the good news."

Once I arrived at the studio and saw Niko's face, I knew the news wasn't what I'd hoped. Niko went on to explain that Flom loved the album and the band, but he felt that we sounded a bit too "dated." Unfortunately, this was a term I would hear a lot over the next few years. Exposed's sound was still what we considered to be commercial hard rock. Some people today would consider us a "hair band," but one of the more muso type bands like Queensrych, not a bubble gum band like Poison. Flom explained to Niko that the music scene was beginning to change and bands like Nirvana, Pearl Jam, and Alice in Chains were beginning to dominate the scene. Nobody wanted to hear operatic type voices anymore, which is exactly what our singer John had.

Everyone wanted to sign grunge bands, which were the exact opposite of what we were and the opposite of what I liked. Grunge was dark, depressing music. I liked happy, feel good music with a positive message.

We were crushed by the devastating news. It was the worst thing we could possibly hear. Not only did he not want to sign us, but he basically told us that our whole genre of music was dead. After this horrible news, I decided that I would try my hand at college. I had no intention of giving up on my music, and I think the main reason I went to college was for my mom.

Even though she was always the most supportive person of my music career, I thought it was time that I did something that would make her proud. I didn't want to go to a music college because my high school burnt me out on that. So, I decided I would go where my brother went. Of course, it hadn't worked too well for me when I attempted to follow in Danny's footsteps back in high school, so I'm not sure why I thought it would be different going to college.

Once I started college, my schedule was absolutely insane. I would leave my apartment in Manhattan at 7:15am to get to my first class at 8:30. I would be in class until 1:30pm then go straight to my job at the hospital. Once my shift there ended at 7:15, I took a train directly to Queens to rehearse with Exposed until around 1am. This was my schedule at least 4 days a week, and needless to say, after one semester of this brutal schedule, something had to change.

I weighed all of my options and came to a pretty easy decision. Obviously, there was no way I was giving up on my music and I knew I needed money to live on so I couldn't give up my job. The only logical thing to quit was school.

Ever since those early days with that devil Sr. Marie, school just wasn't for me. I was just always someone that loved to figure out a better way to do things. And nine times out of ten, I could! I was also someone that didn't like to be told what to do, and that's really all school ever was to me — someone telling me what to do, how to do it. At a very young age, I felt like that controlled way of thinking was actually stifling someone's potential to grow as an individual. I don't want someone to tell me how I should think. Right or wrong, I want to think for myself.

Don't get me wrong, I believe school is one of the most important things for a young mind to grow. Socially it is essential. It also teaches you to function in a controlled atmosphere and shows you the rights and wrongs of interacting in that enviorment. There was just something about my particular teachers that made me rebel a little.

About this time, my grandmother grew very ill and passed away. She had been sick for as long as I could remember. When I was just a baby, she had a massive heart attack and was never completely healthy again. For years, my family and I were in and out of the hospital with her. Once my grandmother passed, my mother was never the same. I always felt a little piece of my mom died the day my grandmother passed away.

My brother had a new girlfriend, Liz, that he moved in with shortly after my grandmother's passing and I had my music that kept me extremely busy. With all of our struggles as a family, my mom at least always had my grandmother to lean on and talk to. Now that she was gone, I think my mom felt very lonely.

Over the next few years, Exposed recorded a few more times and gigged periodically. When Flom told us that our genre of music was dead, we kind of brushed grunge off as a fad that would quickly fade. It did turn out to be a fad, but it did last about 7 years. Eventually, the whole entire live rock music scene was dead and buried. Even though grunge was popular, it was a different kind of music. Nobody was going to see local grunge bands live, and in essence, that was shutting down any and all live rock music clubs.

Looking back, I think it was a combination of all of the club promoters implementing the "pay to play" strategy and grunge music that put the final nail in the live music coffin. Exposed tried to reinvent themselves a few times over those years, but to no avail. First, we attempted to become more of what was considered an "Industrial Band" like Nine Inch Nails and White Zombie. We even changed our name to In The Flesh. Still, we couldn't bring ourselves to become a grunge band, and we thought that changing to a weird industrial type sound might make us more relevant.

This was an ongoing problem during the 90's for my music career. We were always chasing trends. Looking back, In The Flesh actually had an original sound with really new and fresh sounding material. The major problem we still faced was that our singer, John, still sang in that high register that everyone associated with "Hair Bands." As much as we'd changed the sound of our music and our song writing, it didn't matter: the first thing that every record company heard was John's voice. It was always the same comment: "Band is cool, songs are cool, but singer is too outdated." John couldn't take hearing that his voice was always the cause of the band not making it, and he eventually quit.

Around late 1995/96, we contemplated calling it quits, but decided we would give it one more shot. We also decided that we weren't going to chase anymore trends. We would write and play music that we all loved. The first thing to do was to

DOGFISH

find a bluesy singer with a soulful voice — basically someone with the exact opposite sound as John's. After auditioning and meeting many bad singers, we finally found our man. His name was Paul Connaty. Paul had an amazing voice— soulful, bluesy, and powerful. The only thing holding Paul back was his charisma. He didn't have that "IT factor" that a rock and roll singer needed to command the stage and the audience. We knew this when he auditioned, but we hoped that we could teach him that swagger that he was lacking.

We all agreed that once Paul joined the band we needed to completely reinvent ourselves, starting with our name. After much debate and a lot of arguments, we settled on the name Dogfish. There was no real reason, only that Scott had found this cool picture of a dogfish that we thought could work for our new album cover. So, in the winter of 1996, Dogfish was officially formed.

We began writing new music with Paul for our new EP. We consciously decided to be more of a hard rock, no frills band, and we made a promise to ourselves that we wouldn't chase anymore trends. We would just write music that we loved to play and hear. As Dogfish, we recorded two dynamite EP's, both with solid playing, great song writing, and most importantly, soulful singing. We included one of the most unique and catchy songs that I'd ever recorded, "Waterdance." We also did a kick ass cover of Jefferson Airplane's "White Rabbit." Niko once

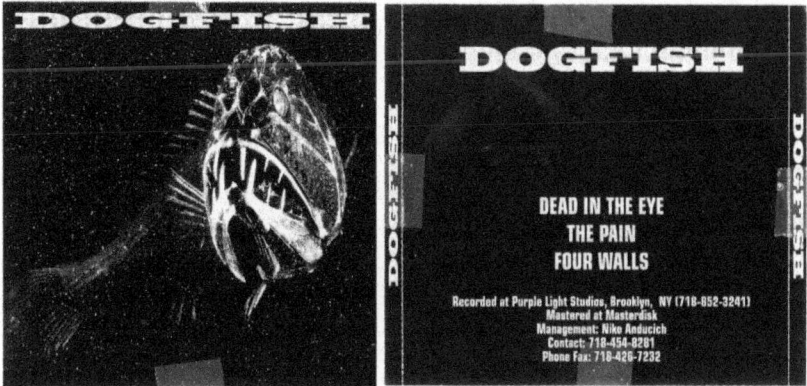

DOGFISH CD 1995

again tried to get us a record deal with all of his industry connections, but it was to no avail. The music scene was still dead for any rock bands not doing grunge. Dogfish lasted two solid years and then we collectively decided to call it quits.

The time I spent in Exposed, In The Flesh, and Dogfish really taught me a lot about the music industry and helped me become a much better musician. My only regret is that we never had any real major milestones or accomplishments that I could look back on and smile.

Dogfish 1995

CHAPTER 16

CHANGING COURSE

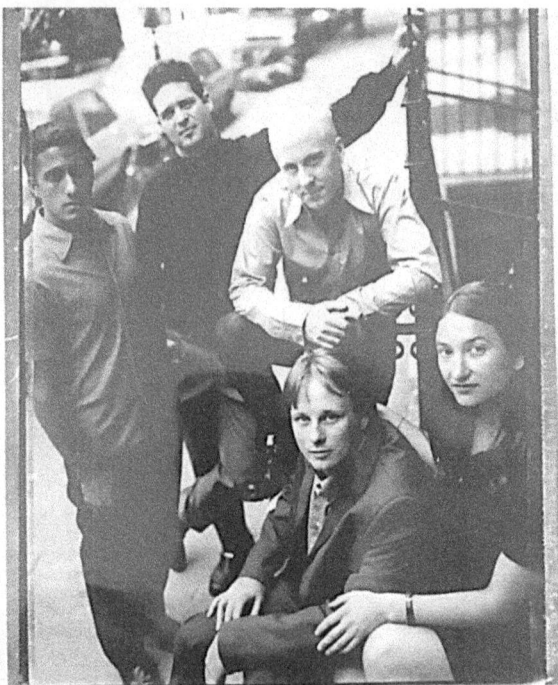

VALENTINE SMITH TMA
Clockwise (l to r): Joe Cassata • Brad Finkel • Stephen Dima • Kimberly Nordling • Bill McGarvey   201-531-048/

My obsession with Kiss never really wavered. I was still a rabid fan and would follow their every move. After the mini reunion KISS had on MTV Unplugged in 1995, they announced that they would be officially reuniting with Peter Criss and Ace Frehley and putting their signature makeup back on. My mind was blown.

Since Eric Carr's passing, KISS was never really the same to me. I always thought the *Revenge* album was a bit overrated. Around this time, I ended up with a bootleg of their most recent album, *Carnival of Souls*. It was very heavy and dark, not KISS-like at all. Of course, I still loved it because it was KISS, but it wasn't like the 70's and 80's KISS that I was obsessed with. Now that Ace and Peter were back and in makeup, though, I knew big things were on the horizon.

The first appearance of a reunited KISS was on the 1996 Grammy awards show. It was surreal and chilling to see the four original members of KISS walk out on that stage looking exactly like they did in 1978. Then more than ever, I realized what geniuses KISS really were. The makeup made them absolutely timeless. It no longer mattered that they were aging rock stars in their late 40's. When they put that makeup on, they were just KISS, instantly transformed into my childhood superheroes. I felt like I was 5 years old again while watching the Grammy's that night.

Shortly after their Grammy appearance, KISS announced a world tour with the first show being at Detroit's Tiger Stadium. I immediately called all of my old friends to try and convince someone into going with me to Detroit. Unfortunately, I had no takers. Even though some of my friends and former band mates liked KISS, no one was obsessed like I was. At that time, I didn't know one single KISS fan that liked them like I did.

Even though I couldn't convince anyone to come to Detroit with me, they all said yes to go to the shows when KISS came to New York at Madison Square Garden. KISS would play four straight nights at MSG in 1996. The day that tickets went on sale I bought as many seats as I could for those shows. I knew between all of my friends I could find people to go with me every night.

Those four nights at Madison Square Garden, watching my heroes, the original KISS in makeup, really rejuvenated me and my drive to make it as a drummer. All I kept thinking to myself while watching was, "Somehow, someway, I have to get up on that stage with them." KISS were my idols. They were larger than life superheroes to me, dare I say "Gods." Now, 17 years after I first saw them at MSG, I felt as though I was at least in the same ball park as them. I knew I could play my instrument just as well and I wanted more than anything to one day show them.

Right after Dogfish broke up, I had to figure out what my next move in the music business was going to be. I didn't want to just blindly keep pursuing my dream. I needed to be focused and smart. Knowing that the rock scene was completely dead, I had to figure out a suitable alternative.

In early 1998, I began combing the music papers again for bands looking for a drummer. By the late 90's, I started to like a few new bands that were on the radio like Oasis, Hootie and the Blowfish, The Goo Goo Dolls, and Train. This was the type of music that I wanted to start playing. Even though I still loved KISS more than every other band combined, I knew that I needed to once again shift my focus into what was being sold and popular at that time.

One ad in particular struck my interest. It was for an "Indie signed band doing retro Pop rock music looking for Drummer." "Indie" was a popular term during the 90's. Independent music (shortened to "indie") is music produced independently from major commercial record labels, a process that may include a do-it-yourself approach to recording and publishing. The term "indie" is sometimes also used to describe a genre (such as indie rock and indie pop). "Indie," for some reason, always gave a band some kind of immediate credibility in the listener's and record industry's eyes. To me, it was all a big joke.

Somewhere along the line, it became uncool to be with a major record label. If you were a so-called "indie band," then you were hip and modern. If you looked like you were a struggling band trying to make ends meet and recording songs about being down on your luck, you were the "It Thing."

Even the major record labels soon became hip to this way of thinking. They would form small "indie offshoots" of their giant main record label to trick the average consumer into thinking the band that they loved was coming to them from a small indie label. And it worked! The public wanted to buy records from bands that they thought were on their same level. I guess people thought they could relate to the music better this way. It was all a farce!

I always wanted the bands I loved to be bigger than life itself — someone to look up to, someone to admire and want to strive to be like — like KISS!

Shortly after answering the ad for the "pop Indie rock band," I received a message on my answering machine. "Hey, Joe, this is Bill McGarvey from the band Valentine Smith returning your call about the drummer wanted ad." After listening to the message, I was a little confused. For some reason, the name "Valentine Smith" sounded like an "80's rock" band name. I guess it was the word Valentine that was throwing me off. I pictured an 80's hair band when I was listening to the message. Even so, I returned Bill's phone call and we chatted a little about Valentine Smith.

I questioned him rather quickly about the name Valentine Smith. I didn't voice my concern about them being an 80's hair metal band, I just asked him what the name meant. Bill went on to explain that Valentine Smith was a name of the main character in the book *Stranger in a Strange Land*, a 1961 science fiction novel by Robert A. Heinlein. It tells the story of Valentine Michael Smith, a human who comes to Earth in early adulthood after being born on the planet Mars and raised by Martians. Me being a huge science fiction and fantasy fan, this intrigued me and made me much more comfortable with the name.

Bill sent out a three-song cassette that he wanted me to learn for the audition. The songs were "Katie's a No Show," "Dress You Up," and "Ahead of Her Time." I was pleasantly surprised when I received the tape. The songs were just what I was looking to get into — sort of a cross between Train and The Beatles. It had a very retro 60's vibe to it. I had no idea what they looked like, but I was hoping their image fit the music. Honestly, I'm not even sure what that means. At this point, I was just very concerned with not hearing the term "dated" or too "80's looking."

Because I still didn't have any image to connect to Valentine Smith, I tried to dress as neutral as I could for the audition. Upon arrival, I liked what I saw. It wasn't necessarily what I liked, but they looked much more contemporary to what the music industry was about in the late 90's. In other words, they looked quite ordinary.

Everyone had short hair and dressed pretty basic. I could also tell they were a good deal older than I was. I was just 24 and these guys all looked to be in their 30's, except for the female violin player who looked more my age. I was okay with all of that because like I mentioned, the music industry was no longer about "image." Actually, let me rephrase that: the music industry was still very much about image except now the "in image" was to have no image at all. Totally ridiculous! But, whatever the industry wanted and accepted at the time, Valentine Smith seemed to fit the bill. There was no way I was going to hear from anyone that this band looked "dated" or too "80's."

The audition went great. They wanted to get to know me a little better, so afterward we went out for lunch a few blocks away. They filled me in about how they were on a small "indie label" that was being distributed by one of the majors, and that they were ready to record their new album. It all sounded great to me. After about an hour of talking, they officially asked me to join.

Valentine Smith
Bill McGarvey - Vocals
Stephen Dima - Guitar, Piano
Brad Finkle - Bass
Kimberly Nordling - Violin
Joey Cassata – Drums

I quickly realized that this "band" was anything but. It was really the Bill and Steve show. It wasn't a band atmosphere at all. I felt like a hired gun from the get go. Bill and Steve were the songwriters and they refused to even accept material from any of the other band members. I think they believed they were like Lennon/McCartney and didn't want anyone else getting any song publishing. It was a very weird vibe from day one.

As much as I tried to be friendly and fun with them, it just felt like strictly business. After a show, I would get a check from their corporation and then be on my way. We never hung out, never had a drink together, and we never talked about anything personal. It was the exact opposite of my time in Playground, and I was really beginning to miss those days.

Even though the guys in Valentine Smith weren't any fun to be around, I stuck it out because I knew that they had a lot of potential. I thought to myself, "Maybe this is how a band should be." If it was all business, maybe there wouldn't be any petty fights to break us up. Every gig and every rehearsal felt like going to a job. It was sucking all the fun out of playing my drums, but I stuck with it.

We began recording the new album in late spring of 1998. The songs that we had slated to record were great. We decided, and when I say, "We decided," I mean Bill and Steve decided, that instead of recording a full-length CD, we would do only a 6-song EP. I was a little upset because a few of the songs they were going to cut from the CD like "Be Happy" and "5'o'Clock Hero" were amazing. But it really didn't matter what I thought.

Right before we began tracking, Bill asked me if I could use the blast sticks I'd been using at a few of our smaller shows to record. Blast sticks were a cross between brushes and sticks, and I sometime used them because we were playing small coffee houses and restaurants. Basically, they made the drums quieter. I didn't know why they would want me to use them in the recording studio, but Steve explained that they were looking for a Ringo-esque sound for the drums on the new CD. They loved the way the blast sticks sounded live and they wanted to recreate it in the studio. Once again, I really had no say. So, I recorded the whole Valentine Smith CD with blast sticks. The biggest problem I had was that the sticks limited my playing. They were essentially five small rods of wood attached to a single handle, which made it virtually impossible to do any ghost notes. As a drummer, ghost notes were a huge part of my playing to create rhythmic undertones throughout songs. Now I was limited to playing just basic solid notes with no texture or dynamics.

Even the recording process was work with Valentine Smith. For some unknown reason, they didn't even want any creative input from the other members of the band. I'm not sure if there was some kind of monetary producer credit thing that they were afraid of, or they were just utter control freaks. I'd probably lean towards the latter. Don't get me wrong, I enjoyed playing with Valentine Smith tremendously. I think it's some of my best and proudest work of my career, but Bill and Steve had a way of making everyone feel like they were unimportant just hired guns, and I guess we were.

Once the CD was completed, I found out that the small "indie label" that Valentine Smith was on was no longer in existence. We would basically be releasing the album on our own with no support or backing.

Even with all of these problems, I was very proud of the CD and being a part of the band in general. This was the first band that I didn't really play heavy rock grooves with. My drum parts were much more intricate and complementary to the songs. In retrospect, they were more "Ringo-esque." Being in Valentine Smith forced me to become a different kind of drummer — not a better drummer or a worse drummer, but an overall more balanced and versatile drummer.

We officially released the self-titled Valentine Smith CD in early 1999. It got rave reviews from the critics. Here's a sample from the *New York Times*: "Valentine Smith has the ability to balance its raw energy and pop hooks with melancholy undercurrents. The band may rely on

Valentine Smith CD 1998

acoustic guitars and violin for folky textures, but their raucous live show proves that it's a rock band at heart."

We also had many write-ups in national magazines and press. Here are a few of the blurbs from such articles:

Described as "classic American pop," Valentine Smith's music has also been compared to early REM, "Waterloo Sunset"-era Kinks, and early solo Paul McCartney.

Sculpted out of the neighborhoods of North Jersey and New York, this five-piece pop band has built a solid fan base touring on the strength of two releases, Back On Earth and Putting In The Peacetime Hours in the past three years. Billboard Magazine put their debut CD on their end-of-year top ten list, while CMJ says that they are "as wide ranging as the Hudson River ... impossible to overlook."

Like I said, even though being in Valentine Smith wasn't what I'd call a party, once the CD was released and I read the reviews and write-ups, I once again remembered why I was sticking it out with them. My ultimate goal was always to be able to play my drums for a living, and this band was the closest I'd been to seeing that become a reality. Yes, it wasn't what I'd always imagined. I'd much rather be with my friends back in Playground and share success with them. But, unfortunately, we couldn't hold it together.

A few months after the CD release, we somehow got a few of our songs placed in TV shows. This was about the time when playing original music on new, hip TV shows was becoming the "it" thing to do. The WB and UPN were both new upstart networks and they were the first to try out original material during their teeny type series, like *Dawson's Creek* and *The Gilmore Girls*.

The first show that played one of our songs was the Don Johnson cop series *Nash Bridges* on CBS. I remember my mom being so proud to hear her son playing the drums for a song on TV. There was nothing better in the whole world than making my mom proud of me. I believe we also had a few songs on some WB shows like *Charmed*, but I was never sure exactly which shows.

Dealing with the guys in Valentine Smith was like pulling teeth. I would have to get all this kind of information from second-hand sources. Can you believe that? They wouldn't even voluntarily tell the other members of the band if/when one of our songs were being played in a TV show. Again, I'm not sure if it was some kind of financial thing, or if they just didn't feel the need to tell us because they felt it was "their band."

Throughout 1999 and into 2000, Valentine Smith played dozens of shows throughout the tri-state area. We even ventured as far as Boston and Detroit. Most shows were just local taverns, coffee houses, parks, and restaurants. These places were a long way off from the parties

Playground used to have at The Crazy Country Club! Valentine Smith just wasn't that type of band.

I hate to say it, but we were more like background music for most of these places. I remember we even played a pizza place in Park Slope Brooklyn that was filled with snobby yuppies. The whole scene just wasn't for me.

In the middle of my run with Valentine Smith, another tragedy hit me and my family. Yukon had become ill and it seemed like he wasn't going to make it. Yukon and I grew up together and he was like a brother to me. I did everything with him. We ate together, played together, wrestled together, and even slept in the same bed together.

A few years after moving to Manhattan, Yukon's legs started to give him trouble. Our apartment was three steep flights up, and it was starting to take its toll on him. Manhattan was no place for a dog his size. He was about 170 pounds at this point, and he was cooped up in a small tiny apartment all day. It was heartbreaking to watch him suffer. I was basically carrying his whole back end up the steps every time I took him out to pee. I didn't mind doing it at all and I would do absolutely anything for him, but it was heartbreaking.

By the end, Yukon could barely stand on his own. We had a vet make a house call because he was just too big to move. When the vet finally arrived, Yukon had begun bleeding from the nose and the vet told us that he was probably bleeding internally and that there was nothing we could do for him. He suggested we put him down. I told the vet that I needed time to think about it and that we would call him tomorrow.

I prayed to God that night to please take Yukon and let him have peace. Selfishly, I couldn't face the decision of having to be the one to put him down. I laid with him on my kitchen floor for the next 12 hours. Yukon's favorite food was my mom's meatballs. Even in this weakened state and bleeding internally, he still loved his meatballs. I fed him as many as he wanted that night.

Finally, the next morning, I called the vet to return to do the unthinkable. I would have to be the one to sign the paper to end my best friend's life. I was sick. I held Yukon in my arms while the doctor administered the lethal shot and cried my eyes out. I hugged him so tightly and told him how much I loved him and how I would never ever forget him. And then he was gone.

My life changed that day. I've talked to Yukon every day since he's been gone. I always look up in the sky and see a bright star and know that it's Yukon staring down on me and watching over me.

Me and Yukon in Greenwhich Village

CHAPTER 17

ALL WORK AND NO PLAY
MAKES JOEY A DULL BOY

By the summer of 2000, I decided I needed a little fun back in my life. Some of my old friends from the Playground days, namely our old mascot/manager Ernie LaMonte, would always rent a house in the Hamptons for the summer.

The Hamptons is a famous beach town located on the tip of Long Island. I would visit one of Ernie's share houses once or twice every summer over the last few years and I always had a great time. In the summer of 2000, I decided to become a full share in his house. This basically meant that I would pay somewhere in the neighborhood of $2,000 for a spot in one of the bedrooms of the house for the entire summer, giving me full access whenever I wanted. Ernie and company always rented a massive place with a giant backyard and in-ground swimming pool. It was just what I needed.

The summer consisted of drinking by the pool all day and then going to a few clubs at night. It was just the distraction my mind needed to get away from the everyday grind of Valentine Smith. I told the guys in the band that I was unavailable most weekends that summer due to family commitments, but I said that if any really important shows or appearances came up I would be able to change my plans.

The Hamptons Crew, 2000-2003

I knew in my heart that all of these small local shows were doing nothing for the band. The CD was a success, but it wasn't getting the traction that we'd hoped for. In my humble opinion, Valentine Smith just really never had a clear goal or a path to achieve such a goal. The band was great, the songs were great, but a band needed more than that: the band needed to put itself out there and network and push the product down people's throats. I think Steve and Bill just thought someone would come and knock on their door. That was never my mind set. If I wanted something, I would go kick the door down and take it, but because they never wanted any input from me or from the other members, I was forced to let them do it "their way." So, I decided to basically take the summer off and do things "my way."

By then I'd been in a band since I was 15 years old and I had never really gotten to let loose and have fun without thinking about business. Don't get me wrong, playing in all of my bands was amazing fun and I had a great time gigging and partying, but there was always an underlining sense that this was work and I couldn't go overboard. The Hamptons was the exact opposite. It was the first time, in a very long while, that I didn't have to worry about "band business." I could just let loose.

The summer of 2000 was a fantastic time with a lot of partying and just being stupid. It was just what I needed. One of the best parts about the Hamptons house was I could really just be myself. As you know, I was always a huge wrestling fan, and wrestling had become popular again over the last three or four years. My childhood hero, Hulk Hogan, was now considered a heel, and guys like Stone Cold Steve Austin and the Rock were becoming popular. As a nightly ritual, after coming home drunk from the clubs, the whole house would put on one giant wrestling match. It was fantastic. I still can't believe someone didn't get seriously injured. We would body slam each other on to the floor, jump off the counter, and "superfly splash" people. I was constantly applying Ric Flair's "figure four" leg lock on unsuspecting victims.

It was just nonstop fun from our arrival on Thursday night until our departure Monday morning.

I would constantly try to talk business with Bill and Steve, but they just never seemed interested or motivated. I'm not sure if they were blowing me off because they thought I was young and didn't know anything, or that they just felt like they had it all under control. It was very frustrating.

2001 was more of the same from Valentine Smith. We played plenty of meaningless shows with no real goal or idea of what we were doing. Once the summer of 2001 came, I decided I would once again do the Hamptons house with Ernie and company.

The summer of 2001 proved even better than 2000. This year Ernie and I plus our friend Billy Zehmisch would be in charge of running our own house. We went and searched for the perfect house and finally found it at 10 Penny Lane. The house was much older and smaller than the year before, but we would be able to get it at a lower cost and have control over who became shares in the house. It was perfect. We even had some of our old Playground boys back partying every weekend. Tommy Snyder was there all the time, along with guitarist Steve Kerasotis. It was another absolutely perfect summer of fun.

In the fall of 2001, I came to a very big revelation: why couldn't I have fun in a band like I was having in the Hamptons every summer? I had it once before with Playground and that's exactly what I wanted again. The business and egos in Valentine Smith were really a bummer to be around day in and day out. I wanted to have fun playing my drums again. I wasn't sure exactly what that meant, but I knew that I needed a side project away from Valentine Smith to fulfill the fun side of my music career. My plan was to stay with Valentine Smith and basically wait to see if we hit it big. But, in the meantime, I would find another band that I could have fun playing with. The hunt began…

I immediately went back to my tried-and-true place to find bands, the music papers. This time it would be *The Village Voice*. I wasn't exactly sure what I was looking for, but I was hoping I'd recognize it when I saw it. After flipping through the paper for a few minutes, I saw an ad that I had to read twice to believe. It said, "KISS Tribute band, doing Creatures of the Night era Kiss, looking for drummer to be Eric Carr."

This was no mere coincidence. This was fate, something I truly believe in, along with the idea that things happen for a reason. This was one of those times. What were the chances of me looking in *The Village Voice* that day and finding a KISS band looking for a drummer to be Eric Carr? I'd never heard of, or seen, any tribute band doing Eric Carr. I called the phone number immediately and spoke to a guy named Ruby.

Ruby Rinekso was Ace Frehley in the band KISSNATION. He explained to me that they were looking for a full-time drummer and that they had a few shows coming up rather quickly. He was very matter-of-fact and to the point — dare I say, business-like, which I found a little odd because at the time I thought a tribute band was just for fun. He told me that he'd email me a song list that I would need to have ready for the audition.

The next day I received three different emails from Ruby, each containing a different group of about 12 songs. I responded to the emails and asked him which of these song groups he wanted me to learn for the audition. He replied that I should learn them all just to be safe. He explained that because KISSNATION was doing Eric Carr and the

Creatures of the Night era of KISS, they needed to know a lot of oddities from KISS' catalog.

Because KISS had so many different versions of their songs, be it on the live albums, studio, or greatest hits, I asked Ruby what versions he wanted me to learn. He replied, "Whenever possible learn the KISS *Animalize Uncensored* video versions." I couldn't believe that's what they wanted. I knew that video like the back of my hand. Every little lick and fill that Eric Carr did on that video I've probably played a thousand times. Like I said, it was fate.

Getting ready for the KISSNATION audition was not only super fun, but very exciting. There wasn't much I loved doing more than playing KISS songs. I rehearsed a few times at the Valentine Smith studio in Hoboken and, as I was playing the songs, I couldn't help but to imagine what it would feel like to be playing these songs in KISS make up and costume. After two rehearsals, I was more than ready. I knew this gig was mine!

I was set to meet the guys in KISSNATION at Funkadelic Studios on west 40th Street in Manhattan. When I arrived, I saw two guys standing in the hallway chatting. I knew right away it was the guys from KISSNATION. Ruby was Asian and had the same exact demeanor as Ace, the same hair as Ace, he was skinny, and he even stood with his legs in a weird twisted pose, just like I'd seen pictures of how Ace stood. There was also a Puerto Rican looking guy standing next to Ruby with a giant afro. He looked just like Gene Simmons even without makeup. His name was Carlos Espada.

It was a little weird and surreal at the same time. I loved Eric Carr, but I didn't go around my everyday life looking like him. Did these guys actually study Ace's and Gene's mannerisms and incorporate them into their everyday life? I wasn't sure, but I wanted to find out more.

Ruby said, "Hey, we are about to audition another guy before you. Can you wait in the hallway while we play a few songs with him?" I waited and listened behind the door. After a song or two, I could tell the guy was a decent drummer, but he wasn't playing anything like Eric Carr. I knew the ins and outs of everything Eric did and this guy wasn't doing any of them. I was extremely confident at this point.

After about 25 minutes, the door opened and Ruby waved me in. The other drummer was packing up while Ruby introduced me to their

Paul Stanley. He had bright, florescent red hair and said with a thick Brooklyn accent, "Hey, I'm Paulie Z."

Once I was all set up and ready to go, I asked Ruby, "What song do you want to start with?" I had all 36 songs Ruby asked me to learn down pat, and I could fire any one of them off first. Ruby paused for a minute and said, "Let's do 'Strutter'." I actually began to laugh out loud. I said to Ruby, "Just so you know, 'Strutter' was not on the list of 36 songs you gave me. I know it, but I just wanted to tell you that" I was kind of annoyed.

Carlos then laughingly yelled at Ruby, "You gave him 36 songs to learn? What are you nuts?" Paulie began laughing and seconds later, Ruby and I joined in. I played the infamous drum intro to "Strutter" and we were off.

I could tell they were immediately impressed. Even though I didn't practice this particular song for the audition, I knew all of the little differences in how Eric Carr played it compared to how Peter Criss played it on the albums. We barreled through 4 or 5 more songs and I was having a blast. These guys sounded like KISS! The singer Paulie Z sounded like Paul Stanley, Carlos sang just like Gene Simmons, and Ruby played guitar very sloppily, just like Ace!

Carlos then said, "Hey, let's finish with 'Black Diamond'!" This was the one thing I was a little worried about. Up until this point, I didn't do a lot of background singing in my bands. I'd done some, but definitely not a lead vocal like "Black Diamond" required. It was a pretty hard song to simultaneously play and sing. I'd rehearsed it, but I didn't have access to the Valentine Smith PA system, so I couldn't rehearse singing it with a microphone.

Ruby then said, "We are doing the big ending like on KISS *Animalize Uncensored*. Do you know it?" The way he asked me always felt like he assumed I didn't know that version and was trying catch me off guard. I responded, "Yes, I know it." He looked surprised and tried to explain more about what he meant like he couldn't believe I'd learned that version. I quickly cut him off and said, "I know that version," then began giving an example of the Tom Tom pattern at the end. Carlos smiled and looked at Ruby and said, "Yup, that's it all right!"

While playing "Black Diamond," I remember thinking to myself, "Wow Joe, you sound a lot like Eric singing this song right now." I'd never heard myself sing "Black Diamond" before and it wasn't half bad. The song is naturally a little out of my range, but Eric would always growl through a lot of it and I was able to mimic that pretty well.

After the audition, the guys seemed pretty happy, but were trying not to let on. All they said was, "Thanks, we'll let you know." All I could do was smirk to myself. I knew that I had the gig. There was no way they were going to find a drummer that could play as much like Eric Carr as me. I thought to myself, referring mostly to Ruby, "I guess even in the tribute band world people had egos."

Sure enough, I got the call the next day from Ruby to ask me to join KISSNATION. Even though I was still with Valentine Smith, I accepted!

This was September of 2001 shortly after the 9/11 World Trade center attack.

KISSNATION
Paulie Z - Rhythm Guitar, Vocals
Carlos Espada - Bass, Vocals
Ruby Rinekso - Lead Guitar, Vocals
Joey Cassata - Drums, Vocals

My first KISSNATION show was only a few weeks away on Halloween night at The Big Easy on 2nd Avenue and 92st in New York City. Musically, I was more than ready, but I still hadn't tried to put on the infamous KISS makeup. When I was a kid, I was Ace Frehley and Gene Simmons for Halloween and then I wore Peter Criss' make up for my sixth-grade talent show, but I'd never attempted to apply my own makeup and I had no idea what I would look like as Eric Carr.

Carlos said that I could use their old drummer's costume and boots and Paulie said he had a wig for me to use. Once we loaded in, set up, and sound checked, it was time for me to attempt putting on the makeup. Carlos sent me a list a few days earlier on what makeup I should buy. He told me KISSNATION used the same exact makeup that KISS used. I thought that was very cool and I was more than excited to go shopping to get it.

I purchased a tub of Clown White, Ben Nye black, and Ben Nye red. I also purchased a few eye liner pencils that Carlos suggested, to draw the outline of the makeup. I wasn't sure what brush to buy so I bought an array of different sizes just in case.

KISSNATION Promo poster 2002

Once we began to apply the makeup, Carlos was the only one to give me any pointers on the right way to apply it. I was assuming that they would all help me a little to make sure that it looked perfect. Paulie seemed to be in his own world and Ruby had an attitude as if he was saying, "Let him figure it out himself. Nobody taught or helped me!" This was exactly the type of stuff that I was trying to get away from by joining KISSNATION. I was applying Eric Carr's KISS make up and was about to do a two-hour show of KISS songs. Nothing could spoil my mood.

When I finished applying the make up and put my wig on, I looked in the mirror and couldn't believe my eyes. I looked just like Eric! It was actually a little creepy how much I looked like him. The other guys in the band couldn't believe it either. We blistered through an amazing two-plus hour set filled with KISS classics and some rare cuts. It was exhilarating to play the songs I grew up idolizing. I had found my new outlet to once again enjoy playing my drums!

Valentine Smith was still active, but nothing was currently happening. It was really the best of both worlds. I would play with

KISSNATION once or twice a month and do the same with Valentine Smith. KISSNATION was for fun and Valentine Smith was business. I still hoped in the back of my mind that Valentine Smith would hit it big, but I knew it was wishful thinking.

Applying the war paint.

After the gig, we all loaded our gear to the sidewalk in front of the club. Paulie had a van and he would be transporting it for us. He would be taking me to the Valentine Smith studio in Hoboken. After about 20 minutes of waiting for Paulie to return from getting the van, we started to wonder what could be taking him so long.

We called his phone to make sure everything was all right, but it started ringing in a bag that was sitting next to our gear. Carlos then said, "That jig probably fell asleep!" Carlos called everyone Jig. "Fell asleep? What do you mean he fell asleep?" I said confused. Carlos went on to explain that Paulie had a bit of narcolepsy. Narcolepsy was a condition that caused people to fall asleep unexpectedly. I still couldn't quite grasp what he was saying. Did he fall asleep walking? Did he sit down on the curb to take a nap? I just couldn't wrap my head around someone falling asleep when he knew we were waiting for him on the sidewalk to pick up the gear.

After another half an hour, we decided we should split up and go look for him. We left one of the KISSNATION roadies, Vic, to watch the gear. We began combing the streets in search for either Paulie passed out in the street or at least maybe his van. After another 30 minutes of searching the streets of uptown Manhattan, Carlos called me on my cell to tell me he found Paulie and the van. He was sleeping with thick white smoke pouring from the engine and filling the inside. If Carlos hadn't found him, he would have probably suffocated. All of this was going on

My first time as Eric Carr.

while he was fast asleep, snoring in the driver's seat, like nothing happened. This was my very first experience with Paulie Z. And the night was far from over...

Paulie and Carlos returned with the van and we finally loaded up our gear at around 4am. Carlos and Ruby didn't even seem that annoyed or surprised. This kind of thing had obviously happened before. They both had very minimal gear that they would leave in Paulie's van until the next gig. After they loaded theirs into the van, they hailed a cab with Vic the roadie, and were on their way home. Unfortunately, my adventure with Paulie Z had only just begun.

Paulie and I were now off to Hoboken to drop off my drums. We jumped on the FDR Drive at 92st and were on our way. About 20 blocks into our trip, thick white smoke once again began to pour out of the engine. Paulie frantically tried to pull over but there wasn't much room on the FDR. We finally were able to get off at the 61st Street exit. We barely made it off the exit when the van completely died.

Instead of pulling to the side of the street away from traffic, Paulie decided to just leave the car in the middle of the street, right off of the FDR exit. He stopped the car and took the key out of the ignition. Thick white smoke was still pouring out of the engine. It turned out that because Paulie had left the car running for about 2 hours while he took a nap, he must have overheated the engine of his old 1988 conversion van. Before I could ask him what we were going to do now, I looked over and he was once again fast asleep.

I thought to myself, "What the hell kind of freak is this? How could he fall asleep in the middle of the street while his van was over heating?" I shook him and asked him "Now, what do we do?" He replied, "We have to wait for the engine to cool down. Then we can try again." He then put his head back and went back to sleep as if he were comfy in his bed.

About 45 minutes later, we tried the engine again to no avail. Now, it was getting close to mid-morning and cars were zipping around us and honking since we were blocking one whole lane off the exit. Even though it's not wise, Paulie decided he would pour water on the engine to speed up the process. It worked, but only temporarily. We finally got off the exit and drove about another 20 blocks when that white smoke began pouring out once again. This process would go on for the next few hours. Every 20 blocks or so the engine would overheat, Paulie would pour water on it, and we would drive a little more. The van finally completely died at around 7am.

We made it to 14th Street, and with the van full of our gear and completely dead, I had no other option. I didn't know the guys in KISSNATION well enough to just leave my drums in their broken-down van like Paulie suggested. Actually, I did know Paulie well enough after the last 5 hours to know there was no way in hell I was leaving my drums in his care. He was liable to fall asleep again and have someone steal all the gear right from under his nose. I decided I would hail a few taxi cabs and load everything into them. This was just about the time when the small mini-van taxis were starting to be on the road, so I was able to get two of those and fit all my gear. I would have to take it all to my tiny apartment in Manhattan and carry it up three flights of stairs. That wasn't the part that bothered me the most. If I'd known that this was going to be the final outcome, I could have avoided the last 5 hours with Paulie and just taken a cab right after the show.

Once I was loaded into the taxis, I asked Paulie, "What are you going to do now?" He said, "I'm not sure. I guess I'll wait a little while and see if it starts again." I got in the taxi and headed home. As I was pulling away, I glanced back at Paulie in the van and saw that he had already fallen back to sleep. This was the end of my first adventure with Paulie Z. Unfortunately, there would be many more to come.

My second KISSNATION show would be in Ohio on November 15, 2001. KISSNATION would fly me out because I had a prior commitment and couldn't drive with them. I was to be godfather to my brother's daughter, Samantha, and the christening was the morning of the show in Ohio.

I would have to baptize my niece, go to the after party, and then go straight to the airport.

Flying during this time was a bit challenging. It was right after the terror attacks on 9/11, and the airports had very tight security. Because I was on a strict time constraint, I wouldn't be able to check a bag. I would just be making the gig as it was, so I didn't have time to wait for my bag in Ohio. I packed my costume, makeup, and a change of clothes in my carry-on bag and that was it.

When I went through the security check at the airport, I was flagged and called over by security. They opened my bag and began examining my makeup. I tried to explain that I was in a KISS tribute band, but they weren't listening. They examined every inch of my bag and closely looked at my makeup, which I happen to be carrying in my 1978 KISS lunchbox. After about a 20-minute detainment, they finally let me board the plane.

Because I was so pressed for time, the plan was for me to apply my makeup in the car that was picking me up at the airport. The car was supposed to be a luxury town car that would give me plenty of room to work in. However, the car that picked me up was anything but. It was a small, old, beat-up two-door Dodge Neon.

I obviously couldn't properly apply my makeup while cramped in this small car. I decided to wait until I arrived at the venue. Upon arrival, Ruby thought it was okay to be upset with me for not being ready and in makeup. I quickly told him, "Ruby, here's a little heads-up: never speak to me like that again". He never did.

The third show with KISSNATION was a "tribute to Eric Carr" show at the Chance Theater in Poughkeepsie. I couldn't have asked for a better experience than to pay tribute to my idol and to one of the main reasons I played drums. I now was sure that joining KISSNATION was the right move for my career. Even though I knew that a tribute band was a dead end, it just felt right to be doing what I was doing. Dressing as Eric Carr and playing KISS songs every night gave me a strange sense of fulfillment and joy that I wasn't getting with Valentine Smith.

Before the Eric Carr tribute show, we met with Eric's sister, Loretta. She was the host for the event and she wanted to meet us and show her gratitude for playing the show in honor of her brother. She was a sweetheart and I was very happy to have met her. I didn't know it then, but years later we would work together to bring to life one of her brother's dream projects, the animated show, *The Rockheads*.

Things were going great with KISSNATION! I was having a fun time and I couldn't have been happier. Shortly after the Eric Carr tribute show, we got invited by Gene Simmons and Paul Stanley to appear at

Tower Records for the official KISS box set release. My mind was once again blown. Gene and Paul knew us enough to invite us to help promote their new box set? I had never met anyone in KISS and this would be my chance to not only meet them, but to be working alongside them to help promote and advertise their new product.

The day of the Tower Records event was surreal. The KISS camp put us up at the Gramercy Hotel in downtown Manhattan. We were to get in makeup and costume there, and then walk over to Tower Records. Once we arrived, it was pandemonium. I hadn't yet experienced a real, full-on KISS crowd while we were in full gear. They went absolutely wild when they saw us, especially because I was Eric Carr.

I always felt that me being Eric Carr was more of a tribute to a fallen hero of mine than it was me impersonating someone. The other guys dressing as Gene, Paul, and Ace always would seem like a cheap imitation of the real thing. But because Eric was no longer with us, people had a different kind of affection and appreciation towards me portraying him.

When I finally got to meet Gene and Paul, I think that they had the same feeling. They seemed a little weirded out by Carlos and Paulie being dressed as them, but they had a sense of gratitude when they talked to me about being Eric. It was as if they were seeing their long-lost friend again when they saw me. It was very overwhelming.

I had grown up my whole life idolizing Gene and Paul and now I was working side by side with them, and they seemed to really appreciate me being Eric. This wasn't one of my "Frozen Moments," but I did realize that something special had happened to me that night.

Shortly after the Tower Records appearance, Gene asked us to appear with him to help promote his new book, *Kiss and Make Up*. This was still all pretty crazy for me. Gene Simmons of KISS was personally requesting us to appear with him to help promote his book. It was as if it wasn't reality.

I know this wasn't the fame and fortune that I'd always wanted, but I still thought it was pretty damn cool that I was able to hang out with one of my childhood idols. In a strange way, it made me want to become his peer and equal more than ever.

Me as Eric Carr with Paul Stanley & Gene Simmons

Even though I had a passion and a love for KISS, I never viewed myself as a "fanboy." I would never ask them for an autograph or anything like that. It was just weird to me. What I wanted was for them to see me play the drums and for them to think I was good. That's the type of fan I was. I wanted to play with KISS; I didn't want their autograph!

The *KISS and Make Up* book signing event with Gene went great. He was kind and appreciative to us throughout the day. He invited us to the after party at a club called Spa in the West Village.

We never ran into Gene at the after party, but we did run into a mega KISS fan that went absolutely bonkers when he saw us. It was none other than Sebastian Bach from the band Skid Row. Sebastian had been a huge KISS fan all of his life, and he immediately recognized that we were in the "Creatures of the Night" era costumes. He went nuts when he saw me as Eric Carr. He said, "Holy shit, dude! You look exactly like Eric! I never got to see him in makeup. This is so F'N cool!" He wanted pictures with us and we started to hang and drink with him. It was a pretty fun and wild night.

One of the few times I was Peter Criss in KISSNATION.

Paulie Z, Sebastian Bach and me at Gene Simmons' after party, 2001.

Chapter 18

STOP CHASING AND LET IT COME TO YOU

KISSNATION meets Paul Stanley and Gene Simmons.
Tower Records 2001.

In December of 2001, Valentine Smith had a show at one of our regular spots called Kroughs in Sparta, New Jersey. It was a bar/restaurant type place that always had a pretty steady VS fan base. We had a tradition of always having a big slice of their homemade apple pie after the show. While I was digging in to my pie, Kim the violinist told me, "I can't believe it's our last piece of Krough's apple pie." I asked, "Why? Is Krough's closing down?" I had no idea what she meant. She then replied, "No, this is our last show." Again confused, I said, "Last show at Kroughs?" She said, "No, our last show. Valentine Smith's last show. Bill or Steve didn't tell you?" Pissed off, I came back with, "No, they didn't tell me!"

That's the type of people I was dealing with in Valentine Smith. They had known it was our very last show and didn't even feel the need to tell me. I never even asked why it was our last show. I was just so over the whole situation. I was having fun again in KISSNATION and I was hanging with all my friends all summer long in the Hamptons. I was actually pissed that I devoted as much time and energy as I did to Valentine Smith. Looking back, I can admit that we made really great music together, music that I still love to listen to today, but overall the experience really left a bad taste in my mouth.

So, 2002 started with me not having an original band to work with. This was the first stretch of time since I was about 14 that I wasn't in an original band. The weirdest part about it was that I was totally okay with it. I was having so much fun with KISSNATION that I didn't miss the everyday grind and business of an original band. It was nice to take a break from the world of trying everything in your power to get signed by a record label every waking moment. With KISSNATION, all I had to do was have fun playing my drums, and that was refreshing.

In May of 2002, KISSNATION was invited to play the Puerto Rico KISS expo. KISS drummer Eric Singer was going to be the special guest. Of course, we jumped at the opportunity. Not only were we going to be going to Puerto Rico all expenses paid, but we got to hang out with Eric Singer all weekend. This was the trip that really made me feel comfortable with the guys in KISSNATION. To say we bonded during this adventure is an understatement.

Growing up in NYC, it was common to "rank" on each other. All that meant was that boys would usually bust each other's balls as much as they possibly could. The classics were always to either make fun of someone's mother or to pick on some physical attribute that you knew bothered that person. Where I grew up in Brooklyn, and with the friends that I had, I became a pretty masterful ball buster over the years.

Being that I was still kind of the new guy in KISSNATION, I hadn't felt completely comfortable enough around the other guys to really let loose. Carlos and Ruby had been together for years and even Paulie had been with them a good 6 months before I joined. They were all very comfortable with each other and would constantly break each other's balls, mine included.

When they busted my balls, I would always just tap my head and say, "Okay, I'm storing all of this in my file cabinet to use at a later date." They would laugh it off like it was really just me not being able to come back with anything. They had no idea who they were dealing with.

I could tell that Paulie and Ruby had probably been nerdy kids growing up; I recognized the tendencies a mile away. They were both quick to put someone down or to try to make themselves look good which to me were all signs of someone being insecure. Carlos was a little more like me.

I had a huge group of friends that were all master ball busters! I've had years and years of practice doing what Paulie and Ruby probably just started doing since they began to play in a band. I was just waiting for the right moment to unleash, and that moment came during the first day of our Puerto Rico trip.

Once we landed and settled in at our hotel in San Juan, we were scheduled for a full day of press all over Puerto Rico in full makeup and costume. Our first stop was Telemundo.

After that we were headed to The Hard Rock Cafe to meet with KISS drummer Eric Singer for a small press outing to promote the KISS expo the next day.

After a few photos, Eric suggested that we all hang out and have lunch. This was our first-time meeting Eric and he seemed friendly and down to earth, but this was at a time when he was also a little bitter at KISS.

Eric was asked to rejoin the band in 2001, after Peter Criss tried to hold out for more money to do the tour of Japan. KISS called Peter's bluff and decided to put Eric Singer in the "Catman" makeup.

Shortly after the Japanese tour, KISS decided to do a show in Australia with the Australia Symphony Orchestra for a new Live DVD and album. The only problem was that KISS decided to ask Peter to do the show instead of Eric. There remains much speculation about why KISS did this; I always assumed it was because they wanted to make sure they were able to play their biggest hit single "Beth," which Peter wrote and sang, with the full orchestra.

Eric was bitter with KISS for asking Peter back, and we could all tell by the way he was talking. It wasn't anything in particular, but he just had a sour vibe about Gene and Paul at this time. One thing he said did annoy me a little. We were discussing the era that KISSNATION was representing, Creatures of the Night, and he made a snide comment about Eric Carr. I asked him what he thought of Carr and he said, "He was Okay. I never understood why he used gloves to play with. What, were his hands too fragile?" I guess he was trying to make a joke, but he seemed almost jealous of Carr in a way. Other than that, Eric was fun to be around that weekend.

KISSNATION ready to appear on Puerto Rico's Telemundo TV

After we finished lunch, we notice a giant 2-foot ice cream sundae over at the next table. Paulie's eyes lit up and excitedly said, "We should get one of those for our table." To which Eric Singer responded, "It looks like you don't need a sundae" then he pointed at Paulie's love handles. They were sticking out due to the nature of the Paul Stanley costume he was wearing, which was basically a belly shirt.

Paulie's mood and demeanor immediately changed. Up until this point, Paulie was as chipper and giddy as I'd ever seen him. He was definitely the "fan boy" type. He was so excited and happy to be having lunch with Eric Singer we thought nothing could bring him down. Boy, were we wrong.

Paulie's shoulders began to slouch, his head went back, and his neck crawled into his torso like a turtle. He then began to actually pout. Carlos asked, "Jig, what the hell is wrong with you?" Paulie then responded in a feeble pouting voice, "The Eric Singer called me fat." (I'm not sure why Paulie addressed him as "The Eric Singer", but it just added to the hilarity of the story.) He looked like someone had just run over his dog with a car. We thought he was going to cry at any second. This was the opening I'd been waiting for. I relentlessly ripped into him about Eric Singer making fun of his love handles. I had the whole table, including Eric, in tears with laughter. All the while, Paulie was cowering lower and lower in his seat. Ball breaker Joey had arrived.

After lunch, Paulie pulled me aside outside of the Hard Rock Cafe to explain to me why he was so upset. I pretended to be deeply concerned as I listened to his heartfelt story. Paulie proceeded to confide in me that when he was younger, his father and many other people used to call him "Fat Boy." I held in my laughter and excitement about hearing this new development and said, "Paulie, that's horrible. Tell me more." Paulie told me a few other childhood stories and then we went back inside to join the other guys. Before we got within 10 feet of them, I blurted out while laughing, "Guys! Paulie's dad used to call him 'Fat Boy'!" I tried to restrain myself, but I just couldn't hold back this spectacular information. This absolutely crushed Paulie: he had confided in me and I had betrayed him. The real Paulie was beginning to show his face. We found out rather quickly that he could dish it out but he couldn't take it.

That was the first rule of trash talk. If you dish it, you better be able to take it. The second rule was don't "sell it," which was an old wrestling phrase that I always used. All it meant was that if someone said something that bothered you, you shouldn't let on that it bothered you because that gave them ammunition against you. If you didn't "sell it" or let it bother you, they had nothing they could use. Paulie was definitely "selling" this!

The next day we went to lunch before getting ready for our appearance and performance at the Expo that evening. Our tour guide, Jose, took us to a small restaurant off the beaten path. It was a real local place in the middle of nowhere. Paulie was still in a sour mood from all of the shenanigans that went on the day before, and he wouldn't stop talking about it. Finally, Jose, who had been very quiet up until this point, asked Paulie, "You know what they call that, right?" Paulie said, "call what?" Jose responded, "They call those Chichos." Then he grabbed Paulie's love handles. This sent Paulie into a frenzy. He jumped up and proclaimed that he couldn't take it anymore and that he was quitting the band and leaving!

He proceeded to leave the restaurant and walk down the lone dirt road to nowhere. As he was walking and got further and further away, we just laughed harder and harder. We could almost hear the theme from the old Incredible Hulk TV show playing while he walked that lonely road...Dun dun dun dun....Dun dun dun dun..dun.

Of course, Paulie didn't quit. We picked him up about a mile down the road and headed to the Hard Rock to get ready, but he was still quite upset. While we were getting ready, he wandered off for a little bit. Carlos and I had to use the restroom and what we found inside was the final straw. Paulie had Eric Singer cornered in the restroom, pinned up against a urinal trying to explain to him that Eric had hurt him so much by calling him fat. The sight of Paulie, who is about 6'3", looking down on Eric Singer, who's about 5'6", was absolutely comical. Eric looked terrified. We quickly came to his rescue and pulled Paulie out of there.

Eric must have felt bad because later when we were in our dressing room, putting on our costumes, he came in to hang out. He proceeded to tell Paulie all of the tricks that Paul Stanley used to hide his gut. He showed him how Paul would use double sided tape to keep his belt piece over his love handles. Paulie couldn't believe it. He said with a slight stutter and quiver in his lip, "You … you mean that Paul Stanley needs help hiding his love handles too?" This somehow made Paulie feel better — that his hero and idol suffered from the same problem he did. I realized during the KISSNATION trip to Puerto Rico that Paulie Z was a real mental case.

The show at the expo went great. I later heard from the person who ran the expo that Eric Singer was really impressed with my drumming and said I was easily the best drummer in any tribute band he'd ever seen. Now I just needed to get Gene and Paul to see me play one day!

In the late summer and early fall of 2002, KISSNATION was approached by VH1 to film the pilot episode of a new show they were developing called *Mock Rock*. It was a reality show about tribute performers. We, of course, accepted. I knew that there was a very low ceiling for a tribute band and that I couldn't fulfill my dreams playing other people's music, but these amazing opportunities were impossible to pass up and I was enjoying the great run we were having. The plan was for VH1 to follow us around in our everyday lives to see what kind of people we were, and then focus on what kind of planning and hard work it took to put on a tribute show.

I wasn't really into them filming my private life at home. My mom was starting to get sick pretty regularly with her breathing and I didn't think it was a good idea. Instead, I just had them follow me on a few drum lessons that I did. Looking back, I wish I had let them film my mom for the show. It would've been so great to have her talking about me growing up as a KISS fan on the TV show.

KISS drummer Eric Singer teaching Paulie Z how to hide his love handles in Puerto Rico, 2002.

It was pretty fun filming. I had never done anything like this and I was really enjoying it. We had the film crew and the main producer, Angela Quilala, following us to our gigs and to an appearance at the NY/NJ KISS expo. They filmed our every move: footage from our dressing room, when we were applying makeup, always wound up being the best content. Because the four members of KISSNATION were all different ethnicities (Carlos was Puerto Rican, Ruby was Indonesian, Paulie was Jewish, and I was Italian), somehow the conversation always turned racist. Now when I say racist, I mean in a joking manner towards each other.

After our Puerto Rico trip when I finally unleashed my ball breaking abilities, I became the lead dog when it came to trash talk. Because of this, the cameras always seem to fall on me. The only problem we were having was that the producer, Angela, kept telling us that the footage was hysterical, but they couldn't use most of it because we were either cursing or being too racist. We just couldn't help ourselves. We loved to bust each other's balls.

After a few months of filming, we were invited to Los Angeles by VH1 to attend a screening party for *Mock Rock*. It would be held at the world-famous Whisky a Go Go on the Sunset Strip. We were also scheduled to do a special performance at the event. I had never been to L.A. and was super excited to play the Whisky where all the famous L.A. bands got their start, like Van Halen, Motley Crue, and Ratt. If they were a big rock band in the 80's, chances are they started at the Whisky. Again, I knew that we were just a dopey tribute band, but we were doing some really cool shit!

KISSNATION UNMASKED!

The trip to L.A. was an absolute blast. All of the shenanigans that went on in Puerto Rico carried over. Paulie was a little thicker skinned at this point and the ribbing was more evenly distributed. I fell in love with L.A. right away and being flown out by VH1 to screen our very own TV show made it extra special. And all of this because I played drums and I loved KISS.

One of the very first things we saw in L.A. when were at The Whisky was singer Avril Lavigne riding down the street on her skateboard. I know what you're thinking: "Big deal," but at that time Avril had a huge song, "Skater Boy," and it was just wild seeing her riding her skateboard on Sunset Strip like a regular kid. L.A. was just like that.

VH1 put us up at the Beverly Hills Hotel. It was one of the best hotels in L.A., and it was where all the TV, movie, and rock stars stayed.

We felt pretty cool walking in. We weren't just a tribute band anymore. When someone asked who we were, we could legitimately say, "We're a band filming a special for VH1." Pretty cool!

On the day of the party, we would get to The Whisky early for a sound check. It felt magical as soon as I got on that stage, much like years earlier when I played L'amour with Playground. The Whiskey was the West-Coast version of L'amour, only even bigger!

The party was to be mid-afternoon. VH1 told us that for our performance, they were going to have the club opened to the public early so we had a good-sized crowd. They told us that the screening would follow shortly after the performance. We finished setting up and did the sound check at around 2:15, with the performance scheduled to begin around 3:30. It was time to start the hour-long process of applying makeup. Periodically, we would peek downstairs to see if the club was filling up yet, but it was completely dead every time we checked. We were a little bummed, but still happy to be at the Whisky and for the screening of our new TV show after the performance.

Our roadie/tour manager/photographer, Victor Lim, always introduced the band, and this night would be no exception. As we waited in the dressing room, which was on the second floor of the Whisky, we heard that familiar battle cry "You wanted the best. You got the best, the hottest band in the world: ...KISSNATION!"

When we emerged from the dressing room to take the stage, the scene was quite different than the last time we checked. The Whiskey was now packed from door to door. We couldn't believe our eyes! What happened? Not only was it now packed, but it was with young people and pretty girls, which if you've ever been to a KISSNATION show or any tribute show for that matter, you'd know it's usually filled with older, middle-aged people.

We didn't have time to question our good fortune. We took the stage and exploded into our blistering KISS show. The crowd was extra enthusiastic and we felt their energy. Not only were we playing at the infamous Whisky A Go Go, but the crowd was great, and we were there in honor of our brand new VH1 TV show. Things couldn't get any better. Or so we thought.

Towards the end of our set, while we were playing the song "Lick It Up," I noticed Carlos acting a little overly excited. I then glanced at Paulie and he also looked a little giddy. Carlos then came close to the drums and mouthed, "Look up!" and then he pointed. I was still a little confused and didn't notice anything out of the ordinary. Then I saw Ruby pointing up towards the balcony where a spotlight had just come on. Under that spotlight stood none other than Gene Simmons and Paul Stanley of KISS!

Wow! One of my childhood dreams was coming true right before my eyes. The air suddenly got thick, my breathing slowed down, and I could feel my heart beating. The moment began to freeze as I watched Gene and Paul smile down on me. For so many years and countless times, these roles were reversed: I had always been the one watching them on stage performing. Whether it was the first time when I was 5 years old at Madison Square Garden or the time when Jimmy and O'Grady and I took the bus from Port Authority by ourselves when we were 13 to go see KISS at the

***KISSNATION** in front of the infamous Rainbow Bar and Grill in Hollywood, CA.*

Meadowlands in New Jersey, I had always been the one in the audience watching Gene and Paul. Now, Gene and Paul were watching me play my drums to their songs.

I smiled in that "Frozen Moment" like I had never smiled before. As I slowly let the moment slip back into real time, I noticed the other guys in the band grinning from ear to ear.

We finished "Lick it Up" with a bang and only had the rock and roll national anthem left to do. Paulie quickly took to the mic and preached, while he looked up at Gene and Paul, "Besides my Bar Mitzvah, this is the greatest fuckin' day of my life!" That put a huge smile on Gene and Paul's face and we blasted into "Rock and Roll All Night."

The crowd went berserk! We never had more fun playing that song than we did that night. Somewhere towards the end of the song, it became a little unhinged due to all of our excitement. We got completely turned around at the end of the song and I had to quickly play an odd time measure to sync us back up. It worked, and we ended right on target.

As soon as we ended, Gene and Paul came up on stage to greet us and shake our hands. Paul then grabbed the microphone and said, "If we ever decide not to go out on tour, we'll just send these guys in our place." Gene then came over to me and said what a great job I did saving the ending by flipping it back around. I couldn't believe it. Not only had he heard what happened, he recognized and complimented how I fixed the problem.

Shortly after we got off stage, we went back to our dressing room and started high-fiving and hugging each other. We couldn't believe what was happening. Gene and Paul joined us a few moments later with the VH1 crew filming everything. They told us the whole story of how VH1 had contacted them and that they had watched a video of ours and absolutely loved it. We talked with them for about a half an hour about everything from our performance to Gene making fun of Carlos's hair. Even Gene and Paul got in on the "KISSNATION ball busting."

Tommy Thayer, who years later would replace Ace Frehley on guitar, was with Gene and Paul, filming their every move. Back then, Tommy was in charge of a lot of KISS's videography and producing their DVDs. Paul then told me that he couldn't believe not only how much I looked like Eric Carr, but how much I played and sang just like him. It was probably the greatest compliment I'd ever gotten in my life. To have one of my idols not only see me pay tribute to my drumming idol Eric Carr, but to then say that I played just like him was absolutely amazing. Gene and Paul then bid farewell and we were left to ponder what had just taken place.

Paul Stanley telling me that I sing and play drums exactly like Eric Carr on VH1's Mock Rock.

Angela, our producer, came in to talk to us about everything that had happened. She informed us that there was actually no screening for the show at all. The whole L.A. trip was a trick to get us to play in front of Gene and Paul as a surprise ending for the pilot episode of *Mock Rock*. Even the audience turned out to be actors and extras that were hired just to film the show. We couldn't believe it: what a great way to end an amazing trip and an amazing time filming for VH1.

The whole experience had been one of my favorites of my life. Unfortunately, KISSNATION's episode of *Mock Rock* never officially aired on VH1. The show didn't get picked up for series and they shelved the pilot. Luckily, they sent us the final cut to see and keep for ourselves. It turned out amazing and it's one of the things that I most cherish having done. It was my first real taste of filming and acting, and it provided me great preparation for so many things to come.

Shortly after we returned from filming for VH1 in L.A., Paulie mentioned that his original band was looking for a drummer. He asked me if I would be interested. I hadn't really heard any of Paulie's original material up until this point and I asked him to give me a recording to listen to. At the next KISSNATION rehearsal, Paulie handed me a four-song demo that he had been working on with his brother, Dave. I knew Dave really well already because he was often at our KISSNATION shows. Dave seemed cool enough and he was supposed to be a really good bass player. The songs on the Demo were "Takin Me Down," "Liar," "Wait," and "Head Up." They were going by the name of CO2.

To be honest, I didn't think much of the demo. The production quality was pretty crappy, and the songs weren't very memorable. The only song that I thought had any merit was "Wait." I could tell from the songs that they had a bit of a grunge influence; they weren't heavy, per se, but they sounded more in the vein of bands like Audioslave, Soundgarden, and Stone Temple Pilots. When I asked Paulie about this, he quickly confirmed that those were some of their biggest influences. Those bands were definitely not bands that I liked listening to or wanted to sound like.

Over the next few weeks, Paulie consistently bugged me to go and jam with them. I never really told him I didn't like the demo; I just kept putting him off. If nothing else, though, Paulie can be persistent and downright annoying when he wants something from someone. Because I constantly saw him at KISSNATION rehearsal and gigs, there was no way to avoid the subject. Finally, I just gave in and said, "Yes, I will come and jam."

I would discover years later that this was always Paulie's tactic to get what he wanted: torture someone and wear him down until the person said "yes" just to get Paulie to stop. It was always my intention to just go down this one time, so I could get him off my back.

Over the next few days, I learned the songs on the demo. Still, after a half dozen listens, none was sticking in my head. I also didn't care for any of the drum parts on the songs, especially the song "Head Up," which had a weird floor tom pattern in the verse that I would never write.

I asked Paulie later that week at KISSNATION rehearsal what had happened to their old drummer. He told me that his name was Ike and that he just wasn't a full-time musician looking to make it in the business. He also said that he and his brother had just started working with a producer friend of theirs named Bob Held, and he thought they should find another drummer. This new tidbit of information piqued my interest, so I asked him to tell me more about this producer and about his involvement in the project. Paulie went on to tell me that Dave met Bob Held while auditioning for the blues guitar player Joe Bonamassa. It turned out that Dave wasn't right for that gig, but the producer liked him and his playing and asked him if he had any original projects. Dave lied and said yes. At that time, Dave and Paulie weren't really playing together, but Dave lied and said that he had a band with his brother, Paulie. Shortly after, Bob helped them produce their 4-song demo, and while tracking they realized that they needed a new drummer, since Ike was more a finesse player where they wanted more of a John Bonham-type. Paulie quickly suggested me.

I jammed with Paulie and Dave for the first time in the late fall of 2002. I wasn't excited to go, but I did want to meet and talk with this producer they were working with to see if this was legit and what their plans were for the immediate future. Unfortunately, when I arrived at the studio, Bob the producer wasn't there. Over the next few hours, we plowed through the four songs they gave me. I added a little bit of my own feel to it and the songs definitely became a little more groovy and powerful. Paul and Dave seemed excited and wanted to set up the next time to play. Because I didn't have any other original projects going at that time, I thought, "Why not?" I figured I would at least jam with them until I met this producer guy, Bob.

At the next KISSNATION show, Paulie and Dave's producer friend Bob was there. I assumed he came down to check me out and to make sure I was a good drummer. Bob seemed like a nice enough guy when I met him, even though he wasn't what I pictured. (For some reason, I pictured a guy in a suit, very businesslike and professional.) Bob Held was anything but that: he was a bit overweight, schlubby guy, but, he seemed like a big teddy bear and was very nice. Bob Held was what people in the industry would refer to as a name dropper. At any opportunity he would mention the name of a pseudo-celebrity/musician that he either worked with or knew. Because I had just met him, and I guess he was trying to swoon me a little, Bob dropped names a plenty that first night.

After the KISSNATION show, Bob and I spoke for a while and I was impressed by his accomplishments in the business. He mentioned producing Joe Bonamassa and also said he produced a few albums for former Rainbow/Yngwie Malmsteen singer Joe Lynn Turner. This was all well and good, but it really didn't sell me yet on actually joining Paulie and Dave on a full-time basis. At the end of the conversation, probably strategically on Bob's part, he mentioned that he was good friends with Paul Stanley of KISS. This, of course, made my radar go up, and I think Bob knew it.

He then began to tell me that he spoke to Paul Stanley earlier in the week and mentioned to him about this new band he was working with. He told Paul that he was possibly going to be getting the drummer from the KISS tribute band KISSNATION. He reminded Paul that he had seen KISSNATION at the Whisky in L.A. for the VH1 show *Mock Rock* a few months prior. What he told me next is what solidified me finally joining with Paulie and Dave: "Paul Stanley told me that I should grab that drummer in KISSNATION immediately and that he thought he was fantastic!" I couldn't believe what I was hearing. Paul Stanley had actually told him personally that he thought I was "fantastic"!

I am a person that totally and whole-heartedly believes in fate. Everything that I had been through up until this moment in my music career was all leading me to a certain destination. Me finally being fed up with the business side of the "music business," because of my dealings with Valentine Smith, led me to answer the ad for the drummer wanted for KISSNATION. This, in turn, led to me playing the Whisky in front of Paul Stanley and Gene Simmons, which led to Paul Stanley telling Bob Held that he should grab me because he thought I was fantastic. It was fate!

Even though I was still wasn't 100 percent sold on their music, enough things were aligning to convince me to give it a shot. Once I told Paulie and Dave that I was in, we started to think of a name for the band.

Since Paulie, Dave, and I were all big fans of action figures and toys of all kinds, we all had an extensive collection of 80's action figures, anything from *Star Wars* to wrestling to He-Man. Because of this, we started to think of ideas for the band that had something to do with toys. The first idea for our band name was TOYZ spelled with a Z. We even went as far as thinking of stage show ideas involving toys. We had an idea of dressing the whole stage up like a toy store and us being some kind of life-size action figures. As ridiculous as this sounds, it fit with what we all loved. We all loved KISS and toys, and we thought this could be a way to merge the over-the-top KISS stage show with our love of toys. As you can imagine, this idea didn't last long.

Like I mentioned, Paulie's last band and the first incarnation of this band was called CO2. Paulie threw out one day that maybe we should just call the band ZO2 instead, switching the C for a Z because of Paulie and Dave's last name, kind of like Van Halen. We all just kind of agreed and went with it. Later, we thought of another meaning. Paulie and Dave's dad and uncle had a band in the 70's with an Italian drummer, Joey, they called "Z." So, ZO2 would be the new incarnation of "Z" formed in 2002. ZO2. So, towards the tail end of 2002, ZO2 was officially formed.

CHAPTER 19
THE BEGINNING OF ZO2

ZO2 taking their first set of promo pictures at our studio on 38th street in NYC.

Once I officially joined ZO2, I moved my drums out of the Valentine Smith studio and into ZO2's studio on 26th Street in Manhattan. It was a place called "The Green Door." Shortly after moving in, Paulie and Dave informed me that we had to take a little break due to the fact that Dave was leaving to go on tour with a band called TSO.

I asked, "What the hell is TSO?" Dave said, "It's short for Trans-Siberian Orchestra." I wasn't disappointed at all. I still wasn't really into ZO2's music, even though I felt a good energy when we played. I thought to myself, "Great, I could use a break from these guys."

Before Dave left, the guys confirmed that when Dave returned, they were headed, with Bob the producer, to a big music convention out in L.A. called NAMM. I had never heard of NAMM, but apparently it's where musicians gather to check out all of the new gear that's coming out the following year. They wanted me to come because they said it was a good place to meet people and talk up the band. I thought, "Talk about the band? The band was barely even a band yet." The convention fell right on my birthday that year and I just couldn't see myself spending money to go to some lame music convention with Paulie and Dave. Playing with them was okay, but spending my birthday with them, away from my family, wasn't going to happen.

As 2003 started, I was still playing pretty regularly with KISSNATION, but we hadn't had any of the high-profile gigs like the year before. It was starting to seem like we'd plateaued, and that the VH1 filming and having Gene and Paul see us play was the pinnacle of our success. We'd reached the ceiling and there was no place left to go.

Because KISSNATION was in sort of a down swing, we decided not to rehearse as much. Since we had more free time now, ZO2 began to rehearse once a week in KISSNATION's place. We began writing new songs so we could eventually play live. At that time, all we had were the 4 songs from their old demo. Bob Held would usually come to the rehearsals to help generate ideas for new music, and this at least made it feel more professional and focused. Somehow having a seasoned producer in rehearsal made it worthwhile for me to go every week. It also kept Paulie and Dave focused. They had a tendency to argue about the smallest little things and it would cause rehearsals to last forever.

I was quickly learning that Paulie and Dave were strange. Some things they did would cause me to question why I was playing with them. Paulie always gave me a ride to my apartment in the West Village after rehearsal. One night, we went to a nearby deli and Paulie bought a sandwich for himself. Once we got into the van and started driving, Paulie began to eat. Dave, who was in the front seat next to him, asked for a bite of his sandwich. The way I grew up, this was nothing out of the ordinary. My friends and I would always share things like that. If we all went out to dinner, the gracious thing to do was to offer someone a taste of your meal. This was the moment I realized that Paulie and Dave were very different than I was, and grew up differently too. Paulie looked flabbergasted that Dave would even ask for a bite of his precious sandwich. After a few minutes of arguing, Paulie told Dave that the bite would cost him 50 cents. Dave protested the price tag, and Paulie then pulled the van over on 7th Avenue to begin breaking down exactly why

50 cents was the correct price for a bite. After about 15 minutes of this intelligent discussion, Dave finally agreed and gave Paulie the 50 cents. Unfortunately for me, though, this argument was just getting started.

Once Dave paid for his bite, they began the discussion of how big a bite would be allowed. This went on for another 15 minutes until they agreed upon bite size. It didn't end there: Dave took hold of the sandwich and took what Paulie deemed "too big of a bite." Paulie screamed in outrage and began demanding more money for the bite that Dave had taken. At that moment, I decided to get out of the van and walk the rest of the way home. I don't even think they noticed I'd left. As I walked away, I thought to myself, "What the hell have I gotten myself into playing with these two maniacs?"

Sometime in February of 2003, ZO2 was forced to move studios. Our old room at the Green Door building on 26th Street was about to become unavailable. We found a monthly room in the Manhattan Music Building on 8th Avenue between 37th and 38th Streets. We would be sharing the room with a few other bands and musicians, and we would all split the days each month.

We would rehearse on Tuesdays and Thursdays. Once we moved into the music building, we started to focus on writing new material.

Inside ZO2's rehearsal studio. Notice KISSNATION's KISS sign in the background.

After about a month, we decided to record a quick demo just to assess the songs and the arrangements.

Early ZO2 promo shot. For some reason Dave thought we should always have our shirts off. Lol.

I had just recently purchased an electronic drum kit and we decided to record the drums on that. I bought the top-of-the-line Roland V drum kit. It was the best purchase I'd ever made! Before being thrown out of my two homes in Brooklyn and being forced to move to Manhattan, I'd played my drums every single day. Since moving to Manhattan, I had no way of practicing unless I went to a rehearsal studio. With my newly purchased electronic kit, I could finally practice anytime I wanted.

Dave came over to my apartment one afternoon and, while my mom was watching TV in the next room, we digitally recorded the drum tracks to 5 songs for our demo. It was incredible! Because my drums were all digital, they went directly into Dave's laptop and into Pro Tools. Recording drums had never been easier or quieter. The songs we recorded that day included:

1- Identity
2- Verge of War
3- Center of the Universe
4- 12 o'clock
5- I Don't Mind

None of the songs were particularly good. A couple had catchy parts, but as whole they were a bit of a mess. As great as the V-drums were, they sounded fake, especially the cymbals, but this demo wasn't meant to be shown around or anything; like I mentioned, it was just to evaluate where we were with our original songs.

During this time, Paulie and Dave were also very into odd meter changes, something I was not a fan of. I thought music was all about two things: groove and melody. They were still young song writers and I think they were trying to impress other musicians with the odd time signatures. After that first demo, I quickly put a stop to that. Even though we all agreed that none of the songs were amazing, we thought we had enough ready to book our first gig.

A few days after the demo was complete, Dave said that he had the perfect first gig for us. The Trans-Siberian Orchestra was having a special night where their members could showcase their original acts. It was called "TSO Originals Night" at the Cutting Room in NYC. Paulie and I said, "Sure, why not," but Bob wasn't as quick to agree. He didn't think it was a right mix for us to play with the other members of TSO. Dave and Paulie absolutely disagreed and I still didn't even know enough about TSO to bring any kind of opinion. Even with Bob's hesitation, we decided to do the show. So, on March 6, 2003, ZO2 played its very first gig at The Cutting Room. We were still really raw and didn't know what kind of direction we were headed in.

My fashion style was basically the same as it had been since the eighth grade. Paulie and Dave both had short hair and Paulie's was a bright fluorescent red. Our look was as mish-moshed as our songs. We opened with the first song the three of us had written together as ZO2 called "Identity." It was a very odd opener.

To open the show, Paulie and Dave were crouched down as low as they could go and then as the intro to "Identity" slowly built up, they slowly rose to their feet. When the song finally kicked in, they jumped and began flailing around the stage. It was strange, to say the least.

Immediately following the opening song, we did the ZO2 opening that everyone is now familiar with: "Hello, We Are, ZO2." It felt so weird doing it in second place, even back then. I believe in 2003 we did it this way for the first few shows. We actually even did a good-bye version right before the last song using the same melody as the intro. It went something like this: "Goodbye, Goodnight, We Love You."

The show went okay and we got a good response from the crowd. My lifelong friend, Scally, was in attendance. To this day, he's the only person who has seen me play live with every one of my band incarnations.

I didn't stick around long after the show because I was leaving at 5:30 am the next morning to go to my good friend Ernie's bachelor party in Key West, Florida. By the time I packed up my drums, had a drink, and drove to Brooklyn to meet the other guys who were going to the bachelor party, it was almost 4 am. I never did get to sleep that night— not a good way to start a bachelor party weekend.

Once I was in Key West, I really didn't think much about the gig that I had just played. ZO2, at that time, still felt like a little side project I was just doing to keep busy. I was enjoying my time with my Hamptons friends and still playing with KISSNATION.

ZO2's first show. The Cutting Room, NYC 3-6-03

The bachelor party trip was wild! We drank the whole flight to Key West and were feeling pretty good by the time we landed. I was awake for about 48 hours and drinking for about 12 of those by the time we decided to go out on that first night. Needless to say, I was already a little delirious by the time we got to the bar to start partying for Ernie. By the time 4 am rolled around, the whole crew broke off into smaller groups. After about 10 more Sambuca shots, my friend Lu Lu and I decided to call it a night. Once back at the hotel I was informed by everyone that our friend Tommy (former singer from Playground) got himself thrown out of the hotel earlier. I couldn't believe no one tried to help him or even cared that he got thrown out. I told my roommate Carmine that I was going down to the front desk to straighten everything out!

I can't quite remember the next 15 minutes, but I know I got into a big argument with the front desk attendants. What was said or done? I have no idea. I went back up to my room and informed Carmine that I think we might all be getting thrown out of the hotel. Carmine laughed it off and jokingly said, "I'm not going anywhere unless the police throw me out. Two seconds later there was a loud bang on the door: "This is the police! Open up!" Sure enough we were all getting thrown out of the hotel, about 20 of us in all, due to whatever I did while I was attempting to "straighten everything out" in the lobby.

One of the guys we were with was a transit cop in NYC and was able to cool the situation a little. Now only the people in my room had to immediately leave the premises. Carmine snuck into one of the other rooms while the police were making me pack my bags. So the only person getting thrown out now was me!

The police proceeded to escort me off the premises. That's where I found Tommy along with my friend Spider still outside arguing with the police. Once we were together, the police informed us that if we were caught on the premises again we would immediately be arrested.

Because the rest of the bachelor party was still staying at this hotel and because we didn't want to miss out on any partying, the next afternoon Tommy and I decided to buy disguises and sneak back into the hotel.

It worked like a charm, at least until we decided shed our disguises to go in the pool. The hotel manager recognized us immediately and rushed over screaming that he was calling the police. Tommy and I quickly grabbed our stuff and got the hell out of there.

I would give anything to see the security footage of me in the lobby that night trying to "straighten everything out!" I can only imagine.

Upon returning from my trip, I was surprised to hear that ZO2 had already booked our next few shows. The second was at The King's Lounge in Long Island, and the next few shows were all pretty uneventful. The crowds were very sparse. We were just trying to figure out who exactly we were as a band.

Because I never thought of ZO2 as a serious project, and I felt like KISSNATION had reached its peak, I decided to spend most of the summer of 2003 with my friends in our rental house out in the Hamptons again. It turned out to be one of the best decisions of my life.

Tommy, Spider and me wearing our disguises after getting thrown out of our hotel in Key West.

My Family

Christmas time with The Cassatas!

Vacation Time

One of my favorite pictures ever.
My family facetiming me right before
I hit the stage with The Great Comet

Madalyn & I on our wedding day

Madalyn with her Mom & Angelina

With my little girl Angelina

With my boy Joe

Flying like superman with my Grandpa 1979

Me and my big brother Danny

Me and my Mom

Me and Yukon

My mom, baby Yukon and me

Angelina with her Mom, Grandmother
and Great Grandmother

Me & my big brother Danny 1987

30 years later at my wedding 2007

Me and Danny at my 8th grade graduation

My father , Danny & I at Danny's wedding

Me, Mom & Danny at my Hampton's house. Summer 2002

Christmas eve with my brother Dan & his beautiful family

Madalyn & I on Halloween

Maybe the best present I ever recieved.
World's greatest dad championship belt!

1988

2018

My grammar school friends. 30 years of friendship

Me & my lifelong buddy Scally

Me & the boys at Phils wedding

Me & my buddy Brian O'Grady

Age 8

Age 18

Age 28

Age 38

Me and the boys all dressed up at Daly's wedding 2002

On our way to Jimmy's Bachelor party on a cruise to Nova Scotia. This was taken a week before the twin tower attacks on 9/11/2001

Getting ready to go to the
Boardy Barn in the Hampton's

We constructed a 20 foot beer funnel

Flexing & funneling by the pool.

My first solo promo shot

Playground at Rockaway Studios

Me as Eric Carr with Gene Simmons & Paul Stanely

Sevenwiser at the Wind-Up Records release party

KISSNATION'S last show 2004

Playing arounfd on Eric Singer's KISS set

The BIG KIT!

My Ludwig Vistalites with Rubix Kube

KISS, POISON & ZO2 drums

ZO2 & KISS on the Rock The Nation Tour

ZO2 on the road fighting over food as usual

ZO2 & POISON

**The drummers for the Rock the Nation Tour
Rikki Rocket, Eric Singer & Joey Cassata**

ZO2's First Show at Arlene's Grocery

Brooklyn boys

Dave Z controlling the crowd like only he could

A rare Z Brothers promo shot

Playing a Z Brothers concert so I took my girl Angelina with me

Super Hero poses for Casino Logic CD

About to hit the stage in Dallas on the KISS Tour

Z Rock promo poster

IFC Red Carpet with Bethenny Frankel, Constantine Maroulis and Sabastian Bach

Playing to a sold out crowd of 14,000

Having fun with Kim Kardashian on the Red Carpet

Backstage shenanigans with Twisted Sister

FROM "ROCK 'N' ROLL" ... TO "ROCK-A-BYE-BABY".

Z ROCK

SUNDAYS 11:30 PM

iFC series, uncut.

SEASON 2

Z ROCK season 1 & 2 DVD promo poster

A cupcake cheers with Dave Navarro in Z Rock

Getting thrown out of the casino on Z Rock

With Frank Stallone & Andrew Gottlieb

Z Brothers Promo Picture

A wacky Z Rock photo shoot

A bizzare Z Rock photo shoot

ZO2, Daryl Hall and Lynn Koplitz

Going over Z Rock scripts with Sabastian Bach

Anthrax's Joey Belladonna & ZO2 doing our QUEEN pose

Jamming on Z Rock with Dave Navarro

Z Rock producers with John Popper

Hanging with NSYNC's Lance Bass

On the set of Z Rock with Chris Barron

Chapstick Commercial?

On set laughs with Dee Snider

The new Stallone brothers...Joey & Frankie!

Having a few drinks with Chris Jericho

Playing Wiffleball with Bret Michaels

Mick Foley teaching me about tough love

Jamming with Mike Portnoy on his monstrous kit

This would be one hell of a band!
ZO2 & Ace Frehley

Trying to take down NFL
Hall of Famer Warren Sapp

Joeylicious & "Rowdy" Roddy Piper

Singing the Russian national
anthem with Nikolai Volkoff

Joeylicious co star,
comedian Rachel Feinstein

The last ZO2 show

ZO2 had so much more to do. RIP Dave Z

Almost 300 shows played with
Josh Groban

Angelina watching me on Broadway

Or Matias & Myself on our way to Europe

Recording the Great Comet

The Great Comet band outside of Radio City Music Hall
about to play the Tony awards

Wrestling has many legends...

He's not one of them!

Wrestling with Joeylicious

It's been amazing filming with all of my child hood heroes for Wrestling With Joeylicious

Playing a sold out show at The Great Comet on Broadway

VICTOR

Doing voicovers with Gilbert Gottfried

12 TONY AWARD NOMINATIONS INCLUDING BEST MUSICAL

The Great Comet led all Tony nominiations with 12!

CHAPTER 20

SUMMER LOVIN'. HAD ME A BLAST

In late April, I attended my friend Ernie's wedding rehearsal dinner and I thought it would just be another night out with the guys. Then something entirely unexpected happened; I fell in love.

Ernie's wife, Colleen, had a bunch of girls in her bridal party and one in particular caught my attention. Her name was Madalyn. She was beautiful and exactly my type. She was a petite little Italian girl with long curly hair — as cute as can be. I noticed her first in church while we were going over what to do at the wedding.

No one was really paying attention to the priest while he was talking, especially me and the two guys I was with, Steve and Tommy from my old Playground days. We had already been drinking for a few hours over at Steve's apartment before arriving at the church.

Once the rehearsal at the church was finished, we were all heading over to a bar/restaurant called The Salty Dog. I quickly grabbed my friend Carmine to walk with me, then I saw Madalyn walking out the door. I wanted to make sure she was going over to the dinner.

Once at The Salty Dog I started to do what I do best. No, not play the drums — get people drunk! I was hoping that Madalyn was a drinker. It was really the only shot I had because I hated small talk with girls. My way of talking to her was to order shots and then do them with her. It worked like a charm.

At one point, I ordered a tray of 18 black Sambuca shots. Sambuca had always been my shot of choice ever since my buddy Damien would steal a bottle from his parents' basement every Friday night back when we were 14 years old.

Everything was going according to plan. Madalyn was getting tipsy and I was already drunk. I then used my pick-up line on her, which is still discussed as legendary. Just to set it up correctly, Madalyn was about 5'2" and 105 pounds. So, being the ball buster that I am, I said to her, "You know, you could be a plus-size model if you had a pretty face." Her face dropped and then I suddenly felt a burning pain on the top of my head. The bride-to-be's mother hit me over the head with her cane after hearing what I had just said to Madalyn. I think Madalyn thought it was funny. After another few hours of flirting, Madalyn left. I didn't get her number or anything. I just hoped I'd see her again at the wedding. I couldn't stop thinking about her over the next few days and I couldn't wait to see her again.

I know people think I'm outgoing and extroverted, but I'm actually very shy around someone I care about. The only way that I could open up was, of course, to have a few drinks. Fortunately for me, all the guys in the wedding party liked to drink as much as I did. We started drinking right after breakfast on the morning of the wedding.

Once we got to the church, I got to see her again. She looked beautiful in her bridesmaid dress. Her hair was up and her face was stunning. After the ceremony, we spent an hour or so taking pictures with the entire wedding party. Madalyn and I continued to flirt the whole time. Things were going great again. After the pictures, the guys and girls split up to head over to the wedding reception.

Once at the reception, we all met back up in the bridal suite. This is when the bride, Colleen, gave me some really bad news. I asked her where Madalyn was, and she said she had to meet her date down at the cocktail hour. I was devastated. I couldn't believe it. But, I wasn't going

Madalyn and I in the wedding party where we met.

to let that stop me. Not to brag, but I had never chased after a girl in my whole life, but I wasn't going to let this one get away so easily.

Once Madalyn came back up to the bridal suite, I immediately confronted her in a very playful manner. I said, "What is this I hear, you have a date?" She knew that we had been flirting the whole time and she was very apologetic. She went on the explain that it was just some guy she asked to the wedding. She didn't care about him being there. I told her, "If you want to get away from him at any time in the night just give me "the high sign" and we'll meet in the bridal room." I then mimicked the old classic "Little Rascals" TV show high sign that they would give each other. I put my hand under my chin and wiggled my fingers in a waving motion. She said, "Okay, I got it!"

I had no idea if she was serious or not, but at least I had a little hope left. Right after the best man speech, I tried to catch her eye. The problem was that she was sitting on the other side of the room with all of the bride's guests. I finally caught her eye and quickly flashed her the

The Little Rascals High Sign.

"high sign." This was it. If she didn't respond, I knew my chances of getting her were over.

To my overwhelming surprise, she flashed it back at me. For two people trying to be inconspicuous, the high sign probably wasn't the best way to go about it. But, I didn't care. I quickly got up and went to the bridal suite where she joined me moments later. As soon as she entered, I grabbed her and kissed her. I can still feel and taste that very first kiss we shared that night. It sounds cheesy, but it felt like it was right out of some corny movie when fireworks would go off as two people kissed. It was magical.

We continued the same shenanigans throughout the night, every 20 minutes or so. Either she or I would flash the high sign and we'd meet up in the bridal suite. After a while, her date started to get suspicious and began looking to see where she was going. I had my friend Carmine stand guard at the door just in case.

I made sure that I didn't leave the wedding without getting Madalyn's phone number so I could ask her to come to my Hamptons house which started soon.

A few days after the wedding, I scheduled a meeting with all of the people involved with the Hamptons house. I told them that we needed to go over the bills and the general rules for guests. It was really all a

Madalyn and I in the Hamptons Winery, 2003.

sham. I just wanted to see Madalyn again, but was too shy to ask her out on a one-on-one date. I figured if I could see her again with everyone around, it would be more comfortable. It worked like a charm. Once she was there, it felt just like the wedding again– no awkward date conversation, no weird silences. It was like I'd known her my whole life. I'd never felt like this before. It just felt right.

I also used this opportunity to invite her to come to the house whenever she wanted. She said that she'd love to come and I became excited and nervous all at the same time. This would be the start of one of my favorite summers of all time.

The summer of 2003 consisted of me spending every weekend with Madalyn and all of my friends in the Hamptons, then during the week I started writing new material with ZO2. The band only had access to the shared rehearsal room on Tuesdays and Thursdays. Paulie, Dave, and our producer, Bob, decided we needed to make a full-length, professional sounding CD with all the bells and whistles, an idea I was completely against for many reasons. I didn't see the need for a full-length CD: what would that do for us? If the idea was to get picked up by a record label, then all we would need is a demo.

Lastly, it was going to cost a small fortune to make and record. I found out Bob was asking for $10,000 to produce the CD. I couldn't believe it. I told the guys that there was no way we should be paying Bob all that money and spending thousands more to make a CD. I was financially responsible for my mom at this point, and there was no way I could afford such a thing, nor did I want to.

Paulie and Dave said that they would front the money, all to be paid for on credit cards. I could pay them back at a later date. I still voiced my vote against doing it, but because I didn't have to come up with the money right away and because ultimately, I was outvoted (which would become a regular occurrence), I went along with the plan to record a full-length CD. We would start writing extensively every Tuesday and Thursday, from 8pm until the wee hours of the morning during the summer of 2003.

It was the perfect mix of fun and work. All week I would be rehearsing with ZO2 and writing for the album, then I spent every weekend partying with my friends and falling more in love with Madalyn. In fact, towards the end of the summer, Madalyn and I were officially "in love" and ZO2 had the right songs for the album; things were starting to come together.

Right in the middle of all of this, Paulie and Dave informed me that they had been approached by another band called Sevenwiser to play a showcase for a big record label. I told them, "Of course, you should do it." I was genuinely excited for them. I thought this was a huge opportunity for them. I'd been working my whole life to play in front of a record label. I didn't think they should pass it up.

A few days later at ZO2 rehearsal, Paulie and Dave informed me that the showcase went great and that the band got signed to Wind-up Records. I was so happy for them. What amazing news! But they didn't seem that happy. They said that they were undecided about whether or not to play with Sevenwiser or to continue on with ZO2. Paulie was especially skeptical because he would only be playing guitar in Sevenwiser and not singing. Basically, neither was sure if he wanted to be back-up musicians for someone else's band or do his own thing.

I personally thought they were crazy. They had a band signed to Wind-up Records that wanted them. Wind-up was very popular at this time. They had the hugely successful Creed as clients and just recently released Evanescence first CD. They were slowly becoming the "It" label. I told them both, "Why not go and play with Sevenwiser and see how it goes? Worse case, you can use that to further ZO2." I thought it was very sound reasoning and advice. They said that they'd have to think it over and would decide in the next few weeks.

About two weeks later, Paulie and Dave said that they got a call from the manager of the band that was signed to Wind-up. He had been to a ZO2 show while scouting Paulie and Dave and mentioned that he also really loved my drumming. It turned out that they were now potentially looking for a new drummer and wanted to know if I would be interested in coming down to audition. Of course, I immediately said yes, which I think took them by a bit of a surprise. I never pretended or misled any band I've ever been in. My ultimate goal was always first, and my friendship and loyalty to any particular band was always second. I'm not sure why they were so surprised that I was interested in auditioning for a band that was signed to a major label. Hadn't I just given them that exact advice only a few weeks prior? I received the Sevenwiser demo a few days later and began learning the songs. I actually really liked the material; it sounded contemporary and in line with what was happening in the rock music world in 2003. It was definitely very radio friendly.

I went to the audition in early August 2003. Paulie and Dave were also there because they still hadn't decided exactly what they were going to do. I met the singer, Jon Santos, guitarist Joe Bell, and their manager/producer Sandy Thomas. All of them seemed nice upon my first meeting, and the audition went perfectly. Not only did I know all of the material, but I had been playing with Dave on bass for over a year now and it was pretty easy to lock in with him. I got a call the next day inviting me to lunch.

I wasn't nervous for the meeting, but I definitely knew that this could possibly be the moment I'd worked my whole life for: a shot at being in a band on a major label. All the years of shopping for a record deal could possibly be coming to an end. I met with Sandy and Jon at Figaro Cafe in the village. That was my go-to spot. It's even where I scheduled the semi-fake Hamptons house meeting so I could see Madalyn again. I thought returning might bring me some good luck. Sandy started off by saying that not only did he love my playing, but he really loved the chemistry that Paulie, Dave, and I had together. He then offered me the job on the spot.

I didn't want to show my excitement, so I calmly said that if the offer was contractually good, I would definitely be interested. They were offering me more of a hired gun position and not the role of full band member. I assumed it was the same sort of deal they were offering Paulie and Dave. I was totally okay with it as long as the guaranteed money was good. I also assumed that's why Paulie and Dave weren't as quick to accept the offer. Sandy said that he would have a contract drafted for me within a few days. I still didn't want to celebrate, but I was very happy and excited. I thought to myself, "This was the break I'd been waiting for".

Sevenwiser
Jon Santos - Vocals
Joe Bell - Lead Guitar
Paulie Z - rhythm guitar
Dave Z - Bass
Joey Cassata - Drums

That same night, I went to ZO2 rehearsal and told the guys that Sevenwiser had offered me the gig. I thought they would be happy, but instead they told me that they had decided earlier that day not to take the Sevenwiser gig. I couldn't believe what I was hearing. I told them I thought they were making a huge mistake and explained it could only benefit us and not hurt ZO2. I explained, "If Sevenwiser became huge, then great for all of us. We would then have money and some industry clout if we ever wanted to launch ZO2 again. Worst case scenario,

Sevenwiser bombed and then we could just pick up ZO2 where we left off."

They wouldn't even listen to my suggestion and advice. They both had Bob in their ears telling them that it was a huge mistake to go with Sevenwiser. I'm 100 percent positive that Bob was doing this strictly out of selfish financial reasons. Paulie and Dave listened to everything Bob said like he was God. It would be a battle between us for many years to come.

I think they believed that if they didn't take the offer from Sevenwiser, then surely I would also turn them down. They couldn't have been more wrong. They were absolutely crushed when I told them I was still accepting the offer that was on the table — not only crushed, but shocked that I would do that. I told them that I would still record the album and do any shows we had booked as long as it didn't conflict with Sevenwiser. At one point, Paulie even said, "We never should have even told you that they were interested in you as their drummer, then none of this would be happening." That was the difference between us. I was genuinely happy for both of them when they told me about Sevenwiser. In complete contrast, they were actually upset with me for wanting to do it.

I think Paulie and Dave thought they had something to prove. Even though they weren't much younger than I was, ZO2 was going to be their first real band. Yes, they had been in other bands and Dave was even with TSO, but ZO2 was something that they decided they were going to start from the ground up and build into something. I had already been through starting a band from ground zero a dozen times before. I'd also been through the countless number of shitty gigs and years of chasing the illustrious "Record Deal." Paulie actually said to me that he didn't want a record contract yet. He said he wanted to go through the years of struggle because he felt he had to pay his dues. I had already paid my dues a thousand times over and I was ready for the record contract and to fulfill my dream to finally start making money as a professional drummer.

We used to argue this point all the time. Us both being huge KISS fans, Paulie would try to argue that KISS, and bands like KISS, had really paid their dues before making it! That's what he wanted and he thought that's what I should want. My response was always the same:

bands like KISS did pay their dues to a certain extent, but nothing compared to what guys like me went through.

When KISS released their first record, Paul Stanley was only 22 years old! I'm sure he paid some dues by playing in bands for a few years, but I had started gigging at the age of 14. I was now approaching 30 and was still grinding every day, trying to make it in the music business. That's 16 years of dues! 99.9 percent of people would have long given up their dream after just a few years, but not me!

That's why it's always so comical to me when I read books by mega rock stars and they all preach about "paying their dues." They were all rich and famous before they were 25 years old. How many "dues" did they really pay? Let's see any one of them struggle for 15 years while working as many jobs as possible and helping to support their families. That's "paying dues!" I'd paid enough dues for 5 lifetimes. I was ready for success!

Over the next few weeks, while I was negotiating my contract with Sevenwiser, ZO2 was beginning pre-production on the debut album. Most of the songs were ready to be recorded, and we were scheduled to go into the recording studio to begin tracking in October 2003. I'd also just scheduled tracking for the Sevenwiser debut album for Wind-up records. In fact, I recorded the Sevenwiser record only a few days before recording the ZO2 record. It was all becoming a very strange situation.

Sevenwiser would track their album at Pie Studios in Long Island. I was to be paid a nice amount to track the songs, and it felt really good to finally be part of a professional operation — that was until I got into the recording studio. I recorded my tracks on an old 60's black Öyster Ludwig kit. It was beautiful, just like Ringo's from the Beatles. The first problem I noticed was when we started to get drum sounds.

Getting drum sounds is a very tricky thing. So much goes into it, from the size of the room to the placement of the mics on the drums to the placement of the mics throughout the room. It is a long, tedious process, but a process with which I was very familiar. That's why when we started to get sounds for the Sevenwiser album, the approach of the producer surprised me.

About 10 minutes into getting sounds, the producer said in my talk back mic, "Okay, we got it." I assumed by that he meant, okay, we have signals and now we can start to get sounds. But he meant that he was

Tracking the Sevenwiser album at Pie Studious in Long Island, NY, Fall 2003

happy with the sounds he was hearing. I thought to myself, "Impossible!" I then asked if I could come in and hear what they got. I knew the Ludwig kit I was playing was fantastic, but there was no way they could have gotten sounds in 10 minutes. Sure enough, when I entered the control room, the drums sounded like tin cans. The producer must have seen my face because he immediately got defensive and said, "Don't worry, we are going to use a lot of plug ins and triggers to beef up the sound in post-production." I knew this was the wrong approach and a disaster waiting to happen. It was okay to use those things in post-production but it's imperative to start with a killer drum sound as a base to work off of. I had to go along with it because I was just a hired gun, and the record label was paying for studio time and they wanted to start tracking.

Tracking went smoothly, albeit a little stale and lifeless. I was going to be tracking to Sevenwiser's old demo. They were undecided about whether to re-record some of the other tracks like bass, guitar, and vocals. So, I just basically played along to their old demo with my new drum parts. It was a lifeless session. All of my songs were done in 1 or 2 takes. As soon as my tracks were done, my job was over. Again, this was something I wasn't used to. I can say this: the years with Valentine Smith did prepare me for my first major record label experience. It wasn't the exciting experience of recording my first major label album that I thought it was going to be. I just hoped it sounded okay.

Just a few days later, I began recording ZO2's album at Unique Studios in NYC. From the start, the process was exactly the opposite of the Sevenwiser experience. Paulie and Dave had never really done a big recording for their own band in a major recording studio, so they were excited and extremely energized. What ZO2 was lacking in pure "hit songwriting" it made up for tenfold with sheer energy and vibe. Getting drum sounds for this record was once again night and day different than the Sevenwiser recording just a few days earlier. We spent hours making sure that drums were perfect so that could be used to anchor the rest of the album. And it was...damn near perfect.

Once tracking began, we did it more old-school style and not the lifeless way I had recorded the Sevenwiser album. We attempted to track all the rhythmic instruments at the same time. Even though we were assuming we'd only keep the drum tracks, it was my favorite way to record. In essence, it was the three of us playing live. Paulie was in the control room tracking guitars, Dave was in an isolated booth tracking bass, and I was in the massive main room tracking drums. The very first song we tracked was "Radio."

Everything was going super smooth until we got to the song "Takin' Me Down." This was one of the songs from their old demo and I never particularly liked the drum pattern that the old drummer was doing. Ever since ZO2 started gigging, I had changed the drum pattern to more of what I would play and write. This apparently went unnoticed by Paulie, Dave, and Bob, but when we began tracking, Dave immediately stopped the take and said, "That's not the drum pattern from the demo." I replied, "Yeah, I changed that months ago." This comment caused a bit of a frenzy.

I went into the control room where I was confronted by Paulie, Dave, and Bob. They explained that when writing that original demo, they had worked hard to come up with that drum pattern. Bob went so far as to say that every single kick drum was carefully thought out. I politely explained that they weren't drummers and really didn't know how to write a good drum pattern and that the pattern was very spacious and not groovy. They, of course, liked it because it sounded complicated and slightly off beat. We debated and/or argued about it for the next hour, depending how one looks at it. They were strangely attached to this ridiculous drum pattern. It was already the end of the night, so I told

ZO2 tracking Tuesday's & Thursday's at Unique Studios in Times Square, NYC, 2003.

them that I'd learn the pattern and do it tomorrow. I came in the next morning with a slightly modified version of their pattern. I purposely kept in the few off beats that I knew they were weirdly attached to. Since tracking "Takin' Me Down," I have never played that pattern again, and no one ever even noticed. I thought to myself, "I'm dealing with nut jobs!"

Once my tracking was completed, I still came to the studio every day to be a part of all the other tracking and the mix. Hearing that ZO2 album come together was the first time I started to get really excited about ZO2. There was a raw energy vibe that we really captured.

On one of the last days of tracking background vocals, Bob told us that he had a little surprise for us. A few minutes later, legendary rock singer Joe Lynn Turner walked through the door. Joe was famous for his days in Richie Blackmore's Rainbow and singing with Yngwie Malmsteen. At first, we thought he was just there to say hello, but Bob informed us that he was going to be laying down some background vocals to our song "Dirty Water." Up until this point, I thought Bob was just a name dropper and someone that liked to exaggerate about the people he knew and worked with. Actually, I still thought he was that person, but at least bringing in Joe Lynn gave some validity to his boasts.

Joe Lynn's vocals definitely made the choruses much fatter and warmer, but having him on the album was more to give ZO2 a bit of street cred. I knew in the grand scheme of things having Joe Lynn sing some background vocals on our album meant nothing. But, to the outside world and to everyday people, when I mentioned we had Joe Lynn Turner from Rainbow singing on the album, they immediately took us seriously. It was just the way of the world. Perception is reality.

This was a weird time period. As ZO2 was getting more and more excited about the album and talk of the future, in the back of everyone's mind, especially mine, we knew that I was also a member of Sevenwiser. Both albums wound up being mixed, mastered, and finished at the same time. The quality wasn't even close: the ZO2 album sounded warm and powerful while the Sevenwiser album sounded tinny and thin. Bob did an outstanding job producing along with Gary Tole as the engineer. But there were still two very big things in Sevenwiser's favor that I just couldn't overlook: they were signed to a major label and their songs were all radio friendly. I was at another crossroads in my career, and I knew I'd have to make a big decision.

Luckily, I wouldn't have to make that decision anytime soon. After both albums were finished, it was time for Dave to leave on tour with TSO again. This gave me a few months of straight Sevenwiser rehearsals without having to somehow split my time with ZO2. My contract hadn't been fully ironed out with Sevenwiser yet, and the next few months were pretty stressful trying to get it done.

Joe Bell, Sevenwiser's guitarist, introduced me to a lawyer named Gary Adleman who would be negotiating our contracts for us. In November 2003, Sevenwiser also hired two new members to replace Paulie and Dave.

Negotiating my contract was difficult. Sevenwiser's manager/producer, Sandy Thomas, was a real jerkoff. He was the type of guy that would yes you to your face and then do something completely different behind your back. It was important for me to get the right deal because I was becoming more and more financially responsible for my mom.

About 6 months prior, she had a collapsed lung and was officially diagnosed with emphysema. She wasn't doing well at all and I knew this was my shot to not only take care of her, but to possibly get her out of that stupid little apartment in the city and maybe buy her a house back in Brooklyn. It was all I wanted now. I didn't care about being a "rock star" anymore. It was more about being able to take care of my mom, the one person who had taken care of me all my life. I knew the only way I would be able to do that was through my drums.

Paulie, Dave, and Bob never understood that I needed that financial stability for my mom. Once Dave came back from TSO, and if I had the right contract negotiated, my mind was made up: I would leave ZO2 and stay with Sevenwiser.

Madalyn was a paralegal at a law firm in Manhattan and she was a real wiz with contracts and wording. Even though I had a lawyer, Madalyn was the one to constantly make changes and negotiate my contract for me. Gary was always surprised at all of the intelligent things Madalyn asked for and put into the contract. Finally, after about two months of negotiations and dozens of hours on the phone with Sandy, the contract was finished and signed. There was one major clause that I wanted in: I wanted a way to be able to terminate my contract at any point. I remained skeptical about Sandy's intentions after the two months of negotiations. I started to have a funny feeling in my gut that he was up to no good. I insisted on the clause and they obliged.

Once Dave returned from the TSO tour, ZO2 began playing a residency at Arlene's Grocery in NYC every Monday night. It was perfect. Sevenwiser was still in extensive rehearsals for a possible upcoming tour that the record label was putting together, and Monday nights playing with ZO2 wouldn't interfere at all — or so I thought.

While Dave was away on tour, Paulie began to launch the official ZO2 website: **ZO2.com.** It was filled with live pictures of the band performing along with pictures from our recent photo shoot with the legendary rock photographer Mark Weiss. Mark was mostly known for photographing all the biggest rock acts of the 80's, including Twisted Sister, Motley Crue, Van Halen, Metallica, and even KISS! Dave had known Mark through TSO and Mark agreed to do a photo shoot with us. This was a huge opportunity that we couldn't pass up. I have to hand it to Paulie: the website looked fantastic. The problem was that it was a little too fantastic for Sevenwiser's manager Sandy.

Sandy was still bitter that Paulie and Dave chose to do their own thing instead of joining with him and Sevenwiser. It started to become this crazy competition between them. Once Sandy saw the amazing looking ZO2 website with all of the stunning photos that Mark took along with the live shots, he basically lost his mind. He had to do something to slow ZO2 down because Sevenwiser was moving at a snail's pace. I didn't know it at the time, but the reason why they were moving so slowly was because of Sandy. It turned out that he was torturing Wind-up Records with every little detail.

ZO2 photo shoot with legendary rock photogragher Mark Weiss. 2003.

The night that Sandy saw the ZO2 website he had his assistant/lacky, Andrew, call me and demand that ZO2 take down all pictures and references of me in the band. I actually laughed at first because I thought he was kidding. He wasn't. I demanded to talk to Sandy directly.

All of a sudden, Sandy chimed in. The weasel had been listening to my and Andrew's conversation the whole time. He began screaming like a lunatic over the phone, to the point where if he had been in front of me, I would have knocked him out. His demands were absolutely outrageous! Not only did he want me to take down any picture that included me from the ZO2 website, he wanted me to stop playing with them altogether, and he demanded that I didn't play live in public with them anymore.

I tried to keep my cool as much as I could and responded by saying, "You have no right to take away a source of income if you and Sevenwiser aren't paying me yet." Sevenwiser's pay didn't start until the "tour" officially began. Once it did, they would pay me while I was out on the road and then a retainer while we were off. I told him, at that point, he had the right to tell me not to play with ZO2 if and only if it interfered with Sevenwiser's schedule.

My calm demeanor sent him into more of a frenzy, but he knew I was right; still, Sandy wouldn't back down easily. He had to get something out of me and do something to hurt ZO2.

So he approved of me playing for now, but still demanded I take the pictures down. He said that if Wind-up saw that the drummer for their new band Sevenwiser was in a big photo shoot with the famous rock photographer Mark Weiss, as an obvious member of another band, that they would flip out. I knew it was all bullshit and he was just on a power trip, but I decided to placate to him and agreed that I would get Paulie to remove the photos. I refused, though, to take down the live shots. Sandy agreed.

The next day I had to call Paulie to tell him the news. He was crushed. His worst fears were beginning to come true. He knew that eventually the time was going to come that I had to go to Sevenwiser full time, but I guess he was just in denial. Before Paulie agreed to remove the photos, he, Dave, and Bob wanted to talk to me.

I had assumed that they were going to give me an ultimatum and that I had to choose ZO2 or Sevenwiser. I couldn't fault them for this. It was obnoxious of me to ask them to remove the photos from the website. Even though Sandy was just being an asshole, I couldn't jeopardize my record contract, and my financial future for myself and my mom, just to avoid hurting Paulie's and Dave's feelings. I was fully prepared to make the choice that night and it wasn't going to be what the guys in ZO2 wanted.

When I got to the studio, Bob began by saying how valuable he thought I was to ZO2 and that he didn't want to lose me. I kept waiting for the "but," but it never came. Bob then asked for permission for him to call Sandy directly and talk to him about the situation before removing any pictures from the website. I told Bob, "I think you're wasting your time. Sandy is a jerkoff and he's on some kind of power trip. There's no way to change his mind." Bob still suggested that he give it a shot.

We actually decided to call Sandy on the spot. I heard the whole conversation. Bob basically tried to reason with Sandy. He said, "Listen, Joey's a great drummer and we both want him. Let's just both use him. There's no conflict. If he's under contract with you then you get first priority, but if you aren't using him let us use him for gigs and some label showcases." Sandy wasn't having any part of it. He began screaming on the other end, "Who do you think you are? You cannot use my drummer that's under contract with me and Wind-up Records for showcases at other labels. I will be a laughing stock if I allowed that to happen!" Bob kept his cool and tried to reason with Sandy, but Sandy was like a rabid animal. I gained a lot of respect for Bob that night. He fought for me and tried to keep me as a member of ZO2. I never forgot it.

Unfortunately, Bob's idea didn't work. I was again expecting the ultimatum, but it never came. I went straight to Paulie's house and sat with him as he reluctantly agreed to take the Mark Weiss photos down from the website. He was clearly very upset.

After I left Paulie's house, I decided that I wasn't going to let Sandy get away with anything else. I just knew more was to come. He was on a power trip that wouldn't end until ZO2 was no more. If I was having this much trouble now, what would happen when it was time to actually get paid? Dealing with Sandy was one of the worst experiences I ever went through in my entire musical career.

Sure enough, the morning after I made Paulie remove all of the agreed-upon photos, I got a voicemail from Sandy's lackey, Andrew. It said that I was in violation of my contract and that *all* photos and any mention of me had to be removed from ZO2's website and advertising. I was in shock! I'm not sure why because I knew more was coming, but I never thought it would be the next morning and a complete contradiction of the agreement Sandy and I had just made. I called Sandy back in a rage!

Of course, Andrew picked up and I began to scream at him: "This is ridiculous. I did exactly what Sandy wanted and now he wants more. What the F is his problem?" I screamed. Once again, it turned out that the coward was secretly listening in on the conversation and then decided to chime in. He also began to shout: "I can't be made a fool of. I don't want that fat asshole Bob Held calling me and telling me what I should be doing." Then he started to make demands: "You get those photos down within the hour or your fired!"

I was fuming! I wished he was in front of me. We would have brawled right then and there. I fired back with just one comment: "GO FUCK YOURSELF!" And I hung up the phone.

So, depending on how you look at it, either I quit Sevenwiser when I told Sandy to go fuck himself or he fired me because I didn't do what he wanted. Either way, later that day I received a letter saying that our contract was now null and void. So much for my big record contract deal. What a joke.

I went straight to the Sevenwiser studio in Williamsburg, Brooklyn, to pick up my gear. I brought it to the ZO2 rehearsal room and on the way I called Dave and Paulie to tell them the good/bad news about what had just transpired. I was back in ZO2 full time.

As disappointed as I was about the whole Sevenwiser situation, I also had a strange sense of relief once it was over. I wanted to have that record contract so badly that I compromised a lot of who I am. A younger version of myself would've knocked that prick Sandy out months ago. I should have never let him treat me like that or talk to me the way he did. He was hanging that golden carrot in front of my face and I just couldn't stop chasing it. There's an amazing lyric by the Australian band The Kin that goes, "You're looking for gold, when sitting on diamonds." Maybe I had my diamonds right underneath me the whole time in ZO2. I had just turned 30 and I knew ZO2 was going to be one of my last big pushes to finally make my dream come true. I planned on going at it 1,000 percent

My gold record for SEVENWISER'S appearance on the Punisher soundtrack.

Original photo for the inside of the SEVENWISER CD. I was taken out before it's official release.

CHAPTER 21

ROCK THE NATION

ZO2 continued to build our residency on Monday nights at Arlene's Grocery into the happening place to be. It started to feel like my old Crazy Country Club days with Playground. It started to become "a thing."

On March 8, 2004, we had a release party for the debut album *Tuesdays & Thursdays*, titled after the days of the week on which we rehearsed and wrote the album. Just a few short weeks later, I got an email that would forever change my life.

On the morning of Monday, April 12, 2004, I woke up like it was any other morning. Madalyn had stayed over the night before and was getting ready to leave for work. I decided to check my emails on the computer while she was getting ready. I had an email from Lynn Lendway, Bob Held's wife, who sometimes helped out on day-to-day activities with the band, but by no means was she a co-manager or anything at this point. The email was addressed to me, Paulie, and Dave. It went something like this:

"Hey guys,

It's Lynn. I wanted to see what you were doing this summer. I hope you all aren't too busy because ZO2 just got 40 dates opening up for KISS on their summer tour!!!"

I had to read it a few times to even grasp the concept of what it said. I would not let myself get too excited until I understood more. I called Madalyn over to read it and she didn't seem that excited. In her defense, we had only been dating for about 10 months and this email said that I would be going away on tour for 3 straight months. After her initial skepticism, she cheered up a little. I still didn't.

Then I told my mom, who was making us all breakfast, what the email said and she freaked out! My mom had really understood what this could mean to me. It was basically my dream come true. Next to actually being the drummer in KISS, this was the ultimate for me. Even though Madalyn and I were already deeply in love in under a year, she couldn't understand all of the work, practice, blood, sweat, and tears that I'd put into my drums. She didn't understand how big KISS was to me, but, my mom was there from the beginning. She was there at Madison Square Garden in 1979 when I first saw KISS, she was there when I bought my first KISS album, and she was there through all the months and years of me practicing my drums to KISS albums. She was the one who gave up her bedroom after we lost our first house so I could have a place to keep practicing to someday fulfill this dream. That day had finally come!

Even though I stopped myself from 100 percent celebrating yet, I saw tears well up in my mother's eyes. The sight of her with tears of joy and pride for her baby boy made me happier than the actual news of getting the KISS tour. I'd always known that family was the most important thing, but that day reassured me that without family and someone to share your dreams with, your dreams would be empty.

I called Bob right away to confirm that this email wasn't some kind of twisted joke. He immediately confirmed and told me how such a thing had transpired. As mentioned, Bob was pretty close friends with Paul

Stanley. Bob always told stories about how he got an old band he used to produce/manage called 40 Foot Ringo a few gigs opening for KISS. I'm not sure if I ever truly believed him.

Apparently, after we finished our album, Bob had sent Paul Stanley a copy to not only listen to, but to also put it in his head that if KISS ever needed anyone for a one-off gig to give ZO2 a call and they wouldn't disappoint.

KISS was already scheduled to kick off their summer 2004 Rock The Nation tour with Poison as the opening act. A few different rumors also had former Motley Crue bassist Nikki Sixx's band, Brides of Destruction as the third band on the bill. Something happened that caused either Brides to be fired, or they pulled out of the tour last minute at the beginning of April. Rumors were going around that it was because Nikki Sixx refused to tour in the opening slot in front of Poison. Others say it was because KISS fired them due to drug use. It really didn't matter. All that mattered was KISS had a last-minute opening slot on their upcoming tour, and Paul Stanley gave our manager Bob Held a call and asked him if ZO2 wanted it!

It was amazing to consider the different set of circumstances that had led to this exact event. All of the hard work throughout the years burned me out at one point during the Valentine Smith years. Then, I decided to enjoy playing my drums again, which led me to KISSNATION, which ultimately led me to ZO2 and straight back to KISS. It's funny how everything always came back to KISS. Even the disaster with Sevenwiser turned out to be a blessing in disguise. If Sandy wasn't such a douchebag, I probably would have stayed with them and then possibly missed out on this KISS tour.

I never give Paulie and Dave enough credit. They had a vision to make a full-length album and finance it themselves. They were set on not waiting for things to come to them and doing it all ourselves. I was absolutely against it. The circumstances that led ZO2 to make that album now had brought us to this moment: the KISS tour!

Without that album and without Bob getting it to Paul Stanley, none of this would be happening. I always give credit where credit is due. Paulie and Dave deserve a lot of credit for funding that whole album, which wound up costing upwards of $30,000. And, I also give major credit to Bob Held. His contacts and his pushing us to do the full-length album got us the KISS tour. Now, it was time to make the most of it!

The Rock the Nation tour was set to begin on June 10, 2004, which gave us less than two months to figure out how the hell we were going to pull off this monumental task.

Believe it or not, Paulie and I were still gigging with KISSNATION during this time. But we knew once we got the KISS tour that we couldn't do it anymore. We broke the news to Carlos and Ruby and finished up the last few shows we had already scheduled.

It was bitter sweet. It was amazing knowing that ZO2 was going to the next level and going on tour with KISS, but in a strange way I was going to miss my time in KISSNATION.

The only small disappointment was that the tour wouldn't include original KISS members Ace Frehley and especially for me…Peter Criss. They had both recently been replaced by Tommy Thayer and Eric Singer. I was still thrilled beyond belief but having my Idol, Peter Criss on that tour would have really been the cherry on top.

It was unheard of for an unsigned band like ZO2 to be on tour with a major act like KISS. We had no label behind us for tour support money, and we had never done a major tour before. We didn't know all of the logistics that went into it, but, we were soon to get a crash course.

Once the tour was confirmed, Bob's wife, Lynn Lendway, came on board officially as a co-manager. This was totally okay with us. Lynn had worked in the record industry for years and even spent a few years working directly for KISS. She would be the person to start spearheading all of the things that had to get done before the tour started. The first thing we had to figure out was transportation.

Luckily, KISS's road crew was going to be transporting our gear from show to show. That was one major obstacle out of the way. Now, we just had to figure out how the band, Bob, a tech, and the Z's little brother Brian, who was coming along to film and document the entire tour, were going to travel across country for the next three and half months. We knew right away that a tour bus was completely out of the question due to financial reasons. Paulie, Dave, and Bob decided to rent

Promo poster for the KISS "Rock the Nation" tour.

a large SUV Ford Explorer with a third row of seats in the back. It was going to be a miserable summer with 6 people and luggage traveling almost 20,000 miles, or at least that was until I found the answer to our prayers one night when I was at Madalyn's brother Joe's house in Staten Island. Parked in front of his house was an old RV camper. A light bulb immediately went off in my head. That was exactly what we needed.

I started to research what an RV would cost to rent for the summer. It turned out that because traveling across country was what an RV was intended for, it was only a little bit more expensive than renting the Explorer. In the long run, it would actually save us money. We would now be able to skimp on many of the hotel rooms we were planning to rent and just sleep in the RV. Another luxury was that we could also bring along an extra person to help with the driving.

Because Paulie and Dave were already bringing their brother and their other friend Paul Laplaca was coming as our tech, they asked me to pick who could come help out with the driving. Of course, the first person that came to mind was my lifelong buddy Rob Scally.

Scally had been there for every band I'd ever been in. He had been there to buy KISS albums and to see KISS and for wrestling time and time again. I couldn't think of anyone better to bring along to share this amazing experience with.

I called Scally excitedly to not only tell him the news about the KISS tour, but to ask him to come along. He was excited beyond belief and knew that this was a dream come true for me. Unfortunately, he couldn't come on this once-in-a-lifetime experience because he had just recently become a firefighter and there was no way to take off for three months. He was crushed that he couldn't be there with me, but we both understood. In hindsight, it was probably much better that Scally didn't come. He and I would have gotten into way too much trouble!

I had to figure out someone to bring who would not only be responsible, but who was available for the entire summer. I then thought of the perfect person, another lifelong friend who had just gotten laid off from his job, was responsible, and didn't drink and party enough to get me into trouble. I called Anthony Muscarella whom we all called Musk. Musk would basically be a jack of all trades for us on the tour. Driver and security guard, offering help to break down gear — whatever we needed him to do, he was ready to help out.

Most of all Musk brought me a slice of sanity while we were on tour that summer. Like I mentioned, Paulie and Dave were very different from me. Whenever they drove me crazy on tour, I would grab Musk and we would hang out either playing Wiffle ball or just exploring the arenas.

We were now almost set to hit the road. It would be me, Paulie, Dave, Bob, Brian Z, Paul LaPlaca, and Musk. The next step was to try and find

Dave Z, Musk and Paulie Z picking up our RV on the day we left for the KISS tour.

some endorsements for gear and try to get some kind of sponsorship for the tour to help us offset some of the costs.

The next two weeks consisted of making non-stop phone calls. Everyone was in charge of trying to get their own music gear endorsements and then we all had delegated other tasks to carry out. Since I had found the RV, I was in charge of trying to find a company that wanted to put its logo on it as advertising to help sponsor the tour.

Tour buses and even local city buses had mesh bus wraps that companies paid to wrap the entire bus in as a huge advertisement. We thought we could get someone to do the same to our RV. Musk and I would spend the next few weeks trying get it done, but to no avail.

Next, I would to try and find a drum company that would endorse me for the tour. My first call was to my dream company, Ludwig. Ludwig was a brand I'd always wanted to play. All of my drum heroes played Ludwig drums, including Eric Carr. I cold-called Ludwig one afternoon and asked to speak to the artist development department. As luck would have it, they connected me to the head of artist development, Todd Trent. I went into detail to explain who I was and that I was about to embark on a tour with KISS. Todd seemed interested and asked me what I needed and that he'd love to help me out.

At that time, I was really looking for something to help make me stand out while we were on stage. I knew I was only going to be traveling with a small, four-piece kit but I wanted something different. I remember seeing a recent picture of Tommy Lee of Motley Crue and his drum kit. He had an enormous bass drum that I just thought looked incredible. I had no idea what size it was, but I described this to Todd and he understood right away what I was thinking. Todd said that they didn't have anything like that in stock as a loaner and because we were on such a time constraint, Todd said that it would be impossible to make something like that so quick. He offered me a basic kit to use for the tour, but I stupidly declined. I figured I already had a basic kit and didn't need the one from Ludwig.

A few weeks before we would be leaving for tour, Madalyn surprised me with a trip to Mexico to celebrate. It was amazing. I knew she was a little worried about me going on tour, but I knew that she was the one for me and I would never do anything to jeopardize that. The day before we left for Mexico, Bob informed us that we had a new show booked at the Funky Monkey in Long Island. I told Bob that the new show conflicted with my trip to Mexico. Shockingly, he asked me to get back a few days early so I could make the show. I actually laughed out loud at this obscene request. Of course, Paulie and Dave agreed with Bob that I should come back early. I said, "Do you hear what you are actually asking me to do? You want me to change my trip, my flights, and leave my vacation early just to come back and play a no-name dump of a club out in Long Island that was booked after I already had plans." This was the first time, and unfortunately not the last, that Bob would attempt to interfere in my personal life.

If ZO2 didn't have the KISS tour coming up in just a few weeks, I would have told Bob and the guys absolutely not. Since I didn't want to ruffle any feathers right before spending 3 months with these guys, I gave them an option I was sure they would turn down. I told them that it was going to cost me almost $500 to switch my flights on such short notice. I knew the gig in Long Island was paying us maybe $200 tops so there was no chance they were going to agree. Sure enough, Bob said that it was worth it to pay the extra so we could do the gig. I thought, "Of course, he said yes! He was going to make Paulie and Dave, and ultimately me down the road, pay for it!" Bob was extremely generous with other people's money.

The KISS/Poison/ZO2 Rock the Nation tour would start in San Antonio, Texas, on June 10, 2004. We would all meet at Paulie's apartment in Brooklyn to load the RV. We were all so excited loading

ZO2 and KISS's tour itinerary books.

the RV with snacks, drinks, pillows, and blankets — and we even figured out a way to rig a small TV and a DVD player to the sink. We knew this was going to basically be our home for the next three months and we wanted to make sure that we had everything we needed.

Even though I was about to embark on an experience of a lifetime, I was still slightly hesitant to get too overcome with joy. It all still felt a little too good to be true. There was always something in the back of my head that thought that when we arrived in Texas for the first show they either wouldn't know who the hell we were, or we would be playing as a side act in the parking lot or something. Until I was on that stage, KISS's stage, hitting the first note to our intro, I wasn't going to fully believe it was happening.

The plan was to leave 3 days before the first show. Texas was about 1,500 miles from Brooklyn and we planned on stopping 2 nights at hotels. We were so pumped and excited to get there that we wound up driving straight for the next 35 hours, only stopping to eat and pee.

I'm the type of person who never gets nervous before an event or a big show, mostly because I know before I ever do a gig that I am uber-prepared. I always thought it was silly to be nervous if you were ready and happy to be there. Excited? Yes! Nervous? Never. But this event was different, not because it was the biggest thing I'd ever done, but because of all the unknowns. And this time I was nervous — not to play in front of 20,000 people or to meet my idols. I was nervous that I would be disappointed that all of this would somehow not happen.

On the day of the first show, I was still a little unsure of what kind of greeting and reception we would get. Would they even be expecting us? If they did, would they welcome us? How would the guys in Poison and KISS feel about having some young, unknown band on tour with them? There were just so many questions going into that first day; it was pretty overwhelming. But, the biggest question still was, is this really happening?

On the morning of June 10, we arrived at the Verizon Wireless Amphitheater around 9am, which was three hours before our call time. We wanted to get there early to assess our surroundings and figure out what the procedure was going to be every day. I'm sure I was the only one still questioning if we were really going to be opening for KISS later that night.

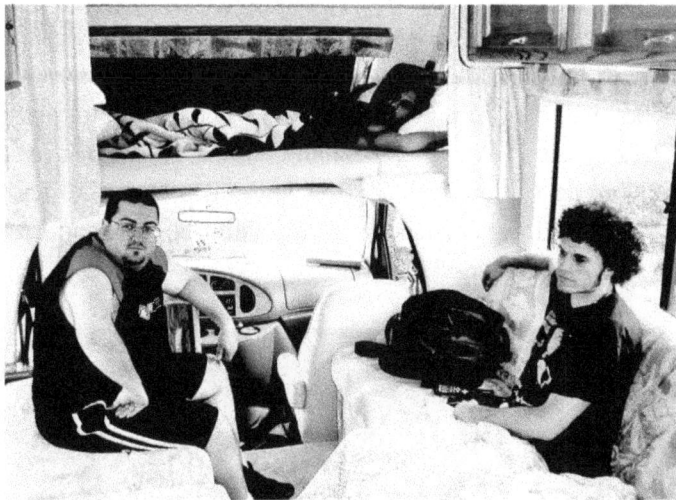

Inside ZO2's RV! This was home for three months.

Once we arrived, we were greeted by Patrick Whitley the production manager. Patrick was a dry Englishman that was in all honesty a little scary — not physically scary, but scary in the fact that he really held ZO2's fate in his hands. Bob, Paulie, Dave, and I all walked up to him to introduce ourselves. I had a lump in my throat. This was the tell-tale moment. If he was expecting us, than all was okay; if he wasn't, then this might be the moment my dreams are crushed.

Bob politely said, "Hello, sir, ZO2 reporting for duty." Patrick paused and gave us all a look over and said, "Who?" My heart sank. I thought to myself, "Oh no! How could this be happening? He had no idea who we even were." Patrick looked up and said, "Just kidding, fellas, good to see you!" I'm not sure there had ever been a greater sounding sentence in the history of the world. He then said, "Let me show you guys the stage."

Patrick then passed us off to one of the stage managers, Mike "Spragoo" Sprague. He brought us out to the center of the stage and began to show us exactly where our gear would be going every night. I didn't really hear much of what he was saying; all I could see were the massive arena and the thousands of seats as I looked from center stage. Then I turned around and saw the enormous KISS logo and KISS's gear all set up right behind me. I just couldn't believe I would be playing in front of that every night.

While "Spragoo" was showing us around, a familiar face came over and introduced himself. He was wearing tight blue jeans, a bandanna, and a cowboy hat. Yes, you guessed it: Bret Michaels from Poison. He said, "What's up guys? I'm Bret, welcome on board!" He was as sweet and as welcoming as could be. If Bret knew who we were and was greeting us, I guess it was official. I could finally start to breathe a little. This was "really happening!"

Dave, Paulie, Bob Held, and me standing on the KISS stage for the very first time. June 10, 2004.

Next, it was time to go backstage and see what it was like. In all the years of me being a huge music fan, I had never been backstage at a concert. It wasn't like it is today with bands offering meet-and-greets and special backstage tours. When I was growing up, backstage always meant "party!"

The first stop backstage was catering. Paulie and Dave didn't drink at all so the one thing that we all had in common and could enjoy together was eating like animals. After we filled our plates with as much food as humanly possible, I heard a familiar voice. Standing two feet away from us were Gene Simmons and Paul Stanley. Paul and Bob immediately exchanged some pleasantries, then Bob called us over so we could meet.

Paulie and I had already met them when we filmed *Mock Rock* for VH1 but we had had our KISS makeup on then, so I'm pretty sure that Gene and Paul never even realized it was us from KISSNATION. Not that we were embarrassed by it or anything, but we just never even brought it up to them. Paul seemed friendly enough, giving us all a fist bump. He didn't really like to shake hands because he was a bit of a germaphobe. Gene, on the other hand, couldn't have been friendlier. He immediately said, "Stand back a little. Let me take a look at you boys." He then pointed at Dave and me and said, "These two look like rock stars. This one," pointing at Paulie, "looks like he should be in college." We all erupted in laughter except for poor Paulie, who was completely crushed. Just like Eric Singer had done to him in Puerto Rico, Gene destroyed him on the very first day of the tour.

SHOW SCHEDULE	
SAN ANTONIO	THURS, JUNE 10, 2004
DOORS:	5:00 PM
ZO2:	7:00 - 7:30 PM
POISON:	7:50 - 8:50 PM
KISS:	9:15 - 10:45 PM
HARD CURFEW:	11:00 PM

The call times for the first show of the KISS tour.

Once we finished with all of our hellos, it was time to load onto the stage. Once the three of us set up, it was time to get a line check. I'll never forget the first time I hit my bass drum that sunny afternoon in San Antonio. It was the greatest, most powerful thing I'd ever heard. Growing up, whenever I went to an arena to see a band, the first thing I always noticed was how massive the drums sounded. Now it was my turn — my turn to have some kid in the audience notice how powerful and explosive my drums sounded. I was ready.

Minutes before show time, we gathered backstage to tell each other to kick ass and have fun. We put our fists in, looked each other in the eye, and knew we were about to do something magical. Before leaving for the tour, people warned us about the "KISS crowd." I also knew firsthand, having seen them a dozen times, that the KISS crowd wasn't very receptive to the opening band. They wanted to see KISS, and they didn't want to hear or see anyone else. Even the crew had told us to not get discouraged if the crowd booed or didn't respond positively. It didn't matter to me. We were about to hit the stage in front of about 12,000 people and open for KISS! Everything I'd worked for in my life led me to this exact spot. I was going to enjoy it no matter what.

As we walked out onto the stage, people were still filing into the arena. Most didn't even know there was a third band on the bill. They thought it was just Poison and KISS. We went out there to make sure they never forgot us.

Paulie and Dave turned toward me to signal for the first downbeat of our intro. We hit that massive first chord and it felt like the world shook. "HELLO, WE ARE, ZO... 2!!!" The crowd was skeptical but began to take notice during our opening song "Takin' Me Down." I could see people's heads starting to bop during our second song, "Living Now" and by the time we hit our ballad "Dirty Water," I could see the people in the audience focused on the stage and enjoying what they heard.

We were quickly approaching our finishing number "Fly On Your Wings" and I didn't want the night to end. It was all going by way too fast. I almost expected to have a "Frozen Moment" but this was the one time that my adrenaline and sheer joy and happiness overwhelmed me so much that I was finding it hard to focus and slow things down.

During the rumble of our last song, Paulie began to talk to the audience. He thanked them for being there and told them that we would be out by the merch booth selling CD's and T-shirts if anyone wanted to come by and say hello. As the low rumble Dave and I were creating began to slowly build, Paulie asked the crowd, "Are you ready?" The crowd gave a light cheer. He asked again, "Are you ready for a party tonight?" The crowd responded a little more. Paulie knew he had them and asked, "Then, where's the party tonight?" He answered his own question with a scream: "It's here, it's here." As his words became more powerful, Dave and I got more powerful, and as the three of us were pouring every ounce of energy we had into that build, the audience became more energized and started to rise. Right at the moment when we all finally reached our peak together, the song kicked in and the crowd exploded. For the next four and half minutes, the crowd was on their feet and sent us off the stage to a standing ovation and loud roar.

We had done it! Not only had I just lived my dream of opening for KISS, but we actually won the crowd over and kicked ass. We erupted when we all met backstage. High fives, hugs, and tears of joy were flying everywhere. I don't think I'd ever felt that kind of energy, excitement, or adrenaline in my life.

This would go down as the all-time, number one greatest show I'd ever played in the history of my career. I don't believe it could ever be or will ever be topped. We all did it together, and right here in the pages of this book I want to formally thank Paulie, Dave, Bob, and Lynn for helping make my dreams come true. I'll never forget it. Thank You!

We were still flying high and celebrating when we realized that the night had just begun. We had to rush to pack up our gear so we could get out to the merchandise stand to meet the crowd and hopefully sell a few CD's and T-shirts.

Once we were done packing our gear, we raced up to the merch stand where they told us they would be selling our stuff. When we got there, we weren't expecting to see what was in front of our eyes. Not only did we have a huge crowd of people waiting for us, but our merch was side by side with KISS's and Poison's. It was a surreal

Opening night of the Rock The Nation Tour!!

moment to see my face on a T-shirt being sold right next to a KISS T-shirt. Wow!

When the crowd of people surrounding the merch stand finally saw us approaching, we were bombarded. I don't think the three of us were expecting such a wild reception. Everyone wanted a piece of us — either an autograph, a picture, or just to chat with us and tell us how much they enjoyed the show. After about 20 minutes of being mobbed, as I was signing someone's CD, another person shouted, "Where can I get that CD?" I pointed and replied, "Right over at that merch stand." He shouted back, "They just told me they are sold out." I was taken aback by that. "We were sold out already?" I thought to myself excitedly.

ZO2's merchandise being sold side by side with KISS's!!

We could hear Poison playing in the background while we were finishing with our autographs and talking with everyone. Once the crowd began to wind down, we decided we wanted to run to see some of Poison's set. Just like when I was a kid and ran everywhere, we did it again. We ran all the way from the merch stand to the front row. The other audience members didn't mind at all that we were there; in fact, they loved it! We were greeted like rock stars, so much so that it became

Meeting young fans always reminded me of myself when I first saw KISS.

a little awkward because Poison was on stage performing and we were getting so much attention in the front row. We had to tell people to stop and watch the show.

Bret saw us right away and gave us a little head nod as if to say, "Good job boys." Guitarist C.C. DeVille and drummer Rikki Rockett did the same. We only got to enjoy the last two songs of Poison's set due to all the time we spent at the merch stand. As soon as Poison said goodnight, we were once again bombarded with fans from all sides. The merch booth a few minutes earlier was one thing, but this was really nuts! Everyone was surrounding us and wanted to talk to us. It was insane and amazing.

We still hadn't eaten anything since lunch at around 1pm and we decided if we wanted to watch KISS, and of course we did, we would have to go eat fast. Our plan was then to come right back to the front row and watch our idols tear up the stage. I had never seen KISS from the front row and I wasn't going to miss this opportunity to see them on the first night of our tour. We told all of the fans around us that we'd be back out for KISS and then to meet us at the merch booth after KISS finished.

Paulie, Dave, and I went backstage to scarf down some food as quickly as possible. We were all still on such a high it was incredible. We told Bob about selling out of CD's at the merch stand and suggested

that he try to get more over there because we planned on heading back after we watched KISS. He said, "I'm on it" and ran off to see what he could do. Bob seemed just as excited as we were. He knew big things were about to happen and he was acting like a little kid too. We were all giddy with the events of the day so far.

As we were finishing our last bite of food, we started to hear a deep humming noise coming from the stage. We knew it was time. Once again, we raced to the front of the stage. There was a large black curtain now hanging in front. As the hum grew louder, a familiar voice began to shout, "All right San Antonio, you wanted the best, you got the best, the hottest band in the world ... KISS!" The arena erupted and so did we.

As soon as that curtain dropped, I was no longer Joey, the drummer of ZO2 that was just playing on the stage in front of me. I was that 5-year-old boy who was eating his hot dog in Madison Square Garden 25 years earlier.

Gene immediately acknowledged us in the front row and began pointing at us and doing a little dance. I think he might have been making fun of Dave's stage dance moves. Paul then pranced his way over and gave us a cool thumbs-up signaling what he thought of our show. "Holy shit!" I thought. I'm watching KISS from the front row and Gene and Paul both personally gestured to us what a great job they thought we did. My 5-year-old self would have fainted. KISS blasted through an hour-and-a half of absolute Klassics.

The plan was to watch the show from the front row until the beginning of the last song, which we knew would be "Rock & Roll All Night." Right before they began, we would start heading back towards the sound man so we could beat the crowd to the merch booth when KISS finally said good night.

As we walked back, I drifted away a little and decided to watch "Rock & Roll All Night" by myself. I wanted to breathe for a second and reflect on this incredible day. I drifted away and found myself looking up into the night sky. This is the exact moment that this book began: this was my "Frozen Moment" at the greatest show of my life. It was a moment solidified in time, and one that I would never forget.

When I finally snapped back into real time, I knew I had to get to the merch stand to see if we could meet with another rush of people on their way out of the arena. The strategy worked perfectly, and we were once again met with a mob of people waiting to greet us!

The first day of the KISS tour worked out so perfectly that we decided to do this exact routine every night for the whole tour. It was the start of one wild and amazing summer. If possible, the next night in Dallas was even better. Gone were the doubts about being part of the tour. We arrived in Dallas ready to conquer, not hoping to be accepted.

The capacity crowd was even more receptive than the night before. All 11,000 fans were on their feet during our finale "Fly on Your Wings." The first night wasn't a fluke. The KISS crowd was not only accepting us, they were loving us!

We were once again bombarded by fans when we went down to the front row to watch Poison. T-shirts & CD's were sold out before KISS ever finished playing and we once again finished the night watching our idols kick ass on stage.

Watching KISS from the soundboard on opening night. Electricity filled the air!

After the show and another trip to the merch stand to meet fans, Bobby brought us in to KISS's hospitality suite. This was basically where KISS could have dinner and relax if they didn't feel like eating in catering with everyone else. There was steak, chicken, fish, and about a half-dozen different types of desserts. We were in heaven. There was nothing better than celebrating a long, amazing show day with a big meal.

As we started to eat, KISS's road crew began coming in and out to shower and to also pick on KISS's leftovers. I guess this was a regular routine for them. Each guy was nicer than the next, and we really bonded with the road crew that night. Everyone was so friendly and nice, until we met Gene's roadie, Spike.

Spike was as uptight and miserable a person as I'd ever met. We asked what was wrong and why he was so down. He explained, "Because my boss is an asshole! That's why!" He began telling us horror stories about how Gene would spit on him, scream at him, and even kick him during the show. We couldn't believe it. Gene, so far to us, seemed like a real sweetheart. After Spike's horror stories, he went into the bathroom to take a shower. We all agreed that we had to find a way to cheer Spike up when he returned.

Once Spike was finished with his shower, we began talking to him again about some of the other stuff he did on the road. He informed us that he was actually the voice behind KISS's famous intro, "You wanted the best, you got the best." He'd been doing it since the reunion tour in 1996! That was all the opening we needed. We got down on our hands and knees and started bowing to him, ala Wayne's World and chanted, "We're not worthy, we're not worthy." He finally cracked a smile. Before too long, we had him teaching us how to properly deliver those magical words. That was just who we were — bright-eyed kids enjoying life. I think our youthfulness and happiness was infectious to anyone that came across our path that summer, Spike included.

We received some much deserving news while we were on our way to our next stop. Sevenwiser, the band with which I'd had a falling out, had been dropped by Wind-Up Records a week after their album was released! It turned out that they just couldn't work with that asshole manager Sandy anymore and decided it wasn't worth dealing with them.

I did feel badly for the few guys in the band that I got along with, like Joe Bell and Tudor, but hearing that Sandy was the cause of them being dropped made me happy. It couldn't have happened to a nicer guy. Karma's a bitch, dude!

The next three stops were Houston, Denver, and Albuquerque. Musk and I were in charge of driving the night shift from about 3am to 7am. Musk would drive and I would be in charge of the map. Remember, this is before GPS: we needed a giant map open at all times as we followed the highways across the country.

Musk and I drove the other guys crazy by blasting 80's pop music all night and singing along at the top of our lungs to songs like Culture Club's "Karma Chameleon" or Cyndy Lauper's "Girls Just Want to Have Fun." This drove Bob absolutely mad all summer.

It was before the Houston show that we got to see KISS sound check for the first time. This was something I'd always wanted to experience, and it definitely didn't disappoint. We were the only ones watching and KISS noticed. Paul would shout out to us, "What do you guys want to hear?" We yelled back the obscurest songs possible and they would actually attempt playing them. I think I shouted, "The Oath!" It was like our own private KISS concert and they were taking requests. In a way, this was even more enjoyable than watching them from the front row every night. This private show was quickly added in to our daily routine.

The reflection in my bass drum says it all.

Denver and Albuquerque were more of the same — pure ecstasy every day and night. Every moment was a dream come true. To add to the fantasy, we had lunch with Gene Simmons in New Mexico. It wasn't planned or anything; we were just sitting down at catering and Gene walked in and sat with us. He began telling us, "You know you guys are doing a fabulous job so far." We, of course, thanked him and then gave him a copy of our CD, and he immediately loved the cover. We told him that we were selling out every night and he was impressed. He gladly took the CD and began talking to us about the music industry.

Gene was extremely smart and very intellectual, but he also had a skewed view on things. It was my first real experience having a long conversation with someone rich and famous, and it was enlightening. As down-to-earth as he was, he just didn't think like the everyday person. He couldn't or shouldn't. He'd been rich and famous since he was in his early 20's, for about 30 years at this point. He was constantly surrounded by people that yes'd him to death, which is why he was in shock when we started to debate and disagree with him on some issues. Not only was he in shock, but I could see he was enjoying it. A man like Gene wanted to debate. If you said the sky was blue, Gene would say, "Well, actually the sky is black and the atmosphere just makes it look blue." This turned out to be another thing that we would add to our daily routine — lunch and debate hour with Gene.

We really had an unbelievable schedule that we were starting to build up.

Dave Z controlling the massive crowd

Here is a quick rundown of a typical day with ZO2 on the KISS tour.

A typical day on the KISS tour.

8am – Arrive at the city in which we played that night.

9am – Eat breakfast at the local Denny's or Waffle House.

12pm - Arrive at the venue. Check catering to see what's for lunch. Usually hang with Gene for a little while and debate about something.

2pm - Play a little Wiffle ball or football in the parking lot. Sometimes just throw the football with Bret.

3pm - Start unpacking all the gear and getting it ready for stage.

4pm - Watch KISS do sound check.

5:30 – Do the ZO2 sound check.

6:00 - Pack up our dinner from catering to eat after the show.

6:30 - Get dressed and ready.

7 - 7:30 - Showtime!

7:45 - Pack up our gear.

8:15 – Scarf down dinner as fast as we can.

8:45 - Watch the end of Poison's set from the front row.

9 - 9:30 - ZO2 meet and greet at the merch stand.

9:31 - Run to see KISS in the front row.

10:45 - Watch the end of the KISS set near the sound man.

10:55 - 12:30 - ZO2 meet and greet at the merch stand.

12:30 - Look for scraps at catering to bring in the RV.

1am - Begin traveling to the next city.

2-7am – Switch drivers on and off. Try to sleep a few hours in between shifts.

8am - Start all over again!

ZO2 ready to begin our first day and conquer the world

CHAPTER 22

TURNING IDOLS INTO PEERS

KISS AND ZO2!

After New Mexico, we began to travel up the West Coast, doing shows in L.A. and San Francisco– actually right outside of San Fran in Concord, California. We were flying higher than ever. After that, we had a full travel day to get to our next destination, Portland, Oregon. At about 7pm on the day before the Portland show, we got word that because of a strict sound curfew in Portland, ZO2 had to be bumped from the show. Needless to say, we were extremely disappointed, but the bigger fear was that his would happen more often. Thankfully, this was the one and only time. We decided that we would still go to the Portland show to show our support for KISS and Poison, which turned out to be a very good idea.

Because it was essentially a day off for us, we decided we would just lounge and play Wiffle ball in the parking lot for most of the day. Out of the corner of my eye, I noticed a figure in the distance watching the game. It was none other than Paul Stanley. I quickly jogged over to him and said, "Hey Paul, do you want to play?" Never in my wildest imagination did I think he'd say yes. I was just asking to be nice because I saw him watching. He replied, "Sure, I'll take an at bat."

Paul and I walked over to join the game. I started to pitch to Paul, but it wasn't in my competitive nature to lob pitches in so he could hit them. I threw three straight curve balls and he was out. I couldn't believe that a year ago I was in the Hamptons with my friends playing Wiffle ball every day and now I was pitching to Paul Stanley!

Paul seemed a little agitated by my curves so I let Paulie pitch to him. Before he began, I ran in to catering to grab a few waters for everyone. As soon as I walked in, I saw Gene and Eric. Gene yelled, "Buttafuoco!" Gene always called me "Buttafuoco" because of Joey Buttafuoco from the popular Amy Fisher news story from the 90's. I went over and told them, "Hey, we are playing Wiffle ball outside. Paul's playing. Come and play with us." They said yes right away and seemed genuinely excited.

I think ZO2 was a nice shot in the arm for Paul and Gene. We had this unbridled innocence and youth about us that they enjoyed. Gene seemed like a little kid when I asked him to come and play ball with us.

As soon as I walked out with Gene and Eric, it was official. It had become ZO2 vs. KISS in Wiffle ball! I started pitching a few warm up curve balls to Gene and he couldn't believe how I was making the ball curve. He ducked away from every pitch even though they were hitting the strike zone.

After warm ups, we decided to each pitch to our counterparts. Paulie would pitch to Paul Stanley, Dave would pitch to Gene Simmons, and I would pitch to Eric Singer.

Paulie started against Paul, and his first pitch was a strike right down the middle. Feeling a little brazen and cocky, Paulie told Paul, "I call that pitch my Love Gun. Here comes the Destroyer." Everyone began to crack up. That was until Paul's comeback: "Be careful. We can still throw you off this tour." Paul ripped a single right after that. Thank God!

ZO2 vs. KISS in Wiffle ball!!

Gene was next. He decided to hold the wiffle bat with only one hand and easily blasted a double off Dave. He walked away and gave Paul a high five as if to silently say, "Let's take these kids down." It was now my turn to pitch to Eric. Gene yelled, "Oh c'mon. He's like a professional pitcher!" I laughed and then struck Eric out on three consecutive pitches.

Before it was time for KISS to pitch to us, Bret Michaels, who was off to side watching, yelled out, "Let me get an at bat," as if to say, "I can hit better than those guys." Bret was a known athlete and he was always in the parking lot either throwing a football or having a softball catch. Because of this, they all wanted me to pitch to him — sort of like a challenge to see if I could get him out.

Bret was pretty good at sports, but he was no match for me in Wiffle ball. On the first pitch, I threw him a slow overhand curve. He didn't duck out of the way like Gene did, but his knees definitely buckled a little. Strike one. The second pitch, I threw what looked like the same pitch to the batter, but it was actually a slider low and away. He took a big swing and missed. Strike two. He looked a little upset. I knew it was over before I even threw the third pitch. I then tossed a gentle riser that I knew would end up about two feet over his head, even though it looked like it was right down the middle. Sure enough, Bret couldn't lay off and

Gene Simmons getting ready for the pitch.

it was strike three. He tossed the bat up in the air and said, "Forget it!" I think this also scared everyone else off because KISS also walked away shaking their heads in disbelief. So technically, ZO2 won! Even though I basically ended the game before it began, I couldn't hold back and not "really pitch" to Bret. After that, everyone was scared to play Wiffle ball with me for the rest of the tour.

As amazing as this whole tour and experience had been, this might have been my favorite moment of all. It was just a genuine fun time. Gene, Paul, Eric, and Bret were really having a good time. They had been "rock stars" for so long and had had people bowing down to them for so long that I don't think they could ever just let their guards down and have fun. It was a great day.

After that day in Portland, our relationship with KISS became even closer. Not only would Gene seek us out every day to hang, but KISS would put on a special performance for us every sound check. We even started a little game with Gene and Paul. During sound check, they would continuously try to hit us with picks. Now, over the years, they had both become throwing masters; they could easily launch a pick 40 or 50 rows, and both were dead accurate. We would run in and out of rows ducking and dodging while they shot rapid fire at us. Paul nailed me right in the bridge of the nose one day and made me bleed pretty badly. He apologized backstage and said, "That's why we don't throw picks during the show anymore. People used to get hurt all the time."

KISS's soundcheck got so out of hand after a while that their tour manager Paco had to pull us aside and tell us to please only come out for a little bit during sound check. He explained, "They are performing for you guys every day and loving it. Sound check is running too long and causing the whole crew to be behind schedule." In a weird way, I felt like we gave KISS a shot of youth on that tour. They were like our crazy uncles trying to entertain us every day.

After Portland, we started to head east and play places like Minneapolis, Kansas City, St. Louis, and Detroit. Anyone that's ever been to a KISS concert knows that they have special effects galore. Two highlights of the show are when Gene flies to the top of the arena to sing "God of Thunder" and when Paul soars over the audience to sing "Love Gun." One afternoon while KISS's road crew was setting up, they asked if we all wanted to try out the flying rigs. I think we yelled, "Holy Shit! Really?" all at the same time. This was another dream come true for me. I remember being 5 years old at Madison Square Garden and watching Gene fly into the air. It was magical. And now I would be getting to experience it for myself! There was, though, one problem: I am actually pretty terrified of heights and so I was nervous. But there was no way I was passing up this opportunity.

The first thing the rig tech told all of us was, "Don't grab the wire as you are being lifted into the air." Of course, what's the first thing I did as soon as I was catapulted into the air? Grabbed the wire! I was scared shitless, but excited beyond belief. What an amazing experience it was to fly like Gene!

After we all got our chance to fly on Gene's rig, we did Paul's. This was great but not as exciting to me as Gene's. Paul didn't do this back in 70's so it wasn't as magical to me, but still loads of fun! Paul's set-up was a wire that hung from the rafters with a small step at the bottom. Paul would step up and the rig would fly him over the whole crowd to a small platform on the other side of the arena. Even though it wasn't as high as Gene's, it was even scarier because I wasn't strapped in at all. I had to hold on for dear life or could fall 30 feet onto the chairs on the arena floor.

Paulie's and Dave's brother Brian was the last to go. When he got to the middle of the arena, the person operating the flying machine decided to play a joke and leave him dangling high above the floor for a little while. Brian was screaming, but we were all on the floor laughing … Good times!

30 feet in the air flying like the God of Thunder!

After our show in Detroit, we realized that we had been on the road almost a full month and we hadn't emptied our waste compartment. Even though we had a strict rule of "No Dumps" on the RV, we knew it was still very full of just urine. Luckily, we found the perfect time to empty it. Dave and our tech, Paul LaPlaca, had met a few girls at the show earlier that night and we were parked outside their apartment somewhere in a suburb of Detroit. When we rented the RV, the owner told us the correct protocol for emptying the waste. We were supposed to take it to a truck stop on the highway and hook the large hose to the sewer system. But, because we were just parked and waiting for Dave and LaPlaca, we decided this would be a good time and place to empty it out.

After losing a bet (I'm pretty sure I cheated), Musk and Paulie would be the ones to open the latch. As they got ready to open the waste compartment, I was standing in the RV, leaning out the door watching.

Once they pulled the latch and the drain opened, I was hit with the most putrid odor I have ever smelled in my life. Paulie and Musk began screaming as a rapid river of piss flowed down the street into the nearby sewer. Just then, Dave and LaPlaca were walking up the street toward the RV and began yelling, "Oh my God, what's the smell?" We all jumped back into the RV and got the hell out of there as fast as we could! We heard later that summer that Dave Matthew's tour bus had a major lawsuit against them for dumping their waste tank off a bridge. We were lucky nobody saw us.

Sound check was always an adventure for ZO2. After line check, the sound man always asked us to play a quick song to get levels. We were still such a new band that we really didn't know any cover songs together; the only songs we all knew were KISS songs, and "That Thing You Do" by the Wonders from the Tom Hanks movie. We all loved that movie and watched it about 100 times in the RV that summer.

One day in Nashville, Tennessee, while sound checking, I jokingly began playing the drum intro to KISS' "Love Gun." Paulie and Dave immediately joined in. "What are we doing?" we all thought as we looked at each other. We then gave each other another quick glance, as if to say, "Fuck it," and we continued on.

Midway through the first chorus, we saw Paul Stanley and Tommy Thayer stroll out onto the stage. "Uh oh," I thought. "Are they going to be pissed?" Not only were they not mad that we were doing their song, but Paul grabbed the microphone and started singing the second verse. Tommy joined in right behind with his guitar. I couldn't believe it! "Holy shit! I'm jamming with KISS!" I thought. Paulie then pointed behind me and I saw the KISS logo flashing above me. If I could only zap myself back in time to my 5- year-old self and tell him that one day you'll be jamming with KISS, on KISS's stage – as the KISS logo flashed behind you.

As I mentioned, Paul Stanley was a little bit of a germaphobe, and a few times Paulie tried to sing backup vocals with him. But, sharing the mic clearly made Paul a little stand-offish. I shot Paulie a look of death, as if to say, "If you chase Paul Stanley off this stage because of your dirty breath, I will kill you!" My death glance worked and Paulie quickly got the hint. Just as the solo section kicked in with Tommy taking the lead, Eric Singer walked out on to the stage with his arms crossed. Eric was very confused by what was happening, and I think maybe a little jealous that we sounded so good. We ended the song on a big open chord and I saw Paul Stanley turn back towards me and then look up to the rafters. At first, I had no idea what he was doing. Thank God I quickly realized he was signaling me to do the ending the way KISS did it live every night. He wanted me to play the intro at a fast speed while he pretended to shoot the fireworks in the rafters. I hit the ending and sure enough Paul did his part. It was perfect, like I had played it with him a million times. He gave me a fist bump and said, "Great job!"

Sound check was over and we were flying high. Soon after, the sound man came over to us and said that what we had done was cool, but that he didn't think we should ever play a KISS song during sound check again.

We said, "Why not? They didn't seem to mind." He replied, "Because you guys sounded better than KISS, that's why!" That was our first and last time jamming on a KISS song for sound check.

The night after in Indianapolis, ZO2 had just finished sound check on stage and Gene came out to hang with us to mess around with his bass a little.

We started talking and began asking him some KISS questions, which he loved to answer. Paulie asked, "Hey, why did you guys go back to regular tuning in the 80's but still D-tuned during the live shows?" KISS had always D-tuned throughout the 70's, and all that meant was that they tuned their guitars lower to achieve a heavier, bluesier type sound. This was very common for 70's rock bands.

Gene's response was classic: "What do you mean? We didn't do that. Maybe your CD player is playing those albums at a faster speed." We all began to laugh in disbelief about what he just said. Paulie tried to explain more, but Gene was insistent that Paulie didn't know what he was talking about. Paulie even went so far as to bet Gene $20. The bet was if Paulie was right, then Gene had to pay him $20 and write on the bill, "I was wrong. Paulie Z was right." If Gene was correct, then during our set later that night, Paulie would have to say to the crowd, "Don't bet Gene Simmons. He's always right."

Now the only question was, "How are we going to find out who was right?" Just then, Tommy Thayer walked onto the stage and Paulie quickly asked him the question. Tommy laughed and pleaded the fifth. There was no way he was going to take our side over Gene's. Tommy said, "There's Paul. Go ask him," then he chuckled.

Paulie Z winning $20 from Gene Simmons. Not an easy accomplishment.

We ran over to Paul and posed the same question: "Did you guys tune back up during the 80's?" He responded right away with "Yeah." Gene looked completely baffled and said, "Why would we do such a thing?" Paul responded, "I guess we did it so I could sing higher." Gene looked completely dumbfounded. That $20 bill is one of Paulie's most prized possessions.

After shows in Pittsburgh, Milwaukee, Chicago, Cleveland, and Cincinnati, we arrived in Camden, New Jersey, and were almost back home. Right after lunch, someone from the Poison camp came running over to talk to our manager Bob in private.

He explained that they had a possible emergency brewing. C.C. DeVille had locked himself in his hotel room on some sort of drug or alcohol binge and was refusing to come to the show. This came as a complete shock because as far as we knew, everyone in Poison was clean and sober at this point. I guess not. Bob said, "That's terrible news, but what would you like me to do?" Their tour manager asked if there was anyway Paulie could learn the set by show time.

One of the highlights of the tour. Jamming to KISS's Love Gun with Paul Stanley!

So, for the next four hours, Paulie sat in the RV with his guitar and attempted to learn all of Poison's set, just in case C.C. didn't show up. Thank God, and at the last minute, C.C. arrived and played a flawless show. Paulie let out a sigh of relief. To prevent this from happening again, Poison flew out former Skid Row guitarist, Dave "The Snake" Sabo, to travel with them for the rest of the tour, just in case.

As we worked our way around the whole country, it was almost time for us to get back and play in our hometown of New York! We had two local shows on the tour that all of our friends and family were going to attend. Jones Beach in Long Island and PNC Arts Center in New Jersey.

I would always call my mom and Madalyn to check in to see how they were. Madalyn was sleeping over and staying with my mom a few times a week because my mom had been pretty sick over the last few years. I was so thankful to have Madalyn spending time with her while I was on tour. I wanted more than anything for my mom to attend one of the local shows. After everything she had done and sacrificed for me over the years, I needed to have her there when I played on the same stage as KISS in New York.

Still, she kept telling me that she didn't think she would be able to make it. Her asthma and emphysema made it difficult for her to get around. I remember talking to Gene one day at lunch and I was telling him about my mom. He said, "Tell her we will send a limo for her! Anything she needs." Gene was a mama's boy like I was, and he understood what it meant to me for her to be there. For everyone out there that says Gene is just a money hungry businessman, I can tell you that he has a heart of gold.

Madalyn, with Paulie's girlfriend Kim, came to meet us in Boston and to spend a few days on the road with us. I loved having Madalyn experience this amazing adventure with me. I asked her about what my mom had said about coming to see a show. "I don't think she is going to be up for it," she said. "She wants more than anything to be there but is nervous about her breathing." I knew there was nothing I could do to convince her that she would be okay and that I would make sure she was treated like a queen. I had an all-access pass made for her and even had Gene call her one day to try and reassure her, but it didn't work.

On July 20 and 21, we would finally be playing our hometown. While we were local, we decided to go home and see our families and sleep in our own beds. The first night I arrived home, my mom and Madalyn greeted me with a little celebration. They made posters with

"Congratulations!" on them and drew me all these amazing pictures. I felt so loved and overwhelmed with joy.

Right before our hometown shows, we had decided that we would give every person who worked on the tour either a ZO2 shirt or a sweatshirt as a special thank you for all they'd done for us. It turned out be a great move. For the rest of the tour, it looked like the road crew belonged to ZO2, especially in New York! Gene even came up to us and said, "Very smart PR move, giving the crew your shirts. Free advertising. Good work!"

Even though Paul was the one who had given us the shot to come on tour with KISS, by this point, Gene had really taken us under his wing. On days like this, he just seemed proud of us, like a dad who was proud of his boys. The two local shows at PNC Arts center and Jones Beach were incredible! I had a lot of friends and family at both, and I had all-access passes for my brother and his wife, Liz, plus I even got my father a ticket to see the show.

KISSNATION unites backstage on KISS tour.

All my friends from grammar school were coming, along with Carlos and Ruby from KISSNATION. It was so great to have my friends that dressed as KISS in my school talent show many years ago, and Carlos and Ruby from my KISS tribute band there to expeience this with me.

These shows were a true party and homecoming for ZO2. The love and support from our friends and family was unreal. KISS and Poison seemed excited for us as well. Bret was telling me one day about his first "homecoming" show after Poison had "made it," and Paul Stanley wished me luck backstage, telling me to "Enjoy every minute of it." I just wished my mom was there to see it all.

While we were home for a couple of days, we decided to bring the RV back for a quick check up and maintenance. When we originally rented the RV, they went over some instructions with Paulie. One main thing was maintenance on the back-compartment generator.

Paulie had told us that we needed to change the oil after 500 hours of use, but it turned out that we actually needed to change it after every 50 to 100 hours of use. We had completely fried the generator and it would take them 3 to 4 days to replace it.

My old grammar school friends came to see me open for
KISS at Jones Beach.

We couldn't wait 3 or 4 days! We had a show in Scranton, Pennsylvania, the next day. They told us if we needed it right away that we had to take it without the back-compartment generator, which essentially meant no air conditioning. And unfortunately for us, we were headed south on this leg of the tour. Anyone who has ever traveled to Georgia, Florida, or Alabama in the dead of the summer knows AC is a must. It got so bad that at one point, I had to sleep with frozen push-up ices on my head. It didn't really matter, though; we were still having the time of our lives.

Sleeping with flovored ice on my head was the only way to get through the heat of the RV in the south.

My friend Billy and his wife were out of town when ZO2 played in New York so they planned a special trip to Tampa, Florida, just to see a show. I met Billy early in the day to show him around the arena. I began the tour by showing him how the crew set up the stage. As we were watching the crew, Billy pointed and asked, "Why are they taking those lights down?" Sure enough, the crew was taking stuff down instead of putting it up. A few minutes later, we all got word that the show was cancelled due to Paul Stanely's health. It was so hot the night before in West Palm Beach that Paul became dehydrated and needed an I.V. after the show. He was still suffering from that dehydration and was unable to perform in Tampa. Billy had made the trip for nothing.

We were now nearing the end of the tour and we began to hear stories about the headliner's road crew playing pranks on young opening bands. We assumed these were just stories to make us nervous and paranoid, at least until our show in Birmingham, Alabama.

ZO2 began each show the same exact way, with a big open chord and crash. On this particular day, as soon as I hit my cymbals, I was covered in baby powder that had been placed on top of my cymbals. Even though I would now have to play the rest of the show looking like a ghost, I laughed to myself and thought it actually looked like a cool effect for our opening — almost like an explosion with a giant cloud of smoke.

I thought it was a very harmless prank until I realized that because of the baby powder, my hands and sticks had become extremely slippery, causing both sticks to fly out of my hands on the next downbeat. Again, I laughed it off because I knew I had my stick bag attached to my floor tom and could quickly replace both sticks. But when I reached down, I found all of my spare drum sticks duct taped together. So here I was, in the middle of ZO2's first song, opening up for KISS and Poison, in front of 10,000 fans, and I had no sticks. As I frantically began to rip at the duct tape to free a pair of sticks, while trying to keep a beat with my other hand and feet, I glanced to the side of the stage to see Poison drummer, Rikki Rockett, KISS drummer Eric Singer and his drum tech Joey Arias laughing so hard they were in tears!

ZO2 with KISS manager Doc McGhee

Somehow, I got through the rest of the show.

We would play the last show with Poison in Atlanta, Georgia, on August 4. After that, we drove back home to New York to return the RV that had now accumulated almost 20,000 miles. We would then fly out to meet KISS for two more shows in Texas with just ZO2 as the opener.

Poison was great to us through the whole tour. On their last day, they told us they were planning their 30th anniversary tour in a few years and they would love to have us on it. As sad as it was to know we weren't going to see the guys from Poison anymore, we were unbelievably excited because the last two shows of the tour would be just KISS and ZO2.

Once we got home from Atlanta, we had a few days off before flying out to Texas. I missed my mom and Madalyn tremendously, and I loved being back home with them. It was really the first time we had to sit back and enjoy what I had just accomplished. Sometimes that's difficult to do because people are always looking ahead to the "next thing." I always found time to savor those moments.

On August 10, 2004, ZO2 flew out to Texas to meet back up with KISS. Shortly after we arrived at the arena, I was scheduled to do a phone interview with a local radio station. This type of stuff was happening pretty regularly now, and I was doing the phone interview in the backstage/dressing room area when all of a sudden Gene saw me and started screaming, "Yo Buttafuoco! Hey everyone, Buttafuoco is back!" It put a big smile on my face.

The two shows opening directly for KISS were unbelievable. Both arenas were indoors and we got an extra 20 minutes to play. Don't get me wrong, the whole tour was a literal dream come true, but something about seeing just KISS/ZO2 on the billboards and marquee was magical. Having that week off in between really gave us a chance to reflect back on the whole tour and fully appreciate these last two shows. The KISS video crew even professionally filmed the final show in Hidalgo, Texas, for us. We still have to release that full show one day.

We gave everything we had during those final two shows. We had so much energy, and by now we were completely firing on all cylinders. The crowds were massive and electric, and the response for ZO2 was the biggest all tour. Because this was our second trip through Texas, a lot of fans came up to us during our meet and greet and said they came back to specifically see ZO2.

We were once again casually reminded of the possibility of pranks played on the opening band, especially on the very last show. We were told that we should watch our gear at all cost.

The road crew relayed to us stories of different practical jokes they had played over the years. They said, "One time we tied fishing wire to every single piece of gear on the stage and then one by one lifted it to the rafters. By the time the opening band finished their set, they had no gear left!" We became so paranoid that after our final sound check, we never left the stage. We stayed there for another hour. We ate dinner on the stage and guarded our gear. We saw people from the crew after the show and we basically laughed and said, "You didn't get us because we stayed on stage and guarded our gear all day. You couldn't prank us!" They all started laughing and said, "Yeah, that's the prank!" They got us after all.

That last night in Hidalgo was something I'll never forget. During our final song, "Fly on your Wings," I experienced another "Frozen Moment." Somehow this one was a little different than all of the others; it was as if my whole journey of being a drummer was coming to a climax. I was on stage, on the last show of the tour, during the last song, opening for my idols KISS, in front of 15,000 screaming fans. I knew I had a long career ahead of me, but I realized that even if I never did anything else beyond this moment, I would still be forever happy just being able to reflect back on this magical experience with KISS. For the next 4:18 seconds, I gave every bit of passion, energy, and heart that I had building inside of me since I first saw KISS 25 years earlier. I know it's cliche, but I literally left everything I had on the stage that night.

ZO2 walking off stage for the last time on the KISS tour. Hugging and thanking KISS production manager Patrick Whitely.

A few minutes after we got off stage, we were greeted by the guys in KISS who were about to take the stage themselves. They embraced us and said, "Great job, guys." Eric gave me a big hug and said, "See 'ya down the road." I thanked Gene for everything they did for us and I told him that I would never forget it and maybe I could even return the favor one day. He said, "Nothing would make me happier, Buttafuco." And just like that, the tour was over.

CHAPTER 23

LIFE AFTER TOUR

My view from behind the drums at the last show of the KISS tour in Hidalgo, Texas.

Adjusting to everyday life after we got home from tour was difficult. While on the road, everyone was always ready to get us whatever we needed. Food, drinks, and just help with whatever we wanted or needed. On top of that, we had 10 to 15,000 screaming fans every night who adored us. To put it simply, we were catered to at every level. Now, not having that kind of attention 24/7 was a hard thing to come down from.

Playing locally again around New York City was another big adjustment. I had gotten accustomed to playing big arenas and sheds with 10 to 15,000 fans every night. I really didn't want to have to go back to playing all of the same clubs I'd played a hundred times.

Bob was trying to get us on the Scorpions/Tesla tour shortly after the KISS tour, but it never came to fruition. Because we didn't get that tour, Dave decided he was still going to go out with TSO starting in October, but before he left, he called to say that he might have a cool opportunity for me.

★ ★ ★ *JOEY CASSATA* ★ ★ ★

Dave asked if I'd be interested in playing with the Trans-Siberian Orchestra. He explained that they were essentially looking for a back-up drummer to be on call in case of emergency. All I would have to do is learn the set, practice with the other back-up players a few times, and get paid to sit home just in case they needed me. It sounded like the perfect gig, but first I would have to audition for one of the co-founders and current touring keyboardist Bob Finkle, as well as their talent manager, Dina Fanai.

It turns out that Bob and Dina were both at the Jones Beach ZO2 show and they really liked my playing and my look. They asked Dave to get me to come down for an audition. I was to learn three songs for the audition, "Mad Russian Christmas," "Ornament," and their biggest hit, "Christmas Eve Sarajevo." Dave warned me that they had to be perfect and that they were very, very strict about tempos.

In early October 2004, I went to SIR studios and met with Bob and Dina. Before I even began playing they told me that they loved the ZO2 performance at Jones Beach and wanted me to do some of the stuff I was doing on stage. I was a little confused and said, "What stuff"? Dina replied, "The stuff with your arms over your head, the stick twirls, you know just be flashy."

It was so funny: not long ago, in the 90's, this sort of thing was absolutely frowned upon. No one was allowed to be a flashy drummer. People thought it was a joke. But, on the KISS tour, I finally got to be myself again and do all the things I loved doing while I played. I stole most of my tricks from one of my biggest drumming influences, Robert Sweet from Stryper.

ZO2 got to open for Stryper a few times over the years and I got to hang with Robert a lot. He even told me after sound check one day that he thought I was better than him, which sounds crazy coming from one of my idols.

I played the three songs and tried to be as flashy as possible. It was a little weird because I was the only one in the room while Bob and Dina stared at me. It felt a little awkward twirling and throwing my sticks in the air, but if that's what they wanted, then that's what I was going to give them.

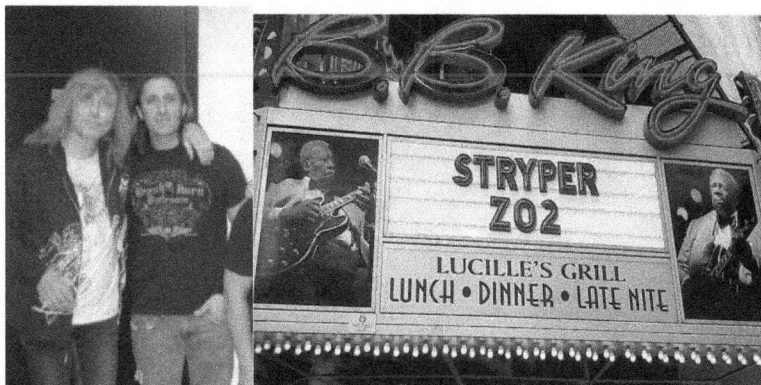

Robert Sweet of Stryper and me, hanging backstage at BB Kings in NYC.

After the three songs, Bob Kinkle jumped on the piano and asked if I could play along to a new song they were working on. It was called "Christmas Nights in Blue." He played the feel and we jammed for a few minutes. Shortly after, Bob and Dina thanked me for coming and said they would be in touch. They didn't show much emotion and I had no idea how I did. I thought it went as well as could be expected.

Dave called me a few days later and asked, "What did you say to Bob?" I wasn't sure what he meant and came back with, "What do you mean?" "You must have pissed him off somehow because he didn't like your attitude," Dave replied. I was immediately trying to play back everything Bob and I talked about, but there wasn't much. Bob was a slightly strange individual with a dry personality. He seemed sweet and nice, but his personality was definitely a little out there. After my long pause of trying to figure out what I said to insult Bob, Dave said, "Just kidding! They loved you. You got the gig!" I almost smacked Dave right through the phone!

This was great news! I just needed to make a little more money playing drums somehow to go with the new TSO money.

Paulie's and Dave's full-time jobs besides ZO2 was being children's entertainers. They called themselves "The Z Brothers." They sang children's songs at schools and were hired for private birthday parties. I couldn't believe it, but they actually made really good money doing this. I thought to myself, "Why not give it a shot?"

I called my old Playground bandmate, Steve Kerasotis, and asked him if he was interested in trying it with me. Steve had just quit his job at Verizon and said, "Absolutely!" Steve and I knew someone who worked in a school and they just happened to be looking for someone to teach a music program, but it was really to be more entertainment than teaching.

TSO Rehearsal in Omaha, Nebraska.

Now, I was set with the money I'd get from singing to kids and being the back-up drummer for TSO. This was incredible for me. For my entire life, the main goal had been to make a living as a musician and not have a regular 9 to 5 job. This was the first time that it was actually happening. It might not have been exactly what I imagined after going on tour with KISS, but I was still enjoying every second of it.

As much as I absolutely loved the KISS tour, it was hard to leave my mom for that long. And now I also had the girl I loved, Madalyn, with whom I wanted to spend every waking second. I'm not sure I would have really wanted to go out on that Scorpions/Tesla tour if it had happened. I loved being home with Madalyn and my mom way too much.

Once Dave got back from the TSO tour, ZO2 picked up business as usual. We started a regular residency on Monday nights at Arlene's Grocery. This worked out great because we had begun writing our second album, and the Arlene's residency was a great way to battle test all of our new material.

We even went out to California for the NAMM convention and did a mini-tour up the coast of California with Alex Skolnick from the band Testament.

While at NAMM, I got back in touch with Todd Trent from Ludwig

ZO2 playing our residency at Arlene's Grocery in NYC 2004.

drums. Todd was the one willing to give me a kit for the KISS tour, but I stupidly turned him down because he didn't have exactly what I was looking for at the time. Now, I wanted to revisit a possible endorsement with Ludwig drums. Todd said that he could start me out at a "cost level endorsement," which meant I would technically be an official "Ludwig Artist," but I wouldn't get anything for free; I would get it at cost. It wasn't exactly what I was hoping for, but I couldn't pass up the opportunity to endorse my favorite brand of drums. While at the NAMM show, I also bought my first Ludwig Black beauty snare drum right off the showroom floor.

During 2005, ZO2 kept busy with a lot of local shows and a few bigger ones, opening for some big-name acts. One such act was Bent Brother, otherwise known as "Twisted Sister." Twisted was just starting to get back into the mainstream and touring regularly, but they had yet to do shows in their signature makeup and outfits. Because of this, they would play random shows as their alter ego, "Bent Brother."

Our manager Bob was good friends with Twisted's guitarist, Jay Jay French, so he secured us the opening slot. I'm not sure how Bob was as a manager, but he had some great connections and got us cool gigs because of them. In fact, in the back of my mind, I was always a little worried about what would happen when all of Bob's connections/friends dried up. The other problem with his connections were that they were all with older bands. Don't get me wrong, I loved it! After all, he did make my dreams come true by getting us the KISS tour! Twisted Sister had also been one of my favorite bands growing up. I'm just not sure a young band like ZO2 was really prospering from these types of shows.

We did get to open up for former Rainbow singer, Joe Lynn Turner because Bob had produced a few of his albums. We played back-to-back shows with Joe Lynn, first at the Chance Theater in Poughkeepsie and then at Double D's in Morristown, New Jersey. Both shows were amazing, but the main reason I'm telling this story is because there was a special guest in attendance at The Chance show watching us from the balcony — none other than former KISS guitarist Ace Frehley!

Ace was really there to see Joe Lynn, but we saw him watching ZO2 and looked to be digging it. It was a thrill to play in front of one of my all-time heroes, but the real thrill came the next night at Double D's. After ZO2 got off stage and before Joe Lynn Turner started, I went to the upstairs area to hang out and grab a drink when all of a sudden there was a tap on my shoulder. I turned around thinking it was just a random fan, but my eyes couldn't believe who was standing in front of me. It was Ace! He said, "Hey, you're that drummer from last night!" I was caught totally by surprise: not only was I suddenly in a conversation with Ace Frehley, but he knew exactly who I was. I said, "Yeah! I saw you watching us at the Chance. What did you think?" In that funny, high-pitched voice Ace replied, "Great man! I love your groove!" Then he asked, "Whatcha drinking?" I told him I was drinking scotch and he raised his glass and we said, "Cheers!" Just then Joe Lynn's set started and it cut my conversation with Ace short. I walked away thinking, "Wow!" Moments liked these made it all worthwhile.

Me and KISS guitarist Ace Frehley!

The second ZO2 album came out much more naturally. We now understood who we were and what we should sound like. I always thought the first album was more of a mish-mosh of all different kinds of songs. On this second album, we made a conscious effort to sound one particular way. I always liked to describe our sound as a mix between Aerosmith and Zeppelin.

The original title for the second album was going to be *Return 2 OZ*. Get it? 2 OZ is ZO2 backwards. We even had the whole concept for the cover, and the plan was, we would try to recreate a scene from the *Wizard of Oz*, but with us dressed as rock versions of the characters. Paulie would be the Scarecrow, Dave would be the Tin Man, and I would be the Lion. The girl from the cover of our first album, who we named Sue Z, would be Dorothy. It all sounds pretty ridiculous now, but we were all very into it back then.

Right before we planned on doing the elaborate photo shoot for the "Return 2 OZ" concept, we changed our mind and decided to go with what got us here.

We all loved the first album cover and agreed that we should go with another classic pin-up girl. Judas Priest had their iconic covers, Iron Maiden had Eddie, and ZO2 had Sue Z. The name of the album would be *Ain't it Beautiful*.

ZO2's second album, Ain't It Beautiful.

A few months prior to its release, I had a long talk with my mom and decided I wanted to propose to Madalyn. She was overwhelmed with joy and couldn't have been happier. My mom and Madalyn really bonded while I was on tour, and she was so happy that I was going to ask her to be my wife.

I decided I would take Madalyn on a beautiful vacation to the Dominican Republic for her 30th birthday and ask her to marry me on the beach.

I've probably said this a dozen times already throughout this book, but I'm not a person that ever really gets nervous, but that night on the beach I was definitely nervous. It wasn't because I thought Madalyn would say no, but because I knew my life was about to change forever. I remember leaving her on the beach in a hammock and telling her that I'd be right back. I went up to our hotel room to get the ring and I also guzzled a bottle of wine. When I returned, I was definitely a little looser and ready to start the next chapter of my life. Madalyn said yes, and we were as happy as could be.

Shortly after I got engaged, my mom's health got much worse. She was constantly in and out of the hospital and just like my grandpa was diagnosed with severe emphysema. Her breathing had been pretty bad my whole life, so I was used to this.

During one of her hospital stays, my mom kept complaining about something in her eye. She said it felt like there was a film or coating and that it was driving her crazy. It turned out that she had something called "macular degeneration."

Basically, her retina was slowly starting to deteriorate. At first, it was only in one eye and then it started in the second. This, on top of her breathing, made my poor mother's life miserable. She couldn't really leave the apartment because it was hard for her to walk due to her breathing, and the only things that gave her any solace was to watch "her programs" on TV and to read. Now with this macular degeneration, both

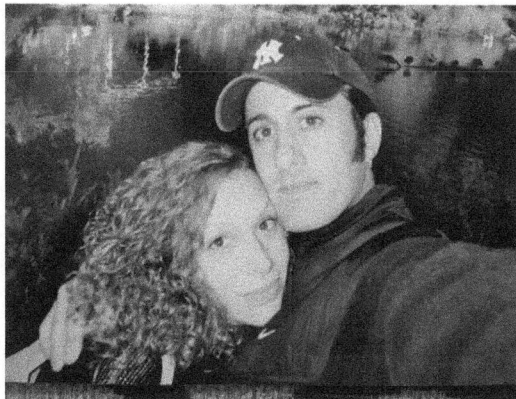

Madalyn and I shortly after getting engaged in Punta Cana, Dominican Republic 2005.

of those activities were becoming impossible. I couldn't understand why this was happening. This woman had given her whole life to her family, sacrificed everything for her sons, and now she was being tortured. I was furious at the world and God.

Once the macular degeneration really started to take over, it seemed like her breathing got much worse as well. I always felt it was because she just couldn't fight anymore and that her mind began to give up. My mom was the strongest women in the whole world, but not being able to breathe, and now being almost blind, was too much for her. Over the next 15 months, she was in the hospital more than she was out.

Ain't It Beautiful would first be released in early 2006. We were super pumped with the album and I was very happy with the drum sound, especially the sound of my new Black Beauty snare. Songs like "If You See Kaye," "She Believes," and the title track "Ain't it Beautiful" are, in my opinion, some of ZO2's best songs.

ZO2 had also just recently transitioned from our Monday night residency at Arlene's Grocery to a special monthly show we called "ZO2's Rock Asylum." This was Paulie's brainchild. In essence, because the music scene was still pretty flat in NYC, he wanted to create our own happening rock scene. His idea was to gather up all the up-and-coming hungry bands in the area and promote the hell out of one night a month with ZO2 as the headliner. He even had the idea of trading shows with out-of-town bands so that they could come to NYC and play in front of a great crowd, as long as they would reciprocate the same for when ZO2 went to their town.

I give Paulie a lot of credit. It was a great idea and he worked his ass off to make it "the place to be" every month. That's the type of personality Paulie had: he needed a project to work on with a tangible goal on which he could focus all of his manic energy. If Paulie didn't have "a project" to focus on, he thought keeping busy, just to be able to say to himself, "We are working hard," was the smart thing to do. Paulie and I have had many arguments over this exact way of thinking, but Rock Asylum was NOT one of those times.

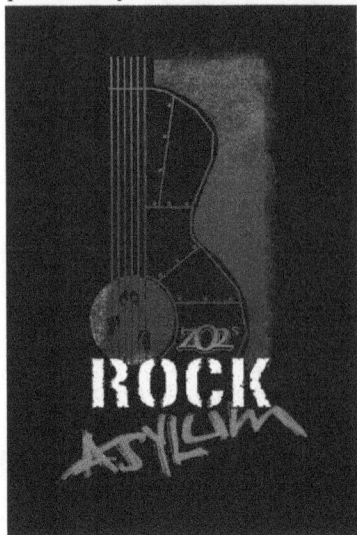

I always felt playing random, sporadic shows was not only useless but could actually hurt the band. Once we finished the KISS tour, Paulie started to book as many random gigs as possible just to "stay busy." I think it was the way he coped with coming down from the high of the tour. My argument had always been that if we played a random empty place in Ohio just to say, "We are playing and keeping busy," it actually hurt us in the long run. I always thought that working "smart" was more important than just working "hard." Driving 10 hours to play for 20 people wasn't the problem. I had no problem working as hard and as tirelessly as anyone. It was more about perception. The old term "perception is reality" is 100 percent accurate.

We had created a level of fame and success by touring with KISS, and I firmly believed playing a random show for 20 people started to take away the credibility that we worked so hard to achieve. I was happy that Paulie started Rock Asylum so he could stop thinking that we just had to appear like a busy band by playing shit holes across the country. In fact, ZO2's Rock Asylum started to create a real buzz throughout Manhattan: any and every band wanted to be a part of it, and we constantly had to turn people away at the door due to the club being sold out.

This type of branding and gigging worked. Creating a buzz in a small club and making it into "the place to be" was the best way to create a following. Playground did it years prior, and now it was ZO2's turn. We were already local celebrities because of the KISS tour, and now everyone wanted a piece of us because of Rock Asylum.

This picture perfectly sums up my time with these two goofballs.

CHAPTER 23 B

ALL YOU CAN EAT

Because Paulie and Dave never drank alcohol, our biggest vice while we were on the road was always…FOOD! We would eat everything and anything we could find. One of our main things that we loved to do were eating contests. I believe the very first one was after we all saw the Nathan's Hot Dog eating contest on TV. After a show at Arlene's Grocery in the East Village of NYC, we decided to have our own Hot Dog eating contest!!

ZO2 and a few dozen friends went to the world-famous Gray's Papaya on 8th street and 6th avenue to begin the festivities. The winner was whomever could eat the most hot dogs in 10 minutes. Paulie and Dave were huge eaters but they both didn't realize that hot dogs had been my favorite food when I was a young kid.

For some crazy reason the Z brothers decided they wanted condiments on their hot dogs. I went plain dog and bun. Once the clock started, I jumped out to a quick lead devouring 3 hotdogs in the first minute. Paulie, surprisingly fell behind right away, but Dave was right on my tail. As we approached the 10-minute mark my stomach was actually feeling great but my jaw was killing me!! Paulie was way behind at this point and Dave was about one and half behind me.

The timer sounded and we were instructed to stop eating. The final tally was Paulie 9 hot dogs, Dave 13 and a half, and the winner.....Joey with 15 hot dogs in 10 minutes!!

The big ZO2 Hot Dog eating contest!

Immediately after, I decided that I didn't want the calories from 15 dogs sitting in my belly. I had to watch my girlish figure after all. So, I went out onto 8ᵗʰ street and proceeded to throw every bit of the 15 hot dogs up all over the street. (Kids don't try this at home. It's very unhealthy) Weirdly I could always throw up on demand. Dave was in shock and asked me "Why the hell are you throwing it all up?" I told him "Because I don't want all those calories!" He looked completely dumbfounded and asked "You mean if I throw it up, I won't get the calories? That's amazing!! Why doesn't everyone do that?" I responded by saying "Some people do. It's called Bulimia stupid!" We both had a big laugh.

I have this whole contest on video, including the disgusting aftermath. I'll definitely put it on YouTube one day for everyone to get a laugh. This was just the beginning of countless eating contests over the next 10 years.

The TV show Man vs. Food was just becoming popular and whenever ZO2 hit a new town we would always look to see if there were any challenges that the host, Adam Richman did on the show. We had a great time trying these. We succeeded at some and failed at others, but always had a ball eating either way!

One of my favorite places to eat in L.A. The Griddle.

Those big challenges were fun, but I always enjoyed the spur of the moment bet that would happen at a rest stop at 3am. One-night Dave bet us that he could eat 75 McDonald's chicken nuggets. And sure enough he did it!! After he ate the nuggets, he attempted to purge himself like I did with the hot dogs. Unfortunately, Dave didn't have my gift of vomiting at will. Thank god he didn't, because the noises that came out of him in the bathroom stall at the rest stop, while trying to vomit for the next half hour, were some of the funniest things I have ever heard in my life.

Not to be outdone by his little brother, the next day Paulie bet that he could eat 7 McDonald's Double Quarter Pounders with cheese. Yes, you read that correctly .... 7 doubles, that's 14 burgers!! What was even worse, this was only about an hour before ZO2 was going on stage. Whether Paulie completed the challenge or not, either way this was going to be great! Paulie's only condition was that the burgers had to be made fresh. So, we ordered 3 double quarter pounders and told the McDonald's cook to be ready for when we needed more. I think some of the workers and cooks at these places enjoyed seeing us try these

Making pizza at my favorite Pizzeria of all time...Joe's Pizza!!

ridiculous eating challenges just as much as we did.

I could definitely beat Paulie in a head to head speed eating challenge, but when it came to quantity, Paulie was the man to beat. And he proved it this night. Paulie ate the 7 double quarter pounders with cheese with relative ease. And even more surprisingly, he sang amazingly at the show only 20 minutes later. He always says he thinks all the McDonald's grease helped coat his throat.

Another fun challenge was when I said I could eat 2 full boxes of cereal. Paulie and Dave took that bet but with one stipulation, they had to pick one of the boxes of cereal. I agreed. I picked one of my all-time favorites, Fruity Pebbles. They picked something that they thought

A fan gave us a giant Rice Crispy treat to eat after a show.

would be impossible to eat a full box of, Shredded Wheats. I remember sitting at a diner while they ate their diner food and I devoured 2 full boxes of cereal. People looked at us like we were absolutely insane. No,

we weren't Motley Crue doing drugs until they were in a stupor, we weren't AC/DC drinking until they passed out, we were ZO2 eating until we were ready to burst!!

Some of the other eating challenges that went on through the years included….Dave eating a dozen Dunkin' Doughnuts (Not the best idea being that Dave was diabetic), Paulie and I eating a full pie of Pizza each at Joe's Pizza in L.A. Paulie was actually still hungry after the pie and ordered two more slices. I even ate a full jar of peanut butter one night on a bet. Dave disgustingly ate 100 oysters once! I still think this might have been the worst out of all the challenges. The guy who had to shuck the oysters (open them) was so pissed off! Haha.

Even our fans would bring us a feast after shows. They would bring cookies, cakes, doughnuts, anything that was terrible and fattening they would bring for us. Finally, we asked people if they really wanted to feed us to try and bring us healthy snacks. So, they started to bring us giant shrimp platters! I remember eating a 100 platter of shrimp each one night!!

The weirdest thing someone gave us to eat was a jar of red liquid with some kind of mushy substance inside. I swear that it looked like a jar with a bloody organ inside, they told us it was something called "Blood Pudding." We decided to pass on that one after legendary rock singer Joe Lynn Turner told us a horror story of his. (Actually, I think Dave still tasted it). Joe said that a young fan brought him a homemade baked cherry pie one show. Joe had a piece of the delicious pie later that night and never thought another second about it. That was until he saw the same fan at a show months later. The young female fan asked Joe if he enjoyed the pie she had made for him. Joe told her that it was delicious and he thanked her for baking it for him. The fan was suddenly very excited that Joe had eaten her pie and creepily said "Now we will be together forever." Joe asked "What do you mean together forever?" The young girl creepily giggled and told Joe that she had put her own blood into the pie and now she would be inside him forever. Needless to say, after hearing that story I never ate another homemade, fan made food item again. Amazingly enough, this did not deter Paulie and Dave. They continued to eat everything and anything that the fans brought them.....Hahaha.

For Dave's 30th birthday, we got him something he'd wanted his whole life. What's that you ask? A new car? A new bass? Cool new

Dave's 30th birthday wish. Swiming in a pool of Twinkies!

jewelry? Nope… he wanted to swim in a pool of Twinkies and eat his way out!! Yes, you read that correctly. A 30-year-old man wanted to swim in a pool of Twinkies and eat his way out.

So, we bought a small blowup pool and filled it with about 500 Twinkies. Do you know how long it takes to open 250 packs of godamn Twinkies!?? A looong time, that's how long! Dave was in absolute heaven when he opened his eyes and saw the pool of Twinkies. He proceeded to jump in, splash around (more like squish around), and dunk his head underneath the 500 Twinkies like he was going underwater. He then sat there for the next 45 minutes and ate as many smashed up, squashed Twinkies as his little heart desired. A perfect 30th birthday in his eyes.

Over the years ZO2's eating habits became almost legendary. There have been so many occasions that we ate enough for 10 people. I remember being in LA playing a few shows with Chris Jericho's band, Fozzy. We were playing at The Whisky a Go Go on the Sunset Strip and Fozzy was doing a meet and greet and had it catered with food and drink. Of course, ZO2 was invited to take part in the festivities and I think Fozzy immediately regretted it. Most bands would have taken advantage of the drinks, but ZO2 dove right into the food. I remember someone saying that the three of us ate more than all of Fozzy's meet and greet guests combined.

Another time when we opened for Dream Theater, we hung out with drummer Mike Portnoy after the show in their dressing room. He also made the mistake of telling us to "help ourselves" to whatever we wanted. He still repeats this story today, of how we ate EVERYTHING in their dressing room in under 5 minutes!

Paulie even started bringing his own Tupperware containers to shows so he could fill up in catering. When we opened for KISS in Lake Tahoe, we were all in catering together and Paulie pulled out his Tupperware and started filling up. Gene and Paul were standing next to him and looking at him like he was a maniac. Secretly I think Gene appreciated the idea and thought it was genius.

One of my all-time favorite ZO2 food stories was when we were in LA for the NAMM music convention and had dinner with the guys from

Anthrax, Avenged Sevenfold, Mike Portnoy and Chris Jericho. We all went to an Italian restaurant called Buca di Beppo. We had an absolute feast and of course Paulie, Dave and I ordered way more than everyone else.

Once the massive bill arrived, Jericho kindly said that the meal was on him. Paulie said absolutely not and that ZO2 wanted to put in their share.

Earlier that day while we were at our hotel, Paulie noticed a 20% off coupon for Buca di Beppo on the coupon rack near the front desk.

So, after the whole table filled with rock stars heard Paulie demand that ZO2 chip in "their share" of the bill, they witnessed him go into his wallet and present Jericho with his coupon. The table erupted in laughter. Of course, Jericho refused to use Paulie's coupon but Paulie was very insistent. Finally, Jericho reluctantly agreed.

The waitress took the check, coupon included, and we all left to head over to Mike Portnoy's performance at the Sabian show. Jericho unfortunately had to wait to sign the bill.

Later that evening when we all met up again, Jericho came over to Paulie and started jokingly yelling at him. Paulie didn't understand what could be so wrong. He proceeded to tell us that he was completely mortified when the waitress returned with the bill for him to sign and informed him that unfortunately "his coupon" was expired. We laughed so hard that we couldn't breathe.

CHAPTER 24
I'D TRADE IT ALL FOR ONE MORE MINUTE

On April 9, 2006, Paulie and Dave played a random kids birthday party as the "Z Brothers," much like they did almost every weekend. We would sometimes do parties all together, but on this particular weekend I had another party already booked with my partner, Steve.

Paulie and Dave were approached after the party by one of the kid's fathers about their rock and roll look and sound. The father asked, "Hey, you guys don't look like kids' entertainers. What's your deal?" Paulie responded, "We are actually a rock band. We just do this on the side to pay the bills. We are playing BB King's in Times Square this Tuesday night. You should come and see us!" The father handed them his card and said, "Maybe I will."

★★★ START WITH A DREAM ★★★

Nobody gave much thought to this encounter at the time, but we would tell that exact story hundreds of times in interviews over the next few years. The father's name was Brian Stern, an agent at the biggest talent agency in the world, William Morris.

Mr. Stern did in fact attend the ZO2 show at BB King's, and afterwards he came over to tell us how great he thought we were. I was still in a fog, because of everything that was happening with my mom, and Paulie and Dave brushed it off as just another fan. We introduced Brian to our manager Bob and left them to talk.

Bob began to pitch the band to Brian in hopes of Brian being able to get us into the William Morris concert touring division. Brian cut Bob off at the pass and told him that he didn't work in live booking; he worked in the TV department. He told Bob that's why he was there that night. He loved The ZO2/Z Brother dynamic. He referred to it as "a Superman/Clark Kent thing." Bob immediately shifted course and said, "Okay, let's do a TV show!" Brian told Bob to write up a small treatment and that he would take a look.

Bob filled us in on the encounter during our car ride home and we all laughed it off and said, "Yeah right, we will do a TV show." It was completely out of our minds two seconds later. It was totally inconceivable to us that we could have our own TV show. Who the hell would give three knuckleheads from Brooklyn their own TV show?

In November of 2006, my father passed away. He had been diagnosed with severe cancer a few months prior. I got a call from my brother one morning that he had passed. My first thought was how strange it felt to know he wasn't around anymore, even though I'd only seen him twice over the previous year — once at my engagement party and once I visited him in the hospital a few days prior to his passing. I didn't feel any real remorse until his actual wake.

During my father's wake, my cousin Monsignor Cassato. I know what you're thinking, "That's spelled wrong!" All of the Cassata's spelled our last name slightly different. When our relatives came over from Italy, the people at Ellis Island would sometimes get the spelling of people's names wrong. Anyway, The Monsignor was giving a last speech before closing my father's coffin. He mentioned that he spoke to my father quite often about his sons, Danny and Joey. I assumed he was just giving a generic speech, because obviously my father didn't really talk about us. He hardly knew us. Then, something he said struck a nerve: he mentioned how my father would brag about his son Joey going on tour with KISS and how proud he was of him. I'm not exactly sure why, but this was the first time that I felt emotional since he passed. I broke down in tears for a few minutes. I guess it was thinking of my father being proud of me when I always assumed he never even liked me.

Shortly after my father died, I got a nice and much needed break from ZO2 because Dave left to go on tour with TSO. It was nice to have this time off from the band so I could spend the holidays with my family. It was especially nice this particular year with my father just passing and my mom being so sick.

After a beautiful two months with my family, in January of 2007, ZO2 went back out to L.A. for the NAMM music convention. We had a new tradition of playing the Viper room on the Sunset Strip whenever we went out there, along with another tradition of going to the Rainbow across the street from the Viper Room for a post-show feast.

On this particular night, while we were feasting on the greatest mozzarella sticks/squares in the world, we found out that Prince did a surprise private show at the Viper Room minutes after we left the stage. So, in a weird way, ZO2 opened for Prince that night.

During this trip to NAMM, I also officially became an A-list Ludwig endorser. Todd Trent, head of Talent relations, saw the dedication I had to the Ludwig brand and also saw that ZO2 was showing a lot of promise. He handed me the new Ludwig 2007 catalog and told me to pick out a kit and it would be free of charge. I was so proud and taken aback to be officially welcomed into the Ludwig family. I'd been watching my hero Eric Carr play Ludwig's since I was 6 years old and now they wanted me to endorse their drums. It was a real honor and dream come true.

Upon returning from L.A., I went straight to my new apartment in Brooklyn where I recently moved in with my fiancé, Madalyn. To my joy, Madalyn had a surprise birthday party waiting for me!

A few months prior, Madalyn and I found a great duplex apartment in Brooklyn. It had been 15 years since I was thrown out of my house in Brooklyn and now I was finally able to return. It felt amazing. Even though I now lived with Madalyn, I still spent most of the time in Manhattan to take care of my mom when she wasn't having one of her lengthy hospital stays. It was a very hard time for me, split between starting my new life with Madalyn and taking care of my mom.

The biggest and best surprise she could ever give me was that my mom was there for my surprise party! She had been too sick to even see my new apartment when we first moved in, but somehow she told Madalyn that she wasn't going to miss my birthday no matter what. It was almost as if she knew something that the rest of us didn't.

I was happier than I'd ever been that night when I came home to find my surprise party with my mom. My brother had just also had his third daughter, Michelle, and this would be the first time my mom was able to see and hold her. I cherish that night more than almost any other: it was the last time my mom would be semi-healthy and with her whole family. Shortly after, my mom was rushed to the hospital and never came home again.

A few days after my birthday, my mom called and sounded completely out of it. This was fairly common at this point because she would sometimes take too much of her medication.

My brother and I always got upset and told her that she had to be

Mom celebrating my 33rd birthday with family in Brooklyn.

more careful. I was heading in to the city to do a few things and was planning on staying with her most of the day anyway, so I took a shower, ate breakfast, and headed in. When I arrived, I found my mom in a pretty bad state. I still assumed she had just taken too much of her medication. I called my brother, who was at work a few blocks away, to come over.

My mom was getting very dependent on the hospital during this time period. I think she felt safe there. Now she was insisting that we call an ambulance, so we did, which was happening a few times a month now. The hospital would admit her for a few days and then discharge her. This time turned out to be very different.

The ambulance arrived and the first thing they always checked was her blood oxygen level. Her level was always a little low but this time it was extremely low and the EMT seemed very concerned. Usually, they took their time with my mom, but on this day they treated it much more like an emergency and rushed her straight to the ER. I went in the ambulance and upon arriving at the ER, they told my brother and I that they had to ventilate her. I didn't understand what was happening: I knew what ventilate meant, but I didn't understand why they had to do it. I thought my mom had just taken too much medicine. I began to panic.

The doctor explained that my mother's disorientation wasn't caused by too much medication; it was because her mind wasn't getting enough oxygen. They had to ventilate her immediately. I couldn't believe what was happening. I knew my mom was very sick, but never even thought of something this bad happening. My world was tossed into turmoil.

My mom stayed on a ventilator for the next few weeks, completely unconscious. To make matters even worse, she was in the exact same ICU room in which my grandfather had passed away years earlier. I stayed with her everyday holding her hand and talking to her. I knew she was scared and I tried everything to comfort her and tell her I was there with her.

Even after a few weeks, I still never contemplated her dying. I thought this was just a bad attack and the ventilator was going to help her lungs rest and heal. The doctors told us that they felt that we should try to take her off the ventilator. They explained that it wasn't helping her condition by keeping her on it. In fact, it was only deteriorating her body faster. They told us to prepare for the worst, and that it was very unlikely she would be able to breathe on her own.

As I stood at the window just outside the room, the doctors began to remove the ventilator. I remember banging on a cabinet and yelling to myself "C'mon, Mommy! Breathe! Please, mom, come back to me!"

The sound of the tube being removed was one of the worst sounds I'd ever heard and still haunts me to this day.

The doctor called us in and informed us that she did in fact start breathing on her own, but not to get our hopes up. Her heart rate was still extremely low and looked to be dropping. Madalyn and I stayed by her side for the next several hours, as each hour showed her heart rate getting just a little stronger. At around midnight, the nurse told me to go home and that she seemed stable for now.

It was a few days, but my mom finally regained consciousness. She still couldn't move her lower body at all though. Even though she looked to be getting better, the social aid people wanted to discuss hospice with us, and I knew that hospice is the place you go to when there was basically no hope of recovery. I said, "No way! You don't know my mom. She will fight and we will do everything we can to get her better."

The next couple of months were some of the worst in my life. My mom would take one step towards getting better and then take 5 steps backwards. I spent every waking hour by her side. During all of this, ZO2 was still keeping busy. I thought about just stopping all together, but I knew my mom wouldn't have wanted that. She would have actually been mad if I did.

ZO2 was in a little bit of a rut at this point. We were far enough removed from the KISS tour to not be able to use that as street cred anymore. Beyond that, our second album was now almost a year old and we were still playing the same old clubs with no real headway.

Our managers, Bob and Lynn, had been trying to get some kind of financial backing, but weren't able to put the right deal together. They had a promising meeting set up with Dave's girlfriend, Terri's father. Terri and her family were very wealthy, and her father owned his own radio station and was sort of an entrepreneur. The idea was to pitch to him to invest in the band. I wasn't at the meeting, but, from the report we got back from Terri, her father thought it was laughable — so much so that he suggested we immediately fire our managers because they were incompetent.

To their credit, Bob and Lynn were persistent and finally found someone that bought into their plan, and even more so than they had hoped: enter Michael Morrison and Michael Wolk. The two Michaels were lawyers by trade, but also loved the music business. They had just recently began managing a band from Boston called Craving Lucy. Bob found out that they were financially backing everything Craving Lucy did and began pitching ZO2 to them.

After a few weeks of meeting with the Michaels, Bob and Lynn convinced them to start their own record label with ZO2 and Craving Lucy as their first two acts. We couldn't believe it! No really, we actually didn't believe it: two millionaires were going to start their own record label with Bob and Lynn running it? It seemed like a fantasy, but sure enough, it happened. The label was to be called Riker Hill Records.

Since our second album was under one year old, Riker Hill would buy it from us and re-release it on their label. On top of that, they would pay us a pretty decent salary.

This was a bittersweet time for me. My mom was basically dying in the hospital while I was finally getting signed to a record label. More than anything I wanted to enjoy it with her. I remember running to the hospital when I got the news to tell her. She was absolutely thrilled. I could see in her eyes how proud of me she was. Even then, lying in the hospital, she showed how much she cared for me.

As my mom continued to get worse, we were getting more amazing news about ZO2. Almost a year prior, Brian Stern had asked us to write

a treatment for a TV show based on ZO2's life. Bob and Lynn drafted a basic concept which told exactly who we were: "Rockers by night, kids' band by day." Stern loved it and had finally gotten back to us to say that he wanted to shop us to production companies to film a "sizzle reel." We all said, "What the hell is a sizzle reel?" We learned it is essentially a demo for TV — a short little teaser about what your show could be. We interviewed a few production companies and finally settled on Mark Mark Productions. They were a small upstart company willing to fund our sizzle reel in hopes of getting the show picked up by network.

We still didn't think there was any possibility of getting our own TV show, but if they wanted to film us we thought, "Sure, why not." The idea was to film us talking about our rocker lifestyle and our kids' entertainment. We would tell a story about a time when both worlds crossed paths. The story would be intercut with flashbacks of the story. Mark Mark took us to a famous BBQ place in Manhattan called Virgil's to film to the interview segment. The Marks had seen how Paulie, Dave, and I liked to eat and they thought it would be good to capture that on film. And it was. During the interview, they brought out tray after tray of food. By the end of the filming, the bill for the three of us was more than for the rest of the 10-person crew.

The next day, we filmed a short scene of Paulie and Dave picking me up on our way to a kid's birthday party. The idea was that they were late because they hooked up with two groupies the night before. Once we arrived at the kid's birthday party, they realized that the groupies from the night before were moms at the party. It was a little goofy, but fun to do. We honestly didn't think this would ever come to fruition.

Shortly after filming the sizzle, we had our official Riker Hill signing party. Bob and Lynn made sure to tell us, "Do not mention filming the TV sizzle to the Michaels at Riker Hill." I wasn't sure exactly why they asked this of us at the time, but we went along with it. We found out much later that Bob and Lynn didn't want Riker Hill to know about the TV show because they were scared they would want a piece. This was not good business. If anything, we needed our label behind us to simultaneously push us. As great as Bob and Lynn were, these were the little underhanded things that began to happen more and more frequently.

Soon after celebrating our record contract signing, we got word from Mark Mark Productions that they began to set up pitch meetings with networks to try and get our show on the air. I'll never forget going to my local Best Buy store and seeing ZO2's *Ain't it Beautiful* on the shelf for the very first time.

It was an amazing moment: after all the years of running to get the new KISS album, I finally got to see my album on the rack!

All during this, I was still spending as much time with my mom in the hospital as I possibly could. She would have a week where she was totally coherent and then get a relapse and end up in critical condition again.

ZO2 signing our first record contract, a moment I waited a lifetime for.

This went on for months. I tried to keep a little focus on the band, but it was difficult; my hero, my first love, was fading away from me before my eyes.

We pitched our show at a half a dozen or so networks, including TV Land, VH1, Comedy Central, and IFC. We got word that both Comedy Central and IFC were interested in possibly developing a pilot with us. Of course, we still didn't realize what a huge deal this was: getting a pilot green light was probably even harder than landing a record contract, and we somehow got both within a few months of each other.

After meeting with both networks, we decided to go with IFC. IFC told us that they planned on making us their flagship show. We were also taking the Marks' advice: they said it was probably better to be the big fish in the small pond over at IFC rather than a little fish in a massive pond at Comedy Central.

A few days later, Bob and Lynn called a meeting to go over our TV contracts. Lynn explained to us that "We will all be splitting a pie of allotted money five ways," and this included Paulie, Dave, Bob, Lynn, and I. Bob also said, "We can't get rich off of a show like this, but it will be able to help move the band in the right direction."

ZO2's Ain't it Beautiful, in stores!

We were still told to not discuss any TV business when the two Michaels from our record label were present. All of this should have sent up a thousand red flags, but I was in a fog because of my mom, and Paulie and Dave were just gullible. The icing on the cake was when Lynn said, "You don't have time or need a lawyer to look at this. I already did and it's all fine. The Marks need these contracts back by tomorrow or we might jeopardize the deal."

I know what everyone is thinking that is reading this. "How stupid can these guys be?" Let me try to explain as best as I can. At the time, the idea of some fantasy TV show still seemed ridiculous to us. Maybe we would film a pilot like we did with KISSNATION for VH1, but there was no way we were getting picked up for a series. I know, that's still no excuse, especially for me! I totally take all of the blame for everything that happened after this. I give none to Paulie and Dave.

Unfortunately, both of them thought of Bob and Lynn as parent figures that would always take care of them. I knew better and never really trusted them, or anyone for that matter. Up to that point, I thought they were good managers and did a lot for us, but I should have never signed anything without a lawyer looking at it first. My mind was completely on my mom and what was happening at home. I also had my destination wedding coming up in the Dominican Republic and was scared to leave my mom. I wasn't thinking clearly, and I think Bob and Lynn knew it and slipped this by me. We signed the papers on the spot and didn't think about it again for a long while.

I was leaving for my wedding on June 5, 2007. Madalyn and I were flying out to Punta Cana, Dominican Republic, and then a few days later my brother and his wife, Madalyn's brother and his wife, and Madalyn's mother and father would join us, all while my poor mother was still in the hospital.

A week before we left, I got a call from Bob that we were scheduled to film the pilot of our show on June 7. I had previously given Bob and the rest of the guys the dates of my wedding and told them that I was obviously unavailable those days. I reminded Bob of this when he called, and he very coldly told me, "You have to change your wedding date."

I absolutely thought he was kidding, but he wasn't. And I wasn't that upset simply that he was telling me this; I was more shocked that he had the balls to even bring that option up to me. Bob knew I was unavailable, and a good manager would have just told the producers way ahead of time so there would be no conflict. But, that's the kind of person Bob was. I told him, "There is no way in hell I'm changing my whole wedding. I'm flying 10 people to the Dominican Republic and it has been booked for over a year." He told me, "We have to film it this day and there is no way out of it." I got very angry and yelled, "Then film it without me!" and I hung up the phone.

I was furious! A few hours later, I got a call from Mark Efman, one of the producers, to talk about it. What he told me next, I flat out couldn't believe. He began with, "Joe, I understand your mom is sick and that you don't think you can make that day to shoot." I cut him off and said, "Excuse me? What did you say?" Mark replied, "Bob explained to us about your mom and that she is sick and that you can't make that day to film."

Can you believe this bastard had the nerve to lie to the network and production company and use my mom's health as an excuse? Later I found out that the reason Bob had never told anyone about my wedding, and then lied about why I couldn't film, was because he and Lynn decided that they didn't want the network to know I was getting married. They thought it might jeopardize how they saw us as a crazy rock band.

I should have fired both of them that day! And, if it wasn't for Paulie and Dave loving them so much, I would have!

After a five-minute conversation with Mark Efman, with me explaining to him the real reason for my unavailability was my wedding, booked for the Dominican Republic, he was totally okay with changing the date. He even said, "Of course, dude! We had no idea! You are not canceling your wedding. That's ridiculous. We will just book it a few weeks later." It was that easy to change it and Bob never even tried. My relationship with Bob and Lynn would never be the same again.

The night before I left for my wedding, my mom took a turn for the worse. Madalyn and I went to spend time with her and to tell her we were leaving to get married the next morning. She was completely unconscious at this point and in really bad shape. My heart was melting with the thought of leaving her lying in a hospital bed and going off to get married. Still, I knew my mom would have wanted it more than anything in the world. In a way, I believe she was holding on until Madalyn and I were officially married so she knew someone would take care of her little boy. I held her hand and gave her the biggest hug and kiss I'd ever given her. I whispered in her ear, "Rest, Mom. I will be alright."

On the morning before my wedding, while already in the Dominican, I got a call in my hotel room at 5:30am saying that my mom had passed away. My world was shattered and I knew I would never be whole again. She hung on just long enough to make sure I was taken care of. Even in her last breath, she was thinking of ways to take care of me.

On June 7, 2007, my mom passed and on June 8, I got married. That day on the beach, as I was marrying Madalyn, I felt my mom's presence more than I've ever felt anything in my life. She was with us. She knew she couldn't be there physically, so she got their spiritually.

As much as my mom took care of me while she was alive, I know she has been my guardian angel every single day since she passed. I love and miss you so much, Mom.

A few weeks after returning from my wedding in Dominican Republic, I had a wedding party in Brooklyn with all of my friends and family. It was a very bittersweet time. I enjoyed myself that night and

Madalyn and I getting married on the beach in Punta Cana, Dominican Republic June 8, 2007.

looked forward to beginning my life with Madalyn, but I couldn't stop thinking about my mom.

I was scheduled to film the pilot to our still untitled TV show at 6:30am the next morning. Paulie and I were both pretty wasted, and we arrived on set feeling a little out of it. Once on set, the producers briefly went over the script outline with us for each scene. Even though I filmed the KISSNATION pilot for VH1, this would be my first real try at acting.

Our show was set up to be what was considered semi-scripted, which meant that we would have a skeletal outline of the plot, but 90 percent of the dialogue would be improv.

Acting came pretty natural to us right away. Paulie, Dave, and I already had huge personalities, so it wasn't difficult for the producers to get us to open up and be ridiculous on camera. We basically played off of one another, which is something we did all day long in our everyday lives anyway. It felt more like reacting than acting. The only thing that took a little getting used to was positioning ourselves in front of the camera exactly where they wanted us to be, without ever blocking another actor or lighting.

We filmed the original pilot over the course of about seven days. It was extremely fun, and we really enjoyed doing it. We still never imagined it would get greenlit for a full season or actually ever air on

Madalyn and I at our wedding party

Paulie Z, myself, and Dave Z at my wedding party.

TV. The finished product was pretty good, and it had some really funny moments, especially any scene with our co-star Big Jay Oakerson. Jay is one of the funniest human beings I've ever been around.

It's crazy because he wasn't our first pick to play the gay club owner, Neil. In the months leading up to filming the pilot, the producers would send us tapes of casting auditions from dozens of actors trying out for different roles in our show. The three main roles besides ourselves were for a Manager, Dina, gay club owner, Neil, and my girlfriend, Becky. We watched tape after tape while traveling to shows and tried to pick our favorites. It was so wild watching all of these comedians and actors audition to be in our show.

It's tricky to pick someone based on stupid audition tapes, where

Twisted Sister guitarist Jay Jay French starred in the original unaired Z Rock Pilot.

actors sit in front of a camera and are asked to read lines. It's ridiculous and impossible to show your real personality this way. Any actors reading this, don't get discouraged when you don't get a part after filming one of these dumb audition tapes. They show the producers nothing! Paulie, Dave, and I actually picked all different people to play the co-starring roles in our show than who ended up getting the parts. For instance, Jay Oakerson's video was terrible and extremely unfunny. But, the producers must have seen something in him while talking to him, and they gave him a shot. He wound up being perfect for the role and stole the show in our original pilot episode.

Once our TV Pilot was done filming, it was back to business as usual for ZO2: we played as much as possible and traveled quite a bit. We even got to open for Brian Johnson and Cliff Williams from AC/DC and then jam with them during the encore, Highway to Hell.

All of these gigs were still so surreal to me. I was on stage playing with the rock legends that I grew up listening to. All of my dreams were coming true. I had toured with all of my favorite bands, I had just gotten a record deal, and ZO2 had just finishing filming a pilot for a TV series for IFC.

I would have traded it all for just one more minute with my mom...

CHAPTER 25

Z ROCK

Right before Dave and I began rehearsals with TSO in the early fall of 2007, we got word that IFC had picked up our show for a whole season. We were super thrilled and unbelievably excited. We were set to begin filming sometime in February 2008.

For some reason, Bob always had something against TSO. I think he felt threatened that he didn't have full control over Dave. Every chance he got, he would bad mouth TSO, calling them all washed up 80's rockers or has-beens. Bob decided to take advantage of getting the TV show picked up for a full season, and having the new Riker Hill record contract, by telling Dave he didn't want him going on tour with TSO this year.

This was ludicrous! 95 percent of our fan base was either people that knew Dave from TSO or people that saw us on the KISS tour. But, of course, Dave listened, like he always did, and he agreed not to play with TSO that year.

I always thought of Dave as a goofy kid. He was just always happy-go-lucky, without a care in the world. I admired that quality about him, but I also thought it hurt him in these types of situations. He was easily manipulated. I wish Dave would've taken a stance once in a while, but he was more than happy just going with the flow.

Bob and Lynn needed full control over Dave and Paulie. They always had Paulie and now they finally got Dave. They knew they could never get me, and that secretly pissed them off. I thought it was a terrible move. This was jeopardizing Dave's future and was disgusting of them to demand it.

Paulie and Dave never really grasped the concept that Bob and Lynn worked for us, not the other way around! There was no way the TSO tour, which ended in late December, was going to interfere with the TV show we were set to film in February.

In January 2008, we were asked by three-time World Series champion manager Tony LaRussa to perform at his Animal Rights Foundation, A.R.F, charity event. Tony and his family were big fans of TSO and knew Dave and ZO2 because of that, which is more proof that TSO was important to the success of ZO2. Tony flew us out to San Francisco where it would be Z02 and Motley Crue singer, Vince Neil, performing.

Tony and his family treated us like real celebrities from the moment we landed. He had a limo waiting for us at the airport and he and his family all greeted us personally at the hotel upon arrival at 11:30pm.

On the day of the charity event, ZO2 sound checked and it must have freaked Vince Neil out a bit. He was originally set to headline the event, but shortly after hearing us, he decided that he wanted to go on first and left us to close the event. LaRussa was upset with Vince.

Legendary baseball manager Tony LaRussa's family and ZO2 in San Francisco, 2008.

Obviously, Vince was who the people were coming to see, and LaRussa thought it was pretty crappy of him to change time slots just because he felt intimidated by a young band.

It's amazing: Tony LaRussa and Vince Neil, two really rich and famous people who brought completely different ethics and morals to the table. Vince was nice enough to us backstage, but we could tell he was awkward and uncomfortable.

After the performance, Tony invited us to an after-party at a ritzy club. Knowing I was a big Yankees fan from a conversation we had earlier, Tony came over to me at the party and we talked baseball for over an hour. He even told me a story of how he was supposed to be the one to replace Buck Showalter as Yankees manager right before Joe Torre took over in 1996.

Overall, it was a spectacular experience and I remember thinking to myself, "Wow, all these great things are happening and now we get

ZO2 and Motley Crue lead singer Vince Neil right before showtime.

to fly home and film our own TV show." Life was getting crazy — in a good way.

Once we got back from San Francisco, we had to come up with a name for our new TV show. Paulie, Dave, and I suggested *Ain't it Beautiful* so we could use that song as the official theme, but the executives at IFC didn't really like it. After a few weeks of going back and forth and not really agreeing on anything, the head of the IFC, Evan Shipiro, sent out an email that the show would be called *Z Rock*. It's funny: we all completely hated it at first and thought it sounded very cheesy. But now, I could never imagine the show being called anything else.

Season one of *Z Rock* was written like this: we all got together with the producers, Mark and Mark, and head writer, Andrew Gottlieb. Paulie, Dave, and I would just tell stories of real shenanigans that went on in the band. This became the skeleton that Gottlieb then used to write each episode.

The plan was to film season one out of order, starting by filming episode 4, which starred Gilbert Gottfried. Upon arrival on set for the first day of filming, Paulie, Dave, and I felt like we had officially entered the land of Oz.

As amazing as touring with KISS had been, we knew right away this was bigger and that it was a completely different animal. The first

Wearing Tony LaRussa's World Series rings

shooting location was inside a mansion that would play as Gilbert's house for the episode. There were about 2 dozen crew members, including hair, makeup, drivers, writers, producers, and network executives — all of them on site because of us.

It occurred to me how different this was from the KISS tour, when we were there because KISS had brought us along. On the set of *Z Rock*, we were the stars! Everyone catered to us. It was absolutely incredible.

Before we began filming for the first episode (which was really the fourth), we sat down and had a table read. Essentially, all of the main actors, producers, and the director sat down to review the script together. One of the stars of this particular episode was well-known stand-up comedian Greg Giraldo. Greg showed up completely whacked out of his mind. He tried to sit with us for the table read and couldn't even hold the script. He was a mess. They had to take him back home and let him sleep it off. I think he was also pretty wasted most of the other times we filmed, but this was the only time he was completely unable to act.

Unfortunately, years after *Z Rock* wrapped, Greg overdosed. It was very sad.

The very first scene I shot for *Z Rock* was Becky and me talking on the couch about an engagement ring. All the producers told us was that Becky should start calculating how much money I would need to have to buy her an engagement ring. The rest was improvised between me and the actor-comedienne Alison Becker.

I was still a little unsure and nervous about what they wanted. This was not only my first scene of the season, but it was my first scene

The first day of filming Z Rock.

without the other two schmucks. At one point, during one of the takes, I asked Becky, "Who came up with this ridiculous tradition of an engagement ring anyway?" She answered, "I don't know, Jesus"? I said, "Jesus? What did he make a wooden ring"? As soon as I said it, I heard the whole production staff laughing in the other room. From then on out, I never felt awkward or uncomfortable filming again.

The schedule ZO2 was on while filming *Z Rock* was grueling, but at the same time exhilarating. Our call time on filming days was usually 7am and we would sometimes film until midnight. That made for a 17-hour day! We loved every minute of it, except for the old cliché that I'm sure everyone knows: "Hurry up and wait." We found out it was very true. It always seemed like an emergency that we get to set, get in wardrobe, get in our makeup, and be ready! Then, as soon as we were ready, the director usually made us do something for about 2 minutes and then sit around for the next 3 hours. Trust me, we weren't complaining. We were on the set of our very own TV show, which means we were in heaven.

After a very tiresome and long week of filming, ZO2 would still play shows on the weekend, sometimes even leaving straight from the *Z Rock* set to make it to a gig. It was insane! On one such weekend, ZO2 was set to open for the 80's rock band L.A. Guns in Pennsylvania. We had just come off a crazy week filming *Z Rock*, and now we had a four-hour drive to go play a show.

We had played this part of Pennsylvania many times before, and we knew we would pack the place. Once we got to the club, we began

Gilbert Gottfried impersonations courtesy of ZO2.

to set up our gear in front of the headliner, L.A. Guns, which was commonplace for the opening band. Usually, the headliner's drummer would use the drum riser and the opener would set up on the floor directly in front.

Just as I was about finished setting up, the road manager for L.A. Guns ran over to demand that I immediately remove my kit from the stage. At first, I asked him, legitimately confused, what the problem was, thinking I had done something wrong.

He started yelling at me, "My singer will not do sound check in front of another band's drum set!" I quickly understood I was dealing with a jerkoff who worked for a has-been 80's band that was on some sort of power trip. He picked the wrong night and the wrong drummer to try this with. I got in his face and started screaming at him, "Who the f**k do you think you're talking to? I will knock your ass out right here! Let's go!" I waved him to come at me.

Now, I'm not really someone who fights a lot or likes to get into fights, but over the years I've had to lay out a few snapper heads. This was definitely a snapper head that needed a beating.

He backed down almost immediately and began back-tracking his words. "You don't understand. My guys need space to sound check." I said, "If they need space, they got it. I'm out of here!" I began packing my drums and was heading out. I knew that without ZO2 there would be no crowd that night. He knew it too.

By then, Bob had come over to try and calm me down and to keep me from leveling this guy. The road manager began pleading with Bob to make me stay, but I wouldn't have it. Bob asked to talk to me and pulled me aside. I said, still heated, "I absolutely refuse to play with these jerkoffs!" The road manager approached and started pulling out money. "Here, here. What will make you stay?" I said without hesitation, "$200!" He handed me the $200 and I said, "And my drums get set up on stage right now." He meekly replied, "Yeah, okay. No problem. My guys will work around them."

Bob repeated that story to everyone for the next year. He couldn't believe how furious I was and how close I was to knocking the guy out; then, seconds later, I was immediately calm after getting the $200. This story was the foundation for what *Z Rock* writer Andrew Gottlieb used for episode 2, starring "The Whitest Kids You Know."

In episode two, ZO2/Z Brothers battle our rival band, Kidtastic. Just like in the real-life situation with L.A. Guns, my character gets into a little scuffle with the other band, but for the fun of TV, I was beaten up at the end. The original plan was to have a member of Kidtastic punch me and knock me out, but I had a much better idea. Still being a huge wrestling fan, I'd always wondered what it would be like to get hit with a guitar just like the Honky Tonk Man used to do to his opponents. Since Kidtastic would have their acoustic guitars in the scene, I thought it was the perfect opportunity to pay homage to the Honky Tonk Man. The producers loved the idea! The scene went as follows: I was supposed to insult Kidtastic by calling one guy's sister a derogatory name for making them ridiculous looking T-shirts. This insult would cause one of their members to lose it and blast me with his guitar. If you've ever seen the Honky Tonk Man perform, you'd know that once the guitar hit his opponent, the guitar would appear to shatter upon impact. I'm not exactly sure how this was achieved, but I do know it wasn't a regular wooden guitar.

ZO2 and The Whitest Kids You Know.

On the morning we shot the scene, I was walking through ideas with head of the props department, Tyler. I asked, "So how did you find out what kind of fake guitar to use? "Fake guitar?" Tyler responded. "No, we couldn't find one of those fake ones that shatter upon impact. But don't worry. I made a few cuts in this one and it should break when he hits you with it." Needless to say, I was a little worried, as were the producers, but less about my well-being and more about whether or not I would be able to act like I was taking a real hit. I explained that I'd been wrestling in "Madison Square Room" my whole life and that I would easily be able to take the hit and make it look fantastic.

We were ready, and the director called action. I delivered my insult to the three members of Kidtastic, each of whom was wearing a T-shirt with one letter on it, the first letter of his name. When they stood next to each other, they spelled out "FAG." I made my obvious comment and turned around to chuckle with Paulie and Dave. As soon as I turned, I was blasted in the head with a real wooden acoustic guitar. It almost legitimately knocked me out, but I didn't let on. I'd been waiting to take a guitar shot ever since I first saw Honky blast the Macho Man 20 years prior.

I knew I had nailed the take, but the director yelled "Okay, one more time just to make sure we have it." I probably already had a slight concussion, and now I had to do it again. On the second take, we went through the whole thing again and, right as the guitar hit me, one of the pieces of wood cut my face pretty badly. Even though I now definitely had a concussion, and I sported a pretty nice cut on my face, I was having the time of my life!

The first season of *Z Rock* was an unbelievably exciting time. We were potentially on the verge of superstardom and each episode of filming got funnier and more outrageous with guest stars like Dave Navarro, John Popper, Dee Snyder, and Joan Rivers.

My favorite episode from season one was episode 8, the first episode that we shot on location overnight. The whole cast, crew, and network went to Mohegan Sun Casino in Connecticut. We arrived the night before filming was to start, and I brought my old buddy Scally along for the trip. Scally and I stayed up until 4am drinking and gambling. My call time the next morning was 6am. I remember one of the producers, Lyndsey, banging on my wall when she heard me walk in at 4am, yelling, "You better be ready by six!"

This episode was really great because Paulie, Dave, and I got to film our own story arcs inside the episode. This, along with episode 7, really built on our individual characters and helped us understand what our character's role in the show was. My scenes were super easy and fun. All I had to do was sit at a blackjack table and gamble. It was always my belief, or maybe superstition, that the only way a person can win at a casino was to make a lot of noise, so I incorporated this into my scene.

The end of the episode was supposed to have Joan Rivers fooling around with Van Halen lead singer, David Lee Roth. At the last minute, because we were behind schedule, David Lee Roth had to back out. We still ended the episode with Joan Rivers exiting Van Halen's dressing room while wiping her mouth.

David Lee Roth did leave us three tickets to attend the Van Halen concert that night at Mohegun Sun. Right after filming, Paulie, Dave, and I ran top speed through the casino to catch the final three songs of Van Halen's set — what a perfect way to end a perfect weekend.

The first season would end on a cliff hanger when our nemesis John Popper double crosses us and sabotages our new major record contract. We loved the way it ended because it really felt like we were going to get a second season. But, of course, that still would depend on the ratings.

Filming a scene of Z Rock with my lifelong buddy Scally.
Priceless!

Once the filming of the show was complete, we still had to come up with the opening and theme song. ZO2 were pitching hard for the opening song to be "Ain't It Beautiful" from our current album, but the head of the network wanted a brand new song with the title of the show in it. ZO2 did have a recent demo recorded called "Big Release" and we thought the music was perfect. Now all we needed were the lyrics.

Bob and Andrew Gottlieb constantly butted heads. One of the show's main themes was for us to play original kid's songs at kids' parties. Each episode called for a different song, such as our birthday song "Blow it Hard" or our Bar Mitzvah song "Shalom Means Goodbye." For some reason, Bob always gave Gottlieb a hard time and told him, "The band won't write another song this week." I'm not exactly sure of the reasoning; I think he was just a control freak.

Finally, Gottlieb was fed up with the arguing and he decided that he himself would write some of the songs for us to perform. Bob countered with saying we wouldn't perform anyone else's songs, and this of course left a sour taste, not only in the writer's mouth, but also the producers' and the network.

We encountered the same problem when it came time to write the lyrics for the *Z Rock* theme song. Paulie, Dave, Bob, and I came up with parts of the chorus, but most of the stuff we submitted for the verse wasn't good. It was too contrived.

The head of the network wanted the song to be very quick and easy and to tell the story of the show. Finally, we got a phone call from Gottlieb saying that Evan, the head of IFC, wrote the lyrics for the verse and that we were required to use them. Bob fought it a little, but finally gave in because the network head was making the call.

Years later, I found out that Gottlieb had actually written the lyrics and told Bob that they came from the head of the network. This was just the beginning of the problems among our managers, the network, and producers.

In early July 2008, just weeks before the premiere of *Z Rock*, IFC flew us to L.A. to attend the TCA convention. TCA is short for

Joan Rivers exiting Van Halen's David Lee Roth's dressing room.
Z Rock Season 1.

Television Critics Association. We stayed at the Beverly Hilton Hotel and we were treated like kings.

IFC paraded us around like we were the biggest stars on the planet. They held a private concert for all of the TV critics, with an after-party to follow. Three boys from Brooklyn were having the time of their lives. We were like big kids in a giant candy store.

While in my hotel room in L.A., I saw the very first commercial for *Z Rock* on MTV. I couldn't believe it! I quickly called the other goofballs to tell them and we all went crazy! I had always heard stories of bands hearing themselves on the radio for the first time. This was that feeling times 1,000! It was the first time that it all seemed real. We had put so much work, time, and effort into not only filming this show, but then to get it off the ground. Actually seeing it on a TV commercial was something I will never forget.

When we returned to New York City from L.A. we had two big surprises waiting for us: two massive billboards were advertising the premier of *Z Rock*! The first was right outside the Lincoln Tunnel, and the second was right across the street from the world's most famous arena: Madison Square Garden!

Z Rock premiered on IFC on June 25, 2008, and it was instantly the highest rated original program in IFC history. The roller coaster had officially started down the tracks. We were more than ready for the wild ride ahead.

Right after the second episode of *Z Rock* aired, we flew out to Mountain View, California, to play with The Scorpions and Sammy Hagar. This was a massive show with about 25,000 fans. Even though *Z Rock* was still pretty new, it was quickly becoming a cult hit in the rock world. People went absolutely ballistic when they saw us. Believe it or not, most people didn't even realize we were an actual band until they saw us perform. They thought we were just actors on a TV show.

Right before we took the stage, Sammy gave me a bottle of his Cabo Wabo tequila to thank us for being there and then told us to have a kick ass show. I even got to party with former Van Halen bassist, Michael Anthony, after the show. Michael was playing bass with Sammy and we enjoyed quite a few whiskeys together after the show. He is a super cool and down-to-earth guy.

The next stop on our wild ride in 2008 was Lake Tahoe, Nevada, where we once again opened for KISS. Kiss was currently on their Alive 35 tour celebrating the release of their monumental album *Alive*. When we arrived at the arena in Tahoe, we were greeted with open arms. It was almost as if the young kids KISS had taken on tour with them four years ago had made good. The crew, sound, camera, wardrobe — everyone, really, congratulated us on the success of *Z Rock* and told us that they loved the show.

Later in the day, at catering, we saw Gene and Paul. Gene immediately yelled out, "Buttafuco!" as if seeing an old friend. Paul told us he watched the first few episodes of *Z Rock* and thought it was really funny. Gene said the same. They both seemed proud of us. In a way, I think they felt like we were their boys that they sent out into the big world and we'd made something of ourselves. I also couldn't pass up the opportunity to give them each a copy of our new *Z Rock* (adult activity) coloring book. They both got a real kick out of it.

Going from gig to gig, we practically live in our van. Stuff gets lost in there all the time. Help us find the following objects: Joey's Bongos, Panties, Paulie's Brush, Alarm Clock, Condoms, Balloon Animal, Demo CDs and Drumsticks.

Z Rock Coloring book.

During our set that night, we decided to play a cover song we'd been playing for a while and was always a big hit. It was Rush's "Tom Sawyer." We figured that if any KISS fans didn't know who we were, this song might win them over. The song went over great and the crowd of over 12,000 really loved it. When we got off stage and headed back to our dressing room, all the guys from KISS were giving us shit for playing the Rush song. Gene even started doing a whiney impression of Geddy Lee's voice. We all got a big laugh out of it and it actually felt great that KISS was now so comfortable with us that they were picking on us like we were their little brothers.

Playing Tahoe with KISS was such a different experience from when we did the "Rock the Nation" tour four years earlier. I think that on the first tour, KISS felt like they were doing us a favor by taking us out with them — and absolutely were. This time, because of *Z Rock*, it felt more like we were a legit opening band that had our own fan base. It was incredible!

Soon after playing with KISS in Tahoe, I was asked to be a "celebrity guest" on a new MTV game show *Silent Library*. A very young Justin Beiber had been the guest the week before. *Silent Library* was a show where a bunch of people had to sit through ridiculous pranks and or scenarios and try not to laugh. If they could hold their laughter in, they would win money depending on the severity of the prank.

In my skit, I was set to come out and play the drums on some fat guy's naked torso. He and his friends/fellow contestants had to try not to laugh while I beat him with sticks for almost a minute. Because this had to be a spontaneous performance to get a real reaction from the contestants, I had an earbud piping in the producer's instructions. Once I began drumming on the guy's belly, the producer began calling out orders in my ear: "Work his nipple! Now his crotch! Finally he said, "Big finish ... really hit him hard!" It was a crazy fun day. I remember thinking to myself, "How the hell did I get here? I'm playing drums on a guy's nipple on MTV!"

Shortly after our West coast trips with KISS, Sammy Hagar, and The Scorpions, ZO2 played in Virginia at a cool club we played quite regularly called JAXX. We were in our hotel room when we got word

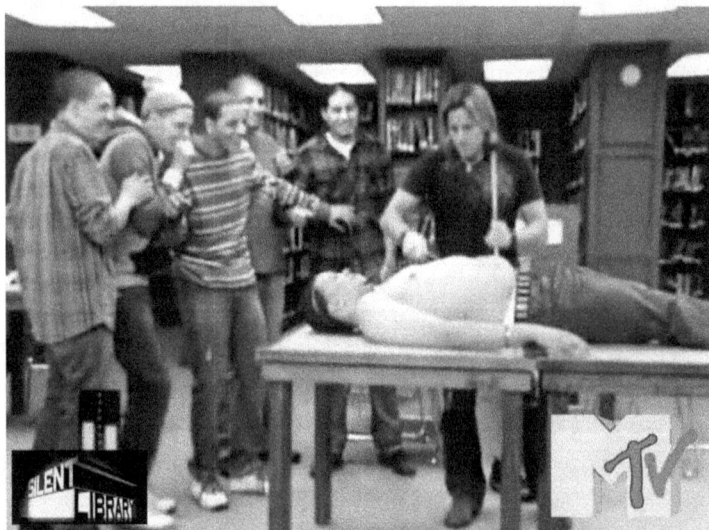

Drumming on a guy's nipples on MTV's Silent Library.

that *Z Rock* was officially picked up for season 2. The three of us were so excited that we began jumping on the beds like little kids. There was only one small problem: we wanted to have a brand new album to coincide with season 2 of *Z Rock*, and we definitely weren't ready.

The next few months consisted of writing all of the new material for ZO2's third album which was named after a phrase I created and used all the time: *Casino Logic*. The phrase referred to justify a crazy way of thinking. For instance, if a person goes to the casino to gamble and loses $500 but had $1,000 worth of fun, then he was really ahead $500. That's "Casino Logic."

The process of writing *Casino Logic* was much different than writing *Ain't it Beautiful*. With *Ain't it Beautiful*, we had the luxury of battle-testing all of our new material on the road. For *Casino*, we needed to at least have an album tracked before we even began filming season two of *Z Rock*. Overall, I think this created a slightly less organic sounding album than *Beautiful*.

We had done a lot of traveling since season one of *Z Rock* and were now super excited to begin work on our third album, *Casino Logic* and the second season of our TV show!

Just some of the ZO2 merchandise that was available.

CHAPTER 26

THE TOP OF THE WORLD

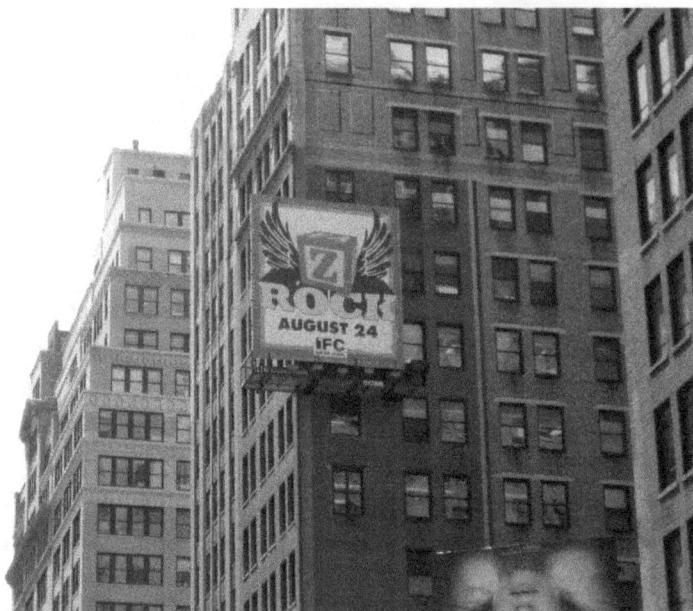

Z Rock billboard across the street from Madison Square Garden!

Around this time, relations with our record label, Riker Hill, became very strange. Our managers, Bob and Lynn, were also Chief Operating Officers of the label and were starting to act shady. They were segregating more than ever the two owners of the label, Michael Wolk and Michael Morrison from anything *Z Rock* related; it was even to the point where they would tell us to make sure "not to invite them to the set for filming." This struck me as odd and manipulative: why wouldn't they want the heads of the label to be on set of our TV show? It was different than when we began filming the first season and they made us keep the fact that we had our own TV show a secret. *Z Rock* was now a HUGE hit and of course, everyone knew about it, especially our own record label! Bob and Lynn were hiding something, but I couldn't figure out what.

When we began tracking *Casino Logic*, it got even more suspicious. Now that we were signed to a label, it was in our contract that Riker Hill would pay for the recording of our next album. Right before tracking began, Bob and Lynn told us that they wanted us to pay for the album because Riker Hill had refused. We couldn't understand how or why our label would refuse; after all, this new album was going to be promoted on the second season of our hit TV show. We were also now instructed to not have ANY contact whatsoever with our label. Our weekly salary checks also stopped.

Years later, we found out that Riker Hill did in fact want to pay for our new album with the amount stated in our contract. Bob and Lynn took it upon themselves to try and negotiate an obscene amount of money for the album and Riker Hill stood firm at their offer, which coincided with what was in our contract. We also found out that Riker was losing a lot of money, mainly on the exorbitant salaries that Bob and Lynn were making. Riker wanted to essentially fire Bob so they didn't have to pay his large salary anymore.

Years later, the head of the label told me that Bob basically did nothing at the label and was a waste of money to keep on. I believe this triggered the bad blood between Riker Hill and our managers. Talk about a conflict of interest! That's why we were always kept away from talking to anyone at Riker Hill.

Bob and Lynn assured us to just lay out the recording costs and that Riker Hill was in breach of contract and that we would get a new bigger deal with a major label. I feverishly protested. I had just paid back Paulie and Dave almost $40,000 for fronting the first album and touring costs up until we got *Z Rock*. I was not about to go into debt again on Bob's and Lynn's word, especially since Bob and Lynn never laid out one single dime from their own pockets for anything.

Paulie and Dave listened to whatever Bob and Lynn said and decided they would once again put all of the album's costs on their credit cards. They never even questioned them about why! On top of that, Bob had the balls to approach us with another producer contract that had us paying him another $10,000 to produce *Casino Logic*! This is where I started to lose my mind and put my foot down.

I remember telling Paulie and Dave, "If they are expecting us to blindly front the cost of the album without any real explanation as to why our label, whom they were COO's at, weren't paying for it, then Bob and Lynn should pay for a big chunk of the album themselves. Bob should only get his producer fee if we get the record funded down the line, not upfront!"

This became a big battle. Paulie and Dave couldn't understand why I thought Bob and Lynn should help pay for the album. I tried to explain: "Bob and Lynn aren't telling us exactly why Riker Hill is refusing to pay and they also have as much to gain as we do, especially Bob who is co-writer on every song!

ZO2's third release, Casino Logic.

By no means was I saying that Bob and Lynn should pay for the whole album, but if they were asking us, in good faith, to trust them, I thought they should take some of the risk also. Of course, I was outvoted again.

The one and only thing that Paulie and Dave agreed with me about was Bob's $10,000 producer fee. We agreed that if Bob wanted to produce the album then he would only get his producer fee if/when we got an advance for the album, from either Riker Hill or another record label. After a lot of arguing, Bob eventually agreed to these terms, even though, years later, he would try to sue us for that $10,000 producer fee. Sad.

Just to paint the picture for everyone: Bob and Lynn were our managers, but both also got salaries as the COO's at our now estranged record label, Riker Hill Records. They were also both getting paid as executive producers on *Z Rock*, getting 2/5 of our *Z Rock* money, and taking an additional 20 percent managerial cut of all the money we were getting paid. On top of that, Bob now wanted his producer fee of $10,000, which he wanted us to personally lay out! All of this smelled really bad to me. It wouldn't be until the end of season 2 of *Z Rock* that I would be able to put all of the pieces together.

In December 2008, right before we began filming season 2 of *Z Rock*, ZO2 had two shows with Twisted Sister at the Nokia theater in Times Square. Twisted was always one of my favorite bands growing up, and it was such a great experience playing with them in our home town. Of course, Twisted still had a huge following, but coming off the success of season 1 of *Z Rock*, ZO2 also had a huge crowd during those Nokia theater shows. Between this and the KISS show we had played out in Tahoe, we really began to feel the impact *Z Rock* was having.

ZO2 and Twisted Sister!

These shows were also very special because we had become really close friends with all the guys in Twisted Sister. Jay Jay had been in the original unaired *Z Rock* pilot. Dee was in one of the most popular episodes from season 1 and was also set to appear along with guitarist Eddie Ojeda in the first episode of season 2. We had been guests on Mark "The Animal" Mendoza's radio show numerous times and we were very friendly with drummer A.J. Pero.

Bob had been friends with Jay Jay for a long time and we always thought he was very friendly with the other guys as well. Years later, we attended the 30th anniversary of Twisted's landmark album *Stay Hungry* and we found out that Mark and A.J. actually detested Bob, and Dee did as well, to some extent.

Mendoza would always fool around with us and say that he was going to kick our ass or beat the crap out of us. It was his way of playing. On the night of the 30th anniversary, he asked us where our "asshole manager" was? We all started to laugh as always. He then got really serious and said, "No, I mean it. I don't want to see that jerkoff here tonight." Paulie replied, "Wait, are you being serious?" That's when Mendoza and A.J. began to tell us all about how they really hated Bob for many years and just could never say anything because he was friends with Jay Jay. We couldn't believe it. I was starting to hear this type of stuff about Bob more and more frequently from all sides.

I wouldn't have changed a thing up until this point, but I couldn't help but notice all of the things that were going on around me. Something wasn't right.

Right after the Twisted shows in January 2009, Paulie, Dave, and I took our annual trip to Los Angeles for the NAMM music convention and another appearance at the TCA convention to promote *Z Rock*. I had just gotten a new rep at Ludwig, Victor Salazar, wo was a huge fan of the show. Victor called me right before our trip to NAMM to introduce himself and to ask if there was anything I needed from Ludwig for *Z Rock* season 2. Even though I had just recently received a brand new Champagne Sparkle kit from Ludwig, I mentioned that I was thinking about getting a new kit for the new season. Never in a million years did I think that he would say yes, but I figured, "What do I have to lose?" Victor immediately said, "Yes absolutely! What did you have in mind?" This caught me totally off guard, but luckily I knew the Ludwig new catalog like the back of my hand and responded, "I was thinking either a Red Sparkle or an Amber Vistalite." Victor quickly responded, "Why not both?" The perks of *Z Rock* were unbelievable.

Upon our arrival at NAMM, we were bombarded. Anyone and everyone knew who we were. As big of a hit as we thought *Z Rock* was,

My red sparkle and amber Vistalite Ludwig kits given to me for season 2 of Z Rock

in the music community, it was almost a phenomenon. NAMM was filled with musicians who could really relate to everything that we did on the show — driving in a van with all of our gear, arguing, crappy gigs, and getting screwed over. It was all relatable to this demographic and they certainly let us know it. We couldn't walk 10 feet without someone stopping us for a picture and autograph or to just tell us how much they loved *Z Rock*.

I also found out that Ludwig was honoring me by including me on their 100th anniversary banner. They placed me right in between two of my favorite drummers of all time, Eric Carr of KISS and John Bonham of Led Zeppelin! I was blown away.

Ludwig had scheduled me to do a signing with some of the artists on their roster. I, of course, was thrilled and honored to be a part of something like this, but I didn't really think anyone would care about me when guys like Alan White from YES, Dave Lombardo from Slayer, and Jason Bonham, the late great John Bonham's son, were standing next to me. Boy was I wrong.

Once the signing began, almost every person in line not only knew me, but said that I was one of the main reasons they waited on line. It got so nuts at one point that Jason Bonham, who had no idea who I was, asked me, "Who do you play with again? Everyone seems to love you!" I told him I was on a TV show called *Z Rock*. He said, "I'm going to have to check that out." Life was good and about to get even better.

Ludwig's 100th anniversary poster. I'm between 2 of my all-time favorite drummers, Eric Carr and John Bonham!

One evening after NAMM, while we were having dinner, I got a call from Madalyn that would forever change my life. Madalyn said, "I think that the pregnancy test I just took said pregnant." I began yelling, "What do you mean, you think?" A few months prior, Madalyn and I had decided that we wanted to try and have a baby. We couldn't wait to start our family and this could be the beginning!

Madalyn replied to my yelling, "I can't read the little symbol that says positive or negative on the test perfectly." I told her to run the store and get one of the tests that say on them "YES" or "NO"! About 30 minutes later, she texted me a picture with the test that said "YES"! I was the happiest man on earth. I couldn't believe I was going to be a dad. I wanted to shout the good news as loud as I could, but we decided to wait until Madalyn was further along to tell anyone.

Once I returned from L.A., Madalyn and I celebrated and were excited beyond belief, but it would be a few months before we could find out if it was a boy or a girl. In the meantime, I began filming the second season of *Z Rock*. Still, filming the second season was nothing compared to the joy and excitement I was feeling. I WAS GOING TO BE A DAD!

The success of the first season of *Z Rock* was unexpected. When we began filming season 1, we really had no expectations and didn't really even care that much about the story lines. Season 2 started off completely different. Now that *Z Rock* was a bonafide "hit show," expectations were very high. We knew we had to make season 2 even better than season 1.

The first day of filming was a blast. It was so good to see everyone again and begin working. The very last scene of the first day was scheduled to be a fight between me and Harry Braunstein, played by comedian Greg Giraldo. In the script, my girlfriend Becky, who I haven't seen in months, shows up at a party we are playing and kisses Greg's character Harry Braunstein. The scene was pretty simple: I had to throw a couple of fake punches and then he was going to tackle me. Easy enough, right? Wrong!

After Greg and I did all the hard moves, Paulie and Dave were supposed to lift me off of him to break up the fight. As I was getting up, my boot slid on the kitchen tile floor, my whole knee twisted, and the whole room heard a loud "pop"! I screamed, not only from the pain but from the horror of what I knew had just happened. I had torn the ACL in my left knee.

I was devastated. I went straight to the ER where they scheduled me for an MRI early the next morning. The results confirmed what I already knew: torn ACL and a torn meniscus in my left knee. This was only our first day of filming. What the hell was I going to do?

Even though I was one of the stars of the show, they couldn't wait for me to have surgery and heal to begin filming again. That would have taken months. I did what I always did. I picked myself up and pressed forward. I decided I would hold off on surgery until mid-season so we could figure out a way to actually write it into the script. In the meantime, I would just hobble around the set and figure out a way to get all my scenes done. I was back on set the next morning! I also played a ZO2 show with one leg just 3 days later. Let's

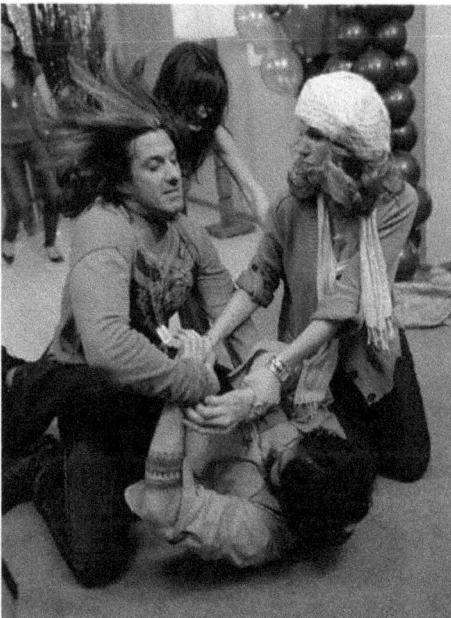

This is the shot where I tore my ACL. Me, Lynn Koplitz and Greg Giraldo.

see a sports star or movie star tear their ACL and go back to work the next day. Never happen! I wasn't going to let anything stop me.

When I told the producers my plan, they couldn't believe that I planned not only to keep filming, but also to not compromise even one shot. Anything they needed me to do, I figured out a way to do it. When I arrived on set the next morning, my knee looked 5 times its normal size from the trauma and the swelling.

The first scene we shot was when Neil comes to visit me at my new "nursing job." The scene took about 3 hours to shoot and I was standing the whole time. Needless to say, season two was off to a rough start for me.

Even though I was injured, I was super excited about this second season. The scripts were calling for much more character development for me, Dave, and Paulie. Because IFC was looking to become an ad-based channel (that is, add in commercials), it was also trying to clean *Z Rock* up a little. We didn't have any more nudity and focused more on actual funny story telling rather than shock value. Some people will say this hurt the show and made it less "Rock and Roll," but I thought the show became much stronger.

In a weird way, me being injured actually led to a lot of funny little changes in the scripts. For instance, in episode 2, Paulie and I were

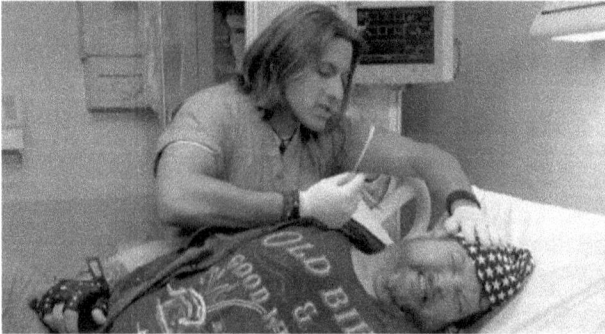

The first scene I filmed after tearing my ACL.

supposed to bring our "dates" to the ice- skating rink and skate with them. Obviously, I couldn't skate with a torn ACL, so we changed it to me standing on the side while my date, Bethanny Frankel from *The Real Housewives of N*ew York, fed me hot dogs while I made fun of Paulie skating. The scene ended when I bribed a little fat kid on the ice with a bacon wrapped hot dog to check Paulie over the boards. It became an instant classic!

Bethenney Frankle feeding me bacon wrapped hot dogs.

One morning, at the beginning of filming episode 3, I arrived on set and thought I was in some kind of weird alternate reality world. It was about 6:30am and as I walked in, I had to stop at the doorway and take in what I was witnessing. I saw Frank Stallone with a guitar and a small amplifier strapped to his belt. He was singing his big hit "Take You Back" from *ROCKY*. While Frank was roaming around by himself singing, Mini KISS, a group of little people that dressed like KISS, were running around the room at top speed for some unknown reason. Mind you, filming for the day had not yet begun. This was just happening while everyone was arriving to set that morning. All I could think was, "Who has a better job than me?"

This was a really fun episode to film in general. Paulie and Dave would always tease me that I looked like Frank Stallone. The joke was that I wasn't handsome enough to be his brother Sylvester Stallone.

People would always ask me, "Who is the craziest rock star or comedian you guys filmed with?" To everyone's surprise, my answer was always the same: "Frank Stallone!"

*Frank Stallone was easily the craziest guest star that appeared on
Z Rock.*

Season 2 also had my two favorite episodes, "Jailhouse *Z Rock*" and
"Z Wrestler." Season 1 had a great underlying storyline connecting the
entire season. For season 2, though, IFC wanted more stand-alone
episodes because they would work better as re-runs. "Jailhouse *Z Rock*"
brought us back to the hometown of Jay Oakerson's character, Neil. In
the episode, ZO2 was scheduled to play a show with Poison singer Bret
Michaels in Connecticut. On the way to the show, we made a pit stop
through Neil's hometown where hilarity ensued.

One of my all-time favorite scenes was when I had to distract a
priest by giving him my confession. The actor who played the priest,
David Martin, was very stiff and it was hard to get any lines out of him.
I was so completely comfortable acting and in front of the camera at this
point that I just took control of the scene. I remember hearing the whole
crew laughing and causing us to lose some really funny takes. There are
a lot of great bloopers from that scene.

One of my favorite scenes that I filmed for Z Rock.
Joey's confession!

My favorite blooper, which actually made it in the episode, was when Neil hit the priest with the egg. When we shot that scene, Mohammed from the props department was standing about three feet from the priest. He was supposed to lightly hit the priest in the chest with the egg. Instead, Mohammed wound up like he was Roger Clemens and nailed him directly in the face. The whole cast and crew were in shock.

As soon as the director called cut, the priest looked at Mohammed with a disgusted look and said, "I guess you missed." I remember hiding behind a tree with one of the head executives of IFC and crying with laughter. The set was so much fun every single day. We were having the time of our lives.

The end of the episode was supposed to have us hand deliver a specially requested soup to Bret Michaels. We were all scheduled to film one night when ZO2 actually played with Bret at Mulcahy's in Long Island on March 19, 2009.

Bret had been in touch with our producers and was excited to be on the show. We arrived to Mulcahy's with the whole *Z Rock* crew to film the scene. For some reason, however, Bret decided he didn't want to get off his bus. This really surprised us: not only was he really cool with us

A great Z Rock blooper that was so good it made the episode.

during the whole KISS/Poison tour, but we had just hung out with him the night before and were talking about filming.

This was one of my first real dealings with someone famous throwing a little diva fit, besides the incident with Vince Neil in San Francisco. Bret just got it in his head that night that he no longer wanted to film. He told our producers that he was a little under the weather and wanted to rest. Not only was this hurting the final scene of the episode, but this just wasted thousands of dollars because the whole *Z Rock* crew was there ready to film.

Gottlieb quickly rewrote the scene on the fly and we instead had Paulie chasing after Bret's tour bus with the soup. I never looked at Bret the same after he screwed us over that night.

Writing our scenes for season 2 was much different than season 1. I had become friendly with head writer Andrew Gottlieb and his assistant writer, Sam Brenner. Dave and I would play poker with them on set for hours every day in between takes. During those hours, we would always discuss scripts and ideas, and we would tell jokes. This meant I ended up having a much larger impact on not only my character but the show in general.

One early morning while we were getting ready to film the priest scene in "Jailhouse *Z Rock*," Gottlieb, producer Mark Efman, and I were playing poker and discussing upcoming episodes. Everyone knew that I loved professional wrestling. Efman said that they were planning a wrestling themed episode where Paulie, Dave, and I dressed as 80's wrestlers like Hulk Hogan and "The Macho Man" Randy Savage. He also mentioned that they were in talks with Ric Flair to be the celebrity guest for that episode.

Of course, I was immediately excited about the possibility of not only working with a legend like Ric Flair, but about filming a whole episode dedicated to one of my favorite things in the world, wrestling! But, I had a much better idea than dressing like 80's wrestlers...

I suggested to Gottlieb and Efman that Paulie, Dave, and I dress as our original wrestling characters. Efman said, "What do you mean, original?" I went on to explain that I'd been doing my "Joeylicious" wrestling character for years. They loved the idea and that's how the "Joeylicious" episode of *Z Rock* was born.

We found out shortly after that Ric Flair couldn't do the episode due to a scheduling conflict, but the producers had secured another famous wrestler, Chris Jericho, as the guest star. I was definitely disappointed that I wasn't going to get to work with Flair. He had always been one of my all-time favorite wrestlers growing up. Of course, I knew Jericho, but he was definitely more from the newer class of wrestlers. I always liked him in WCW and thought his promos were great.

The weekend before we filmed "Z Wrestler," we all headed back to L.A. for the "Spirit Awards" that aired on IFC every year. This was our first experience being part of an awards show and we were pretty excited. Because the Spirit Awards were on IFC and *Z Rock* was their flagship show, Paulie, Dave, and I were asked to present an award that night.

Once we got to L.A., we received the red-carpet treatment all weekend. This was the first time that I really felt like a celebrity. I had never thought of us like that, but now that *Z Rock* was a hit and we were not only going to be mingling with Hollywood A-listers, but on stage in front of them presenting an award, we felt like we belonged.

The day before the awards show, we had a run-through of what we were supposed to do when presenting. We each had a few lines to read from the Teleprompter. The only problem was that the lines were very straight, not funny, and just not "us."

We had dinner and drinks with everyone from IFC that night and we were telling the president of IFC, Evan Shipiro, that we didn't love what they had written for us to say on the awards show. He said, "Then don't say it! Write something else."

"Are we allowed to do that?" we all asked. He went on to tell us that "IFC asked you three to present an award to show off your unique personalities and tell the world about *Z Rock*. Be yourselves and come up with a little bit that will leave people saying, 'I have to see their show!'" We all agreed and knew the exact bit that we were going to use.

When we arrived at the Spirit Awards we were immediately greeted by our guide for the day. She ushered us to the red carpet to greet the press and take hundreds of photos. Each celebrity had their own guide that would steer them in the right direction through the press and event activities. It was an amazing experience: I've seen dozens of red-carpet shows on TV and always wondered what it would be like to actually walk one.

Dozens of photographers were screaming out names to get stars to look at them so they could get the best shot. This worked great when they were trying to get a picture of one celebrity, but in our case there was three of us, so I don't think there is one picture where we are all looking in the same direction. IDIOTS!

After the red carpet, they guided us to the "Swag Tent." We had no idea what a swag tent was, but we were eager to find out. Once inside, we saw dozens of stations showcasing all sorts of different products, anything from toothpaste to new smart phones to vacations. Our guide explained, "Just go to each station and sign up for anything you want."

We still weren't sure what she meant exactly. We asked, "What do you mean, sign up?" She further explained, kind of joyously because she had just realized we'd never done this before: "Everything and anything in there is free." We ran into the room like kids on a Toys 'R Us shopping spree!

It was so weird seeing Elaine from Seinfeld standing next to me signing up for free toothpaste. It made no sense: these millionaire celebrities didn't need free things, yet each and every one of them were in the room with us, each getting as much stuff as possible. It was a fun experience.

After the swag tent, we were taken to our table. Because IFC ran

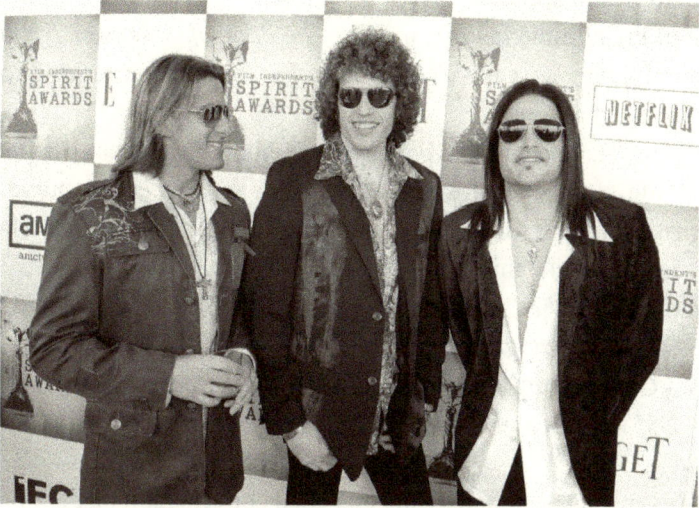

ZO2 on the Red Carpet at the Spirit Awards

the whole show, our table was right against the stage, dead center — basically the featured table. All other tables were slightly behind us. Seeing people like Alec Baldwin, Jessica Alba, and Mickey Rourke all sitting behind us was really quite extraordinary.

After watching a little bit of the awards, we were escorted backstage to get ready to present the award in the Best Cinematography category. After doing a few minutes of press, we started to get ready in the dressing room alongside of Christina Applegate, who was very sweet and nice to us. Paulie looked like a lovesick puppy when he met her, since he was a huge *Married with Children* fan and had had a crush on her since he was a kid.

As we made our way to the stairs and up to the stage, I told the other guys not to walk too fast because I still had a pretty bad limp from my torn ACL. As we started to go over our routine, who stood behind us but Cameron Diaz, who was set to present right after us. She laughed at our bit and told us, "Don't be nervous guys. I love it and you will do great." She was super sweet and friendly — and also extremely skinny in person.

We heard the host, comedian Steve Cohan, announce, "From the hit IFC show *Z Rock*, here are 7O2." We came out from behind the curtain to a mild applause except for a screaming Eric Roberts, the star of one of my all-time favorite movies *The Pope of Greenwhich Village*. Apparently, he was a big *Z Rock* fan. We were all set to go into our newly scripted routine.

Paulie, Dave, and I had prepared something that actually happened in real life. Just like most of our *Z Rock* scripts, even our award presentation for best cinematographer was based on real life. The bit went something like this:

Paulie - Hi we're here to present the award for best choreography.
Dave – No, cinematography.
Paulie - Choreography, Cinematography, whatever, the point is mute.
Joey - Did you just say mute? The word is "moot" stupid. You should be mute!

This was taken straight from an actual conversation that Paulie had with Gene Simmons years prior on the KISS tour. The bit got a huge laugh, and we got to present the award for best cinematography to the movie *The Wrestler*! Overall, it was a perfect night that I will remember forever.

At the after party, I even got into a pretty heated argument with *Buffy the Vampire Slayer* star Eliza Dushko. It turns out Eliza was a big Boston Red Sox fan and I was a big New York Yankees fan. We had a friendly argument about who was the better team. I obviously won that discussion.

After the Spirit Awards, we still had one more night in L.A. with everyone from IFC. They planned a small dinner and get together to celebrate our success at the Spirit Awards. They all seemed proud of us and thought we came across very funny, natural, and ridiculous — exactly what they wanted.

Even though they weren't invited and IFC actually didn't want them there, Bob and Lynn came along for the whole trip. It was as if they didn't want us to be alone around the network, the producers, or our label. Curious...

Midway through dinner Bob got an interesting and exciting call. It was from the now head of A&R at Universal Records, Jason Flom. Earlier in the book, I talked about Flom, who was once the head of A&R

ZO2 presenting at the Spirit Awards.

at Atlantic Records and my former band, Exposed, was trying desperately to get him to sign us, only to be told we were "too 80's."

It turns out that Flom had been a huge fan of *Z Rock* and wanted to sit down and talk with us. Even though the dinner that IFC was having was mainly in our honor, we couldn't pass up an opportunity to sit down with the one and only Jason Flom.

We met him at a small place in Beverly Hills. He greeted us like he knew us, and in a way he did, from *Z Rock*. He was nice and we talked for around two hours about everything and anything. Jason wasn't a big drinker, so we all decided to have giant milk shakes during the meeting. I'm sure this was quite a ways off from when he used to have meetings with bands like Twisted Sister or Skid Row back in the day.

We played it cool and never really talked business with him. It felt like he was just trying to feel us out. I guess we felt pretty good because Bob got a call the next day before we left for the airport that Jason had a great idea about him appearing on *Z Rock* and really signing us to a record contract, on the air, during the episode. If the Spirit Awards appearance had us flying high, this now sent us into outer space!

Once we returned to New York City, we received an invite from Joan Rivers to guest star with her on NBC's *Celebrity Apprentice*. Joan was doing a challenge against the other contestants, and we appeared on the show with her to help sell cupcakes. It was a very fun experience.

The day after filming *The Apprentice*, it was time to get back to filming *Z Rock*. Filming the episode "Z Wrestler" was one of the best moments of *Z Rock* for me. Not only did it really showcase me, but it also let me play this alter ego I'd been wanting to be since I first saw wrestling come on my TV that fateful Saturday morning back in 1983. The world would now finally be introduced to JOEYLICIOUS!

As soon as Chris Jericho came on to the set, we knew it was going to be a fun week of filming. He immediately made fun of us to break the ice. The three of us, who were all now dressed as our wrestling alter egos, Pulled Pork Paulie, ChippenDave and Joeylicious, greeted Jericho and he started laughing at us. He said, "Why the hell are guys wearing cups?" Paulie quickly responded, "Why, wrestlers don't wear cups?" Jericho laughed even harder, " No, we don't wear cups!" Dave chimed in, "Then, how do you protect your nuts?" Jericho, still laughing, replied, "You guys are exactly like you are on the show!" It was the perfect way to break the ice. It turned out that Jericho was a huge fan of *Z Rock* season 1 and was thrilled to be on the show. Chris was hysterical and an absolute joy to work with.

The episode was directed by Brad Hall from *Saturday Night Live* and husband of *Seinfeld*'s Elaine, Julia Louis Dreyfus. "Z Wrestler" was filled with so many bloopers and laughs behind the scenes that it was easily my favorite episode.

The scene when I first see Chris Jericho at the birthday party was completely improved by me. The idea was for me to get excited because my character was a big wrestling fan and a huge Chris Jericho fan. I took it to the next level. Up until this point in *Z Rock*, it could be said that I played the most normal character. I was more of the "cool Italian drummer," while Paulie and Dave were goofier and more childish. That was about to change.

When my eyes first saw Chris Jericho entering the room, I started to scream like a little girl at a Backstreet Boys concert in 1999. I began jumping up and down, clapping, and practically weeping. We got everything and more that we needed on the very first take.

When Brad Hall called "Cut!" on that first take, the whole room absolutely exploded with laughter. No one was ready for, nor could they believe my over-the-top hysteria. They loved it! After the scene, Brad told me that it was one of the funniest things he'd ever seen.

That's a pretty big compliment coming from someone who starred on *Saturday Night Live*!

It's the perfect example of turning a negative into a positive. When I tore my ACL, I could have easily gotten down and took off a few episodes of *Z Rock*. Instead, I fought through the pain and discomfort on set and wound up filming, in my and many others' opinions, one of the best episodes ever of *Z Rock*.

The day after filming "Z Wrestler," I had surgery to repair my torn ACL. They used a cadaver's ACL. The plan was for *Z Rock* to halt production for one week, then resume as planned.

The opening of the next episode "Z My Baby" showed Paulie and Dave picking me up from the hospital. In the episode, I explained my injury to them like this: "I went to the store to pick up some walkin' AROUND pork and while trying to reach a beautiful soppressata that was hanging from the ceiling, I slipped on a can of olive oil. A classic Italian injury."

The episode was filled with guest stars galore including NFL Hall of Famer Warren Sapp, rock DJ Eddie Trunk, and the band Steel Panther, who we would face off against in a "Battle of the Bands." I

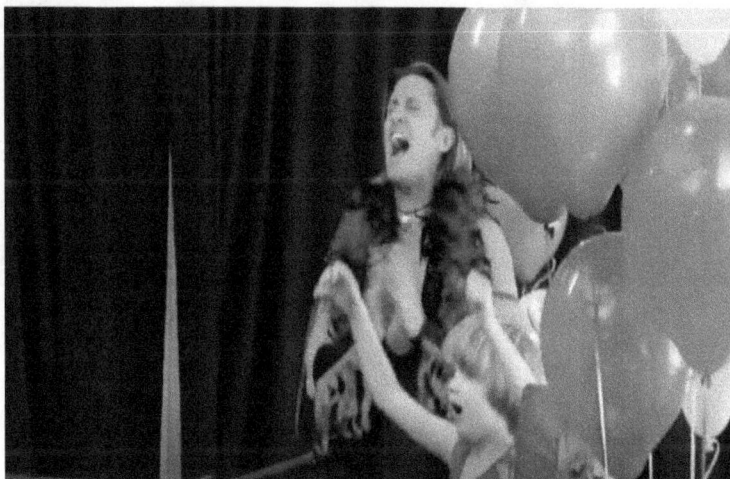

No one was ready for my over the top performance during "Z Wrestler!"

spent the whole episode confined to a wheel chair, and ZO2 had Warren Sapp fill in on drums.

Somehow, even me having surgery worked out. Me being in the wheelchair made us come up with a lot of new crazy ideas for story lines, and they worked perfectly! For anyone that has had ACL replacement surgery, you know for the first few weeks you are in excruciating pain, completely immobile, and in need of extensive rehab to get back into walking shape. But I fought through all of that, filmed on the set of *Z Rock* every day for 16 hours, and instead of taking a lunch break I would spend an hour at rehab.

I'm not sure anyone — the producers, the network, our managers, Paulie, or Dave—ever really realized how hard it was for me to do that every day. I never complained or made an issue of it. Whatever they needed me to do, I figured out a way to do it.

Chris Jericho flexing with ZO2 on the set of Z Rock.

Joeylicious!!

CHAPTER 27

SOMETHING'S NOT RIGHT IN PARADISE

It was right around this time that I started to see a lot of tension on the *Z Rock* set, mostly among the producers, the network, and our managers, Bob and Lynn — Bob especially. He would constantly interrupt takes to correct the most minute detail pertaining to the music business. He would even go up to the network to explain to them that there were certain things Paulie wouldn't do because it made him look ridiculous, which would in turn hurt ZO2 and his "rock star" image. It was starting to drive the network and producers crazy!

Paulie even made Bob go to the network and complain on his behalf that his name wasn't top billing for our newly released season 1 DVD on Amazon! I was listed first, simply because the three of us were listed in alphabetical order. Can you believe that? Bob made the network change it so Paulie was listed first. Not only was this psychotic of Paulie, but Bob was my manager too! He should have told Paulie "no," but Bob had Paulie in his back pocket so he placated to this kind of insanity!

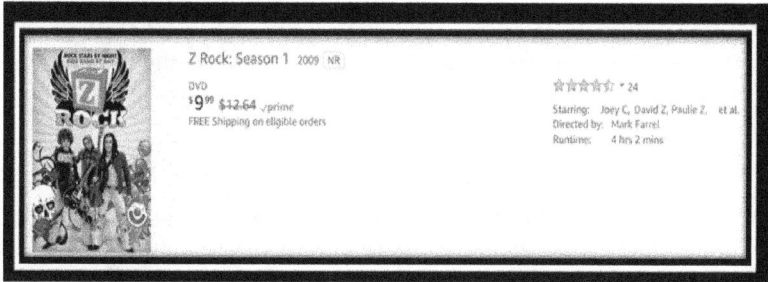

The actual listing of the Z Rock DVD on Amazon before Paulie made them change it so his name was first.

We used to refer to Bob as "The Cradler" because every time Paulie threw one of his diva fits about something, Bob would hold him in his arms and cradle him to make it all better.

One time while we were on the road, we had checked into our rooms for the night. I usually roomed with Dave, and Bob would room with Paulie. A few minutes after settling in, Bob came knocking on our door and told us that we had to switch rooms because Paulie's bed was too close the ground. We laughed and said, "Excuse me?"

Bob went on to explain that there was dust in the carpet and Paulie's bed was too low and he couldn't be that close to the dust because it would affect his voice. Needless to say, I slammed the door and went to sleep.

Can you believe the insanity that was going on? Bob wanted us to switch rooms because Paulie's bed was "too low"! Maybe this is why Paulie went along with whatever Bob said. Bob cradled him like a baby.

For some reason, ever since we started *Z Rock*, Bob and Lynn never realized that it was a TV show and not real life. This went so far that they hid my wedding from the network because they thought the network wouldn't like that I was getting married because on the show we played three single rock and rollers. It was so ludicrous! We were actors on a TV show and the network couldn't care less about our personal lives. Bob and Lynn were so obsessed with controlling ZO2 that they were beginning to hurt *Z Rock*. And, I was starting to hear about it often, on set and behind the scenes.

I remember one instance in particular when one of the IFC executives stormed off the set. We were filming a scene for episode 8, "*Z Rock* this Town." It was the end of the week and we were filming the final few scenes; we were way behind schedule and needed to get a lot more done in the hour we had left to film or it would send us into mega overtime that the network had to pay for. We are talking tens of thousands of dollars.

During one of the takes, Lynn Koplitz said a line about the singer Dido reaching number one on the Billboard charts. Bob came storming in during the take to announce that Lynn cannot say that. The director didn't know what happened, and asked, "What's wrong?" Bob proceeded to lecture the director that Dido did not reach number one but only number three, so Lynn couldn't say that because it wouldn't be accurate. Right then and there, the IFC executive stormed off set in a fit of rage.

This was a reflection on us as well. Since Bob was our manager, the network and producers had put up with him on set for almost two full seasons. After this, Bob had finally sealed his own fate.

The set was very uncomfortable over the last few episodes.

The scene that was the beginning of the end for Z Rock

Tensions were running high because of Bob and Lynn, and it was about to get worse for us. Bob and Lynn told us that Jason Flom had offered ZO2 a record contract, but they didn't think we should take it. Mind you, we were still technically under contract with our old label, Riker Hill, but we weren't getting any updates on what was happening. Bob and Lynn would flat out tell us, "Don't worry, we'll handle it." Paulie, Dave, and I wanted to know why we shouldn't accept Flom's offer.

They explained that Flom was offering what the industry calls a 360 deal, which meant the record company would get a little piece of everything we did, including record sales, touring, and merchandise. This was pretty standard at the time because in 2009 everyone stopped buying CDs and just streamed or illegally downloaded everything; therefore, most record companies wanted a cut of other revenue outlets from artists.

I voiced my opinion: "I think we should absolutely take it!" To have someone like Jason Flom not only offer a deal, but also appear on your TV show to sign you, was a huge opportunity. He was going to champion the band because he loved *Z Rock*. With Universal Records promotion and touring behind us, it was well worth it to give them a 360 cut.

The band we had just filmed with, Steel Panther, just recently signed the exact same deal with Flom and still to this day are doing fabulously, touring everywhere and selling a ton of records.

Paulie and Dave, of course, sided with Bob and Lynn, and we actually turned down the deal. I was once again outvoted. Flom wasn't happy, and it kind of spoiled his whole appearance on the show. He still appeared, but it was just a small little part that ultimately ended when John Popper landed on him

Record company mogul Jason Flom filming a scene for Z Rock

trying to escape from a prison window. Not the big contract signing on air that he wanted. A HUGE wasted opportunity!

On June 7, 2009, we had the *Z Rock* season 2 premiere party at Webster Hall. ZO2 was firing on all cylinders and we put on one of my favorite shows of all time. It was the pinnacle of all we'd done up until that point. We were surrounded by friends, family, and fans.

As we hit the stage and rang out our all too familiar opening chord, I had another "Frozen Moment." My mind let me stop everything and breathe in this amazing accomplishment. I looked up at the balcony and saw Madalyn standing there, pregnant with our daughter, and it made me the happiest man in the world.

I was living my dream, not only career wise, but I was also about to be a dad. It was a perfect night.

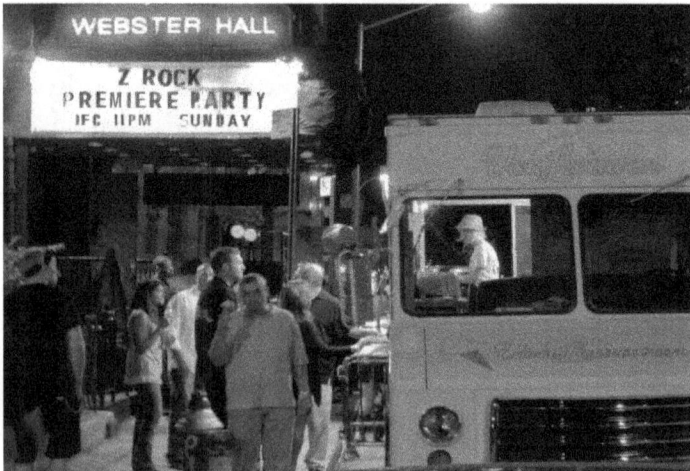

Outside of Webster Hall before the Z Rock season 2 premier party!

After filming concluded on Season 2 of *Z Rock*, I remained very friendly with the producers and network, more so than with the other guys. I got along really well with them and began having meetings with them about the possibility of season 3.

During these meetings, it was brought to my attention that none of them knew that our managers Bob and Lynn were commissioning us on our *Z Rock* salary. They were appalled to find this out.

It turned out that Bob and Lynn were "double dipping." They were not supposed to be getting a salary from the network and commissioning our salary as well. It wasn't 100 percent illegal, but it was extremely immoral and highly unethical!

The producers went on to explain that when we initially signed our *Z Rock* contract, the producers told our managers that they had an allotted salary for the band — a "pie," if you will, to be split three ways. Unknown to us, Bob and Lynn wanted to be paid as executive producers, but the production company explained that it was irregular for the talents' managers to be paid as executive producers, and there really wasn't any allotted money to pay them.

Bob and Lynn negotiated to be cut into our "pie" and to have it split five ways instead of three. The producers didn't care how we split it and said, "If it's okay with Paulie, David, and Joey, it's fine with us". Of course, the producers assumed that Bob and Lynn told us the full situation and if Bob and Lynn were going to be paid as equals to us then they wouldn't also commission us. They were wrong!

Looking up into the balcony at Webster hall and seeing Madalyn watching while pregnant with my daughter is one of my happiest moments ever.

We were never even informed that there was supposed to be only a three-way split among Paulie, Dave, and me. Bob and Lynn presented the offer from the beginning as a five-way split.

To break it down, Bob and Lynn got paid the same salary as we did. Not one of them as "our managers." Both! And then they took 20 percent of our money as well. Wow! I tried to explain all of this to Paulie and Dave, but they wouldn't listen. Bob and Lynn were in such control over them that they couldn't see straight. Well, I was starting to see crystal clear!

I even told Paulie and Dave that I had been talking to the network and producers about all three of us getting a producer credit next season.

If you can believe it, they both said, "No. Why would we get producer credits? We don't want to step on Bob and Lynn's toes." There was only one word that I can use to describe what was happening... BRAINWASHED!

I was also regularly meeting with IFC executive, Debbie DeMontreux. Debbie absolutely loved us and *Z Rock*, and she was fighting to get us a third season. But, there was one main obstacle that she needed to clear with me first. Debbie explained that "if" there were to be a *Z Rock* season 3, Bob and Lynn would be banned from the set. She said they were too disruptive and caused too many problems. They could still function as executive producers because of the contract they had signed, but they would not be allowed anywhere near the set or at the IFC offices. This was a non-starter if we didn't agree.

IFC was also furious with Bob and Lynn because in every press event or interview we did, those two always instructed us to only say ZO2, never stating the show's title. Execs from IFC would go crazy when they read interviews with us on red carpets or in print and it would only say "Paulie, David, and Joey from ZO2," never even mentioning that we had a TV show called *Z Rock*. It would be like an actor doing press for his TV show but only talking about a new movie he was starring in. It was so counter-productive. After a while, IFC just stopped setting up press events for us. They were fed up!

Hanging with Kim Kardashian on the red carpet.

IFC were the ones setting up and paying for all of this press for us, and stupidly we listened to Bob and Lynn, basically shooting ourselves in the foot. Bob and Lynn tried to keep us segregated from IFC and our label as much as possible, knowing that if we ever actually talked with either, they might end up in trouble. And they were right!

Debbie and our producers, Mark Efman and Mark Farell also suggested that we demand that they not commission our salary in addition to getting paid as producers. I knew I had to convince Paulie and Dave of all of these points, but I thought they would never go for it.

Luckily, Paulie was slowly starting to come around and see the light. After I explained how Bob and Lynn were double dipping and how the network was demanding that they be banned from the set, a little switch went off in his head that started to make him see things differently. I also insisted that we finally retain a lawyer to look at our *Z Rock* contracts. Once I got Paulie to bend a little, Dave was easy, even though he never really came around to seeing the truth about Bob and Lynn; in every case, he went along with whatever his big brother said. Once our new lawyer looked at the contract, he immediately reiterated everything that I was told about Bob and Lynn "double dipping."

We decided that we wouldn't even tell Bob and Lynn until we secured the third season. We did, however, let IFC know that we were okay with them being banned from set. Debbie scheduled a huge production meeting with all of the producers, us, and the network, for mid-September 2009. She assured us that the Bob and Lynn issue wouldn't be brought up in the meeting.

The meeting was going really well, and we were all discussing different things that could bring costs down and speed up shooting schedule. It was all sounding very positive — that is, until Paulie started to speak.

Paulie was always a bit of a diva, but at this point, he had really gone off the deep end. He stood up and basically demanded that he have a trailer to change in on set every day. I saw the producers hang their heads as if to say, "We are fighting to keep this show on the air and this idiot Diva is demanding his own trailer." I don't think Paulie's antics really had any weight in IFC's decision, but it definitely didn't help. All we could do was wait and see if IFC decided to bring back *Z Rock* for season 3.

Whatever happened with *Z Rock*, I had made a decision to not have Bob and Lynn represent me in my acting career anymore. After their call to turn down Universal Records and all of the new information I had discovered about *Z Rock* salaries, I no longer wanted any part of it. I didn't even want them as my music managers, but I knew Paulie and Dave would never agree to that. My plan was to sign on with Brian Stern, the agent whom Bob and Lynn told us we didn't need.

Don't misunderstand: Bob and Lynn did some wonderful and amazing things with ZO2. They got us the KISS tour, put together a record label that ultimately signed us, and were instrumental in helping us launch *Z Rock*. We would not have been where we were without them, but somewhere along the line, they forgot that they worked for us, not the other way around. Instead of all of us being a team and working together as a unit, they thought Paulie, Dave, and I did nothing and deserved no recognition at all and that they were the sole reason for our success.

Bob even told us that the three of us never made any sacrifices for the band, that only he and Lynn did. What sacrifices was he talking about? I have no clue! He quickly forgot that Paulie and Dave laid out all of the money for our first two records and the whole KISS tour, and that I just recently paid them back every cent that I owed them. Meanwhile, Bob and Lynn never once laid out even a single penny for anything.

People always like to say that Bob was to ZO2 what Bill Aucoin was to KISS. In some ways, that was accurate, but the biggest difference was that Aucoin funded every single thing KISS did on his personal credit cards for the first 3 or 4 years until KISS ALIVE hit big, going hundreds of thousands of dollars in debt because he believed in KISS. That's sacrifice!

In complete contrast, Bob would make Paulie pay for his meals and his metro card just to write a song with Paulie, even though Bob was co-writer! That's a fact, and that is the difference between Bill Aucoin and Bob Held.

Bob actually told us one day that they didn't need us to make *Z Rock* and that it was all his idea. He actually had the balls to say, "We could have made *Z Rock* with actors. We didn't need you three." This was one of the conversations that put me over the edge.

We said, "Your idea? It's 100 percent based on our real lives!" The one and only reason the show was ever even a thought was because Paulie and Dave happened to play a birthday party that a TV agent was attending! Two things sold the show to IFC: 1) the concept, which was kids' band by day, rock band by night, and 2) Paulie's, Dave's, and my personalities, none of which Bob and Lynn had any creative input on. Bob and Lynn wrote a small 2-page treatment and now they thought they had created the show and were the masterminds behind everything. Wrong!

I officially had had it with them after that conversation! And I think Paulie and even Dave to a certain extent never looked at them in the same light. Now that IFC was going to ban them from the set, I had an easy way to break the news to them that I didn't want them representing me anymore. Unfortunately, I never got the chance to tell them.

CHAPTER 28

I SEE EVERYTHING SO DIFFERENTLY NOW

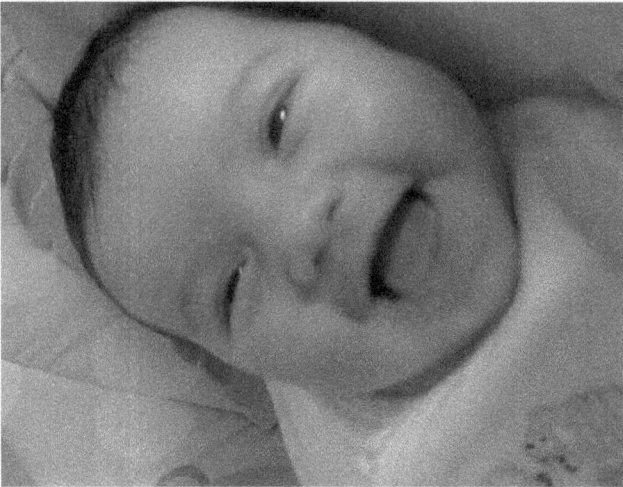

My angel ANGELINA

October 1, 2009 would be one of the happiest days of my life. My little angel Angelina was born. Madalyn and I arrived at the hospital on September 30. Mad looked ready to pop, and if she didn't go into labor soon the doctor was going to begin inducing.

After almost 24 hours in the hospital, on the morning of October 1, the doctor began inducing with a drug called oxytocin. All seemed okay for the first few hours: Mad received a spinal, which numbed her entire lower body. I've never seen a needle so big in my whole life, but she took it like a champ. I was so proud of her, and she was doing great.

Suddenly, Mad's blood pressure started to drop a bit which caused some concern with the nurses. They slowed down the medicine they were giving her to induce, and her blood pressure stabilized. But every time they began a new dose, the same thing happened. When her blood pressure dropped, she looked completely out of it. It was now dangerously low for her and the baby. Finally, Dr. Mukerji decided,

"Let's not take any chances." He decided to do a C-section to remove the baby.

I was starting to get very nervous. Everything was happening so fast. While they rushed Mad into the OR to begin the surgery, she still looked really out of it. I kissed her and told her I'd be right with her the whole time. The nurse threw a hospital gown at me and said, "Put this on!" As I was putting it on with one hand, I was calling Mad's mother with the other. "Come up to the hospital quick. The baby is coming!" Mad's mother and father hung up and rushed right over.

Once in the operating room, I started to feel even more nervous. All I cared about was Mad and the baby's health. There was a large blue curtain that separated half of her body and half of the room. I was with Mad on one side and the doctors and nurses were on the other side performing the operation. After only a few short minutes, Dr. Mukerji said that he could see the baby. The first thing he said was, "Wow, what a head of hair on this baby!" After a few pulls and wiggles, I heard a loud cry and my Angelina had entered the world. Angelina Marie Cassata was born on October 1, 2009, at 8:05 am and weighed 7 pounds, 12 ounces.

I'll never forget seeing my little girl for the first time. I had this sudden and uncontrollable urge to grab her and protect her from the world. I still have that exact urge today whenever I see her. She is my light, my sunshine, my heart, my love, my joy — my little angel Angelina.

As soon as she was born, I immediately saw the world differently. Everything I did from that moment on was to make sure my Angelina had a good life. I had such a new perspective on life in general. It was wonderful.

I immediately saw so much of my mother inside of Angelina, physically and especially spirituality. I am a firm believer in people's spirits and energy living on. I am beyond positive that a piece of my mom is inside of my angel Angelina. Maybe that's why she had to leave me — so that she could live on and be with me through my daughter.

Even though Madalyn and I were beyond happy to have our little Angelina, we had no idea how to take care of a baby. I remember the first time the nurse brought Angelina to us to talk about feeding and changing. She told us, "After every few little sips, you have to burp her."

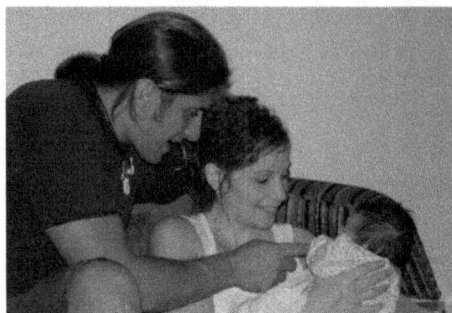

Madalyn and I holding our baby girl, Angelina.

We kindly asked, "How exactly do we burp her?" The nurse laughed and quickly showed us. I loved every second we spent learning something new and how to take care of our baby.

I remember when Madalyn's mother saw Angelina for the first time. She couldn't believe how dark and chubby she was, and with a head of jet black hair. She even jokingly asked Madalyn, "Are you sure she's your baby?" After a few days, we took Angelina home with us back to our apartment in Bensonhurst, Brooklyn.

Every moment of my life up until this point had been thinking about playing drums and "making it" in the music business. The moment Angelina was born, all of my priorities changed. All I wanted was to keep her safe and provide for her. Ultimately, I hoped I could do this by still playing my drums in some fashion. But, I would have become a garbage man if I had to. As long as my family was safe and provided for, that's what really mattered now.

A few days after Angelina came home I received some bad news. *Z Rock* writer Andrew Gottlieb called me to congratulate me on the birth of my daughter but also let me know that *Z Rock* would not be returning for a third season. This news would've normally devastated me, but I was holding my baby Angelina at the time, giving her a "ba ba," and somehow she made everything okay.

Of course, I was upset that *Z Rock* would be no more, but it was more because of me being able to provide for my family now than caring about becoming a rock/TV star.

Over the next several months, our producers, Mark Mark productions, tried to land *Z Rock* a new home. We actually had an offer from VH1 that we were ready to accept, when all of a sudden, personnel at the network changed and decided not to pick up *Z Rock* after all. Unfortunately, this was the beginning of the end for ZO2.

CHAPTER 29

PUTTING OUT THE TRASH

After almost another full year of playing clubs without much else going on, I had a long talk with Paulie and Dave about Bob and Lynn. I told them my plan to not have Bob and Lynn represent me in anything anymore. I tried to explain that they hadn't done anything for us as actors. Instead of trying to get us more work or even appearances, Bob was too busy on set yelling about Dido not being number one.

I also had just begun writing my own scripts for a cartoon called *Victor* which I was developing with my old Playground bandmate, Tommy Snyder. I would not have Bob and Lynn sticking their nose in it. Along with our lawyer Barry Pearlman, I finally convinced both of them to at least make some changes to our existing contract that was about to expire at the end of November 2010.

Our contract stated that they got 20 percent of everything we did in all forms of entertainment. Because of this ambiguous wording, they were probably entitled to take 20 percent of Dave's and my TSO salary, even though up until that point, they never did.

I also explained to Paulie and Dave that even though their "Z Brothers" CD was made before signing with Bob and Lynn, anything that was in the kids' world was up for grabs, simply because of the way the contract was worded. The contract just had a blanket statement saying they were entitled to 20 percent of everything we did! Ludicrous! All I wanted was it to be more specific, and this finally opened everyone's eyes, or at least they began to squint a little.

Paul and Dave agreed to have these points more clearly ironed out in a new contract. The only problem was that there was a stipulation in our existing contract that stated we would automatically renew unless we delivered something in writing by a certain date. Before we were able to figure out the exact changes we wanted put in the new contract, we first had to send a certified letter stating that we were not renewing our old contract.

Bob and Lynn received the letter on Thanksgiving morning. I absolutely agree it was terrible timing and that it looked like we weren't renewing because *Z Rock* was cancelled, but that wasn't the case at all. I actually had decided that I didn't want to renew over a year ago, during the filming of season 2. Paulie and Dave still wanted to keep them as our managers, but they wanted to add a few stipulations to the contract. That was the reason we sent them the certified letter.

Bob and Lynn called a meeting shortly after receiving the letter and Bob led off by saying, "We are not changing even one word in the contract!" I'm not sure where he got the balls to think it was okay to start off a business meeting that way, but he did and I couldn't have been happier.

Maybe Paulie and Dave would finally realize who we were dealing with: two people who thought they held all the power and that we were nothing without them. They could screw us over and do whatever they wanted and we didn't have the right to even question them. Bob's and Lynn's true colors came out that night.

The pair knew I spearheaded this whole thing. After the meeting, I found out that when I got up to use the bathroom, Lynn secretly said to Paulie and Dave, "Okay, let's find a new drummer." I couldn't believe it. Stuck up, conceited asses.

After the meeting, Paulie started to show signs of coming around to my way of thinking. He never in a million years expected them to say they weren't changing a single word and then suggest they get rid of me. Paulie was almost there, but he needed one more push, and he received it from the most unlikely source.

That January, Paulie went to L.A. for NAMM. I didn't make it because I wanted to stay home with Mad and Angelina. One night while visiting the Rainbow Bar & grill, Paulie ran into *Z Rock* guest star Frank Stallone. As Paulie tells the story, Paulie and Frank sat and talked over dinner for about two hours.

Paulie is someone that wears his heart on his sleeve and he decided to open up to Frank about our current situation with Bob and Lynn. It was risky because Frank had been Bob's friend for years, but Paulie explained the whole situation and how Bob said they weren't changing even one word in the contract. In response, Frank told Paulie that something similar had happened to him many years ago. His manager had also been his long-time friend, but there came a point where he had to let him go.

He told Paulie, "If you feel someone else is not doing right by you or is holding you down, you have to cut ties immediately. You don't want to wake up 10 years from now and say, 'Shit, I wish I would have made a move back then, maybe things would be different'."

Even though I'd been trying to get through that thick Afro of his for years, it only took 2 hours with Frank Stallone to break through. When Paulie returned from L.A., he was officially done with Bob and Lynn.

I wanted to just tell Bob and Lynn, "Okay, if you don't want to change even one word in the contract, then you're fired." That is how I wanted to handle it and how we should have done it. Instead, Paulie decided he didn't want to look like the bad guy, so he came up with this elaborate scheme to draft a contract that he knew Bob and Lynn would reject, just so we could say, "We wanted to keep them as our managers, but they said no to our new contract." I thought it was a ridiculous plan, but of course, Dave went along with it because it was Paulie's idea and I was once again outvoted. Overall, it didn't really matter. There was no way to end our relationship with Bob and Lynn on good terms. Bob had been almost a father figure to Paulie and Dave, and there was no way it was going to end nicely.

Paulie had our lawyer make every change we wanted in the contract, plus a few added things to really tilt things to our side. Once drafted, it was mailed to Bob and Lynn who immediately saw right through Paulie's attempt at deception. The plan completely backfired. Instead of us having the high ground because they said, "We are not changing a single word," they now had the proverbial high ground because they could show everyone our ridiculous contract offer that they promptly rejected. At the end of the day, it didn't really matter to me. Once and for all, we were finally done with Bob and Lynn. Or, so we thought.

After getting rid of Bob and Lynn, it was time for ZO2 to clean up their financial situation. The cost of our third album, *Casino Logic*, was a heavy debt. Paulie and Dave began discussing ways and what percent of gigs and merch would be put against this debt. I cut them off pre-immediately with, "Guys, I told you I was 100 percent against funding that record on your credit cards and I would hold no financial obligation for any of it." After a long and heated discussion, I finally convinced both of them to go bankrupt and to wipe that debt clean so we could have a chance at a fresh start. Otherwise, there was no way to keep ZO2 afloat.

While Paulie and Dave were taking care of all the bankruptcy paper work, I decided to look more deeply into what exactly happened at our old record label, Riker Hill.

I contacted the former head of the label, Micheal Morrison, from whom I'd been completely isolated for over a year per Bob and Lynn's request (demand). Michael and I always got along great. He was a big Rangers and Giants fan like I was, and we often watched games together, which made the whole situation even more awkward when Bob and Lynn started excluding them from everything. Once back in touch, I just asked Michael straight up, "What the hell happened?"

Michael began to break down the whole entire situation for me. He explained, "Bob and Lynn had no idea what they were doing running the label and that everything they originally told Michael Wolk and I, about how they knew how to run a label was a lie". He went on to say, "Obviously a start-up independent label wasn't expected to make money at first, but Bob and Lynn were draining the label dry. Both had enormous salaries, and 95 percent of the time Bob did nothing but go on the road with ZO2 or sit on the set of *Z Rock*. He did absolutely NOTHING for the label."

That was when everything started to blow up. The label told Bob that they would have to stop paying him his salary if he didn't come to the office. Michael believes that this is what triggered all the bad blood, which then snowballed into the end of our relationship. Michael said, "They even hid everything related to *Z Rock* from us. I wanted to try to work with IFC to cross promote or somehow capitalize on *Z Rock*, but Bob and Lynn told me that I wasn't even allowed on set because the network didn't want anyone from the label around". It was all lies.

So for anyone reading this that still thinks it was all ZO2's fault about what happened with Bob and Lynn, think again. This book offers firsthand accounts from one of the heads of IFC stating that "Bob and Lynn would be banned from the *Z Rock* set because they were a hindrance," and I note the head of our record label saying, "Bob and Lynn had no idea what they were doing." Bob and Lynn, over the years, have tried to spin it many other ways, but this is the truth and it's coming from the real sources.

I then asked Michael what happened with the funding for ZO2's third album, *Casino Logic* and he replied with something that absolutely shocked and infuriated me. He said, "Riker wanted to absolutely fulfill the terms of the third album. We were ready to pay the exact amount that was in the contract. Bob and Lynn came back to us and said they would need almost because of promo and touring. Not only couldn't we pay that, we didn't have to. Riker Hill wanted to follow the contract and Bob and Lynn didn't."

I told Michael, "ZO2 was told that Riker Hill refused to pay for the record, period. Never once did Bob and Lynn inform us that Riker was offering the contracted sum for *Casino Logic*." Michael was beyond furious!

Everything was starting to come together. After hearing everything from the people at IFC, from our producers Mark Mark, and now the head of our label, combined with all the underhanded things that I'd experienced firsthand, namely lying about my wedding to the network and our producers, I was now more certain than ever that we ultimately made the right choice by cutting ties with our managers. Years later, I still feel it was one of the best decisions I ever made.

ZO2 would stay together for another 2-plus years and we did some really great things in that time, things that most bands could only dream of. We played huge festivals like M3 with bands like Cinderella, and we

Me holding Angelina at Z02's Rock Asylum.

opened for Stone Temple Pilots at the Tampa Bay Lightning Hockey team season kickoff party. We did other great shows as well, like opening for Stryper, Dream Theater, and UFO.

During this time, we made what I consider to be our two best videos for the songs "No Way Out" and one of our newest singles, "That's What's Up."

"That's What's Up" video shoot.

We also decided to start releasing singles instead of waiting to release another full-length album. One of those singles was "I Will Be Alright," a song I wrote with Paulie about my mom's passing.

I knew my days of traveling in a van with ZO2 were numbered. I wasn't 25-years old anymore without a care in the world. I now had my baby to support and it was getting more and more difficult to leave her. I knew something had to change. I just didn't want to be a full-time touring musician anymore.

ZO2 playing the Tampa Bay Lightning home opener.

CHAPTER 30

RETURNING TO AN OLD LOVE

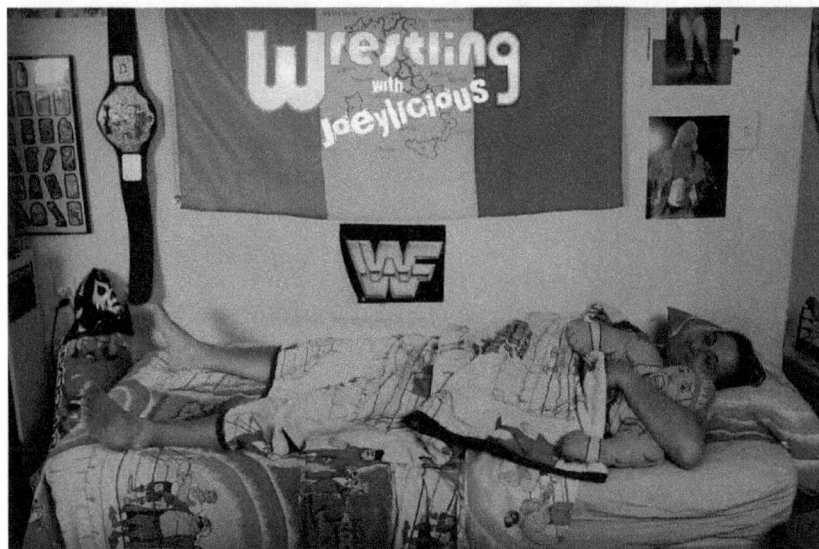

That same January that Paulie was having a heart-to-heart with Frank Stallone, I knew it was time that I ventured out and did more things on my own. I had already begun work on my animated project Victor and now I wanted to take a stab and revisit something that I missed and still loved... wrestling! No, I wasn't going to try and become a professional wrestler, but I decided to try and capitalize on the success of the Joeylicious character that I had created many years ago and that got some great response in the *Z Rock* episode.

I wrote up a small story synopsis and created a fun backstory for the Joeylicious character that was based heavily on my real life. I figured "Based on Real Life" worked for *Z Rock*, maybe it'll work for Joeylicious.

After writing the basic story for the pilot episode of "Joeylicious," I knew I needed to spice it up a little. I remembered that a friend of mine from grammar school, Chris Lynn, was a really talented script writer and I decided to give him a call. Chris and I had the exact same birthday, January 21, 1974, and I called him to grab a drink a few days after to talk about the new project in development.

That night there was a big snowstorm, and we talked for a couple hours about Joeylicious. Chris seemed really into it and was familiar with the episode of *Z Rock* in which Joeylicious appeared. I enlisted Chris to take my two-page story synopsis and come up with a full pilot episode script. What I really wanted from Chris was to capture our youth in the pages of Joeylicious.

Yes, Joeylicious was going to be about wrestling, but more importantly it was going to be about Joeylicious, how he grew up, and the struggles of trying to make his dream of becoming the greatest professional wrestler of all time become a reality. The main characters of the show would be Joeylicious, his life-long buddy Scally, and his mom, Mrs. C.

A few days later, Chris emailed me the first draft of the pilot episode. I couldn't believe how fast he wrote it. I was very excited to read it and hoped for the best. Mid-way through I really started to feel like I was back in my childhood. Chris really had a way of capturing the dialog of our youth. It was perfect! He also retitled the show *Wrestling with Joeylicious* to capitalize on a kind of double entendre. One way of looking at it meant that it was a show about wrestling and about the title character. Another way, and really the way I always think of it, was me constantly "wrestling" with my alter ego, Joeylicious. The next step would be to approach my old *Z Rock* producers to see if they had any interest in *Wrestling with Joeylicious*!

As soon as I emailed Mark Efman the idea, he sounded interested. He also knew that the Joeylicious character was a hit for *Z Rock* and thought we could capitalize on it. He wanted Chris and me to come up to the Mark Mark office as soon as possible to discuss.

Mark Mark eventually agreed to produce a short sizzle Reel for Joeylicious, much like they had done for *Z Rock*. The only problem was that they wanted it to be almost a quasi-reality show and to actually follow me trying to become a wrestler.

Unfortunately, the TV landscape at the time was all reality TV. It was what everyone wanted: it was cheap, fast, and easy to make. That's not at all what I was looking to do. I wanted *WWJ* to be fully scripted with room for improv. This caused a little bit of a rift when it came time to film the sizzle and it didn't turn out as well as I expected.

I eventually pulled *Joeylicious* away from the Marks so Chris and I could do it our way. All the while I was working on *Wrestling With Joeylicious*, ZO2 was still trucking ahead, playing as many shows as possible. I was becoming more and more difficult to work with because I felt that we were back to playing dozens of useless shows, just so it would appear that we were busy. This was always Paulie's M.O.

One of the final straws for me came when Paulie decided he wanted to break ties with the concert booking agent we had recently signed, The Agency Group. I was completely against this.

The Agency Group was one of the biggest booking agents in the country and we had been trying to get them to sign us for years. They were our only hope of getting a big tour and the big marquee shows that I thought we should be doing. Paulie thought the exact opposite. In his mind, if we weren't playing constantly, we weren't working hard enough. He wanted to play every little place that would book us, and for next to no money. Paulie always had a tendency of working "hard" not necessarily "smart."

The Agency Group didn't want ZO2 to play a lot of these places because it essentially hindered some of the bookings they were getting for us. So, once again, and for the final time, I was outvoted. Dave went along with Paulie and we left one of the biggest agents in the country so we could play little dive bars. Insane!

After this, I decided I wasn't going

The cast for the Wrestling with Joeylicious pilot was filled with some familiar faces. Carlos, O'Grady, and Tony Cortes.

to play as many shows with ZO2 anymore. At this time, Paulie also decided he wanted to change the image of the band, and he didn't mean just physically, but musically; he also wanted a shift in overall attitude, thinking we should be a more serious band with meaningful messages in our songs — no more goofy attitudes or funny stuff.

Again, we were on the complete opposite end of the spectrum. I couldn't disagree more! If anything, I thought we should go the exact other direction. We were now known mostly for *Z Rock*. Everyone loved us in the show. We were funny, goofy, and never took ourselves too seriously, which was exactly how we were in real life. I thought at the time Paulie was starting to go through an early mid-life crisis, and I was correct.

Paulie had gotten married the day after my Angelina was born and got divorced shortly after. This absolutely crushed Paulie. Getting divorced on top of the whole disaster with Bob and Lynn, losing our record label, and *Z Rock*'s cancellation sent Paulie over the deep end. Paulie even admitted one night on the road that the main reason he wanted to do so many away shows was because he had nothing to go home to. We had just become such different people at this point in our lives that right then and there, I knew it wasn't going to work anymore.

But I really knew Paulie would never be the same again after we got an offer from our old agent, Brian Stern at William Morris, to do an original Internet streaming show on Warner Brothers' new channel.

Brian told us that Warner Brothers wanted ZO2/Z Brothers to do a comedy show on their new streaming network. It would have put us back in the public eye and possibly even on Warner Brothers' record label since the channel was going to strictly highlight Warner artists. The show would be very much like *Z Rock* but focus even more on the kids' music. It would be a zany, fun comedy show. Shockingly, Paulie wanted nothing to do with it.

Even Dave, who was always on Paulie's side, tried to convince him to do the show, but Paulie outright refused. He wanted to distance himself from goofy, afro-hair Paulie from *Z Rock* as much as he could. He had recently cut his hair very short and essentially cut all ties to that old version of himself.

I just didn't want to be a touring musician anymore. I'd rather be home with my beautiful family.

After this, I had basically checked out of ZO2 land and Paulie and Dave knew it. After another few shows, Paulie called a meeting to tell me and Dave, "Because we all want such different things now, ZO2 should go on a permanent hiatus." I agreed. We discussed in great detail that we would finish the new album that was almost written and release it as a way to end the final chapter of ZO2. We would tell all of our fans that we were taking a long hiatus, but that they might eventually see us again. We all agreed there was no need to say we were "breaking up" or have a "farewell show." We all had a lot of endorsements and there was no reason to jeopardize that by saying ZO2 was breaking up.

During this time, Paulie had changed the old Rock Asylum brand into a "charity" organization. He consumed himself in it. I believe it was just something for Paulie to bury himself in while he was going through a very hard time. I thought it was actually a great thing for him to focus on.

ZO2 had a show coming up at Webster Hall in New York City, but Paulie was billing it under the "Rock Asylum" umbrella. One day on social media, I saw the Rock Asylum show being advertised as "ZO2's final performance." I was furious! It wasn't so much that it was being billed as such, but the fact that ZO2 had a very specific discussion as a band a few days prior to do the exact opposite! To this day, I feel Paulie did it for his own selfish reasons. He wanted to sell more tickets to his Rock Asylum event by using the ZO2 "final performance" card.

I had dozens of people calling me to ask, "What happened? Why is ZO2 breaking up?" I didn't know what they were even talking about until I saw the social media post. This caused a big rift between Paulie and me. I hated to be disrespected and I felt this was a slap in my face. We didn't talk for quite some time. We even had one more show after Rock Asylum down in Maryland that I decided I wouldn't play. ZO2 got a replacement drummer for the very last show.

It's exactly the opposite way that I wanted to end ZO2. I wanted everything we did to be celebrated. I wanted to release our last album, which I thought would have been amazing, by the way. If after that we decided to do a farewell show or shows, we would do it the right way. Instead, because Paulie felt the need to do what he did on his own, without even discussing it with Dave and me, we ended on a complete down. Z02 was no more...

While writing this book, my band mate, my friend ... no, my little brother, Dave Z passed away in a terrible car accident while on tour with one of his new bands, Adrenaline Mob. The band's RV had pulled off to the shoulder on the side of the highway somewhere in Florida to fix a flat tire when an 18-wheel semitruck plowed into them, causing Dave to lose his life.

Dave was one of those people who just always had a good time. He lived life his way, as a big goofy kid. He never had a care in the world, and that goes for money, health, or what he was going to be doing in 5 years. He just enjoyed himself in the moment and never cared about making a fool of himself as long as it made someone else laugh.

After ZO2 ended, I would always ask Dave about what he was planning to do next — what his goals were, his ambitions, whether he was going to buy a house, start a family. He always answered the same way: "I'm perfectly happy the way I am, and with what I'm doing. Why would I buy a house and have to worry about it? I love my little apartment. I love my life exactly the way it is! And he really did.

His fiancé Solina posted a perfect picture and caption of Dave after he passed. "May something in this world make you as happy as jelly doughnuts made Dave."

That was Dave! The happiest man in the world just eating a stupid jelly doughnut!

That's why it was so crushing when he died. I was most sad for him because the life that he loved so much was taken away in an instance. I'm still so angry, sad, heartbroken, and confused about why God would take his life away. WHY??

I always assumed that ZO2 would reunite one day and conquer the world. The next ZO2 album would have been fantastic. Filled with hits and the raw energy that everyone expected from us. I even thought that Z Rock would eventually make its triumphant return. The cult following that it had would surely demand that it resurface in some fashion. Maybe even a Z Rock movie filled with wacky guest stars galore. All I knew was that someday Paulie, Dave and Joey would be back bigger than ever! We had so much more to do together…

Dave Z enjoying life like only he could

I would give anything to be on one more silly road trip with those two idiots. Arguing for hours over where we were going to have lunch or debating about who could eat the most chicken nuggets.

Paulie's 40th birthday: the last time ZO2 was onstage together and the last time I'd see Dave Z.

On March 17, 2017, ZO2 did unit one final time at Arlene's Grocery to celebrate Paulie's 40th birthday. It was so great to be on stage with those two knuckleheads again, and to celebrate all that we accomplished. I am forever thankful that we had that one last night together. It would be the last time I saw Dave.

For 10 years of my life, I had spent more time with Dave and Paulie than I did my own family, and in the process, they became family — a weird Jewish Z version of family, but family all the same. They were both like my little brothers who I loved to pick on. Over those 10 years, I've never argued, debated, laughed, and eaten so much in my life. I will forever cherish each and every moment we spent on stage and in front of the camera together, but more so, all of the moments just kidding around and enjoying life. R.I.P. Dave, I'll miss you everyday…

CHAPTER 31
TAKING CHANCES

Backstage right before my first performance with The Great Comet.

After ZO2 "broke up," Dave joined an 80's tribute band called Rubix Kube with a few friends of ours. They were planning a trip to Germany, Syria, and Kosovo to play for the U.S. military on New Year's Eve. Dave wasn't going to be able to make the trip because he was still on tour with TSO. Their singer, Cheri, contacted me about possibly coming and playing the shows with Rubix. She also asked me if I knew any keyboard players that might want to play the shows. My friend Or Matias that I played in the TSO backup band with immediately came to mind. I contacted Or about the shows and he got on board right away.

The trip to Germany, Syria, and Kosovo with Rubix Kube was very interesting to say the least. When we first arrived on the Kosovo NATO base, we were greeted by a foreign military guard that none of us recognized. We were asked to exit the vehicle so they could search it and us before entering the base. Every guard was holding some sort of heavy-duty machine gun. Or and I looked at each other and pre-immediately regretted our decision to join Rubix Kube on this European adventure.

Once on the base, we met with our guide for the week and he escorted us to where we would be sleeping. I'm not sure exactly what I was expecting, but what he showed us was definitely not it. Each of us would be sleeping in what I could only describe as a large metal container. Picture the back of an 18-wheel cargo truck: that would be where we slept over the next few days. Or and I couldn't help but laugh. The rest of the trip went smoothly enough, and it was cool to say we had played for our troops abroad.

After returning from Europe, I decided I wanted to try my hand at subbing on a Broadway show. Of course, this was a crazy long shot and I knew it was next to impossible to break into that world, but those kind of odds never stopped me before.

I knew a few players in the musical *Rock of Ages* and I arranged to sit and watch one night in February 2013. Just by pure coincidence, Or contacted me that same day about grabbing a drink. I had some time to kill in between teaching drums and going to *Rock of Ages* and I met Or for a quick drink. He was surprised to hear that I was interested in doing a Broadway show.

That small, inconsequential drink with Or would come back to pay big dividends down the road. I truly believe that sending energy out to people and into the world is what creates opportunity.

A few months later, Or called to see if I would be interested in auditioning for a musical/opera that he was going to be playing in called *Natasha Pierre and The Great Comet of 1812*. He said they might be looking to add live drums to the music, which currently only had computer tracks at the time. I honestly didn't know what to say. It sounded like it was definitely not up my alley. I asked him when the audition would be. He said, "The audition has to be tomorrow because we open previews tomorrow night".

I figured there was no way that I was going to go and audition for a show that was opening tomorrow and for which I essentially had to write drum parts. But, I told him to send me the material and details anyway.

Or sent me three songs and the sheet music to look over. When I received them, I was even more sure I was not going to go audition the next day. The sounds were very, very weird, with all sorts of electronic tracks playing throughout. The sheet music was even more confusing. I hadn't read music since leaving high school and because the songs didn't really have drum parts written to them yet, the sheet music was written more for what the weird tracks were playing. It was confusing.

At the time, I was teaching drums in a few private music schools and after thinking about it for a little while, I decided, "What do I have to lose?" If I got the gig, which I thought was a long shot at best, given the half a day I had to prepare, it would be a steady paycheck with me doing 8 shows a week for the whole summer of 2013. I talked it over with Madalyn and she agreed: "Why not?"

I printed out the sheet music and downloaded the three songs, which were "In My House," "The Duel," and "Charming." "The Duel" was the first song I dug into and it was very discouraging. I really couldn't make heads or tails of it. Having never seen or heard the whole show, I could not for the life of me figure out what the hell was going on in the song. I'm not even sure it could be called a song. It was more like this weird, semi-spoken, psychedelic, folky/club thing. The sheet music didn't help either. It had all of the weird track noises written in, which made it impossible to decipher. The only reason the sheet music was of any use for this song was so I could follow along the bars to see where I was in the song.

"In my house" wasn't much better. It was another very weird song with no real backbeat or rhythm to it. Thankfully, the last song, "Charming," had a little something I could sink my teeth into.

After a few hours of prep, I was as ready as I was going to be. It was hard to write anything to these eccentric tracks, especially without knowing what they were looking for. I could only go and be myself and play what I thought might fit into this wacky world.

On May 16, 2013, I went to the meat packing district in Manhattan to audition for *Natasha, Pierre and the Great Comet of 1812*. When I arrived at the address Or gave me, I saw a large, white tent that had been constructed in an abandoned lot across the street from the Standard Hotel. I had no idea what I was walking into.

I did know that my life as a touring musician was nearing its end and that I had to take some chances and make the most out of every opportunity that came my way. I'm confident in myself, my work ethic, my playing, and my personality. I do believe that personality is as important as skill in anything a person does in life. I've met and played with hundreds of musicians over the years, and I would take someone that had a great, fun personality and was a B player over a guy that either had a bad personality or even worse, no personality, and was an A-plus player.

When I walked into the tent, it was nothing like I expected. It was almost like the phone booth in the TV show *Dr. Who*. It was a plain white ordinary tent on the outside, but once inside, I was transported into a magical world. I still had absolutely no idea what the show was about, but after entering into that world, I knew I wanted to be part of it.

The composer Dave Malloy, music supervisor Sonny Paladino, producer Howard Kagan, and Or the music director stood and waited for me to get behind the drum set to begin the audition. As I went to sit behind the kit, I knocked over a 12-foot tall Napoleon painting that was hanging right above the drums. Luckily, I caught it as it fell or it would have caused some major damage. Everyone had a nice laugh and it broke the tension that was looming over the room.

Dave took control of the audition and began asking me to play certain sections of the songs I was given. As we went through each one, I could see Dave and Sonny whispering back and forth to one another. They didn't really give me any feedback.

When it was time to play the song "Charming," they brought out the singer, Amber Gray. I had written a pretty basic drum part that rhythmically synced in with the track as best as I could. The song seemed to crescendo all the way to the last chorus, so upon entering the last chorus, I played a giant drum fill and then came in at almost full volume.

I saw Amber struggling to sing over the volume of the drums. She had never done the song with live drums before and seemed taken aback by them. When the song ended, she turned to Dave and said angrily, "How can I possibly sing over that? It's sooo loud!"

The Great Comet of 1812 tent.

I assumed that was what they wanted and just went for it. I knew my strength was going to be that song and not the other weird ones, so I played what I thought worked. If they didn't like it, there was nothing I could do about it now.

After the audition, Or told me I did great, but that it was really Dave's decision. He said they would get back to me, by the latest tomorrow afternoon.

The next day I was in jury duty in downtown Brooklyn. It was a miserable day of just waiting around for hours. Or called me mid-afternoon and left a message to call him back. As soon as I had a break, I called him to find out my fate. To tell you the truth, I wasn't even sure that I wanted the gig, but I knew I had to start taking chances on new things and seizing the moment.

Or told me that I did great but Dave didn't really want live drums in the show. For a moment, I really wasn't sure if I was disappointed or not. Before I could figure it out in my head, Or yelled, "Just kidding, dude! You got the gig!" My feelings were clear this time; I was extremely excited to begin a new chapter in my musical career with *Natasha, Pierre and the Great Comet of 1812*!

Inside The Great Comet tent always reminded me of the phone booth in Dr. Who.

Or asked me if I could make it back to the tent later that night to see the show and get a feel for it. It was their second "preview show." A play or a musical has a series of "preview shows" before the real opening night, so that cast and crew can work out all the bugs before they lock things into place. Once a show officially opens, it can't be changed.

I told Or, "Sure, I'll be there!" Everything was happening so fast. Once I arrived at the tent later that night, someone ushered me into the wardrobe department, so I could get fitted for my costume. Crazy! I still had no idea what the show even was and I was getting fitted for my costume.

After watching the show for the first time, I still didn't understand exactly what was going on. I knew that it was very different from anything that I had ever heard and definitely different than anything I had ever played. Or wanted me to come back the next day and play a few more songs in rehearsal with the whole band and cast. When I arrived the next day, we played through the few songs that I already knew and had worked on, then we tried a couple of new ones.

I had sheet music on my stand, but I hadn't sight read in a very long time. We played through a wild upbeat song called "Balaga," which I'd never even heard except for once the night before. I tried my best to follow along with the sheet music. We stumbled through it and continued on. After another hour or so, Or and Dave asked me if I thought I could be ready to sit in on a few songs that night.

I was taken aback by this and I didn't want it to seem like I didn't want to play, so I said, "Sure." I assumed they only wanted me to play the original three songs they sent me, but they had something else in mind. They gave me a recording and the sheet music (mostly just what the track was playing) and asked me to try and learn and come up with parts for 5 other songs.

I was a little overwhelmed, but up for the challenge. I took the recording and sheet music and sat in the park for the next three hours trying to absorb as much as I possibly could. I didn't have access to a drum set to rehearse on, so I just tried to memorize what I could.

On the night of May 18, 2013, I played my first show with *Natasha, Pierre and the Great Comet of 1812*. Backstage at the tent, everyone had their own little dressing area. Mine now had my name tag on it with my costume waiting for me. I wasn't set to play on the opening song "Prologue," but would enter shortly after.

As I sat at my station, I experienced a different kind of "Frozen Moment," unlike others I had before. All others up until this point were focused on excitement, accomplishment, and love while this one had a slightly different feel to it. As I sat there and stared into the mirror, I could hear the opening applause for the show coming from 10 feet behind me through the red velour curtains. I knew this moment marked a change in my life.

I could feel a big opportunity in front of me. Or told me that the ultimate goal of the show was to get it to Broadway. I knew as soon as I walked through that curtain that I was taking my first steps to "The great white way." I stared at myself in the mirror during that "Frozen Moment" and told myself, "Go get it!"

My first show was definitely very rocky. Not only did I not know the material as well as I would have liked, but the whole atmosphere inside of the tent was foreign to me. It took a while for me to adjust to the right dynamics to use during each song since this gig definitely did not require me to bang away like I'd been accustomed to while playing with ZO2 in front of 20,000 people. This was more about control and creating mood.

By the end of that very first weekend, I was much more comfortable and confident. Let the summer of 2013 begin!

Musical Director Or Matias, Me, and bassist John Murchinson inside the Great Comet tent.

CHAPTER 32
BE CREATIVE. ALWAYS!

Now that I had steady income from *The Great Comet*, and my days with ZO2 were behind me, I decided to really focus on my two other projects that I was developing. The animated show *Victor*, about an old lovable bigot, and of course, *Wrestling With Joeylicious*.

It's so funny to me when people ask, "How did you know how to develop an animated series?" or, "How did you create "*Wrestling With Joeylicious*?" The answer is that I actually had no idea how to develop an animated series like *Victor* or a live action comedy like *Joeylicious*. I simply had a dream, a vision, and I went out and did it! It was the same scenario as playing my drums: I saw KISS at Madison Square Garden when I was 5 years old and decided from that day I was going to play drums for the rest of my life. Everything that's worth anything in this life takes a tremendous amount of work, sacrifice, and passion.

In the case of my animated show *Victor*, it took many hours, days, and months of research. I can't say the number of books I read on how to develop an animated series or how many online seminars that I watched on how to pitch an animated series. When I want to do something, nothing will stop me from accomplishing that goal. If there is one message above all others that I want my kids to absorb from reading this book, it's that you can do anything you set your mind to, as long as you work hard enough at it and don't let people tell you that you can't do it! The only people that fail are the ones that never try!

When I started up work again on *Wrestling with Joeylicious*, my partner Chris and I admitted that we were never pleased with the original sizzle demo that was filmed with my old *Z Rock* producers. I always felt that it was missing something. I decided I wanted to add some star power the show, and my first call was to my old *Z Rock* co-star, Chris Jericho. Chris and I had become friendly since filming *Z Rock*, and whenever WWE was in town, he'd always hook me up with great tickets.

Jericho and I also had a lot of musical tastes in common. I remember when ZO2 opened for one of our favorite bands, Stryper. Chris called me right after the show to ask me how it went. I told him that I had a long conversation with Stryper's drummer, Robert Sweet, who was a huge influence on my drumming. I told Chris that Robert had watched me play that night and told me after the show that he thought I was a better drummer than he was. Chris started screaming on the phone because he was so excited.

I told Chris about the *Wrestling With Joeylicious* concept and he really liked it. He told me he would absolutely be in it, if/when we got it going. I could have probably asked him for a favor to film a short scene with us now for promo, but I decided I didn't want to put him in that position. I knew another door would open if I just kept knocking.

A few months later, I visited the NYC Comic Con like I did most years. I was there mainly to fill up my comic book collection and try to make some connections for my animated series. Soon after I entered, I ran into an old friend named Brimstone. Brim had been an independent wrestler and a huge fan of *Z Rock*. I mentioned to him about the Joeylicious concept and he asked me if I wanted to meet a few wrestlers who were signing autographs at a nearby table. I, of course, said, "I'd love to."

Brim introduced me to Tito Santana, Brutus Beefcake, and Greg Valentine. They were all very nice and Brim briefly explained to them that I was putting together a new wrestling comedy series. I exchanged numbers with all of them and said I would be in touch.

My first attempt at recruiting wrestling legends to be a part of JOEYLICIOUS. Tito Santana, Greg Valentine, Me, and Brutus Beefcake.

I thanked Brim for the introductions and before we parted ways he said, "Hey, I also have Jimmy Snuka's contact info. Do you want that as well?" Jimmy had been the first wrestler I'd really loved, and I was extremely excited about the possibility of meeting and working with him.

When I got home that night from Comic Con, I began writing a short that involved Joeylicious and Jimmy Snuka! Now that I had access to some of these wrestling legends, my idea was to have them appear in *Wrestling With Joeylicious* as figments of my imagination. This would allow me to put myself and the legends in all sorts of wacky situations. I thought that if I could just film a few shorts with them, I could put together a dynamite sizzle reel that I could pitch to networks.

The next day, I sent an email to the contact that Brimstone had given me for Snuka. It was actually his wife's, Carole, email address. In the message, I explained who I was and that I starred in a hit TV show called *Z Rock*, and that I was currently developing a new project about wrestling. Carole emailed me back quickly and said that Jimmy would definitely be interested.

I couldn't believe it. I was going to be filming with WWF legend Jimmy "Superfly" Snuka for a TV project that I wrote and created! I emailed Chris the outline for the Snuka script so he could work his magic on it. As usual, he didn't disappoint.

I gathered a small crew filled with friends and old colleagues. Scally's wife was going to do makeup, and Scally himself would be on set to help out in any way he could. Almost 30 years prior, Scally had been with me at Madison Square Garden to watch Jimmy Snuka wrestle! I enlisted another longtime friend, Travis Mitterway, to be one of my cameramen.

I really wanted to sort of re-enact Snuka's classic appearance on Piper's Pit. I couldn't pass up the opportunity to write in the script that Snuka would hit me in the head with a coconut.

I stayed up all night before filming, cutting, and getting the coconuts ready for him to smash me with. At the end of the scene, it would be revealed that Jimmy was never actually there and I'd hit myself over the head with a rock.

On August 29, 2013, we filmed the first *Wrestling With Joeylicious* short with wrestling legend Jimmy Snuka. I had sent the script to Jimmy's wife a week prior for Jimmy to learn. Even though the show was going to be partly improv, I still needed Jimmy to learn the basic beats so we could get through it. That's when Jimmy's wife informed me that he couldn't read or write and it might be hard for him to memorize his lines. I told her not to worry and that we would figure it out.

On the day of filming, Jimmy was an absolute gentleman and sweetheart. Even though it was a struggle to get him to say most of the lines we needed him to deliver, the whole day was a dream come true. Because it was so hard to get Snuka to say his lines correctly, I really held his hand and personally helped him with every single word. His wife was very appreciative of how I helped Jimmy that day.

We scouted out the perfect location up in the Bronx. While we were filming, every car that passed screamed out, "Snuka!" He was still a legend. By the end of the day, not only had we gotten some amazing footage but also some even more amazing bloopers. I felt I had made genuine friends in Jimmy and his wife Carole.

While we were editing the Snuka short, I was already setting up our next 2 shoots. This time with Brutus "The Barber" Beefcake and

The man who got me hooked on professional wrestling...
Jimmy "Superfly" Snuka!

Greg "The Hammer" Valentine and then a few weeks later with Tito Santana — more of my childhood favorites. We went through the same process as we did with the Snuka episode. I came up with the initial draft of the script because I knew these wrestlers better than anyone and knew the best way to utilize their unique personalities. Once I had the plot outlined, Chris took over to beef up the dialogue and the jokes. We were working perfectly together.

The Beefcake/Valentine episode would end with "The Barber" giving Joeylicious a haircut. I had everything set. Both wrestlers were coming into town for a local comic convention and we would film around their schedule. I had both wrestlers schedule their flight out of NYC late in the evening the day after their comic convention so that we could film early that morning.

Two days before the scheduled shoot, Brutus called to tell me there must be some kind of mix up. He said he couldn't film the day after the convention because he was flying out early that morning. I was very upset because Greg had spoken to Brutus directly and confirmed that they would both be taking a 7pm flight out of NYC to Tampa. Something started to smell fishy to me.

I told Brutus to give me his flight info and I would change it so that he could fly out later that evening with Greg. I told him that I would cover the extra costs and penalties. Seconds after I suggested this, I could hear whispering in the background. Brutus then said, "You know, if I'm going to do this I really need to be making more money."

I had already negotiated with Greg and Brutus and agreed upon a price. Now that my crew and location were booked, Brutus was trying to squeeze more money out of me. Even though I loved Brutus as a wrestler, I flat-out refused.

I immediately called Greg Valentine to explain the situation. Greg said, "Yeah, that's Brutus. A f'n liar!" I told Greg that it wasn't about the few extra hundred dollars that Brutus was trying to get out of me; it was more the fact that I couldn't be sure that Brutus wouldn't pull another stunt like this the morning of the shoot. I apologized to Greg, but I had to cancel the whole shoot. Brutus' reputation as an ass turned out to be truth.

A few weeks later, we filmed a great episode with Tito Santana. He was an absolute professional and a joy to work with. He arrived on set prepared, and he knew his lines inside and out. He even delivered his signature devastating flying forearm to me to end the scene.

As great as it was to have Tito and Snuka on board and now on film, I knew I needed bigger names to get Joeylicious to the level I wanted it to be. The whole fiasco with Brutus Beefcake really lit a fire under me. I went on a rampage and attempted to contact every wrestler I loved as a kid. Once I had Jimmy on board and on film, my plan was to use his notoriety to lure other wrestlers to the project. Jimmy was still very well liked and respected in the wrestling business.

I reached out first to The Ultimate Warrior, definitely a favorite of mine as a kid so I thought I might as well start at the top of my wish list. Everyone always asks me, "How did you get all those wrestling legends to film with you?" My answer was always the same: it's the same way I've accomplished everything that I've ever done, with hard work, hustle, and determination.

I spent hours upon hours sending emails to find each of their contact numbers or email addresses. For The Ultimate Warrior, I succeeded in tracking down someone who booked Warrior for various projects. This was always my biggest obstacle in getting the wrestlers to film with me for Joeylicious — getting past their agents/managers.

I sent a detailed email explaining *Wrestling With Joeylicious* to Warrior's agent, along with the edited Jimmy Snuka short, and assumed I would get a generic response back. A few days later, I received a long and friendly email from the Ultimate Warrior himself.

Joeylicious and Tito Santana.

Warrior said he was very interested in the project and absolutely loved the comedy in the Snuka short. We exchanged over a half-dozen emails discussing how to best use his character for the show. Once we settled on a few details, I began coming up with the first draft of the script.

About a week later, Warrior emailed me apologizing that he would have to put off any plans to film with us for the time being. WWE had just contacted him about being inducted into the WWE Hall of Fame. Unfortunately, The Ultimate Warrior passed away just 2 days after his Hall of Fame induction.

The three other dream gets for me were Hulk Hogan, Roddy Piper, and Ric Flair. After weeks of gathering the information I would need to contact these legends, I began sending my pitch emails. I was able to get Roddy's personal email, but for Ric and Hulk I could only find agent contact info.

I exchanged a few emails with Roddy and he seemed interested. Because Chris and I were funding all costs, the plan was to film around the particular wrestler's travel schedule. That way, we wouldn't have to fly anyone in or out. We would work around their schedule when they were in town. I researched Roddy's schedule over the next few months and saw the next time he'd be in New York. Roddy was scheduled to make an appearance at a comic/wrestling event near Kennedy airport, and I knew this was the perfect opportunity to get Roddy to film with us. I slightly altered the already existing script we wrote for

Beefcake/Valentine and made it specific to Roddy's character. I sent it to Roddy along with the proposed dates and anxiously waited to hear his response.

The next morning, I woke up to a voice message from the Hot Rod himself! It was surreal to hear Roddy Piper, on my voicemail, talking to me. It was insane! Roddy said, "Hey Joe, it's Rod. Loved the script! Let's make this work. Call back soon. I move fast." After a half-dozen or so phone conversations, I secured Roddy Piper to film with us for an episode of *Wrestling With Joeylicious.*

Because of what happened with Beefcake, I didn't want to get too excited until Roddy was actually on set. I secured my small crew once again. It was filled with friends, former bandmates, and just about anyone that wanted to help out. I also secured a great location for us to film — the basement of one of my drum students on the upper east side of Manhattan. It was to act as Joeylicious' bedroom.

To set the scene correctly, I brought over tons of wrestling paraphernalia from my personal collection, including toys, belts, posters, books, and DVD's. I made the room look very much how my bedroom looked as a kid. The only difference was that the other half of the room would have been my drums and wall-to-wall KISS items!

I also enlisted someone to pick up Roddy from his hotel at Kennedy airport. The team that I assembled to film Joeylicious was unbelievable: each of them went over and above to make this dream a reality.

Once Roddy arrived on set, he was an absolute joy to work with and to be around. He was constantly cracking jokes and telling us old war stories. He learned the script really well and it only took him a few takes to start opening up and understanding the "world" that Joeylicious lived in. By the end of the episode, I was in a kilt just like Roddy's and in a devastating sleeper hold.

The whole day of filming was surreal and amazing. It was one of the most fulfilling experiences of my entire life. All the prep — scheduling, emails, phone calls, script writing, location scouting, getting camera men, makeup, lights, sound equipment — all of it was so new to me, yet somehow I got it all done. I set out to make this TV show with these amazing wrestlers and nothing was going to stop me.

Having fun filming with the great "Rowdy" Roddy Piper.

It just goes to show you, if you put your mind and energy into something, you can really accomplish anything! While driving home later that night, I had another "Frozen Moment." I think it was my first one that happened after the specific moment had already passed. In fact, this one was more of a "Realization Moment." As I was thinking about my day of filming with Roddy, I realized, probably for the first time in my career, that it wasn't about the commercial success or money you made with a project that was the fulfilling part. It was about seeing a dream or vision you have all the way through until it becomes a reality, whether that be playing the drums, opening for KISS, or even writing this book. See what you want to accomplish in your head, figure out all the steps it'll take to achieve that goal, and then work tirelessly, fearlessly, until you climb each one of those steps to make that dream a reality! Don't let anyone or anything stand in your way!

All the while I was filming *Wrestling With Joeylicious*, I was still playing 8 shows a week in *The Great Comet*. It was really the most rewarding time of my life. I was working full-time playing my drums and supporting my family, all while filming a show starring myself and all of my wrestling heroes growing up. Madalyn would always kid around and say, "I know there is no Joeylicious show. You are just finding a way to get these wrestlers to come and play with you and put you in wrestling holds."

As I was doing all of that, I was still working on my animated show *Victor* with my old Playground bandmate Tommy. We had just finished animating our sizzle reel and were ready to start shopping it to networks. I enlisted Rick Van Meter, one of my former *Z Rock* producers, to help. I showed Rick the sizzle for *Victor* and he absolutely loved it. Soon after, Rick set up a meeting with the head of development at Comedy Central.

Comedy Central loved the sizzle and the Victor character, but they asked if we could get some star power attached to the project. They said, "If the creators of *South Park* had brought this in, it would be on the air immediately! That's how much we like it." I now had a new mission: find a star to either be one of the voices in the show or find a big name who would champion the show as an executive producer.

We had created an amazing character for *Victor* named Stymie Midgetawitz, the Hasidic Jewish midget, and I had the perfect person in mind to play him: my old *Z Rock* co-star Gilbert Gottfried! Type casting you say? Maybe.

I was still in touch with Gilbert from our *Z Rock* days. I set up a lunch meeting so we could pitch him the project. Again, nothing happens without hustle and determination. Comedy Central wanted a star, and I was going to give them one of the biggest voice over comics ever!

After showing Gilbert the *Victor* animation and telling him that we wanted him to play Victor's arch nemesis, Stymie, the Hasidic Jewish Midget, he was sold. I knew having Gilbert on board wouldn't be enough. I wanted to actually animate a brand new scene with him so we could really showcase his talents. Tommy and I wrote a small script and we booked Gilbert in a recording studio in Manhattan to record the voices.

Once we started recording, Gilbert gave us so much amazing material that I had to go back and re-do the script and all of the storyboards. We were sitting on gold!

In the meantime, while I was redoing the storyboards to get them ready to be animated, *The Great Comet* had moved from the meat-packing district to the Broadway district. We weren't officially "on Broadway" yet, but our tent was located on 45th Street and 8th Avenue. The word from our producers were that we were just waiting for the "right" Broadway theater to become available so that we could move in. This was now September 2013. A huge billboard hung in Times Square

In the studio doing voices for "Victor" with Gilbert
Gottfried and co-creator Tommy Snyder.

to promote the show! While I waited for *Comet* to move to the Great White Way, I continued with *Victor* and *Wrestling With Joeylicious*. After the high of filming with Roddy Piper, I wanted more! I was still waiting to hear back from Ric Flair and Hulk Hogan's agents, but in the meantime, I decided to try and get a wrestler who was a little bit more in the mainstream eye.

I decided I wanted to reach out to WWE Hall of Famer Mick Foley. It wasn't only about getting big-name wrestlers; it was about getting guys for whom I could come up with a great script, and I had the perfect script in mind for Mick. My usual process once I had a wrestler in mind went something like this: I would write an initial concept/layout of a script, then I would do my research and try to find the best contact info available. I found Mick's agent's info but couldn't get a hold of Mick directly. After numerous emails back and forth with Mick's agent, I was getting nowhere.

Mick's agent told me that "Mick just doesn't have time for a project like this. Thank you, but no thank you". Luckily, it's not in my chemistry to take no for an answer.

I dug deeper and finally got Mick's personal email address from Jimmy Snuka's wife, Carole. Jimmy had been the reason Mick became a wrestler in the first place and I knew that once I explained to him the premise of the show and showed him the episode with Snuka, I'd have him hooked. After sending my first email to Mick, my prediction came

The original Great Comet billboard in Times Square.

true. Mick loved the project and immediately wanted to be a part of it. This is the exact reason I hate going through agents! Once I got to show Mick the project personally, he loved it like I knew he would.

The shoot with Mick would be our biggest undertaking yet. The script that I drafted called for Mick to play all of his wrestling personalities: Mick Foley, Cactus Jack, Dude Love, and Mankind. Each persona brought a unique characteristic to the scene, which I wanted to capture with some crazy camera and editing tricks. I knew in my head what I wanted to see, but I had no idea how to achieve it.

Chris and I had just started working with a young filmmaker named Adam Hada, who we initially brought on board just to edit our Tito Santana episode and then help film the Roddy Piper episode. He did such amazing work that we enlisted him to figure out how we were going to have all four "faces of Foley" on screen at the same time.

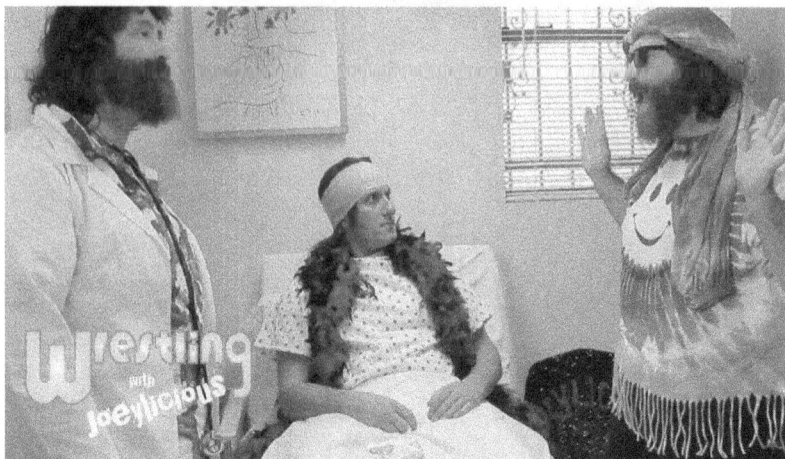

A blast and a big challenge trying to film with the many faces of Mick Foley!

Filming with Mick was just as fulfilling as filming with Roddy and Snuka. It was a little different for me because Mick was a newer generation wrestler and I didn't grow up idolizing him like I did Snuka and Roddy. Still, as far as comedic talent, Mick was by far the sharpest and wittiest wrestler we worked with. Much like when we did voice overs with Gilbert Gottfried for *Victor*, Mick was so great at improv that we kept changing the script on the fly.

Having these wrestlers all do their finishing moves on me had been a real blast. Snuka blasted me in the head with a coconut, Tito gave me a flying forearm, Roddy put me in a sleeper hold, and now I was going to have Cactus Jack beat me with a barbed wire bat, Mankind hit me with a chair, and put Mr. Socko in my mouth. I couldn't think of anything I'd rather be doing.

After filming with Mick, I kind of arranged a shoot with The Iron Sheik. The reason I say "kind of" is because when I spoke to the Sheik's manager Page Magen, he informed me that I was welcome to come and try to get the Sheik to film. I had no idea what this meant and asked him to please explain. Page went on to tell me that The Sheik would be appearing at Caroline's comedy club in NYC, but he never knew what kind of mood the Sheik would be in until ten minutes before the event.

Even with this wild uncertainty, I decided to get my crew together and attempt to film with the man that I loathed those many years ago after he beat Bob Backlund at MSG.

Chris and I came up with a really short, funny script that would take place in the men's bathroom at Caroline's. After taking a few hours to set up the scene with my crew, the Sheik was still nowhere to be found. I finally called Page and asked him what was happening and if the Sheik was willing to film. Page seemed very aloof and kept finding excuses. I told him to call me the second he was in the building.

After another hour wait, Page finally called and said the Sheik was at Caroline's in the dressing room but he didn't think filming was going to happen. I told him I'd be right over!

Once there, Page said "Sorry Joey the Sheik probably won't do it". This was one of those times that I could have just said ok and quit, but I don't have the quit gene in me. I told Page that I wanted to talk to the Sheik myself. He pointed to the other side of the room and said "Be my guest."

I approached the Sheik who was in a wheelchair and pretty immobile. I greeted him very respectfully and explained to him about the shoot that I had lined up. Before he could even get out a word, I grabbed the wheelchair and started quickly wheeling him to the bathroom where my crew was awaiting. He never got the chance to protest. In fact, following close behind us was The Sheik's long-time tag team partner Nikolai Volkoff saying "Hey, can I be in the scene too?" I wish I had a camera rolling for when I was running with the Iron Sheik in a wheelchair with Nikolai Volkoff chasing behind. It was an absolute classic comedy sketch.

Joeylicious meets The Iron Sheik

So not only did I film with the Iron Sheik, we quickly changed the script to incorporate Nikolai Volkoff in as well.

After that amazing experience with the Sheik and Volkoff, my confidence was at an all time high. I decided to once again reach out to my two ultimate gets: Hogan and Flair.

I finally got Hogan's longtime agent on the phone after I sent him the edited Mick Foley and Roddy Piper episodes. He told me that he thought the show looked great and that Hulk had watched and also agreed. It would definitely be something that Hulk would be interested in, but he explained that it would be hard to get Hulk to commit until the show was officially picked up by a network. I totally understood. Hogan's agent also told me, "Feel free to use Hulk's name while you are trying to sell the show. Then once you have a legitimate offer, we will talk again." It wasn't the best-case scenario, but it was still pretty damn cool! I now officially had my idol growing up, Hulk Hogan, as part of a show that I created, *Wrestling With Joeylicious*!

Since I began filming *Wrestling With Joeylicious*, word had started to get out in the wrestling community that I was recruiting 80's legends to join the show. One morning, I woke up and listened to the voice mails on my phone and the first message was a very familiar voice. It was none other than the "Mouth of the South," Jimmy Hart! Jimmy was talking a mile a minute and said, "Hey baby, I heard you're doing a wrestling show. Well, it won't be a show unless you have the Mouth of the South Jimmy Hart baby!" He rambled on for another minute or so and all I could do was listen and smile.

Over the next few weeks, I was getting more and more voice mails from wrestlers about Joeylicious. I know I probably use this word too much, but it was surreal. I'm not even sure how some of them got my number. Guys like King Kong Bundy, The Honky Tonk Man, and The Million Dollar Man, Ted DiBiase, all wanted to be a part of Joeylicious.

Because we already had bigger names on film, like Roddy and Mick, I didn't necessarily need to film with these guys yet. Instead, I called all of them and explained the situation and that I really wanted them to be in the show once we sold it to network. I asked them all to be patient and I'd get back to them soon. But I did get one text message from someone that I wanted to film with as soon as possible.

My phone buzzed one afternoon to signal that I just received a text message. It was from an unknown number and I didn't read it right away. About an hour or so later, as I was glancing at my texts, I realized that I still hadn't read it. When I finally did, I thought it was a joke at first. It went something like this: "Hey Joe, Ric Flair here. Got your number from Carole Snuka, said I should give you a buzz. Talk soon – Ric."

I couldn't believe it: Ric Flair, the Nature Boy, 16- time world champ, just texted me. I called Carole Snuka right away and she told me she mentioned the project to Ric and he seemed interested.

I called Ric back right away. We talked for about 20 minutes. He seemed interested in the show and we talked about a few funny possibilities for the episode. It would involve Ric taking Joeylicious shopping for a new $10,000 suit so I could style and profile like "The Nature Boy."

Ric was ready to film and asked me to contact his agent with all of the details. That's where I hit a little bump in the road. Talking to Ric's agent was completely the opposite of talking to Ric. After a dozen or so calls and emails, I decided to try and bypass the agent and go directly through Ric himself. It almost worked.

I had set up a tentative shoot with Ric the next time he was in town with WWE at Madison Square Garden. Two days before the shoot, Ric informed me that he had to reschedule because he needed to do a round of press with his daughter, Charlotte. Even though I didn't get to film with Ric on that date, he was officially on board with the project, just like Hogan, if and when we sold it.

To this day, I continue to film and write new episodes of *Wrestling With Joeylicious*, with the hopes of getting it picked up by a major network. This is an absolute passion project of mine and some of the greatest, most fulfilling moments of my career. I will never give up on this until *Joeylicious* takes over every TV in the country! And to quote the immortal Ric Flair, "Woooooooo"!

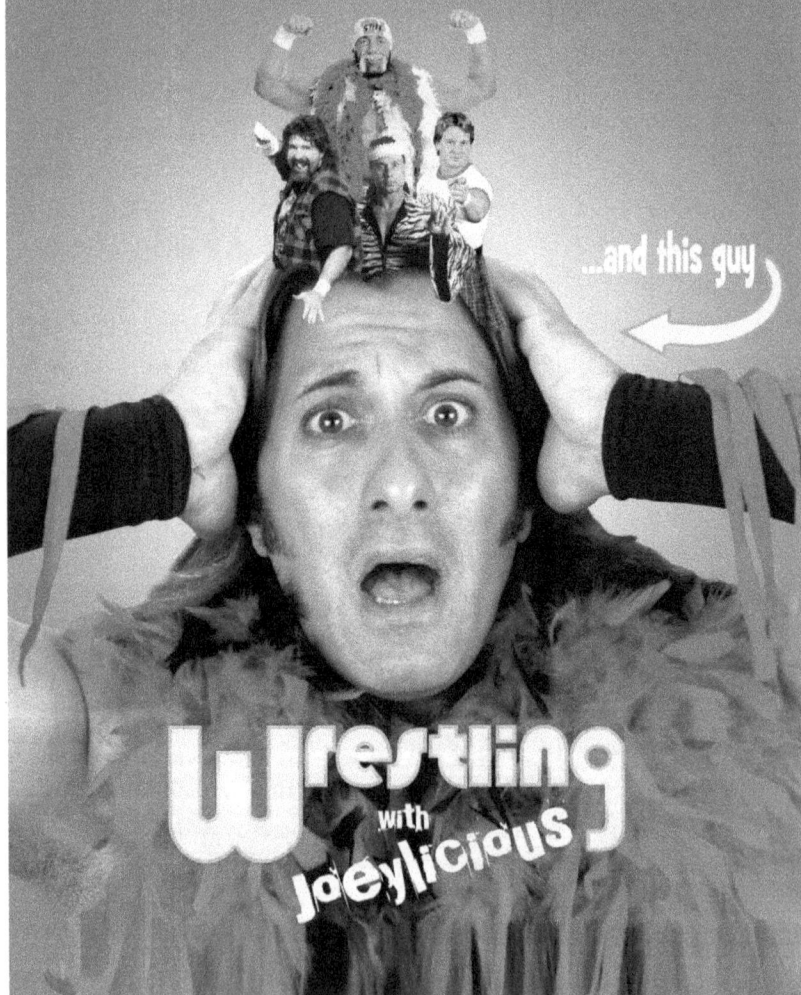

Starring The Legends Of Wrestling...

...and this guy

Wrestling with joeylicious

CHAPTER 33
EVERYTHING I'VE EVER WANTED

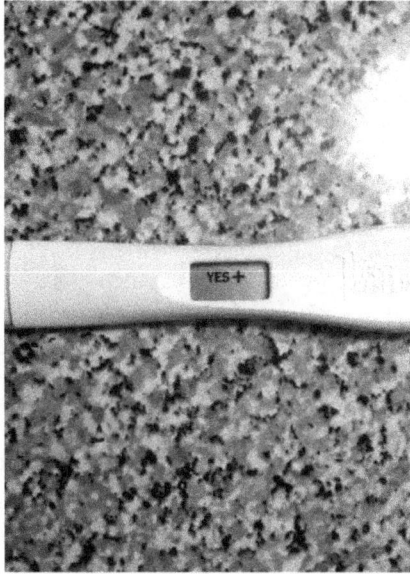

Finding out I was going to be a dad again!

During one fateful night in November 2013, I was backstage during intermission of *The Great Comet* and I received a text from Madalyn. It was a picture of a pregnancy test and it said, "YES!" A few months prior, Madalyn and I had decided we wanted another baby and this was the greatest news ever!

I couldn't have been any happier! When I started the second act of *The Great Comet* following her text, I immediately messed up the first few bars of the song "Letters." I couldn't stop thinking about being a dad again. I was so happy!

Shortly after, we found out that Madalyn was having a baby boy. We were so beyond excited. Of course, he would have to be named Joseph Cassata!

In March 2014, *The Great Comet* ended its off-Broadway run. The producers told us all that they were going to try their hardest to get this show to next level ... Broadway. They didn't have a time frame but asked us to be patient and not over book ourselves so we would be ready when the time came. It was actually much-needed time off, and I was looking forward to spending time with Angelina and taking care of Mad during her last few months of pregnancy. On August 9, 2014, my baby boy Jo Jo was born! I was never happier in my life! Joe looked completely different than Angelina when she was born. Angelina was very dark, chubby, and had a full head of black hair. Joe was white, skinny, and had light blonde fuzz on the top of his head. He was absolutely adorable! My beautiful family was now complete with the addition of my baby Joe.

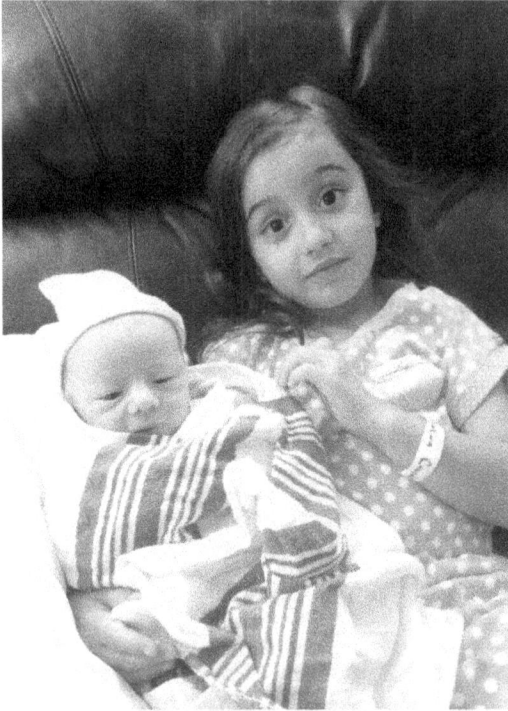

Angelina holding her baby brother, Joe, for the very first time.

A few years prior to Joe's birth, Madalyn's mother passed away. It was a hard time for her and the family. Just like when Angelina was born, when I immediately saw my mother in her, the same thing happened when we had Joe: Madalyn's mom's presence was all over him. It was undeniable. It's been so hard having both our moms gone from our lives, and to know they missed out on enjoying our babies with us. Deep down, though, I know there is a piece of both of our mothers inside our children. It makes me that much happier whenever I look into their eyes.

A very funny thing happened a few days after we took Joe back home to our apartment in Brooklyn. I knew I was in trouble right away. For some reason, the first few days of being home, Joe would always frown whenever I talked; there was clearly something about my voice that he didn't like. At one point, he was crying and Madalyn was trying to console him with his head on her shoulder. I swear on my life that he looked at me and gave me this little sinister smile as if to say, "I was just crying to get my mommy to hug me." I couldn't help but smile.

I know what you're all thinking: there's no way that happened! He's just an infant. But I don't care what anyone says, that was the first day I knew my Jo Jo would be big trouble, just like his Pa!

After a few months of living in our apartment in Brooklyn, we quickly realized that it was shrinking by the second with the addition of our second child. Madalyn, of course, was still working, but I was only teaching part-time and waiting anxiously to hear about the potential

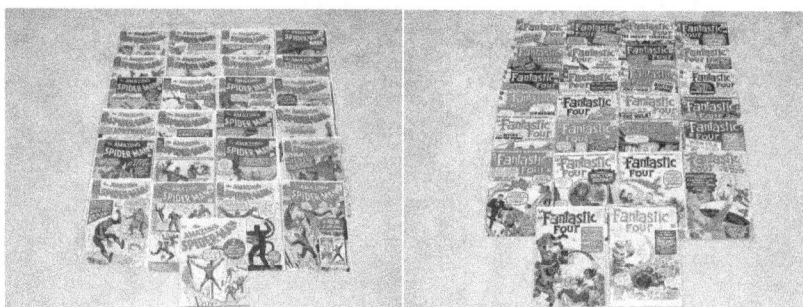

My first 25 issues of The Fantastic Four and Spider-Man.

My Biggest comics...
Spider-Man#1, Fantastic Four #1,
Hulk #1, X-Men #1 & Avengers #1

Broadway move for *The Great Comet*. We knew we needed a change, but we didn't know how we could do it.

Madalyn came to me one day and said, "We are buying a house! I'm not sure where or how yet, but we will have it soon." Ever since I lost my two homes as a kid, my dream had always been to buy a house for my family and I knew just the way I would pay for it.

Since I was 5 years old, my brother and I had collected comic books. We both had massive collections and I remember even as a kid people would always ask, "What are you going to do with all of those comic books? You're crazy!" I would always have the same response: "Hopefully I'll buy my kids a house one day with them." Everyone always laughed.

I contacted a few dealers about selling my collection and they all were very interested. My goal was to sell only my really expensive comics so Madalyn and I could use the money for the house down payment. I had almost full complete runs of *Avengers*, *Fantastic Four*, *The Hulk*, and the first 50 issues of *Amazing Spider-Man*. None of the

Selling my comic book collection To buy my family a house.

issues were in amazing condition, but they all still had tremendous value. I found a buyer quite easily and he agreed on my asking price. I was still going to keep a large portion of my collection, but I would be parting with all of my most valuable comics.

As hard as it was to let go of this piece of my childhood, nothing was more rewarding than knowing the comics I'd been collecting since I was a kid were now going to help me buy my kids a brand-new house. Soon after selling my comics, Madalyn and I found the perfect house in New Jersey. It was everything I could have ever dreamed of and then some. It would be the perfect place to raise our beautiful new family.

One afternoon about a year later, I was on the couch in my new home. Both of my babies were with me, one on each side, fast asleep napping. Just then, everything began to freeze, bringing on what is by far my most cherished "Frozen Moment" yet.

As I sat there on the couch, in my brand new home, holding my two angels, my whole life flashed before my eyes and I realized that every single moment had led me to this exact time and place. That's the moment I decided to write this book. I wanted my babies to be able to read about their Papa's life.

All the bad and hard times along with all of the good ones had led me to be where I was. I had everything I'd ever dreamed of times 1,000! My family makes me the happiest man on the face of the earth, and I had done everything I'd ever wanted to accomplish in my career. In that "Frozen Moment," I realized I'd never been happier or more content in all of my life.

The happiest place on earth for me...Holding my babies.

HOME SWEET HOME.

Joe and Angelina following in their Papa's footsteps

My family is my real dream come true.

Epilogue...

As I sit on a New Jersey Academy bus, in route to NYC Port Authority, I ponder to myself, "How did I get here?" I'm on my way to opening night of *Natasha, Pierre and The Great Comet of 1812* on Broadway! So, again — how did I get here? I've done everything I could have ever imagined doing. I've toured the world, starred in my own TV show, become peers and friends with all of my heroes and idols and, best of all, I have the perfect family waiting for me at home.

Opening night of Natasha, Pierre & The Great Comet of 1812 on Broadway!!

Now I'm headed to what some would say is the pinnacle of being a musician: playing on Broadway in a hit musical. So again, I ask, "How did I get here?" It was a long and tiring road, requiring thousands of hours of practice, thousands of gigs, hundreds of blisters, dozens of auditions, band after band after band. I played with hundreds of different musicians, spent countless hours in the backs of cars, vans, RV's, and tour buses, slept hundreds of nights in shitty hotels — and way too many of those nights on the floors of said shitty hotels. I spent thousands of hours away from my loved ones and traveled tens of thousands of miles. I wouldn't trade a minute of it!

There's no Magic Equation that allows a person to "make it," if there even is such a thing as "making it." You have to work beyond hard and put in the time. A person can become a policeman in 21 weeks in the police academy. Someone can become a teacher after 4 years of college. Twelve years of rigorous schooling can even make someone a doctor. A mother can give birth and raise a child to adulthood in 18 years, but there's no exact time frame that you can put on making dreams come true. The work is never ending. There will be countless obstacles and plenty of times you want to give up, but the only people who "make it" and fulfill their dreams are the ones that NEVER GIVE UP.

I will continue to push forward creatively with all of my endeavors. *Wrestling With Joeylicious* and *Victor* are still two of my passion projects that I will continue to work on every day until I get them to where I want them to be. Plus, there are many other things that I still want to do, like create and write my own comic book series, film a movie comedy about my days in the Hamptons playing Wiffle ball, release this autobiography, and maybe even do a solo album. Whatever my heart desires is out there waiting for me.

Most of all, I look forward to growing old with my beautiful wife Madalyn, while watching our Angelina and Joe grow up together and fulfill their own dreams. So, if my son and daughter made it all the way through this book, after hundreds of pages of their Pa rambling on about his life, there is one thing I never want you two to forget...

Angelina, my heart, and Joe Joe, my soul, you can be and do anything your heart desires if you want it badly enough and if you work hard enough. Freeze those special moments, breathe them in, and hold onto them forever. NEVER GIVE UP!

Start With a Dream...

THE END (for now)

Follow Joey on Social Media

f facebook.com/JoeyCassata.zrock

⊙ Instagram.com/JoeyCassata

🐦 Twitter: @JoeyCassata

▶ YouTube.com/c/SattaEntertainment

Z ROCK All episodes of Z ROCK can be seen at:
facebook.com/ZRock

Wrestling w joeylicious facebook.com/wrestlingwithjoeylicious

JOEY CASSATA
is
Endorsed by:

LUDWIG

pAiSTe

VIC FIRTH®

EVANS® USA
drumheads

sticky bumps

WIFFLE® BALL

www.ingramcontent.com/pod-product-compliance
Lightning Source LLC
Chambersburg PA
CBHW021823090426
42811CB00032B/1999/J